Nelson's Annual

Preacher's Sourcebook

2003 EDITION

Nelson's Annual Preacher's Sourcebook

2003 EDITION

ROBERT J. MORGAN, EDITOR

THOMAS NELSON PUBLISHERS
NASHVILLE

Book design by Mark McGarry, Texas Type and Book Works, Dallas, Texas

Typesetting by BookSetters, White House, Tennessee

Morgan, Robert J. (ed.)
   Nelson's annual preacher's sourcebook, 2003 edition.

ISBN 0-7852-4866-8

Printed in the United States of America

1 2 3 4 5 6 7—07 06 05 04 03 02

Contents

Introduction   xi

Editor's Preface: Biblical Principles on Preaching   xiii

Create a Sermon Series!   xxiii

Contributors   xxv

Calendar Pages   xxx

Sermons and Worship Suggestions for 52 Weeks   1

January 5	*A New Attitude for a New Year* Psalms 42, 43	2
January 12	*Developing Mega-Faith* Mark 7:24–30	8
January 19	*This Ain't the Ritz* John 6:35–40	14
January 26	*Press On to the Prize* 1 Corinthians 9:24–27	20
February 2	*Gideon* Judges 6:1—7:25	30
February 9	*More Precious than Gold* Psalm 19	36
February 16	*Is It Enough to Be Sorry?* Mark 1:2b–3	44
February 23	*Battle Dress* Ephesians 6:10–20	56
March 2	*The Wholeness of Worship* Isaiah 6:1–8	62
March 9	*Glimpses of Jesus in Joshua* Joshua 1:1–2	72

March 16	*A Taxing Decision*	78
	Matthew 9:9–13	
March 23	*Be Still and Know*	86
	Psalm 46	
March 30	*Amazing the Amazing One*	92
	Matthew 7:28–29	
April 6	*The Elder Brother Syndrome*	98
	Luke 15:11–32	
April 13	*Have Faith in God*	106
	Mark 11:20–26	
April 20	*Every Day Is Easter!*	114
	John 20:1–10	
April 27	*Our Burdens, Our Battles, and Our Bibles*	120
	James 1:1–27	
May 4	*Hurry Up and Wait!*	130
	James 5:7–11	
May 11	*Lasting Love on Mother's Day*	136
	1 Corinthians 13:1–13	
May 18	*Joyful Stress*	142
	Philippians 1:18–30	
May 25	*When Jesus Tarries*	152
	Mark 5:21–43	
June 1	*The Old Lamplighter*	160
	Ephesians 5:8	
June 8	*Symbols of the Holy Spirit*	166
	Mark 1:1–11	
June 15	*Faithful Fathering*	174
	Ephesians 6:4	
June 22	*Jonah's Journey*	182
	Jonah 1—4	
June 29	*The Upside-down Kingdom of Jesus*	190
	Mark 10:35–45	

July 6	*The Great Physician's Upper Room Clinic* John 14:28–31	202
July 13	*Integrity in Doctrine* Titus 1:5–9	208
July 20	*The Barnabas Secrets* Acts 11:24	214
July 27	*Easter in July* Romans 6:4	220
August 3	*When Satan Attacks You* Job 1:1–12	230
August 10	*And the Walls Fell Down Flat* Joshua 6:1–27	238
August 17	*Growing, Guarding, and Glorifying* 2 Peter 3:17–18	244
August 24	*How to Iron Out Your Differences* *Without Being Burned* Romans 12:16–18	254
August 31	*Water to Wine* John 2:1–11	260
September 7	*Facing Up to a Challenge* Nehemiah 1:1–4	266
September 14	*Go, Stand, and Speak* Acts 5:17–33	272
September 21	*A Look at the Hereafter* Matthew 7:13–14	280
September 28	*Like Peter* John 6:1–68	286
October 5	*Don't Give Up on Believing Prayer* Luke 18:1–8	296
October 12	*Moving from Pain to Praise* 2 Corinthians 1:8–11	302
October 19	*The Intelligent Designer* Genesis 1:1	310

October 26	*Falling Down, Standing Up, Going Forth* Ezekiel 1:28b—2:3a	318
November 2	*The Bad Girl Who Made Good* Joshua 2:1–21	330
November 9	*A Cure for Nerves* Psalm 23	336
November 16	*No Gains Without Pains* 2 Timothy 2:3–7	342
November 23	*Owl or Eagle?* Psalm 103:1–5	348
November 30	*Caleb, the Magnificent* Joshua 14:6–15	358
December 7	*Loving God with Your Mind* Luke 2:17	364
December 14	*"I Have Come"* John 6:38–40	370
December 21	*Good News of Great Joy* Luke 2:8–20	376
December 28	*The Dream of Beginning Again* Exodus 2:11–15	382

Children's Sermon Suggestions

January 26; February 9; March 23; April 13, 20; May 11, 18; June 1, 22, 29; July 13; August 3, 10, 24, 31; September 21, 28; October 19; November 9, 16; December 21, 28

Special Occasion Sermons

A Communion Sermon: The Tree	112
A Missions Sermon: From Here to Timbuktu	180
A Baptism Sermon: No Other Name	278
A Thanksgiving Sermon: Sweet Peas	354

Classics for the Pastor's Library

Patrick's Confessions	84
Green Leaf in Drought Time / Isobel Kuhn	188
Pilgrim's Progress	236
Robinson Crusoe	308

Conversations in a Pastor's Study

Living with Change in the Midst of Tradition / Peter Grainger   26
Everything for the Cross/Peter Cartwright   126
The Craft of Preaching/David Jackman   292
Confidence in Sermon-building/Timothy Warren   324

Helps for the Pastor's Family

When Sickness Strikes the Pastor's Family   42
Table Talk in the Pastor's Home: Toxic or Terrific?   172
Through a Cracked Door . . .   250

Heroes for the Pastor's Heart

Perpetua: The Quandary of Human Affections   71
Saint Basil: The Man Who Knew the Difference Between
     Fame and Faithfulness   104
E. Stanley Jones: The Man Who Survived Brain Fatigue   151
John Calvin's Farewell Address   158
David Brainerd and the Power of Prayer   253
William Carey: The Power of Plodding   327

Quotes for the Pastor's Wall

Augustine   55
Charles Haddon Spurgeon   201
Martyn Lloyd-Jones   201, 329
John Ker   228
Chuck Swindoll   229
Pacific Garden Mission   263
Mother Teresa   356
Joseph Parker   357
Richard Cecil   394

Techniques for the Pastor's Delivery

Your Lungs Are Only as Healthy as You Are   68
Should We Use Notes in the Pulpit? / R. W. Dale   148
Ten Commandments for a Healthy Voice   295
Preaching: Nothing Can Ever Take Its Place   316

Thoughts for the Pastor's Soul

Ministering the Word to Others When Your Own Heart
     Is Hurting   50

Churches Without Boundaries: Mobilizing and Globalizing
   Your Ministry   196
The Deeper Christian Life   226

Wedding Messages
A Traditional Wedding   388
A Scriptural Wedding   390
A Wedding for God's Servants   392

Funeral Messages
The Twinkling of an Eye   395
He Does All Things Well   397
To Die Is Gain   400

Special Services Registry
Sermons Preached   404
Marriages Log   406
Funerals Log   407
Baptisms/Confirmations   408
Baby Dedication Registration   409
Wedding Registration   410
Funeral Registration   411

Subject Index   413
Scripture Index   415

Introduction

"When I'm in the pulpit," said Martin Luther, "I look at no one but tell myself they are merely blocks of wood which stand there before me, and I speak the word of my God to them."

He was talking about the fear, stress, and anxiety of preaching.

We can all identify, especially because Sundays roll around with tyrannical frequency. Need some help? Here is a personal research assistant, worship planner, brainstorming partner, and an associate who never talks back to you!

Nelson's Annual Preacher's Sourcebook: 2003 provides fifty-two weeks of outlines, worship aids, and a miscellany of other helps, hints, conversations, quotes, and uplifting articles, all indexed for easy use, and contained in both printed form and on CD-ROM.

My thanks go to the highly supportive team of Phil Stoner, Wayne Kinde, and Lee Hollaway at Thomas Nelson Publishers, and to my friend and agent, Greg Johnson of Alive Communications.

I'd also like to send a word of gratitude to **Chaplain (Major) William McCoy,** currently serving at the United States Army Europe Headquarters in Heidelberg, Germany. Bill's testimony and challenge to me on September 2, 1971, when we were college roommates, set me on the path to victorious Christian living and service. To him and his colleagues serving in the armed forces around the world, this book is affectionately dedicated.

Editor's Preface

Biblical Principles on Preaching

Some time ago I found a cache of old audio cassettes I'd recorded in college, some of them containing a handful of my earliest sermons. I took a deep breath and punched one into my player. As I listened I was struck by three things: How biblical the content was, how terrible the delivery was, and how little I've improved!

Through the years, I've read book after book in an effort to preach better, and maybe I have grown just a little. The books have surely helped, as have the advice, the critics, the practice sessions, and the benefit of doing something several times a week, year after year. But one book has helped more than any other—the best homiletics text of them all—the Bible.

Nehemiah 8:8

My favorite verse on the subject of preaching is Nehemiah 8:8. In this passage, the remnant of the Jews in Jerusalem assembled before the Water Gate to hear God's Word. Rabbi Ezra stood on a high wooden platform built for the occasion. Verse 5 says: "And Ezra opened the book in the sight of all the people, for he was standing above all the people; and when he opened it, all the people stood up. And Ezra blessed the LORD, the great God. Then all the people answered, "Amen, Amen!" while lifting up their hands. And they bowed their heads and worshiped the LORD with their faces to the ground."

Then it was time for the preaching and teaching of the law. What was their method? How did they go about this craft of preaching? Verse 8 says: "So they read distinctly from the book, in the Law of God; and they gave the sense, and helped them to understand the reading."

That is preaching—and that is expository preaching: reading the Scripture distinctly, giving the sense, and causing the people to understand the meaning to their lives.

As a ministerial student at Columbia International University, I was drilled on the primacy of exposition as a primary approach to pulpit ministry. As Haddon W. Robinson puts it, "The type of preaching that best carries the

XIV / NELSON'S ANNUAL PREACHER'S SOURCEBOOK

force of divine authority is expository preaching." I view an exposition sermon, in its simplest form, as taking a paragraph of the Bible, reading it distinctly, giving the sense, and causing the people to understand it.

The early Bible translator William Tyndale wrote, "I had perceived by experience, how that it was impossible to establish the lay people in any truth, except
the Scripture were plainly laid before their eyes in their mother tongue, that they
might see the process, order, and meaning of the text."

Why a paragraph? Because in literature the paragraph is the shortest seg-
ment of contextualized content. If you preach from only a verse, it's easy to
take it out of context. You cannot accurately interpret a sentence or a verse of
Scripture except with an awareness of its context, which is the paragraph in
which it's found. By exposing (giving exposition of) the paragraph as a whole,
we increase the likelihood of accurately interpreting and explaining the individual verses and sentences.

Why a paragraph instead of a chapter or a book? It's short enough to cover
in a careful way and easy enough for the people to tuck into their minds and
carry out of the service.

Through the years, I've primarily been a "paragraph preacher," for that
lends itself to exposition, but I'm in the minority. Few preachers still embrace
paragraph exposition as their "default" method of preaching, and many people in the pew do not have a clue as to what an expository sermon really is.

Once in my first pastorate I announced I was going to preach expository
sermons. Afterward a concerned parishioner approached me. He thought I
had said "suppository sermons," and he wanted to know how I was going to
deliver them!

Since then I've tried to use the term "Expositional Sermons."

How do we prepare an expositional sermon? No one has ever put it better than Stephen Olford who divides the process into five steps. We must:
(1) Memorize the Scripture; (2) Crystallize the Subject; (3) Analyze the
Structure; (4) Organize the Substance; and (5) Finalize the Sermon.

Well, actually, one person did put it better than that. The writer of
Nehemiah 8:8 said, "So they read in the book of the Law of God distinctly,
and gave the sense, and caused them to understand the reading." It's as simple as that.

Most of the sermon outlines in this book are expository—uh, expositional—sermons.

1 Samuel 17:38–39

Another passage that has helped me is 1 Samuel 17:38–39 (NIV): "Then Saul dressed David in his own tunic. He put a coat of armor on him and a bronze helmet on his head. David fastened on his sword over the tunic and tried walking around, because he was not used to them. 'I cannot go in these,' he said to Saul, 'because I am not used to them.' So he took them off. Then he took his staff in his hand, chose five smooth stones from the stream, put them in his shepherd's bag and, with his sling in his hand, approached the Philistine."

This has been one of my most difficult lessons, but I've slowly learned through the years that I cannot preach like any other person, using another's style or delivery. I have to be myself and do it as it comes naturally for me.

I don't know why this has been so hard; but as an insecure and impressionable young student, I became a composite of the handful of preachers I most admired. I preached like whomever I'd heard most recently. Only slowly have I developed the ability of sliding off another's armor and going forth with my own slingshot.

One of the preachers I've appreciated through the years has been the Southern Baptist giant, W. A. Criswell. When he died, a Dallas television station replayed an interview in which he told of his call to the First Baptist Church of Dallas. His predecessor, Dr. George Truett, a pulpit giant, had pastored the church for decades before him. No one, it was thought, could take Dr. Truett's place. But young W. A. Criswell came and led First Baptist into its greatest days.

In this interview, Dr. Criswell explained one reason why he had been successful, saying something to this effect: "Dr. Truett was a proper and dignified preacher who quietly stood in the pulpit and, with well-modulated tones, delivered profound messages." Criswell then said, as I remember it, "When I came I was not at all like that. I screamed and shouted and hollered and waved my fists and beat the pulpit. I'd ramble across the platform and down onto the floor. It wasn't a dignified, city-fied delivery, but one thing is for sure—no one ever accused me of being a 'Little Truett.' And that's why I lasted 48 years in the pulpit of that church."

I hope there is never another preacher like me (a widely-held sentiment). Every preacher should be an original. God has never been in the cloning business. The Lord has never made two snowflakes alike, or two planets, or two daffodils, or two orators.

Of course, this presents a difficulty. How can we learn from others, how can we listen to them, how can we study them, how can we benefit from them without running the risk of unconsciously picking up their specific methods or mannerisms?

We must first of all deliberately and consciously avoid any tendency toward imitating the style of another. Early in my training, I wish someone had said to me, "Listen to the greatest preachers in the world, but make sure that you don't stylistically pattern yourself after them. Don't adopt their distinctive mannerisms, voice modulations, particular pronunciations, or characteristic phrases or gestures. Be yourself!"

In his autobiography, hotelier Conrad Hilton told of being elected to the state legislature as a young man. He was nervous about giving his first speech, and he invested much time in study and practice, complete with pre-planned dramatic gestures. One evening, his mother overhead him practicing as, with a flourish, he ended with a dramatic recitation of "The Charge of the Light Brigade," hands flying through the air like trapezes.

"Very nice," she replied, "for poetry. But you'll have to unlearn all this."

"But Mother," he protested. He reminded her that all the great speakers of the day were filled with rhetoric and oratory.

"Connie," she replied, "all those trimmings are sinful. You are hiding yourself behind a lot of gestures. If you're afraid to be *you*, son, you're throwing dust in God's face. He made you. If you have confidence in Him, you'll relax and be just what you are. You'd do better to pray about it than to practice *this*." Whereupon she walked off with his oratory textbook.

Hilton later said, "On the opening day of the legislature, I did pray about it. I faced the crowd, kept my hands at my side and my mouth in a normal line, and said simply what I had to say and sat down. It worked out very well that day. It has ever since. And any time, if I've been tempted to phony it up a bit, I remember that that's lack of confidence in Him, and I'll look pretty silly throwing dust in the face of the Infinite."

May God give us all such mothers, wives, friends, or critics.

Our preaching, in fact, should not be unlike our natural conversation. In his book, *A Preacher's Life,* the old British pulpiteer, Joseph Parker, told of a beloved preacher of his era, a man named Norman Macleod, who was older and somewhat of a mentor. Dr. Parker, 32 at the time, asked the venerable Dr. Macleod to come to his church in Manchester and preach one Sunday. That morning when Dr. Macleod opened the vestry door and saw the great size of the building, he stepped back into the vestry and said, "In what tone must I speak in order to fill that space?" Parker replied, "Adopt a conversational base, and rise and fall just as you feel your sentiment requires." Later, in recalling the sermon, Dr. Parker said, "The great man talked to us, talked straight into our hearts."

"Preaching," commented Joseph Parker, "should be conversation at its best."

Charles Spurgeon said the same thing to his students: "Just go into the pulpit, and talk to the people as you would in the kitchen, or the drawing-room, and say what you have to tell them in your ordinary tone of voice. . . . Nothing can succeed with the masses except naturalness and simplicity."

Of course, there is considerable difference between having a discussion with two people and presenting a discourse to two hundred or two thousand. But in general, one's preaching style should not be too different from his or her conversational style, and a conversational sort of delivery, it seems to me, is always the most natural.

I can improve, of course. I can grow. I can get better. I can mature. But I can't be someone that God didn't intend me to be. I need to like myself, confident in the gifts, personality, and preaching style God has built into me. We've got to be natural in the pulpit. If a person seldom gestures in normal everyday conversation, you probably wouldn't expect many gestures in the pulpit.

Or vice versa. There's a story about an old Jewish peddler who was ambling down a street in Tel Aviv carrying two large watermelons. A tourist stopped him to ask, "Where is Ben Yehuda Street?" The peddler answered, "Please hold these two watermelons." The tourist managed to get them in his arms, and that allowed the peddler to make an expansive gesture with his hands and exclaim, "How should I know?"

Acts 26:1 in the *Living Bible* says, "Then Agrippa said to Paul, 'Go ahead. Tell us your story.' So Paul, with many gestures, presented his defense."

Fight in your own armor, preach in your own style, and be an original. That's the only kind of effective preaching.

Matthew 13:34

There is one preacher, however, whom we *should* emulate. Matthew 13:34 says: "All these things Jesus spoke to the multitude in parables; and without a parable He did not speak to them."

There are three good reasons to season one's sermons with parables, stories, and illustrations. First, they wake up people who have drifted off during the more didactic portions of the message. Second, they keep children tuned in. Third, illustrations enable people to see the practicality of what is being preached. Through the use of stories, illustrations, and quotes people see themselves as in a mirror and are better able to personalize the truth of Scripture.

Hosea was clearly the Old Testament master at this. He used the word "like" sixty times in his brief book.

- *Israel is like a stubborn calf*
- *Your faithfulness is like a morning cloud, like the early dew it goes away*
- *like a twig on the water*
- *like a silly dove*
- *like smoke from a chimney*

When William Carey, the father of modern missions, was seeking ordination from the Baptist church in Olney, England, in 1785, he was turned down after the members heard him preach. One man, a Mr. Hall, said, "Brother Carey, you have no *likes* in your sermons. Christ taught that the kingdom of heaven was *like* to leaven hid in meal, *like* to a grain of mustard, and etc. You tell us what things are, but never what they are like."

All of us need some "likes."

The Scottish pulpit giant Thomas Guthrie said in his autobiography: "I turned to the Gospels, and found that He . . . used parables or illustrations, stories, comparisons drawn from the scenes of nature and familiar life, to a large extent in His teaching. . . . The parts of the Bible I like best are the *likes.*"

That's why we've included a generous assortment of illustrations in this *Sourcebook.*

1 John 2:20

There is an old word, disdained by newer translators and ignored in homiletics books, but beloved in olden days. The King James rendering of 1 John 2:20 says: "But ye have an unction from the Holy One." The Greek word, χρισμα (chrisma), literally means an *unguent* (ointment) or *smearing*; it conveyed the idea of rubbing an ointment into the skin. In terms of preaching, it refers to a special anointing of the Holy Spirit on the message and on the messenger of God.

"This divine unction," writes E. M. Bounds, "is the feature which separates and distinguishes true gospel preaching from all other methods of presenting the truth and which creates a wide spiritual chasm between the preacher who has it and the one who has it not."

Bounds devotes a chapter in his classic *Preacher and Prayer* to this subject, pointing out that *earnestness* is often mistaken for *unction*. "Earnestness and unction look alike from some points of view. . . . Earnestness may be sincere, serious, ardent, and persevering. It goes at a thing with good will, pursues it with perseverance, and urges it with ardor; puts force in it. But all these forces do not rise higher than mere human."

Unction, on the other hand, "is the sweetest exhalation of the Holy Spirit. It impregnates, suffuses, softens, percolates, cuts, and soothes. It carries the Word like dynamite, like salt, like sugar; makes the Word a soother, an arranger, a revealer, a searcher; makes the hearer a culprit or a saint, makes him weep like a child and live like a giant."

Genuine unction, says Bounds, "comes to the preacher not in the study but in the closet."

Luke 6:45

Finally, I've recently taken Luke 6:45 as my golden rule of preaching: "Out of the abundance (overflow) of the heart his mouth speaks." In other words, preaching is overflow. I shouldn't go to the Bible looking for sermons; I go for my own refreshment, enjoyment, and benefit. I drink from the rivers of God as recorded in His revelation, and the congregation gets the overflow. This is Psalm 23 preaching, when our cup overflowth.

The other day during my quiet time, I found two verses I'd never before connected. In John 4:14, Jesus told the Samaritan woman, "Whoever drinks of the water that I shall give him will never thirst. But the water that I shall give him will become in him a fountain of water springing up into everlasting life."

Sometime later, Jesus added to His metaphor: "He who believes in me, as the Scripture has said, out of his heart will flow rivers of living water" (John 7:38). The water of life wells up within us, then spills over and becomes rivers of living water, irrigating and refreshing a drought-stricken world. That is preaching!

Paul loved this concept of the overflowing life:

- For if the many died by the trespass of the one man, how much more did God's grace and the gift that came by the grace of the one man, Jesus Christ, **overflow** to the many!—Romans 5:15 (NIV)

- May the God of hope fill you with all joy and peace as you trust in him, so that you may **overflow** with hope by the power of the Holy Spirit—Romans 15:13 (NIV)

- For just as the sufferings of Christ flow over into our lives, so also through Christ our comfort **overflows**. . . —2 Corinthians 1:5 (NIV)

- All this is for your benefit, so that the grace that is reaching more and more people may cause thanksgiving to **overflow** to the glory of God—2 Corinthians 4:15 (NIV)

- . . . so that through my being with you again your joy in Christ Jesus will **overflow** on account of me—Philippians 1:26 (NIV)

- . . . **overflowing** with thankfulness—Colossians 2:7 (NIV)

- May the Lord make your love increase and **overflow** for each other and for everyone else, just as ours does for you—1 Thessalonians 3:12 (NIV)

As it relates to preaching, this is beautifully expressed in Francis Ridley Havergal's 1872 hymn, the prayer of all who wish to be expositional, natural, illustrative, anointed, and overflowing bearers of the Word, and this is my prayer for all the readers and users of *Nelson's Annual Preacher's Sourcebook: 2003*—

> *Lord, speak to me that I may speak*
> *In living echoes of Thy tone;*
> *As Thou has sought, so let me seek*
> *Thine erring children lost and lone.*
> *O lead me, Lord, that I may lead*
> *The wandering and the wavering feet;*
> *O feed me, Lord, that I may feed*
> *Thy hungering ones with manna sweet.*
>
> *O teach me, Lord, that I may teach*
> *The precious things Thou dost impart;*

And wing my words, that they may reach
The hidden depths of many a heart.

O fill me with Thy fullness, Lord,
Until my very heart overflow
In kindling thought and glowing word,
Thy love to tell, Thy praise to show.

O use me, Lord, use even me,
Just as Thou wilt, and when, and where,
Until Thy blessèd face I see,
Thy rest, Thy joy, Thy glory share.

Create a Sermon Series!

If you would like to publicize and preach a *series* of messages, you can assemble your own by mixing and matching various sermons and sermon outlines in this *Sourcebook*. Here are some suggestions:

Famous Bible Characters
- Gideon (February 2)
- A Taxing Decision (Matthew) (March 16)
- The Barnabas Secrets (July 20)
- Like Peter (September 28)
- The Bad Girl Who Made Good (November 2)
- Caleb, the Magnificent (November 30)

Strengthening Your Home
- Lasting Love on Mother's Day (May 11)
- Go, Show Your Love to Your Wife (May 25)
- Faithful Fathering (June 15)
- Old Advice for New Fathers (June 15)
- Love in Your Home (June 29)
- How to Iron Out Your Differences Without Being Burned (August 24)
- How to Bless Your Children Real Good (October 26)
- How to Keep Your Marriage from Going to the Dogs (November 9)

Getting A Fresh Start
- A New Attitude for a New Year (January 5)
- When You've Made a Mess of Things (February 2)
- Is It Enough to Be Sorry? (February 16)
- God's Gardens (September 14)
- The Dream of Beginning Again (December 28)

Praying for Results
- Hindrances to Prayer (February 9)
- All About Prayer (February 16)
- God's Prayer Requests (June 8)
- Lord, Teach Us to Pray (July 13)
- Don't Give Up on Believing Prayer (October 5)
- Jesus' Little Sermon on Prayer (December 7)

When Sorrows Like Sea Billows Roll
- Four Answers to Sudden Difficulties (January 5)
- Developing Mega-Faith (January 12)
- A Mind-altering Passage (February 2)
- Our Burdens, Our Battles, and Our Bibles (April 27)
- When Satan Attacks You (August 3)
- Moving from Pain to Praise (October 12)

Making an Impact for Christ
- The Old Lamplighter (June 1)
- Doing Something for God (June 22)
- Go, Stand, and Speak (September 14)
- Passing On the Timeless Message (December 28)

De-Stressing Your Life
- A New Attitude for a New Year (January 5)
- Resourced! (February 16)
- Be Still and Know (March 23)
- Joyful Stress (May 18)
- A Cure for Nerves (November 9)

Look Up! Christ Is Coming Back!
- What We'll Be Doing in Heaven (January 5)
- While We Wait (May 18)
- A Look at the Hereafter (September 21)
- Beyond Today (November 2)
- Anticipation (December 14)

Contributors

Dr. Timothy K. Beougher
Associate Professor, Billy Graham School of Missions, Evangelism, and Church Growth, The Southern Baptist Theological Seminary, Louisville, Kentucky

Hurry Up and Wait! (May 4)
"Deo Volente" (May 4)
Faithful Fathering (June 15)
"Choose Your Attitude Carefully!" (August 24)
Facing Up to a Challenge (September 7)
Taming the Tongue (September 28)

Dr. Stuart Briscoe
Minister at Large, Elmbrook Church, Brookfield, Wisconsin

Gideon (February 2)
A Taxing Decision (March 16)
The Barnabas Secrets (July 20)
Sons of Encouragement (July 20)
Like Peter (September 28)
The Bad Girl Who Made Good (November 2)

Dr. J. Wilber Chapman (1859–1918)
Presbyterian clergyman, evangelist, and author

The Six Best Places to Be (April 27)

Dr. Ed Dobson
Pastor, Calvary Church in Grand Rapids, Michigan, and Moody Bible Institute's 1993 Pastor of the Year

Developing Mega-Faith (January 12)
Is It Enough to Be Sorry? (February 16)
Be Still and Know (March 23)
The Upside-down Kingdom of Jesus (June 29)

Integrity in Doctrine (July 13)
It Was for My Benefit (November 9)

Dr. Michael Duduit
Editor, Preaching *Magazine, Franklin, Tennessee*

Loving God with Your Mind (December 7)
The Dream of Beginning Again (December 28)

William Evans (1870–1950)
Bible teacher and author

He Leadeth Me (April 6)

Rev. Peter Grainger
Pastor, Charlotte Baptist Chapel, Edinburgh, Scotland

Water to Wine (August 31)
A Sick Son Healed (September 21)
Pool of Healing (October 5)
Overcoming Lust (November 2)
No Gains Without Pains (November 16)
The Lord Lives (November 30)
Good News of Great Joy (December 21)
Passing On the Timeless Message (December 28)

W. H. Griffith Thomas (1861–1924)
Anglican minister, Bible teacher, and author

Chock Full of Christ (March 23)

Dr. Jack Hayford
Senior Pastor, The Church On The Way, Van Nuys, California

The Wholeness of Worship (March 2)
Symbols of the Holy Spirit (June 8)
Five Reasons to Be Filled with the Holy Spirit (August 3)

Dr. David Jackman
Director, Cornhill Training Course, London, England

Don't Give Up on Believing Prayer (October 5)
Don't Give Up Sowing to the Spirit (October 19)

Dr. D. James Kennedy
Pastor, Coral Ridge Presbyterian Church, Fort Lauderdale, Florida

The Old Lamplighter (June 1)
Love in Your Home (June 29)
A Look at the Hereafter (September 21)
Caleb, the Magnificent (November 30)

Dr. Stephen Lawson
Pastor, Dauphin Way Baptist Church, Mobile, Alabama

Press On to the Prize (January 26)

Andrew Murray (1828–1917)
Dutch Reformed pastor in South Africa and devotional writer

The Elder Brother Syndrome (April 6)
Lord, Teach Us to Pray (July 13)

Albert Ernest Richardson
Nineteenth-century author

Hindrances to Prayer (February 9)

Rev. Kevin Riggs
Pastor, Franklin Community Church, Franklin, Tennessee

The World Is a Dangerous Place (March 2)
Amazing Grace (March 9)
Signs and Sins of Worldliness (March 16)
Are You in Your Right Mind? (March 30)
Things Aren't Always as They Appear (April 13)

Real Faith, Real Friends (May 25)
Living Your Faith in the Workplace (June 15)
The Power of Temptation (July 20)
Party People (August 24)
Secrets to a Happy Life (September 7)
Living with People (November 16)
The Wonder of Christmas and New Year's Day (December 28)

Rev. Charles Haddon Spurgeon (1834–1892)
Pastor, Metropolitan Tabernacle, London

The Joy of the Lord (July 27)
When Satan Attacks You (August 3)
Perfection (October 12)

Rev. Drew Wilkerson
Pastor, Jersey Shore Church of God, Jersey Shore, Pennsylvania

"It's for Your Own Good" (April 27)
Joyful Stress (May 18)
"Give It a Rest" (June 8)
Are You Listening? (June 29)
"Speak Up!" (August 10)
"Harvest Time" (August 17)
Just Great! (September 7)
Be Passionate! (October 12)
Pray! (November 23)
Looking for Christmas (December 14)

Dr. Melvin Worthington
Executive Secretary, National Association of Free Will Baptists

Looking for Laborers (January 19)
God's Glorious Gospel (March 23)
Hell's Horrors (March 30)
Accurate Accounting (April 6)
Our Burdens, Our Battles, and Our Bibles (April 27)

Lasting Love on Mother's Day (May 11)
While We Wait (May 18)
Jonah's Journey (June 22)
Weighed and Wanting (July 6)
The Sequence of Salvation (July 27)
Growing, Guarding, and Glorifying (August 17)
Obedience: Our Obligation (September 14)
Communicating Christianity (Sept 28)
Searching for a Servant (October 19)
Wise Workers (October 26)
Principles for Partners (November 30)

All other outlines are from the pulpit ministry of the general editor, Rev. Robert J. Morgan, of The Donelson Fellowship in Nashville, Tennessee. Special appreciation goes to Jerry Carraway, worship leader of The Donelson Fellowship, for his invaluable assistance.

2003 Calendar

January 1	New Year's Day
January 5	
January 6	Epiphany
January 12	
January 19	**Sanctity of Human Life Sunday**
January 20	Martin Luther King, Jr. Day
January 26	**Australia Day; Superbowl Sunday**
February 1	National Freedom Day
February 2	**Groundhog Day**
February 9	
February 12	Lincoln's Birthday
February 14	Valentine's Day
February 16	
February 17	Presidents' Day
February 22	Washington's Birthday
February 23	
March 2	
March 5	Ash Wednesday
March 9	**First Sunday of Lent**
March 16	**Second Sunday of Lent**
March 17	St. Patrick's Day
March 23	**Third Sunday of Lent**
March 30	**Mothering Sunday; Fourth Sunday of Lent**
April 6	**Fifth Sunday of Lent; Daylight Savings Time begins**
April 13	**Palm Sunday / Passion Sunday**
April 17	Passover; Holy Thursday
April 18	Good Friday

(all **boldface** dates are Sundays)

April 20	Easter
April 23	Administrative Assistant's Day
April 27	
May 1	National Day of Prayer
May 4	
May 11	Mother's Day
May 17	Armed Forces Day
May 18	
May 25	
May 26	Memorial Day
June 1	Ascension Sunday
June 8	
June 14	Flag Day
June 15	Father's Day
June 21	Summer Solstice
June 22	
June 29	
July 1	Canada Day
July 4	Independence Day
July 6	
July 13	
July 20	
July 27	
August 3	
August 10	Transfiguration Sunday
August 17	
August 24	

August 31	
September 1	Labor Day
September 7	**Grandparents' Day**
September 14	
September 21	
September 28	
October 1–31	Pastor Appreciation Month
October 5	
October 12	
October 13	Columbus Day; Thanksgiving Day (Canada)
October 19	
October 26	**Daylight Savings Time ends**
October 31	Reformation Day; Halloween
November 1	All Saints' Day
November 2	
November 9	
November 11	Veterans Day
November 16	**International Day of Prayer for the Persecuted Church**
November 23	
November 27	Thanksgiving Day
November 30	**First Sunday of Advent**
December 7	**Second Sunday of Advent**
December 14	**Third Sunday of Advent**
December 21	**Fourth Sunday of Advent**
December 22	Winter Solstice
December 25	Christmas
December 27	Hannukah
December 28	
December 31	New Year's Eve

SERMONS AND
WORSHIP SUGGESTIONS
FOR 52 WEEKS

JANUARY 5, 2003

A New Attitude for a New Year   *Date preached:*

Scripture: Psalms 42 and 43, especially Psalm 42:5: Why are you cast down, O my soul? And why are you disquieted within me? Hope in God, for I shall yet praise Him for the help of His countenance.

Introduction: You'd like to begin 2003 saying, "This is the year that the Lord has made. I will rejoice and be glad in it!" But perhaps depression, one of the great afflictions of our age, is dulling your spirits. In Psalms 42 and 43, we see how one man exchanged depression for joy to begin a new emotional era in his life.

1. **My Condition.** Three key words describe this man's condition. First, *downcast*. Peterson translates this: "Why are you down in the dumps?" Other translations say, "Why are you so sad?" or "Why are you discouraged?" A second word is *disquieted*. The Hebrew term conveys the idea of an unpleasant sound, a commotion or clamor. It refers to unpleasant music in the soul. Peterson translates: "Why are you singing the blues, O my soul?" The third word is *mourning* (v. 9). The Hebrew is picturesque, meaning "to be ashen, dark and dingy." The reference may be to one's facial expression or to the garments of sackcloth worn by the grief-stricken. Can you identify?

2. **My Circumstances.** The writer was one of the sons of Korah, Israel's renowned musicians and worship leaders. Yet he begins Psalm 42 telling us he feels separated from God. Evidently this man is exiled both spiritually and geographically. He has been taken from Jerusalem, away from his normal ministry in the temple courts (v. 4). Where is he? Verse 6 offers a clue: "I will remember You from the land of the Jordan, and from the heights of Hermon, from the Hill Mizar. Deep calls unto deep at the noise of Your waterfalls." This man is in the far north, at the headwaters of the Jordan, in the foothills of Mount Hermon. The word *Mizar* means "little," perhaps referring to a smaller hill in the Hermon range in the area known as Caesarea Philippi or Banias. Here the springs and creeks plunge from the mountains, crashing and roaring and forming the beginnings of the

Jordan River. Second Kings 14:14 tells of a time when King Jehoahaz invaded the nation of Judah. He swept into the temple, looted its treasures, and took some of the temple workers hostage to the north. We don't know if this is the historical setting of Psalms 42 and 43, but it fits. Perhaps one of those hostages wrote this psalm. Have you ever felt downcast and disquieted? Exiled? Far from where you want to be in life?

3. **My Cure.** This man is determined not to give in to despondency or self-pity. He's going to fight with three lifelines.

    A. **Talking to God.** Psalm 42 begins as a prayer; and as he prays, this man's confidence grows and his courage returns, as we see at the end of Psalm 43.

    B. **Talking to Others.** In Psalm 42:2, he is no longer praying; he is talking to you and me, to his readers, to whoever will listen. There are six billion people in the world, yet we long for someone to talk to. That's why support groups, chat rooms, and bars are so popular. But you don't need a bar or chat room. Find a Christian friend, open up, and share your heart. Ask others to pray with you. We're never as strong as when kneeling side by side with a friend in need.

    C. **Talking to Myself.** The psalmist also learned how to talk to himself. "Why are you cast down, O my soul? Why so disquieted within me? Hope in God . . . !" He is addressing himself. We often *listen* to ourselves when we should *talk* to ourselves. We have negative little voices inside us, playing discouraging tapes in endless loops. We need to

>>> *sermon continued on following page*

APPROPRIATE HYMNS AND SONGS

O God, Our Help in Ages Past, Isaac Watts/William Croft; Public Domain.

O God, Our Help in Ages Past, Tommy Walker/Isaac Watts/William Croft; © 1998 Douglas Publishing/Maranatha! Music.

I Can Be Glad, Larnelle Harris; © 1990 Lifesong Music Press (Admin. by Brentwood-Benson Music Publishing, Inc.).

The Solid Rock, Edward Mote/William B. Bradbury; Public Domain.

The Solid Rock, Don Harris; © 1992 Integrity's Hosanna! Music.

eject those tapes, take ourselves in hand, sit ourselves down, and give ourselves a talking to. We need to learn to preach to ourselves.

Conclusion: If you've been singing the blues, talk to God about it; talk to a good friend; and talk to yourself. Those three lifelines will be like a triangle of triumph and will enable you to say: "Why are you cast down, O my soul? Why are you disquieted within me? This is the year that the Lord has made. Rejoice and be glad in it."

FOR THE BULLETIN

✱ January 5 is the feast day of one of Christian history's strangest charac-ters—Simeon the Stylite, who lived atop a 60-foot pillar for 36 years, until his death in 459, at age 69. ✱ King Edward the Confessor of England died on this day in 1066. ✱ On January 5, 1527, Felix Manz was drowned in the icy waters of the river Limmat in Zurich for preaching adult baptism, becoming the first of many Anabaptist martyrs. His mother and brother watched from the shore. Manz's last words were, "Into thy hands, O God, I commend my spirit." ✱ January 5, 1782, is the birthday of Robert Morison, founder of Protestant missions in China. ✱ January 5, 1811, is the birthday of Cyrus Hamlin, American missionary and educator, founder of Robert College in Constantinople. ✱ January 5, 1906, is the birthday of archaeologist Kathleen Kenyon, the first person to date the remains of Jericho. ✱ On January 5, 1913, evangelist Wilber Chapman and song-leader Charles M. Alexander began a two-year campaign for Christ across various cities in the United States, beginning in Lima, Ohio. ✱ Following her sensational divorce, popular American evangelist Aimee Semple McPherson, 32, resigned her denomina-tional ordination and returned her fellowship papers to the General Council of the Assemblies of God on this day in 1922. ✱ Peter Marshall was elected Chaplain of the United States Senate on this day in 1947. ✱ Pope Paul VI met with Greek Ecumenical Patriarch Athenagoras I in Jerusalem on January 5, 1964, marking the first such meeting between leaders of the Roman Catholic and Greek Orthodox Churches since the 15th century.

STATS, STORIES AND MORE

Depression

- Hans Christian Anderson lived in Copenhagen and wrote delightful books for children that are famous to this day, but he suffered all his life from depression. On one occasion he wrote in his journal, "I have no future anymore, nothing to look forward to, no ideas, I am washed out!"
- Winston Churchill's powerful, determined oratory rallied the morale of England, but he battled depression all his life, which he called the "black dog" that continually attacked him.
- Charles Spurgeon's sermons have been read daily all over the world for over 100 years, but he suffered deep depression.
- The prophet Jeremiah is called "the weeping prophet" because of his struggles with depression. Even our Lord Himself, said, "Now my soul is troubled" (John 12:27), and "My soul is exceedingly sorrowful" (Mark 14:34).

Grace to Help in Time of Need

"One day I was in trouble and oppressed about many things. It was one of those days when everything seems to go wrong. I was trying to get my Quiet Time but was constantly interrupted. Suddenly these words came—I could hardly believe they were in the Bible, they seemed so new to my needy heart— 'Grace to help in time of need.' I found them and read them and marked them with joy, and in that moment, the moment of their coming, I was renewed in strength."—*Amy Carmichael*

Talking to Ourselves

John Stott wrote about Psalm 42 and 43: "It is remarkable to note how the author speaks to himself. He will not give in to his moods. He takes himself in hand and reproaches himself for his depression. He recognizes that his soul is weighed down as by a crushing burden, and inwardly disturbed like the raging of the sea. But why? he asks himself. Within his repeated self-questioning is an implied rebuke. Instead of answering his own questions, or excusing himself, he immediately prescribes his remedy: he must trust or "hope" in God. He must give up his introspection and self-pity. . . . The cure for depression is neither to look in at our grief, nor back to our past, nor round at our problems, but away and up to the living God."

WORSHIP HELPS

Call to Worship:
"I am the LORD, that is My name; and My glory I will not give to another . . . . Behold, the former things have come to pass, and new things I declare" (Isa. 42:8–9).

Pastoral Prayer:
Almighty God, You are the Lord. You are Jehovah. That is Your name, and You will not give Your glory to another. From the outset of a new year, O Lord, teach us to praise Your name, and teach us anew to pray. As someone said, "Prayer changes things—and yet how blind and slow we are to taste and see / the blessedness that comes to those who trust in Thee." Help us to praise You, help us to pray, help us to trust. And may this Year of our Lord, 2003, be a season of praise and progress beyond any we've known thus far. We ask in Jesus' name. Amen.

Scripture Reading Medley:
Why are you cast down, O my soul? And *why* are you disquieted within me? Hope in God. For whatever things were written before were written for our learning, that we through the patience and comfort of the Scriptures might have hope. "And now, Lord, what do I wait for? My hope is in You. I hope in Your word. LORD, I hope for Your salvation.—"The LORD is my portion," says my soul, "Therefore I hope in Him!"

Revive the stones from the heaps of rubbish. Revive us, and we will call upon Your name. Turn us back to You, O LORD, and we will be restored; Renew our days as of old. Now may the God of hope fill you with all joy and peace in believing, that you may abound in hope by the power of the Holy Spirit. (Ps. 42:5; Rom. 15:4; Pss. 39:7; 119:81; 119:166; Lam. 3:24; Neh. 4:2; Ps. 80:18; Lam. 5:21; and Rom. 15:13)

Additional Sermons and Lesson Ideas

Four Answers to Sudden Difficulties

Date preached:

SCRIPTURE: Proverbs 3:5

INTRODUCTION: When faced with sudden difficulty, our hearts often question God's love, but He has answers for all our questions.

1. Lord, how do I survive this trial? "[Take] the shield of faith with which you will be able to quench all the fiery darts of the wicked one" (Eph. 6:16).
2. But this is not just a fiery dart. It's a fiery trial! "[You] are kept by the power of God through faith . . . though now for a little while, if need be, you have been grieved by various trials, that the genuineness of your faith, being much more precious than gold that perishes, though it is tested by fire, may be found to praise" (1 Pet. 1:5–7).
3. But Satan is harming us! "[He] meant evil . . . but God meant it for good" (Gen. 50:20).
4. What do I do? "Trust in the Lord with all your heart" (Prov. 3:5).

What We'll Be Doing in Heaven

Date preached:

SCRIPTURE: Revelation 21–22

INTRODUCTION: Some people visualize heaven as white-robed saints sitting on the edges of clouds playing harps. That's not the picture John gives in Revelation 21–22. A study of those chapters shows that, among other things, these four activities will occupy our attention:

1. Exploring the Golden City. John was given a "city tour" of the New Jerusalem, and his description is given to prepare us for our own trip (Rev. 21:10–22:3).
2. Serving. This is the Bible's most definitive verse about our eternal occupation (Rev. 22:3).
3. Fellowshipping with Jesus. "We shall see Him face to face and tell the story saved by grace" (Rev. 22:4).
4. Reigning with Him. (Rev. 22:5).
5. Worshiping. (Rev. 22:6–9).

CONCLUSION: Just as you study the travel brochures before a trip and try to learn all you can about the destination you're going to visit, so with heaven. Even so, come, Lord Jesus.

JANUARY 12, 2003

SUGGESTED SERMON

Developing Mega-Faith

Date preached:

By Ed Dobson

Scripture: Mark 7:24–30, especially verses 27–29. See also Matthew 15:21–28: But Jesus said to her, "Let the children be filled first, for it is not good to take the children's bread and throw it to the little dogs." And she answered and said to Him, "Yes, Lord, yet even the little dogs under the table eat from the children's crumbs." Then He said to her, "For this saying go your way; the demon has gone out of your daughter."

Introduction: In this story Jesus left the Jewish area of Galilee for the seaport of Tyre, a pagan Gentile area. This was a very un-Jewish and un-rabbinical thing to do, but He knew there was a desperate mother there. Notice the verbs describing her: she heard about Him, came, fell at his feet, and begged His help. Yet Jesus answered her not a word. Her response to His non-response was to keep crying for mercy. Desperate people do desperate things. When you're desperate you don't care what people think, nor do you give up easily. Jesus finally said, in summary, "I've been sent to the lost sheep of Israel. My mission is the Jews. Why take the food of children and give it to dogs?" The word *dog* would be better translated, *little dog* or *puppy.* "It is not right to take the children's bread and toss it to their puppy." Jesus was not being unkind, but making a theological point—His first priority was the Jewish people. "Yes, Lord," the woman replied, "but even the puppies under the table get some crumbs." In other words, "What you're saying is true, but I don't need the full meal. Just a few crumbs will be sufficient." Can you sense this woman's faith? Jesus did. "Woman," He said, "you have great faith!" The Greek word is μεγας (*meg´-as*), source of the English prefix *mega.* This woman had mega-faith! From this story, notice the characteristics of mega-faith:

1. **Mega-faith does not deny the problem.** It is not the power of positive thinking or a way of looking at life through rose-colored glasses. Mega-faith is realistic, acknowledging the challenges, difficulties, struggles, and sufferings.

2. **Mega-faith goes directly to the source of blessing.** As soon as she heard of Christ, she came and fell at His feet. We sometimes depend too much on our own abilities and resources. But great faith knows that beyond our own resources is the source of all power and blessing—God Himself! (See Heb. 4:14–16.)

3. **Mega-faith throws itself at the feet of Jesus.** This was an act of submission, carrying the idea of abandonment to the purpose, plan, and power of God. She didn't come with her own plan and ask Jesus to bless it. She said, "Lord, I give this to You." It's frightening to give up control, but when we yield control to Christ, what freedom comes!

4. **Mega-faith is persistent.** At first, Jesus doesn't answer this woman; and when He finally did answer her, His tone was discouraging. But she kept begging. We should always pray and not faint. Prayer and faith persist, even when God seems to respond not a word.

5. **Mega-faith repeats the word of God.** This woman took what Jesus said, repeated it back to Him, then added a request to it. Great faith is anchored in Scripture.

6. **Mega-faith responds with submission.** "Yes, Lord," the woman said. Those are two very important words in our prayer vocabulary. They acknowledge Him who is in charge, like Jesus in the Garden, ". . . not my

>>> sermon continued on following page

APPROPRIATE HYMNS AND SONGS

Until That Final Day, Dennis Jernigan; © 1991 Shepherd's Heart Music (Admin. by Word Music Group, Inc.).

Burdens Are Lifted at Calvary, John M. Moore; © 1952 Singspiration Music (Admin. by Brentwood-Benson Music Publishing, Inc.).

Faith Is the Victory, John H. Yates/Ira D. Sankey; Public Domain.

God Can Do It Again, Don Moen; © 1976 Integrity's Hosanna! Music.

Have Faith in God, B. B. McKinney; © 1934. Renewed 1962 Broadman Press (Admin. by Genevox Music Group.).

will, but Your will be done." Great faith surrenders the outcome to God, Who knows what is best for us.

7. **Mega-faith is always rewarded.** Going home, this woman found her child whole and the demon gone. Great faith is always rewarded with divine intervention which comes either through a miracle or through a specific message from God that enables us on the journey.

Conclusion: Maybe you're thinking, "That's easy for you to preach, but you don't know what I'm facing this morning." The beauty of this story is that it was not the faith of the demon-possessed girl that brought healing, it was the faith of her loving mother. If you can't muster mega-faith, learn to trust in the faith of those around you. God honors their faith on your behalf. Never underestimate the prayers and faith of others in your behalf. God, grant us great faith. Amen!

FOR THE BULLETIN

❁ After the death of Queen Elizabeth I, the English Puritans petitioned her successor, King James I, for changes in the Church of England. On January 12, 1604, the king convened a conference of church leaders at Hampton Court Conference. During that conference, King James authorized a new translation of the Bible which would later bear his name. ❁ On January 12, 1755, John Fletcher, battling conviction of sin, wrote in his diary: "All my righteousness is as filthy rags. I am a very devil, though of an inferior sort, and if I am not renewed before I go hence, hell will be my portion for all eternity." Shortly afterward, he confessed Christ Jesus as Lord and went on to become one of early Methodism's greatest leaders. ❁ As a youth, George Mueller, something of a rogue, was arrested for sneaking out of hotels without paying his bills. On January 12, 1822, he was released from jail, was later converted, and became famous in Christian history for his relief ministries to orphans. ❁ On January 12, 1836, the HMS Beagle with Charles Darwin aboard reached Sydney, Australia. ❁ On January 12, 1906, the Dow Jones closed above 100 (100.26) for the first time ever. ❁ On January 12, 1957, the Southern Christian Leadership Conference (SCLC) was founded by Martin Luther King and his followers to coordinate and assist local organizations working for the full equality of African-Americans in all aspects of American life.

STATS, STORIES AND MORE

Faith or Peek-a-Boo?

Remember when your kids were young and you used to play "peek-a-boo" with them? They would cover their face and say, "Where are you?" They would think because they covered their face and they couldn't see anybody else, nobody else could see them. It was "peek-a-boo." I think sometimes we think that faith is the equivalent of spiritual "peek-a-boo." If we cover our eyes, if we ignore the problem, if we dismiss the problem, if we avoid the problem, if we try to go around the problem, that somehow it will all go away. But great faith begins by acknowledging I have a serious problem. Faith does not ignore the challenges, the problems, the difficulties, the struggles, the sufferings.—*Ed Dobson*

Another Mother's Earnest Prayer

Ruth Bell Graham, in her book *Prodigals and Those Who Love Them,* records a prayer of her own, knowing from experience the worries of a mother whose children go through difficulties:

Listen, Lord,
a mother's praying
low and quiet:
listen, please.
Listen what her tears
are saying,
see her heart
upon its knees;
lift the load
from her bowed shoulders
till she sees
and understands,
You, Who hold
the worlds together,
hold her problems
in Your hands.

Praying Scripture

Praying Scriptural prayers for our children helps us focus on the positives. In his book *Parenting the Prodigal,* S. Rutherford McDill Jr., writes, "*Hope* is believing that what we want to happen will eventually happen, that everything will eventually work itself out and end up okay. Such at attitude allows you to avoid getting so discouraged that you abandon your child when he needs you the most."

WORSHIP HELPS

Call to Worship:

"For I am not ashamed of the gospel of Christ . . . for in it the righteousness of God is revealed from faith to faith; as it is written, 'The
just shall live by faith'" (Rom. 1:16–17).

Readers' Theater:

Reader 1:   Hear now these Scriptures from Matthew's Gospel.

Reader 2:   Now if God so clothes the grass of the field, which
today is, and tomorrow is thrown into the oven, will He
not much more clothe you, O you of little faith?

Reader 1:   When Jesus heard it, He marveled, and said to those
who followed, "Assuredly, I say to you, I have not found
such great faith, not even in Israel!

Reader 3:   But He said to them, "Why are you fearful, O you of little faith?"

Reader 2:   When Jesus saw their faith, He said to the paralytic,
"Son, be of good cheer; your sins are forgiven you."

Reader 1:   When He saw her He said, "Be of good cheer, daughter; your faith has made you well."

All: Then He touched their eyes, saying, "According to your
faith let it be to you." And their eyes were opened.

Reader 3:   And immediately Jesus stretched out His hand and
caught him, and said to him, "O you of little faith, why
did you doubt?"

Reader 2:   Then Jesus answered and said to her, "O woman, great
is your faith!"

Reader 1:   But Jesus . . . said to them, "O you of little faith, why do
you reason among yourselves because you have
brought no bread?"

Rdrs 1/2:   Jesus said to them, "Because of your unbelief; for
assuredly, I say to you, if you have faith as a mustard
seed, you will say to this mountain, 'Move from here to
there,' and it will move."

All: So Jesus answered and said to them, "Assuredly, I say
to you, if you have faith and do not doubt, you will not
only do what was done to the fig tree, but also if you say
to this mountain, 'Be removed and be cast into the sea,'
it will be done. And whatever things you ask in prayer,
believing, you will receive." (Matt. 6:30; 8:10; 8:26; 9:2;
9:22; 9:29–30; 14:31; 15:28; 16:8; 17:20; and 21:21–22)

Additional Sermons and Lesson Ideas

Looking Up or Giving Up

Date preached:

SCRIPTURE: Luke 18:1–8

INTRODUCTION: Luke 18:1 says, "Then He spoke a parable to them, that men always ought to pray and not lose heart." While we appreciate the ensuing parable, there is great encouragement even in His prefacing explanatory note.

1. Ought. This Greek is δεῖ (pronounced *day*), conveying the idea of necessity. The same word is used in Luke 24:46: "Thus it was necessary for the Christ to suffer. . . ." As it was necessary for Christ to accomplish the atonement through suffering, prayer is necessary for us to avoid fainting.
2. Always is πάντοτε (*pan´-tot-eh*), meaning "at all times, on all occasions, evermore."
3. Pray is προσεύχομαι (*pros-yoo´-khom-ahee*), the standard New Testament word for praying to God. It covers all forms of prayer.
4. Faint is ἐκκακέω (*ek-kak´-eh´-o*), which means "to lose heart, to be faint-hearted, to lose courage, to give up, to collapse."

CONCLUSION: Missionary J. O. Fraser wrote in his journal during a discouraging time: "I'm now setting my face like a flint: if the work seems to fail, then pray; if services and the like fall flat, then pray still more; if months slip by with little or no result, then pray still more and get others to help you." Fraser did, and he reaped a great harvest. Do you have a stubborn problem today? Always pray, and don't give up.

What the Risen Christ Gives Us

Date preached:

SCRIPTURE: John 20:1–23

INTRODUCTION: When Jesus rose from the grave, He met His followers with outstretched hands, and they were full of blessings and gifts. The Risen Christ gives us:

1. Comfort (vv. 10–18). His first words were, "Woman, why are you weeping?"
2. Peace (v. 19). His first words to His disciples were, "Peace be with you!"
3. Gladness (v. 20). John 20:20 says, "Then were the disciples glad when they saw the Lord." This is genuine 20/20 vision.
4. Purpose (v. 21). This is John's version of the Great Commission.
5. The Holy Spirit (vv. 22–23), with all His attendant blessings and benefits.

CONCLUSION: For the Christian, every day is Easter, and the Easter blessings of the Risen Christ are ours moment by moment, throughout all our lives.

JANUARY 19, 2003

SUGGESTED SERMON

This Ain't the Ritz

Date preached:

Scripture: John 6:35–40, especially verse 37b: . . . the one who comes to Me I will by no means cast out.

Introduction: If we visited Paris and strolled like gaudy sightseers into the gilded lobby of the Ritz Hotel at the Place Vendôme, the concierge would look on us with disapproval. The hotel is exclusive, and we wouldn't feel comfortable milling around in our tourist garb. I wonder if some people feel similarly uncomfortable coming to church—or coming to Christ? Does anyone feel unworthy of Christ, thinking their life is too soiled or their past too messed up? The Lord's response: "The one who comes to Me I will by no means cast out." The Greek phrase is emphatic: "I will absolutely never reject—cast out—the one who is coming to me." This verse has comforted many people.

I. **Personal Examples**
   A. While dying, Bishop Joseph Butler fell into uncertainty. A sense of his own sinfulness filled him with terrible concern. A friend, trying to comfort him, said, "You know, sir, that Jesus is a great Savior." "Yes," replied Butler, "I know He died to save. But how shall I know He died to save me?" "My lord," said the friend, "it is written that him who cometh to Me I will in no wise cast out!" Butler's eyes brightened. "I am surprised that, though I have read that scripture a thousand times, I never felt its virtue until this moment. Now I die happy."
   B. A man came to D. L. Moody, thinking his life was so messed up that not even God could help him. Moody quoted this verse: "Him that cometh to Me I will in no wise cast out." The man had further objections, but was finally converted through this verse.
   C. W. F. Thompson was converted by seeing this verse in a Gideon Bible while recovering from a gunshot wound. He later entered the ministry.
   D. John Bunyan was poorly educated, the son of a tinker—a mender of pots and pans. He was godless and his language was vile. One day he overheard some women talking about the Lord. He was impressed by

their words and demeanor, and he craved this kind of life; but, fearing he had committed the unpardonable sin, he sank into depression. One day he found John 6:37. That verse changed his life, and later, in *Pilgrim's Progress,* he used it to point poor Pilgrim to Christ.

E. Charlotte Elliott of Brighton, England, was an embittered invalid. Hoping to help her, a Swiss minister, Dr. Cesar Malan, visited her. Over dinner, Charlotte lost her temper and railed against God. Her family left the room, and Dr. Malan, alone with her, stared at her across the table, saying, "You are tired of yourself, aren't you?" "What is your cure?" asked Charlotte. "The faith you are trying to despise." As they talked, Charlotte softened. "If I wanted to become a Christian and to share the peace and joy you possess," she asked, "what would I do?" "You would give yourself to God just as you are now." Charlotte did come just as she was. Her heart was changed that day. As time passed, she found and claimed John 6:37 as a special verse for her. Charlotte later wrote a poem which was sold across England in a leaflet that was headlined with John 6:37. Underneath was Charlotte's poem, which became the famous invitational hymn: "Just As I Am."

2. **Biblical Examples.** Levi was despised, but Jesus came to him, loved him, received him, and made him a new person. Bartimaus' friends told him to keep quiet, but Jesus heard his voice. A demon-possessed woman

>>> sermon continued on following page

APPROPRIATE HYMNS AND SONGS

Just as I Am, Charlotte Elliott/William B. Bradbury; Public Domain.

Come Just as You Are, Joseph Sabolick; © 1993 Maranatha Praise, Inc. (Admin. by The Copyright Company).

Bring Christ Your Broken Life, Thomas O. Chisholm/L.O. Sanderson; © 1935, 1963 L.O. Sanderson.

Come to the River of Life, Don Moen/Claire Cloninger; © 1995 Integrity's Hosanna! Music/Juniper Landing Music (Admin. by Word Music Group, Inc.).

Eternal Father, Strong to Save, William Whiting/John Bacchus Dykes/Robert Nelson Spencer; Public Domain.

named Mary Magdalene was scorned by her own people, but Jesus made her into a new person.

Conclusion: The operative word is "Come." *Him that cometh to Me . . .* What does it mean to come to Jesus?

- "C" stands for "Confess your sins."
- "O" stands for "Open your heart."
- "M" stands for "Meet the Master."
- "E" stands for "Enter into everlasting life."

FOR THE BULLETIN

✵ January 19, 570, is the traditional date for the birth of Mohammed, founder of Islam. ✵ On January 19, 1563, the Heidelberg Confession, written by Peter Ursinus and Caspar Olevianus, was first published. ✵ Miles Coverdale, publisher of the first printed English Bible, died at age 80 on this day in 1568. ✵ Jonathan Blanchard, founder of Wheaton College and Knox College, both in Illinois, was born on this day in 1811 in Vermont. ✵ Rodney (Gipsy) Smith began the first of many preaching trips to America on January 19, 1889, sailing from Liverpool aboard the *Umbria*. He later wrote, "I landed in New York on a miserably wet Sunday morning, a perfect stranger, not knowing, to the best of my belief, a single soul on the whole vast continent. I took up my quarters at the Astor Hotel and sat down to think what I should do." He later became a sought-after and powerful evangelist on both sides of the Atlantic. ✵ On January 19, 1897, Mel Trotter was converted at the Pacific Garden Mission of Chicago. ✵ The Hymn Society of America (now called Hymn Society in the United States and Canada), was established on January 19, 1922. ✵ At 6 p.m. on January 19, 1942, Father Titus Brandsma of the Netherlands was arrested by the Nazi Gestapo. "Imagine my going to jail at the age of sixty," he told the arresting officer. He later perished at Dachau. ✵ January 19, 1949, marks the death of the gospel songwriter, Charles Price Jones. ✵ On January 19, 1981, Wycliffe missionary Chet Bitterman was kidnapped in Columbia and later executed.

The D. L. Moody Story

A man came to D. L. Moody, feeling that his life was so messed up that not even God could help him. Moody quoted John 6:37: "Him that cometh to Me I will in no wise cast out." The man said, "But brother Moody, I am an alcoholic and a drunkard." Moody replied, "It does not say, 'Him that cometh to Me who is not a drunkard I will in no wise cast out.'" The man said, "But I have abandoned my wife and my children." "That is a dreadful thing," said Moody, "but it does not say, 'Him that cometh to Me who has not abandoned wife and children I will in no wise cast out.'" The man said, "But I have stolen; I have been in jail." "Still," said Moody, "it does not say, 'Him that cometh to Me who has never stolen, who has never been in jail, I will in no wise cast out.' It merely says, "Him that cometh to Me I will in no wise cast out.' That covers you without argument or exception." The man was convinced.

The W. F. Thompson Story

At 17, W. F. Thompson joined the Marines and emerged from boot camp a savage fighter who craved blood. "In combat, I enjoyed killing," he recalled, "especially with a bayonet." After the war, Thompson moved to Raleigh, North Carolina, where he went into business. One Friday a man entered his office and, brandishing a gun, demanded money from the firm's safe. Thompson pursued the man from the building and down the street, but the gunman turned and fired, striking Thompson in the chest and arm. Thompson clung to life through the weekend, but on Monday the doctors urged his wife to call the undertaker. Thompson clung to life and at length opened his eyes and glanced about the room. He spied a Bible open on the bedside table. Reaching over with a groan, he closed it and sank back into a stupor. The next time he opened his eyes he saw the New Testament opened. He managed to slam it shut. When his eyes opened the third time, the book was open again. Summoning his strength, he seized it with his good arm to hurl it across the room. But as the Bible hovered above his head, its pages opened to John 6, and the words of verse 37 hit him like a hail of bullets. Thompson later shared this text when he preached his first sermon at the old Trinity Lutheran Church in Du Bois, Pennsylvania.

WORSHIP HELPS

Call to Worship:
"And the Spirit and the bride say, 'Come!' And let him who hears say, 'Come!' And let him who thirsts come. Whoever desires, let him take the water of life freely" (Rev. 22:17).

Scripture Reading Medley:
"Come now, and let us reason together," says the LORD, "Though your sins are like scarlet, they shall be as white as snow; though they are red like crimson, they shall be as wool. Ho! Everyone who thirsts, come to the waters; and you who have no money, come, buy and eat . . . without money and without price. Why do you spend money for what is not bread, and your wages for what does not satisfy? Listen carefully to Me, and eat what is good, and let your soul delight itself in abundance. Incline your ear, and come to Me; hear, and your soul shall live. Come to Me, all you who labor and are heavy laden, and I will give you rest. Let him who thirsts come . . . let him take the water of life freely. (Isa. 1:18; 55:1–3a; Matt. 11:28; and Rev. 22:17)

Benediction:
Now may the Lord use us this week to extend and strengthen His kingdom for Christ and His glory, in Jesus' name, Amen.

Additional Sermons and Lesson Ideas

Brain Transplant

Date preached:

SCRIPTURE: "Let this mind be in you which was also in Christ Jesus" (Phil. 2:5, NIV; see also Prov. 15:25).

INTRODUCTION: How often we have trouble with our thoughts—anxious thoughts, immoral thoughts, mistaken thoughts. Perhaps you need a "thought transplant."

    1. Our Thoughts
        A. Evil (Gen. 6:5; Matt. 9:4; 15:19, NIV).
        B. Godless (Ps. 10:4).
        C. Futile (Ps. 94:11).
    2. God's Thoughts
        A. Higher (Isa. 55:8–9).
        B. Precious (Ps. 139:17).
        C. Deep (Ps. 92:5).

CONCLUSION: May the Lord give us the mind of Christ, helping us think as He thinks regarding matters on our minds today. This "brain transplant" is the essence of sanctification and is accomplished by letting His word dwell richly with us (Col. 3:16). He sanctifies us through His truth (John 17:17).

Looking for Laborers

Date preached:

By Melvin Worthington

SCRIPTURE: Matthew 9:35-38; John 4:34–38; 1 Corinthians 3:5–9

INTRODUCTION: One of the issues the church grapples with is the need for laborers. Various methods have been devised for recruiting workers. While it may not be wrong to use a number of methods to discover, direct, and deploy workers we must never lose sight of God's way.

    1. The Lord of the Harvest. The Lord of the harvest knows the *state* of the harvest, the *shortage* of workers, and the *source* of the workers.
    2. Laborers for the Harvest. The Lord *directs* His disciples to pray to the Lord of the harvest. The Lord is responsible for the *deployment* of personnel. The Lord also *designates* the placement of personnel.
    3. The Laws of the Harvest. The laws of the harvest include the *sovereignty* of the Sovereign, the *supplication* of the saints, the *sending* of the servants, and the *sharing* in the success.

CONCLUSION: Laborers are needed for the harvest. The simple sufficient solution to the shortage of servants is to pray to the Lord of the harvest.

JANUARY 26, 2003

SUGGESTED SERMON

Press On to the Prize

Date preached:

By Steven J. Lawson

Scripture: 1 Corinthians 9:24–27: Do you not know that those who run in a race all run, but one receives the prize? Run in such a way that you may obtain it. And everyone who competes for the prize is temperate in all things. Now they do it to obtain a perishable crown, but we for an imperishable crown. Therefore I run thus: not with uncertainty. Thus I fight: not as one who beats the air. But I discipline my body and bring it into subjection, lest, when I have preached to others, I myself should become disqualified.

Introduction: Perhaps the most dramatic scene in sports is the marathoner's last lap at the end of a grueling 26-mile race. As the fatigued figure presses to the finish line, the crowd in the Olympic stadium cheers him on. Straining every muscle, the runner pushes through the tape and, before the watching world, is awarded the prize. Drawing from this athletic imagery, the apostle Paul compared the Christian life to a grueling marathon, an event well-known to first-century Christians. Writing to Corinthians, believers who lived only ten miles from the famous Isthmian games, he challenged them not merely to enter the race of faith, but to go "all out" and run so as to win. God wants winners! In our present sports-crazed society, perhaps no biblical metaphor better illustrates the reality of living for Christ. What are the keys to victory?

I. **Determination** (v. 24). One can't win a marathon with halfhearted effort. The runner must have a will to win, a strong resolve. It isn't enough to be in the Christian race. Rather, once entered, we must take our spiritual life seriously, pushing to the limit, deeply committed. This is not speaking of salvation or earning entrance into the race; it is calling us to make whatever sacrifice is necessary to win the victor's crown at the end. The most coveted prize of the Roman Empire was the *stephanos,* the laurel-like wreath placed on the head of the champion. Made of leafy greenery, the victor's crown brought instant fame, tax-exemption, and free education. Calling for our total commitment, the apostle Paul writes, "They do it to obtain a perishable crown, but we for an imperishable crown." If a marathoner would be so dedicated to win a withering pine wreath and short-lived fame, how much more ought we be determined to gain the eternal, imperishable crown?

2. **Discipline** (v. 25). In the ancient games, victory depended on the athlete's rigorous training. Every runner entered strict training under the watchful eye of an official. Marathon runners were known to work out for years— lifting weights, running laps, regulating sleep, restricting their diet. Self-control means we must exercise mastery over our lives, foregoing some pleasures, pursuing other disciplines, all for the sake of winning. We must be committed to the basic spiritual disciplines of the Christian life— Bible study, prayer, and meditation *(see 1 Tim. 4:7–8)*.

3. **Direction** (v. 26). The marathon course was clearly marked, winding through the landscape, and the runner needed to stay on course, his eyes on the goal. Paul said that he wasn't running aimlessly or uncertainly, without a goal. The divinely designed track of God's will is clearly marked by His Word. It is a narrow path that includes every aspect of our lives. Winning the prize requires seeking direction from Scripture and following the course it requires.

4. **Denial** (v. 27). Athletes had to give up certain comforts and to "punish" their bodies, foregoing a life of ease and bodily impulses. The same self-denial is necessary for the Christian. After making that point in verse 27, Paul shifted metaphors from running to boxing, saying that we must beat

>>> sermon continued on following page

APPROPRIATE HYMNS AND SONGS

Come, Christians Join to Sing, Christian H. Bateman; Public Domain.

Dare to Run, Harlan Moore/Joel W. Smith; © 1989 Lillenas Publishing Company (Admin. by The Copyright Company.).

Find Us Faithful, John Mohr; © 1987 Jonathan Mark Music (Admin. by EMI Christian Music Publishing.).

I Will Run to You, Darlene Zschech; © 1996 Darlene Zschech/Hillsong (Admin. by Integrity Music, Inc.).

It Will Be Worth It All, William J. Gaither; © 1967 William J. Gaither, Inc. (Admin. by Gaither Copyright Management.).

our bodies, wielding a series of knockout punches to fleshly desires. We must resist temptation, mortify sensual lusts that would defeat us, and remain pure. Even Paul feared that having preached to others, he would be disqualified, referring not to the loss of salvation but of reward.

Conclusion: After the race, every runner was brought to stand before the raised, wooden platform in the middle of the track that supported a throne-like seat for the judge. Each athlete would be crowned, passed over, or disqualified. So it will be for us as believers in Christ (2 Cor. 5:10). Every step of the Christian life has eternal importance. Right now counts forever! Let us run with growing antici-pation of that moment when we will stand before Christ.

FOR THE BULLETIN

✱ On January 26, 1564, the decrees of the Council of Trent were confirmed by Pope Pius IV in his "Benedictus Deus." ✱ Two Scottish Christians, Isabel Alison and Marion Harvie, were executed together on January 26, 1681, for their faith. Marion, 20, wrote, "Farewell, brethren! Farewell, sisters! Welcome my lovely, heartsome Christ Jesus, into Whose hands I commit my spirit." ✱ St. Paulinus of Aquilei, prominent eighth-century priest, led a busy and fruitful life until his death in 804. His bones were deposited in the church of Friuli, Italy, but were later moved because of renovations. On January 26, 1734, amid great pomp, the remains of Paulinus were reinterred under the choir in the chapel of the great basilica of Friuli. ✱ Cyrus McCormick went to Chicago with $60 in his pocket, invented the reaper, and became a millionaire. On January 26, 1859, he married Nettie Fowler, a radi-ant Christian. When Cyrus died 26 years later, Nettie devoted her vast wealth to evangelical missionary projects. ✱ January 26, 1885, marks the death of General Charles Gordon, British military genius and devout Christian, slain at age 51 by Sudanese troops in Khartoum. ✱ London pastor Joseph Parker wrote this in his autobiography about the passing of his wife, Emma: "On January 26th, 1899, I entered upon my old age, for at 9:30 that night the life of my life, the heart of my heart, ascended to the right hand of God." ✱ The first General Assembly of the Church of God convened on this day in 1906. Headquartered today in Cleveland, Tennessee, the Church of God is the old-est Pentecostal denomination in the United States.

The Marathon

This race called the marathon began almost 2,500 years ago when a Greek soldier, Pheidippedes, was dispatched to run to Athens with news of victory from the battle of Marathon. After running through the night, he delivered the news just before collapsing dead from overexertion. Instantly, Pheidippedes became a national hero, a symbol of patriotism and dedication. Thus the "marathon" was born.—*Steven J. Lawson*

Eyes on the Prize

An aimless runner, one who lacks clear direction, will never win. If he is to capture the crown, he must compete with a certain knowledge of the track that is set before him. With singular purpose, Paul ran God's race for his life. His stated goal was to advance the gospel and win as many people as possible to Jesus Christ. We, too, must have this goal to win others to Christ if we are to run with aim. Let me ask you: Are you running with divine direction and eternal purpose? Do you have this fixed goal clearly in mind? Whatever you do, stay on track with your life.—*Steven J. Lawson*

From Charles Swindoll's *Living Above the Level of Mediocrity*

Several decades have passed since my unforgettable days in boot camp. But some of the lessons learned back then are still with me—lessons like listening to the right voice, like ignoring the movements of the majority, and like being disciplined enough to filter the essential from the incidental. The ramifications of this kind of discipline have been life-changing. They include, for example, committing myself to excellence while many are comfortable with the mediocre, aiming high though most seem to prefer the boredom of aiming low, and marching to the distinct beat of another drummer while surrounded by a cacophony of persuasive sounds pleading for me to join their ranks. Remember the way James Russell Lowell put it:

> Life is a leaf of paper white
> Whereon each one of us may write
> His word or two, and then comes night.
> Greatly begin! though thou have time
> But for a line, be that sublime—
> Not failure, but low aim, is crime.

WORSHIP HELPS

"Let all with heart and voice / before His throne rejoice / Praise is His gracious choice. / Alleluia! Amen!" (From *Come, Christians, Join to Sing* by Christian H. Bateman.)

Scripture Reading: 1 Timothy 4:6–10
If you instruct the brethren in these things, you will be a good minister of Jesus Christ, nourished in the words of faith and of the good doctrine that you have carefully followed. But reject profane and old wives' fables, and exercise yourself toward godliness. For bodily exercise profits a little, but godliness is profitable for all things, having promise of the life that now is and of that which is to come. This is a faithful saying and worthy of all acceptance. For to this end we both labor and suffer reproach, because we trust in the living God, who is the Savior of all men, especially of those who believe. These things command and teach.

Benediction:
To Him who is the blessed and only Potentate, the King of kings and Lord of lords, who alone has immortality, dwelling in unapproachable light, whom no man has seen or can see—to Him be honor and everlasting power. Amen (1 Tim. 6:15–16).

Kids Talk

What is your favorite exercise? Do you like push-ups? Sit-ups? What about running? Have any of you ever won a race? Why do we exercise our bodies? Yes, so we'll be strong and healthy. God gave us our bodies; we must take care of them. He also gave to each of us a mind and a soul, and it is even more important to take care of those. How do we "exercise" our souls? By reading the Bible and praying each day, and by being kind and helpful to others.

Additional Sermons and Lesson Ideas

Perhaps This Year!

Date preached:

SCRIPTURE: Acts 1:9-11

INTRODUCTION: As January draws to a close, it's good to remind ourselves again that this may be the year Christ returns. At the Ascension, two angels told the disciples that He would return "in like manner" as He departed. That implies:

1. His Return Will Be Physical. "This same Jesus . . . will so come in like man-ner." It will be a bodily return, as literal, physical, and bodily as His Ascension.
2. His Return Will Be Visible. He was taken up before their very eyes, as they watched intently. (See Zech. 12:10; Rev. 1:7; Mark 14:62; Matt. 24:30.)
3. His Return Will Be in the Clouds. Many scholars believe the clouds receiv-ing Him were the Shekinah clouds of God's glory. He will come again in like manner. (See Dan. 7:13; Matt. 24:30; 26:64; 1 Thess. 4:17; Rev. 1:7.)
4. His Return Will Be to the Mount of Olives. The place whence He left. (See Zech. 14:2-9.)

CONCLUSION: Are you ready for that day? He will come physically, visibly, in clouds of glory, to the Mount of Olives. And we shall behold Him, face to face, in all of His glory. Think of *that* the next time you see a cloud in the eastern sky.

God's Answer to Turmoil

Date preached:

SCRIPTURE: Psalm 2

INTRODUCTION: The word "turmoil" has been around in the English language for about 500 years, describing a state of confusion, agitation, or commotion. That's the kind of world we're in. But God doesn't want us to live in agitation, confusion, or turmoil. He provides an antidote in the second Psalm.

1. The World Plots (vv. 1–3). The world is in turmoil because it is in rebellion against God and against His Anointed One, His "Messiah." This is a messianic psalm, and it is one of the most frequently quoted in the New Testament.
2. The Father Laughs (vv. 3–6). Here is one of the few times in Scripture where God is said to laugh; it isn't a laugh of pleasure but of rebuke.
3. The Son Rules (vv. 7–9). This passage is repeatedly quoted in the New Testament, referring to Christ.
4. The Spirit Warns (vv. 10–12). Under the inspiration of the Holy Spirit, the narrator warns us to reverence the Son.

CONCLUSION: The answer to turmoil is found in taking refuge in the Lordship, the rule, and the reign of God and of His Anointed.

Living with Change in the Midst of Tradition

An interview with Rev. Peter Grainger
Charlotte Baptist Chapel, Edinburgh

You pastor a traditional church in the heart of Edinburgh. Would you tell us a little about the history of the church and about your predecessors?

Charlotte Baptist Chapel is right in the heart of the city of Edinburgh. Our history extends back nearly 200 years. The church was founded by Christopher Anderson, a contemporary of William Carey, who was interested in missionary work and Bible translation. But 50 years after he finished his ministry, the church had difficulties and was reduced to 30 members. It was, frankly, about to close. But a group of people had a vision for revival. There is a famous story that the secretary of the church at that time would take his small son to church on Sundays and say to him, "Can you see the crowds?" The son would say, "Dad, there are no crowds. There's almost nobody here." But the man would say, "I can see the crowds." He believed that God would revive the church. The church called a man called Joseph Kemp, who came and called the church to prayer. Kemp had visited the Welsh revival in 1904, and here at Charlotte Road, a real revival came with a thousand people being converted every year for several years afterward.

Who followed Kemp?

A great Bible teacher, Dr. W. Graham Scroggie. He had a long ministry of Bible teaching and ran a Bible school in midweek attended by hundreds of people. He was followed by another man who was a charismatic figure, the Rev. J. Sidlow Baxter, who went to be with the Lord only a couple of years ago. When Baxter was here, they hired one of the biggest theatres in town, and every summer for three months, after church on Sunday, they would fill it with 2,000 people and he would preach and play the piano. He was followed again by another great Bible teacher, Rev. Gerald Griffiths , then by Alan Redpath who came through like a whirlwind. He was followed by Derek Prime, a wonderful Bible teacher, and I began my pastorate here in 1992.

So you've got a rich tradition, and there are a lot of benefits to that. There may be a downside in terms of the ability to make changes.

Yes. The preaching of the Word of God is central to all we do—the Word preached systematically and expounded week-by-week, year-by-year. That's at the heart of everything. The difficulty comes with changing things that surround that—that is, the Christian subculture, bringing it up-to-date, relating to contemporary society, whose knowledge and understanding of the Christian faith is increasingly minimal. In our church, for example, we have people who have no knowledge of the Bible. When I first came here, there were no Bibles in the pews and people argued—one understands why—that people should bring their own Bibles to church. But we have students from all over the world—postgraduates, Muslims, Hindus, goodness knows what. They don't know one Bible from another. So it is important to provide Bibles in the pews for them, although that was a change that aroused feelings. Now, we have just introduced the use of screens and PowerPoint so we can highlight what we are preaching and explain it clearly. Our goal is to become all things to all men so that by all possible means we might save some. The issue most churches wrestle with is that of music, and people argue about the kind of music we want to sing and so on. We've tried to diversify our music. We have all sorts of different styles, and we try to be tolerant of one another. But it can be quite a battle.

What advice would you give a pastor in a traditional setting?

Change always takes a lot longer than you think it will. I was previously in a newly planted church where we could change things fairly quickly without much argument. There was no tradition to argue from. But here everything takes quite a long time. So, for example, the first major change I introduced was small groups to study the Scriptures. We meet fortnightly in homes. It took a year to introduce it. People were very suspicious. They'd tried it before and it hadn't worked. So we introduced it as a trial, saying, "We'll try it six months, then we'll review, and if it is not working, we'll abandon it."

What happened?

After six months there was no problem, and our fellowship groups have grown in importance in the church because they provide pastoral care. In a church of 1,000 people you can get lost so easily, so the small groups have provided that pastoral care.

Have you had parishioners confront you angrily? Or critical letters?

Whenever you introduce change of any kind, people get upset about it, and certainly we have had letters, some anonymous letters from people who are unhappy about things. I think, though, in all honesty, we haven't lost many people over the years who've left because they're unhappy with what's happening. Most people are tolerant of change if they can see that we are reaching people with the gospel. One of our old people said to me, "I don't really like these modern songs very much, but I'm just delighted to see hundreds of young people there on Sunday evenings and I'll certainly put up with that as long as they keep coming." That's a great perspective on things. And interestingly, few of the younger people are critical of the older music we sing. In fact, they'll often say, "How nice to have one of these older hymns. I really appreciated that and learned something from it."

What advice would you give pastors who need to bring their churches into the 21st century?

Well, it's not easy. It depends on the history of the church, the people you've got, the size of the church—all sorts of factors. I don't say to people, "We're going to introduce modern music this week, or drama,"—or whatever it might be. But I'll say, "What is our goal as a church? If our goal is to be the missionary people of God, then how are we getting on at that? How many of those coming on Sundays are outsiders? How can we make it more understandable to them?" If people understand why you're changing something, they're more willing to accept it.

Second, you've got to take people with you, and therefore I always say, "This is a change we're going to try, and we'll give it a six-month life, then we'll review it." But better to try and fail than not to do anything and stay where you are.

I think also you need grace and wisdom and understanding. So often what people object to is not some theological principle, though they may dress it up in that form. It's actually a threat to their security because their security is in the subculture they've grown up with. We live in a world of rapid change, and for many people the church is the last bastion of tradition, for "nothing changes here"—to quote the hymn out of context. The reality, of course, is that everything changes. But for some people this is a secure place where nothing changes. Everything else in their lives is changing at a frightening pace, and when they come to church and find that it is changing as well, it's not very easy for them.

How do you keep your own anger or frustration from getting the better of you?

I've got an understanding wife. It's a great asset to have a wife you can let off steam to. If you haven't, it's vitally important to have at least a nucleus within the church who knows where you're going and who will help you. If everybody's against you, it's pretty difficult. But we must remember through all our frustrations that it's God who is building His kingdom. Sometimes what we think is important may not be so important after all. We need God's grace and wisdom as we ask Him, "Lord, what are the particular things that need to be changed at this particular time?"

How much change can a traditional church take?

I usually try to introduce one major change a year. One of the problems with our church is that it is an exceedingly busy church. Every night of the week there are things going on, therefore the quality of family life diminishes. A few years ago, I introduced an innovation to the church, suggesting we cancel all activities on Monday nights. I said, "Let's just close the church down on Monday nights—nothing held in church on Monday nights." A lot of people didn't like this. It was a night for committees. We'd always had a prayer meeting on Monday (which we shifted to Tuesday). I can't say whether it's wonderfully successful for everyone, but I do hope it's allowed families to spend more time together. So it's a matter of choosing little steps to achieve a big goal rather than wholesale change all at one go, which alienates everybody. ✿

FEBRUARY 2, 2003

Gideon

Date preached:

By Stuart Briscoe

Scripture: Judges 6:1–7:25, especially 6:11–12: Gideon threshed wheat in the wine-press, in order to hide it from the Midianites. And the Angel of the LORD appeared to him, and said to him, "The LORD is with you, you mighty man of valor!"

Introduction: In Judges 6 we find a character with whom we can identify—Gideon. Some years after the Lord brought the Israelites into the Promised Land, they stopped honoring Him. They began to lose their distinctives, and as a result began to be oppressed by their enemies, particularly by the Midianites who tormented them, especially at harvest time. God's people became beaten down and filled with despondency. The enemy tries to do the same with us today.

1. **Gideon's Despondency** (Judg. 6:1–13). Gideon is a good example of that despondency. He was so terrorized by the Midianites that he threshed wheat in a winepress—the worst place for that task. But the angel who appeared to him called him a mighty warrior (though he wasn't a mighty warrior at all, but a scared farmer). Gideon replied, "If the Lord is with us, why has this happened to us?" Jewish theology taught that God lived among His people, but Gideon's people had begun to look at their circumstances instead of at their theology. When you begin looking at your theology through your circumstances, you soon find your theology shifting. Gideon needed to be reminded that whatever his circumstances, the Lord was with him. You may live in very difficult circumstances, but you must see your circumstances in the light of your theology, not vice versa.

2. **Gideon's Dependency** (Judg. 6:14–24). The Angel said: "Go in the strength that you have, and I will be with you." Gideon's resources were utterly depleted, yet he was commanded to go in the strength he had, though it wasn't much. The more inadequate we are, the greater the likelihood of our being dependent. Accordingly, Gideon built an altar called "The Lord is Peace!" We usually think of peace as the cessation of hostilities or the eradication of stress, but the Hebrews thought of peace as

things being in order. By naming his altar as he did, Gideon was saying: "I'm going to find myself in all kinds of hostilities; there will be incredible stress in my life; but one thing I know—in all my weakness I'll abandon myself to the Lord who will be with me, and things will be in order." Peace isn't the absence of trouble, but the deep-rooted tranquility of order in the midst of trouble (John 16:33). We must daily go in the strength we have (though it isn't much), knowing He is with us in the midst of trouble. Gideon was no longer the despondent Gideon, but the dependent Gideon.

3. **Gideon's Defiance** (Judg. 6:25–7:25). At God's command, Gideon knocked down the altar of Baal, tore down the idolatrous pole of Asherah, sacrificed a bull as an atonement for sin, and began mobilizing his nation against the Midianites. Thirty-two thousand men volunteered, but the Lord said, in effect: "That's too many. The men might get the idea they're a pretty good army, that *they* achieved victory. I can do more with 300 who trust me completely than with 32,000 who don't." God works through a dedicated nucleus, not through the flabby masses. The Lord gave each man an earthen jar, a torch, a trumpet, and a sword. They were told to break the jar, then shout. First the shining, then the shouting. It's interesting to compare 2 Corinthians 4:6–7: "It is the God who commanded light to shine out of darkness, who has shone in our hearts to give the light of the knowledge of the glory of God in the face of Jesus Christ. But we have this treasure in earthen vessels, that the excellence of the power may

>>> *sermon continued on following page*

APPROPRIATE HYMNS AND SONGS

A Mighty Fortress Is Our God, Martin Luther; Public Domain.

Blessed Be the Lord My Strength, Arlys Johnson; © 1980 Zionsong Music.

Declare His Glory, Margaret E. Clarkson/Donald Hustad; © 1980 Hope Publishing Company.

Guide Me O Thou Great Jehovah, William Williams/Harry E. Fosdick/John Hughes/Peter William; Public Domain.

The Lord Is My Strength, Dennis Jernigan; © 1993 Shepherd's Heart Music Inc. (Admin. by Word Music Group, Inc.).

be of God and not of us." The torch of the knowledge of Christ burns in our hearts, but we've got to be prepared to be broken, and we've got to shine before we can shout.

Conclusion: What stage are you in now? Are you despondent? Or has the Lord come to you in your despondency, helping you learn dependency? Or, being dependent on Him, are you beginning to discover He has specific things for you to do? Are you going in His strength to shine and to shout and to put the enemies of the Lord to flight?

FOR THE BULLETIN

❁ Alcuin was raised by schoolmasters in York, England. In the vast library of York's Cathedral School, the boy fell in love with Ambrose, Augustine, Bede, Pliny, and the writers of antiquity. He rose from student to teacher, and on February 2, 767, Alcuin was made a deacon and the school's headmaster. Charlemagne later asked Alcuin to educate his court, train his clergy, and establish parish schools. Alcuin's efforts paved the way for the universities that were soon to rise and made him one of the most famous educators of the medieval period. ❁ George Whitefield departed for Georgia on February 2, 1738, his first preaching trip to the Colonies. He returned to England later in the year to be ordained a priest and to raise money for an orphanage that he later established in Savannah. ❁ On February 2, 1864, Fanny Crosby began her famous hymn-writing career. On that day she met William B. Bradbury, who gave her an assignment to write a sacred song. ❁ Rev. A. J. Gordon died on the morning of February 2, 1895, with the word "Victory" being the last clear word he spoke. It was fitting, for he was a tireless advocate of the "Victorious Christian Life." Gordon, a Baptist pastor, was an associate and friend of D. L. Moody, and one of Boston's most beloved ministers. Among his writings are "When Jesus Came to Church," and the music for "My Jesus, I Love Thee." ❁ On February 2, 1971, Idi Amin assumed power in Uganda, following a coup that ousted President Milton Obote. His reign brought terror to the country and brutal persecution to the Ugandan church.

In a Winepress

In the Middle East to this day, you will see them threshing wheat by harvesting it, then taking it out on a big flat slab or rock where they beat the wheat and throw it in the air, so that the chaff is blown away and the wheat is harvested. The last place you would do this would be in a winepress for the rather obvious reason that a winepress is exactly the opposite of an open threshing floor. A winepress is a carved-out stone in which you put the grapes, and the maidens come and dance around on them, and the juice comes out and the wine is made. Gideon was trying to thresh his wheat in a winepress because he was in despair.
—*Stuart Briscoe*

My dad used to tell of a man who went home one Saturday and his wife wanted him to fix the doorbell. Going down to the local store, he got wire, the bell, and a little battery, and he wired the whole thing up. He thought his wife would be absolutely thrilled. But she complained that she had also wanted him to put up a light at the same time. He trudged back to the store, bought a lamp, and wired it to the same battery. But when he switched it on, nothing happened. He called an electrician friend and said, "Hey, I rigged up this bell my wife wanted and it rings from the battery. But the light doesn't come on." His friend replied, "You don't have enough power, because it takes more power to shine than to shout."
—*Stuart Briscoe.*

"Are you listening, church of Gideon? Let God alone, let his word, his sacrament, his laws be your weapons. Do not seek any other help; do not be frightened. He is with you. Let his grace suffice you. Do not desire to be strong, powerful, honored, respected, but let God alone be your strength, your fame, your honor."
—*Dietrich Bonhoeffer*

"If I had three hundred men who feared nothing but God, hated nothing but sin, and determined to know nothing among men but Christ, and Him crucified, I would set the world on fire."
—*John Wesley*

WORSHIP HELPS

Call to Worship:
"Behold, He who forms mountains and creates the wind, who declares to man what his thought is, and makes the morning darkness, who treads the high places of the earth—the LORD God of hosts is His name" (Amos 4:13).

Pastoral Prayer:
Heavenly Father, God of Abraham, Isaac, Moses, Gideon, and Daniel— The earth is the Lord's, and we know from Scripture of Your concern for the morality—the spirituality—of each succeeding generation. Our generation, O Lord, is in need of grace. Our nation needs Your guidance. Our children need Your mercy. Our times need Your touch. May this be the generation of those who seek You, who seek Your face. Send us revival, dear Lord, and may it begin here, in this very place. Bless our nation, O Lord. Guide our leaders, forgive our sins, renew our churches, and heal our land. We ask in Jesus' name, Amen.

Scripture: Psalm 25:12–15
Who is the man that fears the LORD?
Him shall He teach in the way He chooses.
He himself shall dwell in prosperity,
And his descendants shall inherit the earth.
The secret of the LORD is with those who fear Him,
And He will show them His covenant.
My eyes are ever toward the LORD,
For He shall pluck my feet out of the net.

Offertory Comments:
The word "offering" occurs 803 times in the New King James Version of the Bible. Many of those times refer to the blessings Christ offers us, to His offering of Himself for our sins. But we're also commanded to render God the offering, not only of ourselves, but of our means. Today may I remind us all of these words in Psalm 96: "Give to the LORD, O families of the peoples, Give to the LORD glory and strength. Give to the LORD the glory due His name; bring an offering, and come into His courts. Oh, worship the LORD in the beauty of holiness!"

Additional Sermons and Lesson Ideas

When You've Made a Mess of Things

Date preached:

SCRIPTURE: Jonah 2

INTRODUCTION: Many of our problems arise through disobedience. In Jonah 2, the waterlogged prophet, reeling from God's discipline, prayed about his predicament. A study of his prayer of recovery teaches us:

1. We Must Confront Our Situation (vv. 1–6a). The phrase "I cried" occurs twice, but two Hebrew verbs are used. The first is a general term, but the second implies a specific cry for help, a scream to God. Jonah honestly admitted to God the mess he had made for himself.
2. We Must Come to Our Senses (vv. 6b–7). The key word is *remembered.* "When my soul fainted . . . I remembered the Lord"—like the Prodigal Son in Luke 15, who "came to himself."
3. We Must Compose Our Sermon (v. 8). "What have I learned from this?" is an important recovery question. Here Jonah articulates the lesson God had taught him: "Those who cling to worthless idols forfeit the grace that could be theirs" (NIV).
4. We Must Complete Our Sacrifice (v. 9). Follow through on your vows.

CONCLUSION: Maybe you've made a mess of things and are in the belly of the whale, so to speak. What a place to take the first steps toward reclamation!

A Mind-altering Passage

Date preached:

SCRIPTURE: Lamentations 3:1–26

INTRODUCTION: This is the famous "Great is Thy faithfulness," but before we get to God's faithfulness we encounter great despair.

1. "I Said." In verses 1–20, Jeremiah reveals his inner thoughts of self-pity and misery: "I said my strength and my hope have perished from the Lord" (v. 18). He employs phrases like: affliction, darkness, broken bones, bitterness, and woe; He shuts out my prayer, He has blocked my ways, my soul sinks.
2. "I Recall." In verse 21, the prophet forces himself to alter his thinking. Breaking the cycle of self-pitying thoughts, he says: "This I recall to my mind." He deliberately shifts his mental focus.
3. "I Hope." In verses 22–26, he brings God's compassion, mercy, and faithfulness into the picture.

CONCLUSION: Sooner or later, we all face disappointment, disaster, and despair. We can either let our minds sink, or we can lift our eyes to the Lord whose compassions never fail.

FEBRUARY 9, 2003

SUGGESTED MESSAGE

More Precious than Gold

Date preached:

Scripture: Psalm 19, especially verses 9b–10a: The judgments of the LORD are true and righteous altogether. More to be desired are they than gold.

Introduction: The Antiques Roadshow tells us we often undervalue older items in our attics and basements. How easy to undervalue the old book called the Bible. "The word of the LORD was precious in those days. . . . The law from your mouth is more precious to me than thousands of pieces of silver. . . . The ordinances of the Lord are . . . more precious than gold" (1 Sam. 3:1 KJV; Ps. 119:72; Ps. 19:10 NIV). Psalm 19 tells us that God speaks with two megaphones.

1. **By the Worlds He Has Made** (vv. 1–6). "The heavens declare the glory of God." The stars and sun tell us of God. The sun is 93 million miles away, composed of hydrogen and helium, a literal fireball of remarkable energy generated by nuclear fusion reactions, producing 10 million megatons of energy per second. If it were a little larger, its gravity would pull us into it; a little smaller and we'd drift off into space. If it were hotter we'd burn up; colder and we'd freeze. The psalmist compares the sun to a bridegroom and a runner. What can stellar revelation tell us? That the Creator of the universe is intelligent, powerful, a lover of beauty, and infinite. It gives us general information about God, but doesn't answer the questions "How can I know God?" or "What must I do to be saved?" Suppose you found a box containing a picture-puzzle made up of thousands of pieces. But, opening the box, only twenty pieces are there. You can tell from those pieces that this is a beautiful picture, painted by a gifted artist. You can see the swirls of color and the lines of design. But most of the pieces are missing. To put it together, we need another 31,102 pieces. There is another box, a book containing 31,102 verses. When you open the box of the Bible and study these 31,102 verses, everything falls into place.

2. **By the Words He Has Spoken** (vv. 7–11). Six different titles are given here for the Scripture, six characteristics, and these six effects:
    A. **They convert the soul** (v. 7a). A warden of a prison in a land that wasn't friendly to Christians was married and had a family, but his life was one

of fear. One day two men were incarcerated for preaching. At midnight they were heard praising the Lord. The warden, sound asleep, was unaware of this late-night commotion, but a sudden earthquake flung him from bed. He found the prison in chaos, prisoners free, ruin and disaster everywhere. He shouted, "How can I be saved?" One of those prisoners replied, "Believe on the Lord Jesus Christ, and you will be saved—and your family" (see Acts 16).

B. **They make wise the simple** (v. 7b). Dr. Paul Tournier wrote: "The Bible . . . is a book in which [a person] may learn from his Creator the art of healthy living."

C. **They rejoice our hearts** (v. 8a). Joseph R. Sizoo, former president of New Brunswick Theological Seminary, wrote: "Years ago . . . when my whole life seemed to be overwhelmed . . . one morning quite casually I opened my New Testament and my eyes fell upon this sentence: 'He that sent me is with me—the Father hath not left me alone' (John 8:29). My life has never been the same since that hour. Everything for me has been forever different. . . . Not a day has passed that I have not repeated it to myself. Many have come to me for counseling during these years, and I have always sent them away with this sustaining sentence. Ever since that hour when my eyes fell upon it, I have lived by this sentence. . . . It is the Golden Text of my life."

D. **They enlighten our eyes** (v. 8b). In the movie *Hope Floats,* a song originally written by Charlie Chaplain for his movie, *Modern Times,* says: "Smile, though your heart is aching. / Smile, even though it's breaking.

>>> *sermon continued on following page*

APPROPRIATE HYMNS AND SONGS

For the Beauty of the Earth, Folliot Sandford Pierpoint/Conrad Kocher; Public Domain.

Because We Believe, Nancy Gordon/Jamie Harvill; © 1996 Mother's Heart Music/Integrity's Praise! Music/Integrity's Hosanna! Music (Admin. by Integrity Music, Inc.).

The Bible Stands, Haldor Lillenas; Public Domain.

Holy Bible, Book Divine, John Burton/William B. Bradbury; Public Domain.

More Precious Than, Lynn De Shazo; © 1982 Integrity's Hosanna! Music.

/ Though there are clouds in the sky, you get by." But how? You can smile by the power of God's Word and His promises. They brighten our countenance.

E. **They endure forever** (v. 9a). God's Word produces a fear of God leading to eternal joy.

F. **They lead to righteousness** (v. 9b).

Conclusion: This Psalm ends with a prayer in verses 13–14, that says, in summary: "Lord, forgive the sins I may not even recognize. Restrain me from those I do recognize. And may my thoughts and words be pleasing to you, my Rock and my Redeemer."

FOR THE BULLETIN

❋ In Catholic tradition, this day is dedicated to St. Apollonia, who was martyred in A.D. 249 for not renouncing her faith during the reign of Emperor Philip. Her story was written by St. Dionysius, who reported that Apollonia had her teeth knocked out during persecution. As a result, she is considered the patron of those suffering dental disease. ❋ On February 9, 356, as Athanasius, bishop of Alexandria, led midnight worship, 5,000 soldiers stormed the church. Athanasius calmly asked his assistant to read Psalm 136, then slipped out a side door and escaped to the Egyptian desert. It was one of several exiles for the great preacher, defender of orthodoxy and proponent of the deity of Christ. ❋ During the reign of Mary I, Rev. John Hooper was imprisoned for his faith and sentenced to die. On the morning of February 9, 1555, he was taken to the center of Gloucester, where he was burned at the stake, suffering greatly in the flames. ❋ Today is the anniversary of the famous fire that destroyed the house of Rev. Samuel Wesley in 1709. Young John was saved, "a brand plucked out of the burning." ❋ On February 9, 1744, evangelist George Whitefield, mourning over the death of his infant son, insisted on preaching before the funeral. His text was Romans 8:28. As he finished his sermon, he heard the church bells tolling for the burial service, and he almost broke down. Telling his listeners, *"All* things work together for good," he finished his sermon and headed toward the church.
❋ February 9 marks the deaths of Rev. Henry Melville in 1871 and of Russian novelist Feodor Dostoevski in 1881.

STATS, STORIES AND MORE

The Heavens Declare the Glory of God

- Alan Sandage, who won the Crawford Prize in astronomy, said after years of studying the sky and the stars: "I find it quite improbable that such order came out of chaos. There has to be some organizing principle. God to me is a mystery, but is the explanation for the miracle of existence, why there is something instead of nothing."

- Senator John Glenn, 77, who returned to space in 1998, traveling on the Discovery Space Shuttle, said: "I don't think you can be up here and look out the window as I did the first day and see the Earth from this vantage point, to look out at this kind of creation and not believe in God."

- James Irwin walked on the moon in July, 1971. His trip into space was so moving that he later became a Christian evangelist. This is what he wrote of viewing earth from his space ship: "The earth reminded us of a Christmas tree ornament hanging in the blackness of space. As we got further and further away it diminished in size. Finally it shrank to the size of a marble, the most beautiful marble you can imagine. That beautiful, warm, living object looked so fragile, so delicate, that if you touched it with a finger it would crumble and fall apart. Seeing this has to change a man, has to make a man appreciate the creation of God and the love of God."

- The artist Vincent Van Gogh said "I have . . . a terrible need—shall I say the word?—of religion. Then I go out at night and paint the stars."

His Precious Word

This precious Word of God has made clear many a perplexity, has illumined many a dark road, has cheered many a lonesome way, has soothed many a deep sorrow, has guided and upheld many a faltering step, and has crowned with victory many a feat of arms in the great battle with Satan, the world, and sin.—*Octavious Winslow,* Puritan Baptist

Kids Talk

Show the children something from nature—perhaps a small rock collection, a living plant, a bird's nest, a small pet, or a picture of the stars. Have also a small Bible. Explain that we can learn much about God from His creation, but we also need to learn about Him from the Book He has given us.

Call to Worship:
"My voice You shall hear in the morning, O LORD; in the morning I will direct it to You, and I will look up" (Ps. 5:3).

Pastoral Prayer:
In today's Pastoral Prayer, take time to praise the Lord for details of His creation that we usually take for granted. On the way to church, pay particular attention to the weather, the cloud formations, the rain or snow, the wind, or the stillness of the air. Mention these things to the Lord in a spirit of thanksgiving. Then pray: "For the beauty of the earth, for the beauty of the skies, for the love which from our birth over and around us lies, Lord of all to Thee we raise, this our prayer of grateful praise."

Scripture: Psalm 119:9–16
How can a young man cleanse his way?
By taking heed according to Your word.
With my whole heart I have sought You;
Oh, let me not wander from Your commandments!
Your word I have hidden in my heart,
That I might not sin against You.
Blessed are You, O LORD!
Teach me Your statutes.
With my lips I have declared
All the judgments of Your mouth.
I have rejoiced in the way of Your testimonies,
As much as in all riches.
I will meditate on Your precepts,
And contemplate Your ways.
I will delight myself in Your statutes;
I will not forget Your word.

Benediction:
Let the words of our mouths and the meditations of our hearts be acceptable unto You, O Lord, our Rock and our Redeemer.

Additional Sermons and Lesson Ideas

Hindrances to Prayer
Date preached:

By Albert Richardson, a.k.a. "the Unknown Christian."

SCRIPTURE: Psalm 139:23–24

INTRODUCTION: God wants us to pray, but the devil seeks to hinder us, knowing we do more through praying than through working (Ps. 66:18; Isa. 59:1–2). No sin is too small to hinder prayer, especially the sins of:

1. Doubt. Possibly the greatest hindrance to prayer (James 1:6–8).
2. Self. A full hand cannot take Christ's gifts. Pride prevents prayer, for prayer is a humbling thing. (See Ps. 37:4).
3. Unlove in the Heart. We cannot be wrong with men and right with God (Matt. 5:23–24).
4. Refusal to Do Our Part. When we pray for the conversion of others, are we willing to be the means?
5. Praying Only in Secret. How often our Lord refers to united prayer!
6. Failure to Praise the Lord. 1 Thessalonians 5:16–18 tells us to rejoice, pray, then give thanks.

CONCLUSION: Our text asks the Lord to search us for any prayer-hindering sin, and to lead us in the way everlasting.

Will We Know Each Other in Heaven?
Date preached:

SCRIPTURE: Various

INTRODUCTION: This age-old question comes to our minds especially when a precious loved one has passed away. Several passages of Scripture point to an answer to the question.

1. Luke 24:40—Jesus' glorified body was a real, tangible object, and His disciples recognized Him after His resurrection. Our resurrection bodies, likewise, will be real and recognizable.
2. Luke 16:19-31—The rich man, Lazarus, and Abraham certainly recognized each other.
3. 1 Thessalonians 2:19-20—Paul's joy and crown in heaven was going to be the Thessalonian Christians he had won to the Lord.
4. 1 Thessalonians 4:13-18—The Bible comforts us with the assurance that we will be with our loved ones forever.
5. Luke 9:28-36—Peter and company seemed to intuitively recognize Moses and Elijah.
6. 1 Corinthians 13:12—We shall know even as we are known.

CONCLUSION: It boils down to this: Surely we will be at least as discerning in heaven as we have been on earth. Now we see only a poor mirror image, but then we will see things as they really are—face to face.

When Sickness Strikes the Pastor's Family

By Katrina Polvinen Morgan

A pastor's wife is under the same biblical mandates as all other women. The only difference is that she is married to the pastor. For me, the priority was taking care of the pastor and our family. As the years passed and the children grew, I began teaching Sunday school and leading Bible studies. At one time we had two classes meeting in our home—including one that met in our bedroom!

Just as I was hitting my stride, I began experiencing tingling and numbness in my limbs. The eventual diagnosis was multiple sclerosis. At first, my activities were unaffected and few people knew about my illness. But three years ago it began affecting my legs, and has worsened since.

Instead of becoming sweeter with this trial, I became angrier. The Bible tells us to "be angry and sin not," for "the wrath of man does not produce the righteousness of God" (Eph. 4:26; James 1:20). But anger is insidious and cancerous. At first, I didn't recognize my anger as relating to God. I thought it was a good, healthy antagonism toward my disease, and this was my way of fighting my disability. But it was affecting me in ways I didn't realize.

I'm not sure when God actually started dealing with me about this, but being desperate to move out of the ditch I was in, I begged the Lord to show Himself to me. The Bible says, "You will seek Me and find Me, when you search for Me with all your heart" (Jer. 29:12). The Lord immediately began showing Himself to me and convicting me of sin during the watches of the night.

A part of a verse began popping into my mind, something about losing your life to save it. I had been trying desperately to save my life from going downhill, but the more I tried to save it, the more I was losing it. I looked up this verse and found it five times!

- *He who finds his life will lose it, and he who loses his life for My sake will find it*—Matthew 10:39.

- *If anyone desires to come after Me, let him deny himself, and take up his cross, and follow Me. For whoever desires to save his life*

will lose it, but whoever loses his life for My sake will find it—
Matthew 16:24–25.

- *Whoever desires to come after Me, let him deny himself, and take up his cross, and follow Me. For whoever desires to save his life will lose it, but whoever loses his life for My sake and the gospel's will save it—*Mark 8:34–35.

- *Whoever desires to save his life will lose it, but whoever loses his life for My sake will save it—*Luke 9:24.

- *Unless a grain of wheat falls into the ground and dies, it remains alone; but if it dies, it produces much grain. He who loves his life will lose it, and he who hates his life in this world will keep it for eternal life—*John 12:24–25.

Does God demand from me something He doesn't give Himself? No. The pattern was Christ. The way to glory was the way of the cross. He lost His life to save it. Christ gave Himself away, yet in so doing, not only was His own life saved, but He brought many with Him (Phil. 2:9–11; Heb. 10:12; 12:2).

My responsibility, then, was to lose, to deny, to take up my cross, to follow, to die. It is a daily thing. Every day I must lose my life to His control. As these verses took hold, I experienced a personal revival.

Though I'm constantly having to adjust to my disability, it has enabled me to encourage sick and discouraged people by phone or card. It's difficult for me to teach a class now, but I've been able to write a regular column for our church newsletter. The Lord has given me a ministry of prayer. And I'm still trying to take care of my pastor and our kids!

Many pastors' wives may encounter a crisis at the moment of greatest busyness or productivity, but God is sovereign. He may well use this to liberate her from unknown sins and prepare her for unexpected service. ✿

FEBRUARY 16, 2003

Is It Enough to Be Sorry?

Date preached:

By Ed Dobson

Scripture: Mark 1:2b–3: "Behold, I send My messenger before Your face, Who will prepare Your way before You." "The voice of one crying in the wilderness: 'Prepare the way of the LORD; Make His paths straight.'"

Introduction: If you've ever gone walking or hiking in Israel, you know the paths are crooked, up and down hills, encircling ridges, and around curves. John the Baptist had the incredible task of straightening crooked roads. What message straightens crooked paths? You would think he would have preached a message of celebration: "Get all excited—Jesus is coming!" But his message was all about sin. Verse 4 says: "John came baptizing in the wilderness and preaching a baptism of repentance for the remission of sins." Verse 5 gives the result: "All the land of Judea . . . were all baptized by him in the Jordan River, confessing their sins." This is the straightening that leads to Christ. Let's focus on two words:

1. **Confession.** This word is composed of three Greek terms. The first is a preposition meaning *out of,* indicating something out of our innermost being. The second means *the same as.* The third word, *logia,* means *to speak words.* The idea is that out of our heart we would say the same thing. It is used in a variety of ways in the New Testament. In Luke 22:6, it describes Judas' *consenting* to betray Jesus. In Matthew 11:25, Jesus said, "I *thank* You, Father." Jesus was agreeing with the Father about something. Philippians 2:11 proclaims that one day every tongue will *confess* Jesus as Lord. In today's text, the word occurs in the sense of declaring out of our hearts that we agree with God about our sinful condition. Yet confession is not enough to receive forgiveness. Notice in Mark 1, after confessing they were baptized with a "baptism of repentance."

2. **Repentance.** This means to change your mind or heart. In a physical sense, it means a change of direction. Forgiveness comes when I confess and repent, turning from my sin. Second Corinthians 7:10 contains a formula, a logical progression, about this: "Godly sorrow produces repentance leading to salvation . . . but the sorrow of the world produces death." There are two kinds of sorrow over sin. Godly sorrow, a brokenness over sin, leads to a change of

life and brings deliverance. Sorrow that doesn't lead to repentance doesn't lead to deliverance but to destruction. It's not enough to say, "I'm sorry." I have talked to people who were sorry they got caught. Sorry they embarrassed themselves. Sorry because of consequences. That's not godly sorrow.

3. **Characteristics of Godly Sorrow.** How do we distinguish godly from worldly sorrow? Second Corinthians 7:11 identifies seven characteristics of godly sorrow: "For observe this very thing, that you sorrowed in a godly manner:"
   A. **What earnestness.** This implies taking a matter seriously. Godly sorrow wants to do the right thing. Worldly sorrow wants to avoid further consequences.
   B. **What clearing of yourselves.** This carries the idea of shame for what we have done and a desire to rectify the situation.
   C. **What indignation.** Being genuinely upset at ourselves.
   D. **What fear.** The idea is that it is not easily forgotten. We don't close the door too quickly and go on.
   E. **What vehement desire.** A readiness to see justice done, which includes accepting consequences and punishment for my sins.
   F. **What zeal.** Eagerness to turn things around in our lives.
   G. **What vindication.** This implies a readiness to set things right. The Living Bible says: "You went right to work on the problem and cleared it up."

4. **Fruit of Repentance.** In Luke 3, John the Baptist told the crowds, "You brood of vipers! Who warned you to flee from the coming wrath? Produce fruit in keeping with repentance." The man with two tunics should share with someone having none. The tax collectors must stop extorting money. Unless we

>>> sermon continued on following page

APPROPRIATE HYMNS AND SONGS

If My People, Don Wyrtzen; © 1974 Singspiration Music (Admin. by Brentwood-Benson Music Publishing, Inc.).

Jesus Is Tenderly Calling, Fanny J. Crosby/George C. Stebbins; Public Domain.

Kind and Merciful God, Bryan Jeffery Leech; © 1973 Fred Bock Music Company.

Kyrie Elieson, Jodi Page Clark; © 1976 Celebration.

White as Snow, Leon Olguin; © 1990 Maranatha Praise! Inc./Sound Truth Publishing (Admin. by Maranatha Music).

demonstrate fruit accompanying repentance, we're still a brood of snakes—that was John's message! To really welcome the Messiah, we must confess our sin, agreeing with God about our condition, turning from sin to receive His forgiveness. The result will be fruit suited to repentance.

Conclusion: We sometimes think God flippantly forgives everyone, just because He's God. Even Christians say, "I know my choice is against the teaching of Scripture, but I'm so unhappy; I know God doesn't want me to be unhappy. I'm going to do it anyway and trust Him to forgive." May I remind you that genuine forgiveness cost Jesus His life on the Cross? Get alone with God today and ask Him: Is there something in my life, Lord, that I need to repent? Are there paths needing straightening? May God give us godly sorrow leading to repentance.

FOR THE BULLETIN

❋ On February 16, 600, Pope Gregory the Great decreed the words "God bless you" as the correct response to a sneeze. ❋ Reformer Philipp Melanchthon was born on February 16, 1497. ❋ On February 16, 1688, 26-year-old James Renwick, an imprisoned non-conformist Scottish minister, wrote in a message to his mother: "There is nothing in the world that I am sorry to leave but you. . . . Farewell, Mother. Farewell, night wanderings, cold, and weariness for Christ. Farewell, sweet Bible and preaching of the gospel. Welcome, crown of glory. Welcome, O Thou blessed Trinity and one God! I commit my soul into Thy eternal rest." The next morning he went to the scaffold. ❋ On February 16, 1865, English clergyman Sabine Baring-Gould, 31, published the hymn, "Now the Day is Over," based on Proverbs 3:24. ❋ On February 16, 1923, the burial chamber of King Tutankhamen's tomb was unsealed in Egypt. ❋ On February 16, 1959, Fidel Castro was sworn in as prime minister of Cuba after leading a guerrilla campaign that ousted Fulgencio Batista. Persecution of Christians began shortly thereafter. ❋ Anglican Archbishop Janani Luwum was dragged from his bed at 1:30 A.M. by forces of Ugandan dictator Idi Amin and taken to a compound near the capital where he was forced to strip. He was whipped mercilessly and repeatedly molested by soldiers. Finally Amin drew his pistol and shot Luwum twice through the heart. It was February 16, 1971. Ironically, Protestants in Uganda had been planning for the 100th birthday of Christianity in their country.

STATS, STORIES AND MORE

Teed Off

Recently we were on a family vacation with relatives in Greensboro, North Carolina. My brother-in-law is a member of Forest Oak Country Club, home of the Greater Greensboro Open, the oldest stop on the PGA Tour. One day on the course, we were hooked up with another couple, a man and a woman. Their language was rather colorful, if you know what I mean, but hers was far worse than his. Not only would she use bad words when she made a bad shot (which was nearly every shot), but almost every sentence was laced with horrible language. My brother-in-law kept saying to me on the side, "One of these holes she's going to ask you what you do for a living." I said, "I know, and I can't wait." Fifteen holes later, in that beautiful North Carolina accent, she said, "Ed, what do you do for a living?" I looked at her, smiled, and said, "I'm a minister." I wish I could have taken her photograph! "Oh," she said, "I'm so sorry about my language. I hope you're Episcopalian." I'm not sure what she meant by that. But later her husband took my brother-in-law aside and said, "You really did us in. You should have told us on the first tee that he was a minister. We had no idea. He is such a nice guy, we never thought he'd be a minister." Instantly their language changed. For the rest of the game not another single cuss word, because I was watching them. I guarantee, though, as soon as we left the language went back. She was really sorry, she was embarrassed, but it was not the sorrow Paul spoke about—the sorrow of declaring before God and agreeing with Him about sin, of repenting and turning from that sin to begin a new life energized by the spirit of God.
—Ed Dobson

WORSHIP HELPS

Call to Worship:

"Great and marvelous are thy works, Lord God Almighty; just and true are thy ways, thou King of saints. Who shall not fear thee, O Lord, and glorify thy name? for thou only art holy; for all nations shall come and worship before thee; for thy judgments are made manifest" (Rev. 15:3b–4 KJV).

Offertory Comments:

In 2 Corinthians 8 and 9, Paul encouraged the Christians in Corinth to give generously of their offerings, holding before them the example of the generous churches to the North in the Macedonian region. George Sweeting pointed out, "For the Macedonian Christian, giving was not a chore but a challenge, not a burden but a blessing." Giving was not something to be avoided but a privilege to be desired. "So let each one give as he purposes in his heart, not grudgingly or of necessity; for God loves a cheerful giver" (2 Cor. 9:7).

Scripture: Psalm 51

Have mercy upon me, O God,
According to Your lovingkindness;
According to the multitude of Your tender mercies,
Blot out my transgressions.
Wash me thoroughly from my iniquity,
And cleanse me from my sin.
For I acknowledge my transgressions,
And my sin is always before me.
Purge me with hyssop, and I shall be clean;
Wash me, and I shall be whiter than snow.

Create in me a clean heart, O God,
And renew a steadfast spirit within me.
Do not cast me away from Your presence,
And do not take Your Holy Spirit from me.
Restore to me the joy of Your salvation,
And uphold me by Your generous Spirit.
Then I will teach transgressors Your ways,
And sinners shall be converted to You.

Additional Sermons and Lesson Ideas

All About Prayer

Date preached:

SCRIPTURE: Ephesians 6:18, NIV

INTRODUCTION: This is one of the Bible's great verses on prayer. Notice the use of the word *all*. "And pray in the Spirit on *all* occasions with *all* kinds of prayers and requests. With this in mind, be alert and *always* keep on praying for *all* the saints."

1. On All Occasions. David took this approach. In Psalm 4 he prayed before going to bed. In Psalm 5, before beginning his day. In Psalm 5, when he felt like groaning. In Psalm 6, when he had sinned. In Psalm 7, when under attack. In Psalm 8, when awed with God's creation. In Psalm 9, when happy. In Psalm 10, when God seemed far away.
2. All Kinds of Prayers. Thanksgiving, petition, intercession, praise, repentance. Brief prayers. Long prayers. Written prayers. Spontaneous prayers. Corporate prayers. Private prayers.
3. Always. Prayer should be as constant as an unconscious habit.
4. For All the Saints. Too many of our prayers are all about us. The greater part of our ministry to others is done on our knees.

CONCLUSION: Jim Elliot said, "God is still on His throne, we're still His footstool, and there's only a knee's distance between!"

Resourced!

Date preached:

Adapted from an outline by Charles W. Koller

SCRIPTURE: Philippians 4:10–19

INTRODUCTION: If you need an uplift today, just read Philippians 4 and note its promises. The first half of the chapter gives us Paul's cure for worry. The second half of the chapter contains three great promises for God's children. Through Christ:

1. We Can Be What We Ought to Be (v. 11). ". . . for I have learned in whatever state I am, to be content."
2. We Can Do What We Ought to Do (v. 13). "I can do all things through Christ who strengthens me."
3. We Can Have What We Ought to Have (v. 19). "And my God shall supply all your need according to His riches in glory by Christ Jesus."

CONCLUSION: And all to the glory of God (v. 20)!

Ministering the Word to Others When Your Own Heart Is Hurting

We cannot often suspend our ministries for personal crises, at least not for long. We must plod on, preaching through the pain, and tending to our flock when our own hearts are numbed with anguish. And we must do it without bleeding too much on others, without becoming exhibit "A" in our own sermons, and sometimes without letting too many people into the hurting places of our hearts.

For me, it began with a late-night phone call from a distant city telling me that my college-age daughter was in crisis. That began a prolonged heartache in my life, one that is not fully ended yet, though there seems to be emerging shafts of daylight. At the same time, my wife's multiple sclerosis worsened, and our financial needs hit record peaks due to three kids in college.

It sounds melodramatic even to me, but there were certain moments when I prayed earnestly for the Lord to take me to heaven. It felt as though someone had punched me in the stomach, and I found myself moping around, listless and benumbed, letting my entire ministry be colored by the current crisis.

During this time, our church was growing faster than ever, and the preaching and pastoring demands on me were accelerating, along with an exacting schedule of speaking engagements and writing deadlines. There were times when I trudged through the day too emotionally paralyzed to focus my thoughts, when everything I said or did came from the sole perspective of an anguished heart. Returning phone calls, reading books, attending meetings, giving counsel—these felt like impossible tasks, to say nothing of preparing and delivering sermons.

When Bill Clinton's White House was engulfed in its infamous sex scandal, reporters were amazed at the President's ability to compartmentalize his life, to set the crisis on one burner while he focused his energies on the others. I tried that, but couldn't do it. Nor could I successfully mask my feelings or exhibit a countenance at variance with my heart's pain. Yet I had a calling to keep, a job to do, and a church to lead.

It's Nothing New

Well, it's nothing new. David wrote some of his grandest Psalms when in the severest pain. Paul was at his bravest when stranded on a storm-tossed ship with little hope of survival. Joseph and Mary's deepest crisis produced the world's greatest hope. Ezekiel's wife died just when he needed her the most, and we all know of the trials of godly Job, Daniel in the den of lions, and the three Hebrew children in the furnace.

Furthermore, my friends outside the ministry have struggles as great or greater than mine, and the world doesn't give them much of a break. Parents of an alcoholic son still have to show up for work on Monday morning, even if their weekend was a sojourn in hell.

But I sometimes think those of us in ministry are special targets for Satan. He wants to destroy our effectiveness for Christ, and he knows that our greatest "weakness" is our love for our families and our commitment to the work of God. If he can debilitate us through family or ministry woes, he gloats like a snake swallowing a goat.

Things that Helped Me

But the Lord, calling us "more than conquerors," provides a powerful set of weapons for our benefit. Several things have helped me during the darkest days.

• Journaling. I've kept a journal since college days, and over the past four years I've written hundreds of pages describing my anguish, recording my prayers, and listing the Scriptures God has given me. I routinely record my morning devotions in my journal, but it's especially useful late at night when I'm too tired to pray and too worried to sleep. I write out my feelings, often as a letter to God, and inscribe by hand the verses He gives me to keep me through the night. For me, it's been a tangible way to come into God's presence and to hide myself in the shadow of the Almighty.

• Writing a Personal Book. I also have found inestimable help by writing a book. It isn't one I wrote for others, and whether or not it's ever published is immaterial. I wrote it for myself, and have called it, *Prayers and Promises for a Troubled Parent.* During the last few years, I've read through the entire Bible, listing passages of Scripture that I converted into prayers for my daughter. I wrote out hymns, the words of which were easily changed into prayers for her. I recounted the stories of other parents whose prodigal children have returned to the Lord in answer to earnest prayers. I chronicled some of the greatest lessons God has taught me through these experiences. And I have listed the promises God has given me from His Word. I return to this book nearly every day to remind God—and myself—of the prayers and promises He has shown me.

- Prayer Partners. I thank God for the "Aarons and Hurs" whom He has given me as prayer partners. My mother, prior to her passing, was my greatest prayer partner, and even now I believe her deathless prayers are still at work. But there have been others. Just last week, a friend asked for a list of personal prayer requests for his singles' group to remember at their weekly Bible study. I indirectly alluded to my burden, and he picked up on it, writing back to assure me he would personally devote himself to confidential prayer if I wanted to share more information. I did, and throughout that week his e-mails and prayers were invaluable. It was the week of our silver wedding anniversary, and, as it happened, it was a little volatile with our daughter. I was deeply troubled. My friend wrote back and said, "Relax and let me do the praying. I'll carry the load today. Remember that this is your anniversary—August 28th. On the calendar, that is 8/28, as in Romans 8:28. God has promised that everything that happens today will work for good. Now, I'll take up the praying, and you enjoy the day with your wife." Such friends are more valuable than our daily bread, more precious than gold and silver. While I have tried to keep our situation as private as possible (PK's have it hard enough without everyone in the church knowing of their struggles), a few individuals have been sent from heaven to uplift us to the Throne of Grace. We might have sunk without them.

- Books. The Lord has also ministered to my soul through several books. How thankful I am for Ruth Bell Graham's *Prodigals and Those Who Love Them.* I often read it one-page-a-day during my devotions, or in times of unusual hurt. I've also leaned hard upon that little anonymous classic *The Kneeling Christian,* a copy of which I found in a dusty used bookstore in Florida for seventy-five cents. It would have been a bargain at seventy-five dollars, based on the encouragement it has been in my prayer life. Amy Carmichael's *Edges of His Ways* has also been a daily companion. Just last week after a fitful night I opened to this word: "It seems to me that we are often called to live a double life: in much tribulation (when we think of the poor world); and yet, in the deepest places of our souls, abundantly satisfied." A fourth book I've kept at hand is *Behind the Ranges,* the life-changing story of J. O. Fraser, by Mrs. Howard Taylor. Fraser, a missionary to the Lisu peoples of China, saw remarkable spiritual breakthroughs occur in his work through earnest, protracted prayer. Its applications to me were clear.

- A Patient Staff. God has given me a supportive staff with whom I was perfectly honest regarding our struggles. When things were at the worst, they covered for me, comforted me, prayed for me, and, at times, admonished me.

- Exercise. A psychologist friend talked with me at length one day and insisted I continue my exercise routine. I had no energy for exercise, my depression having drained all my reserves. "But exercise will release the tension *from* your body and endorphins *to* your body," he said. "Both are essential if you're to get through this." Another friend has since called every day to make sure my exercise time is on the next day's schedule. Often when I don't feel I can possibly run or work out, I do it anyway. Afterward, I find my energy and mood elevated at least a little.

- My Wife. Katrina, despite her crippling MS, has been a tower of strength to me. She doesn't worry as much as I do. She has ample faith that God will bring our daughter through these years in His own time. Sometimes we weep together, and we often pray together several times a day. But her confidence and faith exceeds mine. "I don't know what's wrong with you!" she sometimes says when I'm wanting to curl into a fetal position and die. "You act as though God can't deal with this. He loves our daughter more than you do, and she's going to be fine. She's a jewel, and we've committed her to Him every day of her life. He'll bring her through. It'd be so much better if you'd just trust Him!"

- God's Word. An old hymn says, "My heart is leaning on the Word, the Written Word of God." For the past four years, I've leaned on God's Word as never before, and I've found light there for even the darkest days. Even as I write this, I'm thinking of last night. My daughter is away for the weekend, and I don't feel at all good about her trip. Last night my imagination might have wrecked my sleep, but the Lord gave me three words from John 14: *(1) Let not your heart be troubled; (2) Trust in Me; (3) Whatever you ask in*

My Name, I will do. Whenever I'd awaken, I would hear Him, as it were, speaking those words to me, and I was thus enabled to sleep. This morning, He gave me a prayer for my children from John 17: "Holy Father, keep through Your Name those whom You have given me. . . . I do not pray that You should take them out of the world, but that You should keep them from the evil one. . . . Sanctify them by Your truth. . . . For their sakes I sanctify myself, that they also may be sanctified by the truth. Father, I desire that they also whom You gave me may be with me where I am."

Blessings from Burdens

God has meant this trial to strengthen my faith, to drive me deeper into His heart, and to expand my empathy. I've bonded with other parents whose kids are going through difficult times, and I can better relate to those in pain. I have a list of prodigals for whom I daily intercede. My prayer life has made a quantum leap, and I'm slowly learning the secrets of finding refuge in God alone. There have been occasional short-term disruptions in my ministry, but the long-term benefits have already indirectly touched my congregation. I'm exceedingly eager to fully emerge from the valley, but until then He will not abandon me, nor will His promises fail. Sometimes I must minister in sheer faith, preaching when my own heart is breaking, and comforting others when I'm the one in greater need. But Amy Carmichael put it well when she described the panicked disciples on the waters of Galilee:

Looking back on that night the most vivid memory must have been, not the darkness or the weariness, not the great wind and the rough sea, but the blessed Morning Aid that came before the morning. Let us not make too much of the storm in the night.... The wind was contrary unto them then, perhaps it is contrary to us now. But just when things were hardest in that tiredest of all times (between 2 a.m. and 6 a.m.), just then, He came.

The Lord is near. Even when we feel unable to minister to others, He can minister through us. And that's the way it should be anyway. ✿

Quotes for the Pastor's Wall

" *Veritas pateat, veritas placeat, veritas moveat.*

Make the truth plain, make it pleasing, make it

moving. "

—Augustine

FEBRUARY 23, 2003

Battle Dress

Date preached:

Scripture: Ephesians 6:10–20, especially verses 10–11: Finally, my brethren, be strong in the Lord and in the power of His might. Put on the whole armor of God, that you may be able to stand against the wiles of the devil.

Introduction: *The New York Times,* in reporting on a survey by the Barna Group, noted that two-thirds of Americans do not believe in the devil as a living entity. The *Times* called it "a result of fundamental, long-term shifts in the nation's religious culture."

1. **Our Adversary.** Notice how literally Paul dealt with our adversary, presenting him as dangerous on three levels. The first is his *wiles* or *schemes* (μεθοδεία ὁ διάβολος—the methods of the diabolical one). Satan studies us and exploits our weaknesses. It might be a tendency toward lust or pornography; greed and the availability of easy credit; low self-esteem; a proclivity toward addictive behavior; a fearful spirit or short temper. We can be sure that Satan, in effect, has a file with our names written on the tabs and has developed a strategy for our undoing (1 Pet. 5:8). The second level of danger comes from his "storm troopers." Verse 12: "principalities . . . powers . . . rulers of the darkness of this age . . . spiritual hosts of wickedness in the heavenly places." The third danger is "the evil day" (v. 13). In military language this is Zero Hour, when the attack is launched, as we see in Job 1.

2. **Our Attitude.** Paul tells us to *be strong* (ἐνδυναμόω ἐν κύριος καί ἐν ὁ κράτος ὁ ἰσχύς αὐτό). Literally: "Be inwardly strengthened in the Master and in the vigor of the personal strength of Him." When the Communists overran China, missionary Isabel Kuhn escaped on foot with her young son across the dangerous, snow-covered Pienma Pass. Arriving in Upper Burma, she was stranded "at the world's end" without money, unable to speak the language, and half a world away from home. In her perplexity, she made a decision. "The first thing is to cast out fear," she said. "The only fear a Christian should entertain is the fear of sin. All other fears are from Satan sent to confuse and weaken us." Isabel knelt and spread her heart before Him. "I refused to be afraid and asked Him

to cast such fears out of my heart." She then sought "light for the next step," and God led her home. Second, we're to take our stand, a phrase Paul uses four times. This term has military overtones, referring to resisting the enemy and holding a critical position in battle.

3. **Our Armor.** A recent magazine article described modern high-tech body armor, yet it's remarkable how similar it sounded to Paul's list in Ephesians 6. New form-fitting, bullet-resistant fabrics to protect the chest and back, video-display goggles and headgear, a wrist-mounted weapons pod, and so forth are simply modern versions of what the apostle saw on the Roman soldier guarding him. Top to bottom, we have the **helmet of salvation** (v. 17). Satan cannot harm, in any permanent or ultimate sense, those who are genuinely born again. Next is the **breastplate** (bullet-proof vest) **of righteousness**, for there is great protection in a righteous life. **The belt of truth** has to do with those building their lives on the truth of Scripture. Next, the **shield of faith** extinguishes flaming arrows. During World War II in Finland, the soldiers didn't have adequate weapons against invaders, so they learned to fill bottles with gasoline, sand, and soapsuds, and with burning rags in the mouth. These little firebombs became known as Molotov Cocktails. The devil is the original inventor of fiery darts, but see 1 John 5:4. Next are the **boots**, equipping our feet with the preparation of the gospel. Are we available and ready for whatever assignment God gives us? Is our life one of constant alertness and availability? Verse 18 emphasizes **prayer**, our communications gear.

>>> *sermon continued on following page*

APPROPRIATE HYMNS AND SONGS

We Are Strong in the Lord, Dennis Jernigan; © 1989 Shepherd's Heart Music (Admin. by Dayspring Music, Inc.).

Be Thou My Vision, Keith Landis/Mary Byrne/Eleanor Hull/Carlton Young; © 1964, 1994 Selah Publishing Company, Inc./Abingdon Press (Admin. by The Copyright Company.).

I've Got My Armor On, Kevin Prosch; © 1990 Mercy/Vineyard Publishing.

Shut De Do, Randy Stonehill; © 1983 Stonehillian Music/Word Music, Inc. (Admin. by Word Music Group, Inc.).

Soldiers of Christ Arise, Charles Wesley/George J. Elvey; Public Domain.

Having put on these defensive pieces, we're now ready to take up the **sword of the Spirit**—the Word of God. If we are reading our Bibles every day, finding verses to meet the conditions and needs in life, and claiming promises that counter our trials and temptation, the devil will become discouraged with us. He can't do much with people who keep stabbing him with Scripture.

Conclusion: We have a great adversary, but we can withstand him in the power of Christ if we'll keep our armor on. If we let our guard down we're vulnerable and exposed. Keep your armor on, so that when it's all over but the shouting, you'll still be on your feet (see Peterson's translation).

FOR THE BULLETIN

❋ February 23, 155, marks the martyrdom of Polycarp, pastor of the church in Smyrna. When Polycarp was asked to recant his faith, he replied, "Eighty and six years have I served Him, and He has done me no wrong. How can I speak evil of my King who saved me?" ❋ On this day in A.D. 303, a great persecution was unleashed by Emperor Diocletian, prodded by the bitterly anti-Christian general Galerius. Churches were destroyed, Scriptures burned, and Christians were repressed, imprisoned, and killed, making the reign of Diocletian the "Era of the Martyrs." ❋ February 23, 1468, marks the death of Johannes Gutenberg. ❋ On February 23, 1616, the theologians of the Inquisition condemned Galileo for his theory that the earth revolves around the sun. ❋ Thomas Goodwin, English Nonconformist preacher and Puritan writer, died at the age of 80 in London on February 23, 1679. ❋ Bartholomaeus Ziegenbalg, German missionary to India, passed away on February 23, 1719. ❋ On February 23, 1791, after a week of illness, John Wesley, 88, left to preach from Isaiah 55:6 in a village 20 miles from London. It was to be his last journey and his last sermon. ❋ On February 23, 1803, after 20 years of work by William Wilberforce, the House of Commons voted for abolition of slavery in the British Empire. ❋ On February 23, 1950, a revival broke out at Asbury College during a regular chapel service in which the speaker cut his message short due to spontaneous testimonies. The chapel service went on for 118 hours, and the revival continued for weeks.

STATS, STORIES AND MORE

Peter Cartwright was a circuit-riding Methodist evangelist in the 1800s. In his autobiography, he tells of traveling to the Methodist General Conference in Pittsburgh, where he lodged in a particular home where there appeared to be some sort of spiritual dysfunction. That evening, the host asked him to lead in family devotions, but as soon as he began, Cartwright later recalled, "thick darkness fell on me, and if ever I felt the power of the devil physically and mentally, it was just then. I was almost totally blind, literally blind, and the great drops of sweat rolled off my face."

He was so afraid of being unable to read that he turned to Psalm 1, which he knew from memory, but he found his memory as defective as his sight. He somehow stammered through a broken version of the psalm, then suggested the group sing together. He had a reasonably good singing voice, and he rose and started singing a very familiar hymn. But not one person joined him.

"I stopped short, and kneeled down to pray, but in all my life I was never in a worse plight to pray. . . . I then thought my head was as large as a house, and I now thought I had no head at all. It seemed to me that the devil was veritably present, and all around, and in everybody and everything."

The next day at the General Conference he was asked to lead in prayer, but he could hardly get out a few syllables. A dreadful sense of inward paralysis came over him, a foreboding and confusion that rendered him powerless. This oppression lasted for an entire week; and then one night he attended a prayer meeting. "It pleased God that night to roll back the clouds that had covered me in thick darkness." And his old sense of spiritual clarity and vitality returned stronger than ever.

Stand therefore!

When Martin Luther was placed on trial for his views before the council in the German city of Worms, amid high drama he reportedly affirmed, "Here I stand. I can do no other. God help me, Amen."

WORSHIP HELPS

Call to Worship:
"Grace to you and peace from God our Father and the Lord Jesus
Christ. . . . Grace to you and peace be multiplied!" (Eph. 1:2; 1 Pet.
1:2).

Scripture Reading Medley:
The LORD does not save with sword and spear; for the battle is the
LORD's. If God is for us, who can be against us? He who did not
spare His own Son, but delivered Him up for us all, how shall He
not with Him also freely give us all things? Who shall bring a
charge against God's elect? It is God who justifies. Who is he who
condemns? It is Christ who died, and furthermore is also risen,
who is even at the right hand of God, who also makes intercession
for us. . . . We are more than conquerors through Him. . . . For
whatever is born of God overcomes the world. And this is the victory that has overcome the world—our faith. Thanks be to God,
who gives us the victory through our Lord Jesus Christ. Therefore,
my beloved brethren, be steadfast. (1 Sam. 17:47; Rom. 8:31–37;
1 Cor. 15:57–58; 1 John 5:4–5)

Pastoral Prayer:
Our Great and Glorious God, remind us today of those old and
sturdy words of Psalm 46: "God is our refuge and strength, a very
present help in trouble. Therefore we will not fear, even though the
earth be removed, and though the mountains be carried into the
midst of the sea; though its waters roar and be troubled, though the
mountains shake with its swelling." Remind us to be still and know
that You are God. Remind us that the Lord of hosts is with us; the
God of Jacob is our refuge. And for those here today needing this
very present help in trouble, I ask you to display yourself to them,
dislodge fear from them, undertake for them, multiply grace and
peace unto them, and may Satan be soon crushed under their feet.
We pray in Jesus' name. Amen.

Additional Sermons and Lesson Ideas

The Gift of Three Heavens

Date preached:

SCRIPTURE: Genesis 1:1

INTRODUCTION: That there are three heavens is clearly taught in 2 Corinthians 12:2, and as we thank God for all His earthly blessings to us, remember to thank Him for the gift of three heavens.

1. The Atmospheric Heavens—home of birds, clouds, winds, and airplanes. There is a blanket of life-sustaining air that surrounds our globe, and God built into this blanket the phenomenon of weather, so necessary to our life and well-being (Isa. 55:10).
2. The Celestial Heavens—the night sky. While the earth grows old, while empires and nations rise and fall, while all things around us change and fade, the stars continue to shine down upon us. There are more stars in the universe than there are grains of sand on the seashores.
3. The Highest Heaven—where believers will be with God eternally. Paul called it the "third heaven." Solomon called it the "heaven of heavens."

CONCLUSION: We don't know exactly where the highest heaven is located, but we do know how to get there. Jesus said, "I am the way, the truth, and the life. No one comes to the Father except through Me" (John 14:6).

Living in a Rich Neighborhood

Date preached:

SCRIPTURE: John 15:1–11

INTRODUCTION: Today I'd like to take up the role of a realtor and sell you some properties in a rich neighborhood. The word "abide" means to take up residence. Where are the best addresses?

1. "He who dwells in the secret place of the Most High shall *abide* under the shadow of the Almighty" (Ps. 91:1).
2. "The ear that hears the rebukes of life will *abide* among the wise" (Prov. 15:31).
3. "If you *abide* in My word, you are My disciples indeed" (John 8:31).
4. "*Abide* in Me" (John 15:4).
5. "*Abide* in My love. If you keep My commandments, you will *abide* in My love" (John 15:9–10).
6. "He who loves his brother *abides* in the light" (1 John 2:10).
7. "He who *abides* in the doctrine of Christ has both the Father and the Son" (2 John 9).

CONCLUSION: Wouldn't you like to move into these addresses today?

MARCH 2, 2003

SUGGESTED SERMON

The Wholeness of Worship

Date preached:

By Jack W. Hayford

Scripture: Isaiah 6:1–8: In the year that King Uzziah died, I saw the Lord sitting on a throne, high and lifted up, and the train of His robe filled the temple. Above it stood seraphim. . . . And one cried to another and said: "Holy, holy, holy is the LORD of hosts; The whole earth is full of His glory!" . . . So I said: "Woe is me, for I am undone! Because I am a man of unclean lips, and I dwell in the midst of a people of unclean lips; for my eyes have seen the King, the LORD of hosts." Then one of the seraphim flew to me, having in his hand a live coal that he had taken with the tongs from the altar. And he touched my mouth with it, and said: "Behold, this has touched your lips; your iniquity is taken away, and your sin purged." Also I heard the voice of the Lord, saying: "Whom shall I send, and who will go for Us?" Then I said, "Here am I! Send me."

Introduction: The best times for worship are sometimes in the middle of crises or disappointments. Here, amid the crisis of King Uzziah's death, Isaiah learns something about the impact of worship and holiness on our hearts.

I. **Unholiness Is Revealed by Worship.** Isaiah's vision of God's throne gave him a horrible sense of his own unworthiness and sinfulness, and it does the same for us. The Lord's presence makes us aware of our sin. We feel "undone" and "unclean" like Isaiah. But the Lord meets us at our point of need by purifying us. God sent an angel with a hot coal to touch Isaiah's perceived point of unworthiness—his lips. Had he felt his hands were unclean, the Lord would have touched Isaiah's hands. The fire of the coal brought regeneration to the place of impurity Isaiah was most sensitive to. The "fire" of worship:

A. **Refines.** It burns out the residue of what's unworthy.

B. **Consumes.** It takes the bondage out of our lives and burns it up.

C. **Melts.** Our hearts are made soft.

D. **Warms.** Our cold hearts are thawed.

E. **Ignites.** When we've turned off, He turns us back on.

What is the point of your greatest weakness? If we will come to God, in the midst of His holiness, His purifying fire will touch us at that point.

2. **Holiness Is Activated by Worship.** Every time we hear praise going on around the throne of God, we hear, "Holy, holy, holy!" The focus is on God's holiness. We tend to think of holiness as the purity we are trying to achieve, and that God will reject us if we don't. Even among people who genuinely love the Lord, there are those who draw back because they feel unholy, unworthy. There's a natural inclination to avoid worship because of feelings of unworthiness. But the Lord wants us to worship Him because it is there we will find wholeness. There is a root relationship between the words *whole, healthy, wholeness,* and *holy.* When we talk about holiness, we are talking about wholeness. Holiness is God's entirety entering my incompleteness. The only way for that to happen is to come into His presence.

3. **Wholeness Is Restored by Worship.** The word "worth" comes from *axios,* which originally described a coin of full weight. In the ancient world, the coins were made of valuable metals which wore thin rapidly, causing the coin to lose some of its value. That's how Isaiah felt. But God calls us to worship in His presence in order that a transfer of His being into us may take place. Then the worth that has been worn off the coin of our lives— His nature within us—begins to be restored through worship. Worship is the situation in which wholeness is restored. Because of God's worth poured into us, we become worthy.

>>> *sermon continued on following page*

APPROPRIATE HYMNS AND SONGS

Holy, Holy, Holy, John B. Dykes/Reginald Heber; Public Domain.

The Heart of Worship, Matt Redman; © 1997 Kingsway Thankyou Music (Admin. by EMI Christian Music Publishing.).

Holy, Holy, Holy, Gary Oliver; © 1991 CMI-HP Publishing (Admin. by Word Music Group, Inc.).

All I Want, Andy Park; © 1995 Mercy/Vineyard Publishing.

O Worship the King, Robert Grant/Johann M. Haydn; Public Domain.

4. **Mission Is Found in Worship.** The mission of our lives is also found in worship. After the angel purified Isaiah's lips, the Lord gave him a mission. You can only find your direction and intended purpose in the context of worship.

Conclusion: Just as we inherit certain characteristics from our biological parents, so, as we worship, the image and nature of our heavenly Father begins to manifest in our lives. My likeness to my heavenly Father comes from being in His presence. The fact that God is holy relates to our healing and restoration, not our shame and condemnation. His life is already in us, and we will be holy because He is our Father, and He is holy. That's a promise (1 Pet. 1:16).

FOR THE BULLETIN

❀ The Lollards, John Wycliffe's traveling preachers, were early pre-reformation evangelists who were bitterly persecuted. The first Lollard martyr was William Sawtré, who was burned to death on March 2, 1401. ❀ Henry Venn was born on March 2, 1724. He was an Anglican clergyman and close friend of George Whitefield, born near London and ordained in 1749, whose sermons fascinated the industrial and manufacturing classes of eighteenth-century England. ❀ On March 2, 1783, New England evangelist Benjamin Randall was struck with a violent fever, which nearly killed him. He later wrote in his journal, "Through the whole illness, I enjoyed a heavenly calm. I found my faith strong in the Lord Jesus Christ. . . . I laid basking and solacing in divine consolation and felt the streams of heavenly love flow sweetly into my soul. ❀ John Wesley died on March 2, 1791. ❀ March 2, 1848 marks the birthday of Christian entrepreneur, A. A. Hyde, creator of Mentholatum. ❀ American missionary Gustav Schmidt, 39, opened the Danzig Instytut Biblijny in the Free City of Danzig (Gdansk), Poland, on March 2, 1930. It was the first Pentecostal Bible institute established in Eastern Europe. ❀ On March 2, 1979, over 1,100 Christian organizations joined together to form the Evangelical Council for Financial Accountability (ECFA), an oversight agency that helps insure financial integrity among evangelical ministries.

STATS, STORIES AND MORE

Someone Once Said . . .
"As I read the Bible, I seem to find holiness to be His supreme attribute."
—*Billy Graham*

"It does not seem proper to speak of one attribute of God as being more central and fundamental than another; but if this were permissible, the scriptural emphasis on the holiness of God would seem to justify its selection."
—*Louis Berkhof,* in *Systematic Theology*

"Lower our sense of holiness, and our sense of sin is lowered."
—*Dan DeHaan*

"Divine holiness . . . stands apart, unique, unapproachable, incomprehensible, and unattainable."
—*A. W. Tozer*

Holy, Holy, Holy!
Philadelphia pastor James Montgomery Boice once spoke to a discipleship group on the attributes of God. He began by asking them to list God's qualities in order of importance. They put love first, followed by wisdom, power, mercy, omniscience, and truth. At the end of the list they put holiness. "That did surprise me," Boice later wrote, "because the Bible refers to God's holiness more than any other attribute." The Bible doesn't generally refer to God as *Loving, Loving, Loving!* Or *Wise, Wise, Wise!* Or *Omniscient, Omniscient, Omniscient!* But over and over we read the cry of the angels, *Holy, Holy, Holy!*

Go Forth!
Jonathan Goforth became a powerful evangelist throughout Asia, a rarity for a Westerner, and his crowds sometimes numbered 25,000. His Chinese home was open to inquirers—one day alone over 2,000 showed up. Multitudes throughout the Orient came to Christ through Jonathan and his wife, Rosaline. During his missionary career, fifty Chinese converts went out as ministers or evangelists. What led Goforth overseas? Dr. George Mackay, veteran missionary to Formosa (Taiwan), had been traveling across America for two years trying to recruit young men for Asian evangelism. One night as Jonathan, a college student at the time, listened, "I heard the voice of the Lord saying: 'Whom shall I send, and who will go for us?' and I answered: 'Here am I, send me.' From that hour I became a foreign missionary."

WORSHIP HELPS

Call to Worship:
"Holy, holy, holy is the Lord of Hosts; the whole earth is full of His glory" (Isa. 6:3).

Scripture: Psalm 99
The LORD reigns;
Let the peoples tremble!
He dwells between the cherubim;
Let the earth be moved!
The LORD is great in Zion,
And He is high above all the peoples.
Let them praise Your great and awesome name—
He is holy.
The King's strength also loves justice;
You have established equity;
You have executed justice and righteousness in Jacob.
Exalt the LORD our God,
And worship at His footstool—
He is holy.
Moses and Aaron were among His priests,
And Samuel was among those who called upon His name;
They called upon the LORD, and He answered them.
He spoke to them in the cloudy pillar;
They kept His testimonies and the ordinance He gave them.
You answered them, O LORD our God;
You were to them God-Who-Forgives,
Though You took vengeance on their deeds.
Exalt the LORD our God,
And worship at His holy hill;
For the LORD our God is holy.

Benediction:
As we leave from this place, O Lord, may each of us say with the ancient prophet: Here am I, send me. Draw us to be worshipers, and send us to be workers this week. We pray in Jesus' name. Amen.

Additional Sermons and Lesson Ideas

The World Is a Dangerous Place
By Kevin Riggs

Date preached:

SCRIPTURE: Psalm 3

INTRODUCTION: Dates like June 7, 1941, and September 11, 2001, remind us that the world is full of evil. To survive in this dangerous world, Psalm 3 tells us we should:

1. Look to God for Protection (vv. 3–4). Ultimately, the source of all our protection is the hand of God, our shield.
2. Look to God for Security (vv. 5–6). God watches over us as we sleep, and wakes us up each morning.
3. Look to God for Deliverance (vv. 7–8). David compared his enemies to wild animals whom God disarms, rendering them harmless.

CONCLUSION: The world may be a dangerous place to live, but it is also a beautiful place, and a perfect place for the exercise of faith.

This Thing Called Church

Date preached:

SCRIPTURE: Ephesians 1:1 NIV

INTRODUCTION: In the Book of Ephesians, Paul uses fifteen terms to describe the church; each term gives us a different insight into who we are:

1. The Saints (1:2).
2. The Faithful in Christ Jesus (1:1; also see 6:21).
3. "Us Who Believe" (1:19).
4. His Glorious Church (5:27).
5. His Body (1:23).
6. His Workmanship (2:10).
7. One New Man (2:15).
8. Fellow Citizens (2:19).
9. Fellow Heirs (3:6).
10. The Household of God (2:19).
11. A Dwelling Place for God in the Spirit (2:22).
12. The Whole Family in Heaven and Earth (3:15).
13. Children of Light (5:8).
14. The Brethren (6:10, 23).
15. Those Who Love Our Lord Jesus Christ in Sincerity (6:24).

CONCLUSION: What does this do for our church's self-image? We are so special to God that in one book He uses 15 positive phrases to describe us.

Your Lungs Are Only as Healthy as You Are

If preaching is talking, and talking is breathing, than the condition of our lungs—indeed, of our whole body—is crucial to the pulpit ministry. Healthy pastors are better able to withstand the physical strains of preaching. Good lungs are better able to project, to modulate, to whisper, to shout, to sustain the outrushing of hot and holy words.

What would you think of a pastor who allowed his church buildings to crumble? Shattered windows. Peeling paint. Leaking roof. Broken sidewalk. Lawn gone to seed.

Well, then, what of a preacher who lets the temple of the Holy Spirit—his or her body—deteriorate? Paul wrote that our greatest pursuit is the exercise of godliness, but "bodily exercise" also has its place.

The biblical heroes were fit. Consider Elijah's running, Jacob's wrestling and Daniel's healthy diet. Apparently Christ Himself had a strong physique, able to walk long distances, work long hours, and bear great pain. Paul, too, was fit enough to tread water a day and a night in the deep.

Not that we all have to be athletes.

Take me, for example. I can't shoot, sprint, skate, or ski. I'm a terrible dribbler, and I can't hit, one basket out of ten from the free throw line. I can't pitch, punt, hit, or catch. I'm even hopeless at ping-pong and putt-putt.

I've tried hard, but I just strike out. Fumble the ball. Take the count. Foul out. Finish last. Double fault. Don't make it to first base. When I went skiing last year in the Rockies, I had to be rescued by the snow patrol.

But, having learned how to walk and run as a child, I can still stay in shape. We don't have to be Michael Jordans to keep physically toned. Most of us can take the stairs, mow the lawn, or pedal away on the stationary bike.

Bobby Bowers, South Carolina pastor, faithfully visits a gym near his house, lifting weights one day and swimming the next. He has a lot of stamina under his thatch of gray hair.

Ministry, after all, involves much sedentary activity—reading, studying, counseling, attending meetings, doing office work. Much of it is stressful.

"To sit long in one posture, pouring over a book or pushing a quill," Charles Spurgeon wrote, "is in itself a taxing of nature; but add to this a badly ventilated chamber, a body which has long been without muscular exercise, and a heart burdened with many cares, and we have all the elements for a seething cauldron of despair."

Spurgeon was right. I have a cardiac specialist in my church who recently warned me that clergymen are among the highest-risk groups he sees, ranking just below fire fighters.

Dr. Paul Gentuso said that as he traveled around my particular denomination on missionary deputation, staying in homes of many pastors, he found most of them suffering various ills. "I hardly saw a healthy pastor," he said. Perhaps they were neglecting their exercise.

Why Exercise?

Exercise makes us more productive in Christian service. Some people think exercise tires them out, but our fatigue is more often caused by nervous strain than by physical exertion. Exercise provides a way of relieving our bodies of that daily stress and improving their ability to deliver and utilize oxygen. By strengthening the heart, circulatory and respiratory systems, we can perform more work with less effort.

Cardiologist James Rippe, in a survey of top executives, found that two out of three exercise regularly. "For most," he wrote, "regular exercise is taken as seriously as any other appointment on their calendar. The link between a high level of fitness and increased energy, stamina and productivity is critical to them."

Critics said that Italian opera tenor, Luciano Pavarotti, 63, was past his prime, his lungs faltering. But Pavarotti began a daily regimen of swimming, weight training, and walking, plus a new low-fat diet. He shed over 50 pounds, and his magnificent voice is returning full force.

"If you are not healthy," he said, "you are not a good singer." The same, I think, often holds true for preachers.

Exercise also gives us more years to serve the Lord. Dr. William J. Evans of Tufts University, who spent years documenting the health benefits in well-rounded exercise programs, claims that such programs can postpone—even reverse—many of the declines once considered an inevitable part of aging, like shriveled muscles, frail bones, and clogged arteries.

Exercise gives us a better testimony. In two national studies, sociologist Kenneth Ferraro of Purdue University found that religious people in America are fatter than those who aren't. He was surprised by that, for he had expected to find Christians more moderate in their habits since the Bible portrays gluttony as a moral weakness.

But he concluded that, alas, "many firm believers do not have firm bodies."

Exercise also helps us sleep better at night, worry less by day, and it reduces doctor's bills. When California pastor Francis Boyle was in his 50s, he was so ill with hypertension that his doctors advised him to retire. He had a rapid heart rate, high blood pressure, and other stress-related problems.

Boyle decided to start exercising instead. "Now I get up before daylight three days a week and walk for an hour at a pace that makes everything work in my body. I swing my arms so that the blood circulates all over. Then I do my old Army calisthenics, some yard work, and come in to start my day. I feel better at 75 than I ever did at 55."

Why Not Begin Now?

Start with something easy, make a schedule for yourself, and stick with it—walking a quarter-mile, jogging around the block, doing a half-dozen push-ups on the bedroom floor. Slowly increase till you've established a half-hour routine three or four times a week.

Pastor Eddie Hopkins started walking around the block with his wife. He graduated to jogging, then to running, up to four miles a day. Today he still covers four miles, but he's back to a walking pace. "When you get into the routine," he said, "it just becomes part of you."

Running and walking are easy for me because they require only a good pair of shoes. But some days I mow the lawn, visit the health club, or go hiking. I'd like to buy a good bicycle, and I'm thinking about roller-blading, having been inspired by a "missionary kid" in Japan.

I've even considered golf, but I'm suspicious of the health benefits of chasing little white balls in motorized carts.

But enough of me. What about you? Why not put this book down right now—and take a good, brisk walk? ✿

Perpetua: The Quandary of Human Affections

Human affections, dear as they are, must always yield primary allegiance to Christ, as we learn from the example of the famous North African martyr, Perpetua, who so inspired the early Christians that Augustine warned against viewing her story as equal to Scripture. Perpetua was born about A.D. 176 in Carthage, growing up in a well-to-do family. Her father wasn't a Christian, but her brothers and mother were devoted to Christ. Perpetua, bright and attractive, gained a good education and a husband, then a baby boy.

In 202, Emperor Septimus Severius issued an edict against Christians, and presently Perpetua and four other Christians were placed under house arrest. When her father begged her to recant, she pointed to a waterpot and asked, "Father, do you see this vessel? Can it be called by any other name than what it is? So also I cannot call myself by any other name than what I am—a Christian."

She was moved to prison where her father again visited her, begging her with sobs to renounce her faith. She refused. Perpetua and a handful of other believers were then tried in the marketplace where, again, her father appeared, carrying her infant son and begging her to free herself.

Sentenced to torture and execution, the Christians were dragged back to prison. When she asked to see her baby a final time, she was refused. She and her fellow Christians were flogged, but on the eve of her death, Perpetua wrote of God's sustaining presence: "I saw that I should not fight with beasts but with the devil; I knew the victory to be mine."

On March 7, 202, the Christians were marched into the arena where Perpetua was gored and thrown by a savage heifer. Surviving the first encounter, she crept to the aid of a companion. Shortly thereafter, a gladiator pierced her with his sword. When the trembling youth came at her again, she helped guide his shaking sword to her throat. She was beheaded.

Her devotion to Christ so inspired the Christians in North Africa that she personified Tertullian's famous quote, "The blood of the martyrs is the seed of the church." Indeed, through the power of her witness, her chief jailer, Pudens, committed himself to the Lord Jesus. *The Passion of Perpetua,* the history of her martyrdom, inspired many Christians to faithfulness during the Middle Ages. ❁

MARCH 9, 2003

Glimpses of Jesus in Joshua

Date preached:

Scripture: Joshua 1:1–2: After the death of Moses the servant of the LORD, it came to pass that the LORD spoke to Joshua the son of Nun, Moses' assistant, saying: "Moses My servant is dead. Now therefore, arise, go over this Jordan, you and all this people, to the land which I am giving to them—the children of Israel."

Introduction: Have you ever noticed how ticket agents at the airport don't trust us to be who we claim to be? They want to see photo IDs. When Christ showed up claiming to be the Messiah, a lot of people didn't trust Him, but He had a picture of Himself drawn with remarkable accuracy over hundreds of years in the Old Testament. He appealed to fulfilled messianic prophecy to demonstrate the validity of His claims (John 5:39–47). It was His photo ID. Even in the Book of Joshua, for example, we see at least three glimpses of Jesus.

1. **Joshua Himself.** Jesus and Joshua shared the same name. *Jesus* is the Greek version of the Hebrew *Joshua*. According to Numbers 13, Joshua was originally called Hoshea, but Moses changed his name. Why? Hoshea in the Hebrew means *May Jehovah Save*. Joshua means *Jehovah Is Salvation*. Perhaps Moses was led to strengthen Hoshea's name to make it more solid, more durable, and more certain as a personal name for the coming Messiah (Matt. 1:21). These two men not only shared the same name; they had a similar task. Joshua took over after the Law-giver had died and led the people into the future that God had planned for them. Bible teacher Paul Van Gorder points out, "The book begins with the words, 'Now after the death of Moses. . . . Moses represented the law. The people could not enter the land of Canaan until Moses was dead. 'For what the law could not do, in that it was weak through the flesh, God sending His own Son in the likeness of sinful flesh and for sin, condemned sin in the flesh, that the righteousness of the law might be fulfilled in us, who walk not after the flesh but after the Spirit' (Rom. 8:3,4). . . . Joshua led the children of Israel to victory after crossing the Jordan. He was their advocate in time of defeat. It was Joshua who allotted them their portions within the land. All of this beautifully pictures the work of the Lord."

2. **Rahab's Crimson Cord.** The second picture of Jesus is found in a coil of scarlet roping in Joshua 2. In that chapter, two spies secretly entered Jericho and were hidden by a prostitute named Rahab. She had a crimson cord that she tied to the window of her house, which was on the city wall, so the men could rappel down and escape. She said to them, "I know you're going to capture this city. I know God is with you. Please spare me and my family." In reply, the two spies told her to tie the scarlet cord to the window and to bring her family into that room. It would be the only place of safety during the invasion. What a picture of Christ! This world will be invaded by the judgment of God (Acts 17:30–31), and there is only one place can we find deliverance. Just as the Israelites were told to remain in their houses with the crimson blood of the lamb on the doorposts, just as Rahab was told to remain in her room with the crimson cord in the window, so we must be under the power of the crimson blood of Christ.

3. **The Captain of the Lord's Host.** We also have a special pre-incarnate appearance of Jesus in Joshua 5. Joshua meets one who calls himself the "Captain of the Lord's Hosts." When Joshua realized he was speaking with the Lord Himself, he asked, "What message do you have for me?" Instead of imparting military advice, the Captain said: "Take off your shoes. The place where you are standing is holy." That harkens back to Joshua 1:3, where the Lord promised to be everywhere that Joshua set his feet. The pillar of cloud may vanish. The column of fire may no longer be seen. But God's presence was just as real as ever. Your living room is holy

>>> sermon continued on following page

APPROPRIATE HYMNS AND SONGS

Ancient of Days, Jamie Harvill/Gary Sandler; © 1992 Integrity's Hosanna! Music.

We Are Standing on Holy Ground, Geron Davis; © 1983 Meadowgreen Music Company (Admin. by EMI Christian Music Publishing.).

Come, Thou Almighty King, Charles Wesley/Felice De Giardini; Public Domain.

Be Still and Know, Lex Loizides; © 1995 Kingsway's Thankyou Music (Admin. by EMI Christian Publishing.).

Exalt the Lord, Danny Daniels; © 1991 Mercy/Vineyard Music.

ground, for Jesus is there. Your bedroom is holy ground. Your office or classroom is holy ground.

Conclusion: Joshua went forth with a newfound confidence, knowing that even if he could not see the Lord, the Lord was hovering near with His divine armies, ready to fight on his behalf, even as our Lord Jesus Christ said as He ascended into heaven, "Lo, I am with you always, even to the end of the world."

FOR THE BULLETIN

✸ On March 9, 1074, Pope Gregory VII excommunicated all married Roman Catholic priests. Until then, celibacy had only been enforced from time to time and place to place. ✸ Giovanni de Medici, age 13, was made a cardinal-deacon of the church on March 9, 1489. Though he never became a priest, he was elected pope in 1513, taking the title Leo X. His excesses sparked the Protestant Reformation. ✸ On March 9, 1745, the bells for the first American carillon were shipped from England to Boston. ✸ On March 9, 1831, evangelist Charles Finney concluded a six-month series of meetings in Rochester, New York, during which 100,000 people were reportedly converted, including many of the city's leaders. Taverns went out of business, the theater became a livery stable, and the crime rate dropped by two-thirds. The city jail was virtually empty for the next two years. ✸ March 9, 1839 is the birth date of Phoebe Palmer Knapp, Methodist hymnwriter, who wrote the tune to Fanny Crosby's hymn, "Blessed Assurance." ✸ On March 9, 1913, Eberhard Nestle, German biblical scholar, died at 61. Nestle is primarily remembered as a Greek scholar who, in 1898, published the first edition of his Greek New Testament based on the work of leading German and British scholars. In 1904, his text was adopted by the British and Foreign Bible Society in place of the *Textus Receptus*, and became arguably the most widely used edition of the Greek New Testament. ✸ Andrae Crouch wrote "Through It All" on this day in 1971.

STATS, STORIES AND MORE

Fulfilled Prophecy

In his book, *Evidence That Demands a Verdict,* Josh McDowell states, "The Old Testament contains over 300 references to the Messiah that were fulfilled in Jesus," which, he says, "establishes the fact of God, authenticates the deity of Jesus, and [proves] the inspiration of the Bible." McDowell lists 61 specific messianic prophecies and shows how they were fulfilled hundreds of years after they were spoken, and he points out that Peter Stoner, in his book *Science Speaks,* says that according to scientifically accepted laws of probability, the odds against just eight of the prophecies being fulfilled are one chance in ten to the 17th power (100,000,000,000,000,000).

An Urgent Burden

Can you imagine how diligently Rahab sought to get her loved ones into that room? The invasion was imminent, and nothing else mattered to her except to get her father and mother, her brothers and sisters and their children into that upper room. It's the same sort of diligence we see in the apostle Paul as he scurried about the Roman Empire, begging everyone he met to come to Christ for salvation. It's a picture of the burden we should have for our own loved ones who know not Christ.

Holy Ground

When Brother Lawrence, the Carmelite mystic, was assigned to the monastery kitchen, he was unhappy until he realized one day that even the most menial tasks, if undertaken for God's glory, are holy; and wherever the Christian stands—even in a hot, thankless kitchen—is holy ground, for the Lord is there, too. It was said about Brother Lawrence "in the great hurry of business in the kitchen he still preserved his recollection and heavenly-mindedness. He was never hasty nor loitering, but did each thing in its season, with an even, uninterrupted composure and tranquility of spirit."

WORSHIP HELPS

Call to Worship:
"Blessing and honor and glory and power be to Him who sits on the throne, and to the Lamb, forever and ever. Amen!" (Rev. 5:13–14).

Reader's Theater:
Reader 1:   Search the Scriptures!
Reader 2:   You search the Scriptures for in them you think you have eternal life; and these are they which testify of Me.
Reader 3:   But you are not willing to come to Me that you may have life.
Reader 2:   If you believed Moses, you would believe Me, for he wrote about Me.
Reader 1:   O foolish ones, and slow of heart to believe in all that the prophets have spoken! Ought not the Christ to have suffered these things and to enter into His glory?
Reader 3:   And beginning at Moses and all the Prophets, He expounded to them in all the Scriptures the things concerning Himself.
(Luke 24:25–27 and John 5:39–46)

Offertory Comment:
The apostle Paul devoted two chapters, 2 Corinthians 8 and 9, to the subject of stewardship, of the receiving of our financial offerings for the Lord's work. Have you ever noticed how he ended the discussion? The last verse of chapter 9 says: "Thanks be to God for His indescribable gift." He uses the adjective *indescribable* to tell us about God's gift to us in Christ Jesus. But in those same two chapters, what adjectives does he employ to describe the kind of gift we should give in the offering plate? Here are some of the words he uses: *willing, diligent, liberal, bountiful,* and *cheerful.* May that describe our offering to the Lord today.

Benediction:
Now let Thy servants depart in peace, for we have seen Thy salvation. Amen.

Additional Sermons and Lesson Ideas

My Problem Tongue

Date preached:

SCRIPTURE: Various passages in James

INTRODUCTION: The average person speaks 18,000 words a day, and the Bible warns, "In the multitude of words sin is not lacking" (Prov. 10:19). This theme is woven throughout the little Book of James, who warns us of:

1. The Hasty Tongue—James 1:19 and 26
2. The Haughty Tongue—James 2:2-4
3. The Hellish Tongue—James 3:2-12
4. The Hateful Tongue—James 4:11
5. The Heathen Tongue—James 5:12

CONCLUSION: If your problem is your tongue, spend some time reading through the Book of James, underlining his references to the tongue and memorizing some of these verses. Ask God to help you restrain your tongue and give you the tongue of the wise.

Amazing Grace
By Kevin Riggs

Date preached:

SCRIPTURE: Titus 2:11–15

INTRODUCTION: After describing how Christians should live in all aspects of life (2:1–10), Paul reminded Titus of the amazing work of God's grace. God's grace is not a one-time event in our lives. Every day we become more dependent on His grace to survive. God's grace is more amazing than we could ever imagine.

1. God's grace in the past has saved us from our sins (2:11). God's grace, through faith in Jesus Christ, brought us to salvation.
2. God's grace in the present teaches us how to live (2:12). It gives us the power to break free from whatever sin is keeping us down.
3. God's grace in the future prepares us for eternity (2:13–14). God's grace assures us Jesus is returning one day. By being prepared for the future, we have purpose for the present.

CONCLUSION: Our motivation to live a godly life should not be guilt or fear, but love and gratitude for the grace of God. The grace that saved us, teaches us how to live, and prepares us for eternity.

MARCH 16, 2003

A Taxing Decision

Date preached:

By Stuart Briscoe

Scripture: Matthew 9:9–13, especially verse 9: As Jesus passed on from there, He saw a man named Matthew sitting at the tax office. And He said to him, "Follow Me." So he arose and followed Him.

Introduction: The first Gospel was written by Matthew, whose other name, Levi, indicated he had a rich and godly heritage. But he had sadly strayed far from his roots. He was a tax collector, which doesn't mean he was an upstanding employee of the Internal Revenue Service. Israel was an occupied country, and the Israelites were required to pay taxes to Rome. To collect these taxes, the occupying Romans recruited turncoat Israelis as collaborators. They were told, "You can collect any amount of money you wish, just make sure we get our official share. Anything collected over that, you can keep for yourself." So the tax collectors were not only collaborators, but extortionists. They were utterly despised. One day Matthew was sitting in his tax booth on the main road through Capernaum. Imagine his surprise when along the busy thoroughfare came Jesus. Without apology or introduction, Jesus walked up and said with compelling urgency and irresistible authority, "Follow me." Matthew got up and left his booth and his business, and followed Christ. Now, there's little likelihood that when you're sitting at your office desk tomorrow morning Jesus will walk in, tap you on the shoulder, and say, "Quit your job and follow me." Yet He still invites us to be His disciples. His final instruction to the church was to make disciples. The call to discipleship stands to this day. What does that mean?

1. **He Wants Us to Love Him.** He wants to draw us into a loving relationship. We love Him because He first loved us. How do I know Christ loved me? I look at the Cross.

2. **He Wants Us to Trust Him.** In His love, He made certain promises and on the basis of His promises it is possible for us to come to a point of trusting Him. Christ promised that if I commit my future to him, He will

guard it, protect it, and guarantee it. This removes an enormous amount of stress and strain about the future.

3. **He Wants Us to Obey Him.** He has also given certain commands and instructions. There are things we must be aware of, and we must get around to doing them.

4. **He Wants Us to Abandon Our Former Lives.** Matthew left all and followed Christ. This is a sticking point for many who are rather attracted to the Lord Jesus. They are attracted to the idea of having their sins forgiven and to the idea of going to heaven. What they don't find attractive is giving up and walking away from certain things. But have you ever noticed that some oak trees hang on to their old, dried-up leaves no matter how much snow and rain fall? But when springtime comes, without fuss or bother these leaves drop off. Why? Because new life has begun to flow, and as the new life begins to flow in the branches and tendrils, the old things drop off. Don't concentrate on what you have to walk away from, concentrate on the new life, and the old things begin to drop away. That's what happened to Matthew.

5. **He Wants Us to Share Him.** Almost immediately Matthew threw a big bash and invited his friends. Now his friends were from impolite society; the banquet was to introduce them to Jesus. Then at the end of Matthew 9, we read that Jesus saw a large crowd milling around, and He sensed a lostness about them, like sheep without a shepherd. Turning to His disciples, He said, "The

>>> sermon continued on following page

APPROPRIATE HYMNS AND SONGS

Follow Me, Ira Stanphill; © 1953 Singspiration Music (Admin. by Brentwood-Benson Music Publishing, Inc.).

I'm Loving You More Everyday, Becky Pearce/Jimmy Pearce/Charles Aaron Wilburn; © 1991 Jimmy Pierce Music/BMG Music Publishing.

More Like Jesus Would I Be, Fanny Crosby/W. Howard Doane; Public Domain.

All on the Altar, B.B. McKinney; © 1936 Sunday School Board of the Southern Baptist Convention (Admin. by Genevox Music Group.).

Answer the Call, Jon Mohr/Phil Naish; © 1994 Molto Bravo! Music, Inc. (Admin. by Sony/ATV Tunes LLC.).

harvest is very plentiful, but the laborers are few." He was impressing on His disciples the enormity of human need and the fact that the Lord of the Harvest wants to send people out to meet this need in His name. In Matthew 10, Matthew explains this in further detail, and he devoted the rest of his life to sharing Christ. He even became the writer of the first Gospel.

Conclusion: Christ is the *Lord* of the Harvest, and that means He must have charge of our lives. Some years ago, there was a man who used to drive with his little boy sitting on his lap. One day while driving along, the little boy grabbed the wheel. When the little fellow turned the wheel, he turned it the way the father didn't want it to go, and a wrestling match for the wheel began. They took a zigzag course down the road. I want to suggest that the person who grabs the wheel that the Lord of the Harvest is supposed to be holding will find his life taking a zigzag course and maybe ending in a wreck. But when the Lord of the Harvest is in the driver's seat, He takes very ordinary people like you and me—and Matthew—and uses us to do extraordinary things.

FOR THE BULLETIN

✸ On this day in A.D. 37, the Roman Emperor Tiberius, having retired to Capri, died on a visit to the mainland. He was the second emperor of Rome and his reign (A.D. 14–37) provided the political backdrop for the ministry of Jesus Christ and the birth of the church. ✸ On March 16, 1190, the Jews of York, England, committed mass suicide rather than submit to forced baptism. They had sought refuge in Clifford's tower after being attacked by a local mob. ✸ The Fifth Lateran Council, under the leadership of Pope Leo X, issued a special sale of indulgences before adjourning on this day in 1517. ✸ March 16, 1621, marks the birth of George Neumark, a German educator and hymnist. Twice in life he lost everything, the first time by theft and the second by fire. He is the author of, "If Thou But Suffer God to Guide Thee." ✸ On March 16, 1849, Reverend James E. Smith, age 100, became a father with a woman 64 years younger. ✸ On March 16, 1850, *The Scarlet Letter*, Nathaniel Hawthorne's novel about adultery and judgment in Puritan Massachusetts, was published. ✸ On this day in 1851, Spain signed a concordat with the Papacy under which Roman Catholicism became the only authorized faith. ✸ This is the birthday of Dr. Robert H. Bowman, cofounder of Far East Broadcasting Company, born in 1915.

The Four Gospels

When you think of the four Gospels, try thinking in terms of Monday night football. When they replay the touchdown, they do it from one camera angle, then from another, then from another, and then from another. The four Gospels look at the life and times of Jesus from four different angles. It's the story of the Lord Jesus, but told from four different points of view with four different audiences in mind. That's why we get slightly differing angles on the same events. The first of these four Gospels was written by Matthew, who was also known as Levi.

—*Stuart Briscoe*

Levi's Party

When Jill Briscoe was converted at Cambridge University, she went home to Liverpool and wrote letters, inviting all her friends to come over to her home for a special celebration. The invitations said that she had some very exciting news to share with them. Well all her girlfriends assumed that she had gotten engaged. They arrived for this special evening, bringing little presents. "What's he like, tell us." She said, "Just wait till you're all here," and then she sat them all down and told them exactly what Jesus is like. She introduced her friends to Jesus. That is just what Matthew did. Now, actually, some of her friends didn't take very kindly to this. They thought she had gone off the deep end. But two of them came to her and said, "Jill, you were our friend before this and we've no idea what has happened to you. But you're still our friend." Years later both of them became committed disciples of Jesus, too.

—*Stuart Briscoe*

Hymn Story:

William Howard Doane was a wealthy nineteenth-century industrialist who entered the business world at age 16 and was president of his own manufacturing company by age 29. But his real love was music, and he sang solos and directed choirs at various churches around Cincinnati. At age 30, Doane suffered a terrible heart attack which took him to the edge of the grave. As he recovered, he felt God wanted him to devote more of his time to the ministry of Christian music.

He began compiling and publishing hymn books, and writing musical scores for hymns and gospel songs. But Doane didn't feel he could compose words suitable to his melodies, and he was always looking for Christian poets who could write lyrics for the gospel tunes. In November, 1867, in New York, he was asked by Rev. Dr. W. C. Van Meter to write a hymn in celebration of the anniversary of a rescue mission. Doane quickly came up with a melody, but could find no suitable words.

Kneeling in his New York hotel room, he asked God to send him a poem suitable for the anniversary celebration. He also prayed for a poet who could supply an ongoing stream of suitable verse. As he prayed, he heard a knock at the door. Opening it, he saw a messenger boy who handed him an envelope addressed to Mr. William Howard Doane. The letter read: *Mr. Doane: I have never met you, but I feel impelled to send you this hymn. May God bless it. Fanny Crosby.* It was just the hymn he needed and was quickly embraced by congregations around the world:

> *More like Jesus would I be,*
> *Let my Savior dwell in me,*
> *Fill my soul with peace and love,*
> *Make me gentle as the dove.*

Additional Sermons and Lesson Ideas

Signs and Sins of Worldliness

Date preached:

By Kevin Riggs

SCRIPTURE: 1 Corinthians 3:1–4

INTRODUCTION: How healthy is our church? We can learn much from a negative example, and we can detect worldliness in the Corinthian church by observing:

1. Shallow Appetites (3:2)—Milk, rather than the meat of God's Word.
2. Jealousy (3:3)— Taking sides, following human leaders.
3. Quarreling (3:3)—Having their own agendas.
4. Disunity (3:4).

CONCLUSION: These are the branches. The tree itself has one major root, and that root is immature believers (3:1). The best way for our church to remain healthy is for each of us to continue growing in the maturity of Jesus Christ.

Peter's "Be's"

Date preached:

SCRIPTURE: 1 Peter 1:13

INTRODUCTION: H. Edwin Young of Houston once observed, "Being comes before doing. If I'm who I should be, I'll automatically be doing what I should be doing." The apostle Peter would have approved. The word "be" occurs 36 times in 1 Peter:

1. Be Sober (1:13; 5:8). The word literally means "abstaining from intoxicants" but conveys the wider idea of self-control.
2. Be Holy (1:15). This is possible only as the Holy Spirit reproduces Christ's character within us.
3. Be Submissive (2:18; 3:1; 5:5)—demonstrating "loving, intentional selflessness."
4. Be Unified (3:8). The remainder of this verse explains how this is achieved.
5. Be Ready (3:15)—one of Scripture's most practical verses on evangelism.
6. Be Serious and Watchful (4:7)—referring to our prayer lives.
7. Be Hospitable (4:9)—without grumbling!
8. Be Vigilant (5:8—guarding ourselves against the enemy.

CONCLUSION: Our enemy is a prowling lion, but our best defense is not found in what we do, but in who we are—God's sober, holy, humble, eager, watchful, hospitable people.

Patrick's Confession

Only one missionary is honored with a global holiday, and only one is known by his own distinct color of green.

He's St. Patrick, of course, missionary to Ireland.

Patrick was born in A.D. 373, along the banks of the River Clyde in what is now called Scotland. His father was a deacon, and his grandfather a priest. The British Isles were ruled at the time by the Romans, but coastal inhabitants were tormented by Irish pirates who would sweep into their villages, pillage and burn the houses, and kidnap the children. When Patrick was about 16, raiders descended on his own little town. He saw his house afire, then one of the pirates spotted him in the bushes. He was seized (perhaps kicking and screaming), hauled aboard ship, and taken to Ireland, where, like Joseph of old, he was sold into slavery.

Patrick found himself poor and ragged, keeping pigs and sheep, exposed to frost, rain, and snow. His skin weathered, and he grew rugged and strong. His soul also weathered, and he starting thinking more about the God of his father and grandfather. At age 22, Patrick submitted his life to Jesus Christ. "The Lord opened my mind to an awareness of my unbelief, in order that, even so late, I might remember my transgressions and turn with all my heart to the Lord my God, who had regard for my significance and pitied my youth and ignorance."

Shortly thereafter, in vivid dreams, Patrick sensed the Lord telling him, "See, your ship is ready." Mounting a daring escape, Patrick traveled many miles afoot to a harbor where, at the last moment, he jumped aboard a ship. He eventually arrived home, where his overjoyed family begged him to never leave again.

But Patrick couldn't get his Irish captors from his mind. One night, in a dream reminiscent of St. Paul's vision of the Macedonian man in Acts 16, Patrick dreamt of an Irish man who begged him to come evangelize Ireland.

It wasn't an easy decision, but Patrick, about 30, packed up, said his good-byes, and returned to his former captors with only one book, the Latin Bible, tucked under his arm. As he evangelized the countryside, multitudes came to listen. The superstitious Druids opposed him, and he repeatedly escaped assassination plots. But his preaching was powerful. Human sacrifices and slavery eventually ended, thousands were converted, and churches were established.

"For I am very much God's debtor, who gave me such grace that many people were reborn in God through me and afterwards confirmed, and that clerics were ordained for them everywhere, for a people just coming to the faith."

Later in life, a former confidant revealed a sin Patrick had committed as a teenager. We don't know the nature of the sin, but it created a firestorm, and Patrick wrote his *Confession* partly in response.

"I nevertheless wish that my brethren and kinsmen should know what sort of person I am, so that they may understand my heart's desire. . . . I ought to cry out aloud and so also render something to the Lord for His great benefits . . . . I must spread everywhere the name of God so that after my death I may leave a gift to my brethren and sons whom I have baptized in the Lord—so many thousands of people."

His *Confession* is such a gift. Despite being originally written in Latin over 1,500 years ago, it isn't hard reading, and it isn't long. Though a portion of it has been lost to history, what remains is encouraging, priceless, and motivating.

You can't read it without seeing green. ✹

Where To Find Patrick's Confession

Several editions of St. Patrick's *Confession* are available from various publishers, including a paperback edition from Doubleday & Company. Since *Confession* is a brief document, those with access to the worldwide web can easily print it out for themselves. Look for it at www.ccel.org or at www.uk-christian.net/boc.

MARCH 23, 2003

Be Still and Know

Date preached:

By Ed Dobson

Scripture: Psalm 46, especially verses 1–2, 10: God is our refuge and strength, a very present help in trouble. Therefore we will not fear, even though the earth be removed, and though the mountains be carried into the midst of the sea. . . . Be still, and know that I am God; I will be exalted among the nations, I will be exalted in the earth!

Introduction: This psalm was a continual comfort to the Reformer Martin Luther, who used it as the basis of his great hymn: "A Mighty Fortress Is Our God." It can be just as precious to us today if we'll learn its secrets. The author speaks of three things.

1. **A Tight Space.** The psalmist calls God a "very present help in trouble." The Hebrew word translated "trouble" literally means "a tight space." Have you ever been in a tight space, where you're pressed on every side, where your options are limited, your freedom is restricted, or your progress is arrested? The psalmist specifies two such places.

    A. **Uncontrollable circumstances.** Verse 2 says: "We will not fear even though the earth be removed, and though its mountains be carried into the midst of the sea," describing a natural disaster involving storms, seas, and earthquakes. Because God is my help, I will not fear when the foundations are shaken. When we face circumstances over which we have no control, God is our refuge.

    B. **Insurmountable opposition.** In verses 8–9, the psalmist speaks of war, bows, spears, and chariots. He is saying, "When I face an army against which I have no ability to fight, I am still not afraid." Why? Because God, my refuge and strength, fights for me.

2. **A Mighty Fortress.** God uses these troubles to help us say, "I don't know what to do." We are determined people who want to come up with answers ourselves. Faced with a career choice, we get a legal pad, make a pro/con list, then methodically and logically work through choices and arrive at a reasonably good decision. When things go wrong, we know where to go, what books to read, who to consult, and what techniques to

employ. When it comes to the church, we think we know what to do in difficulty. We form a task force, start a committee, do research, set goals, recruit people, and fund the program. We sometimes act as though we don't need God. But we will never really know Him until we humbly acknowledge, "We don't know what to do, but our eyes are fixed on You."

3. **A Divine Strategy.** How do I get help from God? The answer is shocking: We must be still (v. 10). This word means to cease striving, to stop working at it, to relax. God's strategy is counter-cultural. Think about the pace of family life, especially with kids. Running to gymnastics, running to school, dropping them off at church, picking them up, going here, going there. Think about the pace of work. Many of you will open your briefcases and work on stuff for tomorrow morning. Then tomorrow it will be activity after activity, appointment after appointment, phone call after phone call in an endless blur till next Sunday. And there's the church schedule. You may think we sit around dreaming up stuff for you to do, dreaming up programs for you to be involved in, dreaming up meetings for you to attend. When you put it all together, it mitigates against Psalm 46:10. How, then, do we be still?

A. **We do it in our schedules.** We must simplify. Downsize. Find time for our devotions. Find time to rest. Find time for devotional literature and prayer. When our calendars are under the Spirit's control, He always reserves time to be with Christ.

>>> sermon continued on following page

APPROPRIATE HYMNS AND SONGS

A Mighty Fortress, Martin Luther; Public Domain.

Be Still My Soul, Katharina Von Schlegal/Jane L. Borthwick/Jean Sibelius; Public Domain.

Be Still and Know, Anonymous; Public Domain.

The Name of the Lord, Clinton Utterbach; © 1988 Polygram Island Music.

Be Still, David J. Evans; © 1986 Kingsway's Thankyou Music (Admin. by EMI Christian Music Publishing.).

B. **We do it in our spirits.** Release our cares into God's hands. Only He can solve the insolvable, storm the impregnable, and change the unmerciful. Only He can bring sunshine out of storms, and flowers from mud. He can protect you on the outside (God is our refuge) and strengthen you on the inside (God is our strength).

Conclusion: Two old songs come to mind: "A Mighty Fortress is our God, a Bulwark never failing! Our helper, He, amid the flood of mortal ills, prevailing." The other one says: "Be still my soul, the Lord is on thy side." He *is* your mighty fortress and He *is* on your side. And He *does* say: "Be still and know that I am God. I will be exalted among the heathen. I will be exalted in the earth. For the Lord of Hosts is with us, and the God of Jacob is our refuge."

FOR THE BULLETIN

✸ Johann Sebastian Bach, two days old and the youngest in a family of German musicians, was baptized on March 23, 1685. He later became one of Christianity's greatest musicians whose life's purpose was to create "well-regulated church music to the glory of God." When he sat down to compose he often scribbled *J.J.* on his blank pages: *Jesu Juva*—"Help me, Jesus." At the manuscript's end, he jotted *S.D.G.—Soli Deo Gloria*—"to God alone, the glory." ✸ On March 23, 1743, Handel's *Messiah* opened in London. ✸ March 23, 1797, Missionary William Carey, concerned about his lack of converts, wrote his friend Andrew Fuller: "I am sure the work of God must prevail. . . . I know there are only two real obstacles in any part of the earth, viz., a want of the Bible, and the depravity of the human heart." ✸ March 23, 1839, marks the first recorded time the letters "OK" were used, meaning *oll korrect,* in the Boston *Morning Post.* ✸ March 23, 1891, marks the birth of radio Bible teacher, Dr. M. R. DeHaan in Zeeland, Michigan. ✸ On March 23, 1925, Tennessee became the first state to forbid the teaching of evolution. Teacher John Scopes ignored the ban and was prosecuted later in what became known as "The Monkey Trial." ✸ On March 23, 1966, the Archbishop of Canterbury, Arthur Michael Ramsey, exchanged public greetings with Pope Paul VI in Rome—the first official meeting between heads of the Anglican and Roman Catholic churches in over 400 years.

STATS, STORIES AND MORE

"Nor Do We Know What to Do . . ."
Many people believe the background for Psalm 46 is found in 2 Chronicles 20, when King Jehoshaphat faced invasion. In 2 Chronicles 20:12, as he led his nation in prayer, he said: O our God . . . we have no power against this great multitude that is coming against us; nor do we know what to do, but our eyes are upon You." Are you facing uncontrollable circumstances or insurmountable opposition? Are you willing to say, "Lord, I do not know what to do, but my eyes are on you?" God replied through the prophet Jahaziel in verses 15 and following: "Listen, all you of Judah and you inhabitants of Jerusalem, and you, King Jehoshaphat! Thus says the LORD to you: 'Do not be afraid nor dismayed because of this great multitude, for the battle is not yours, but God's. . . . You will not need to fight in this battle. Position yourselves, stand still and see the salvation of the LORD, who is with you, O Judah and Jerusalem! Do not fear or be dismayed; tomorrow go out against them, for the LORD is with you."
—*Ed Dobson*

Under Her Pillow
In 1947, missionaries Dick and Margaret Hillis settled with their four children by the Mule River in the Honan province of China. Nearby, a mission church swelled with nearly a thousand Chinese every Sunday. It would have been a happy time but for the impending war between Chiang kai-Shek and the forces of Mao Tse-tung. One terrible night, the Hillis family found themselves caught in the crossfire. The bombing reached a crescendo one night as each shell dropped closer to the Hillis home. The house next door exploded, killing all the inhabitants, and it appeared the Hillis home would be next. The family huddled in the corner as another shell exploded, sending dirt, glass, and bricks through windows and walls. The house quaked. The children screamed, momentarily deafened. The family prepared for death. But the shelling abruptly stopped, and the Hillises cautiously emerged from their corner. The room was filled with debris, but no one was hurt.

By and by, as Dick tucked each child into bed, he knelt beside Margaret Anne and noticed a dirty scrap of paper stuffed under her pillow. On it was printed in big, childlike letters these words: "God is our refuge and strength, a very present help in trouble."

WORSHIP HELPS

Call to Worship:
"The name of the LORD is a strong tower;
the righteous run to it and are safe" (Prov. 18:10).

Offertory Prayer:
Thank you, Lord, for the grocery stores in our community. Thank
you for real estate, for public utilities, for cars, and for public trans-
portation. Thank you for our clothing, for our stocks, bonds, and
bank accounts. But remind us also that our lives do not consist in
the abundance of the things that we possess. Here, as a token of our
love, we bring You our tithes and offerings. In Jesus' name. Amen.

Benediction:
We confess, our God, that this is easy preaching, but difficult living.
We confess the great disparity between the truth we have seen in
Your Word and the way we most often live. So I pray that we would
raise the level of our living to conform to the truth of Your Word. As
we enter a new week of responsibilities and obligations, grant that
there would be a centeredness in our life whatever the activity
around us, that we would be still and know that You are God.
Dismiss us with Your blessing in Christ's name. Amen.
—*Ed Dobson*

Kids Talk

Have you ever played the "Quiet Game?" Let's all
try to be just as quiet as we can be. Can you be very,
very still for a moment? Uh-oh, I hear someone
breathing! It's hard to be still, isn't it? It's hard for
grown-ups, too. But the Bible says, "Be still and know that I am God." That
means that sometimes you need to turn off your video game or television or
CD player, and play the quiet game all by yourself in your room. Then talk to
the Lord very quietly and pray to Him. We often feel closest to God when
we've turned down all the other noises in our lives.

Additional Sermons and Lesson Ideas

God's Glorious Gospel

By Melvin Worthington

Date preached:

SCRIPTURE: 1 Corinthians 15:1–7; 1 Timothy 1:11

INTRODUCTION: The gospel is God's message *to* the church, and it's His message to the world *through* the church. The word *gospel* is used in the Bible over 100 times. Christ's commission to the church (Matt. 28; Mark 16; Luke 24; and John 20) is to go into the entire world and preach the gospel.

1. The Definition. In proclaiming the gospel it is important that we clearly, convincingly, and correctly set for the *source, scope,* and *sufficiency* of God's gospel.
2. The Design. The gospel confirms the *plight of the sinner, the provision for sin, the power of the Savior, the passion of the Sovereign,* and *the precepts of Scripture.*
3. The Duty. Those who hear the gospel must *appropriate* it, *articulate* it, give *allegiance* to it, and *adorn* it.

CONCLUSION: God's glorious gospel has the intrinsic power to save those who believe it. It is a simple, single, and sufficient message.

Chock Full of Christ

By W. H. Griffith Thomas

Date preached:

SCRIPTURE: Hebrews 1

INTRODUCTION: We know that the entire Bible serves as a sort of biography of Christ, but few passages are so "chock full of Christ" as Hebrews 1. In the preface, the writer presents Christ as:

1. Christ the Heir (v. 2).
2. Christ the Creator (v. 2; see John 1:3; Col. 1:16).
3. Christ the Revealer (v. 3; see Col. 1:15–16).
4. Christ the Sustainer (v. 3; compare Col. 1:17).
5. Christ the Redeemer (v. 3).
6. Christ the Ruler (v. 3).
7. Christ Supreme (v. 4).

CONCLUSION: The Book of Hebrews was written to encourage Jewish believers who were in danger of fainting under pressure. Nothing strengthens us like having our thoughts fixed on Christ. If you're under pressure today, fix your eyes on Jesus (Heb. 12:2).

MARCH 30, 2003

Amazing the Amazing One

Date preached:

Scripture: "The crowds were amazed at his teaching, because he taught as one who had authority, and not as their teachers of the law" (Matt. 7:28–29 NIV. Note: This sermon is based on the NIV text, which is used throughout).

Introduction: The word *amazed* occurs 31 times in the Gospels, usually describing the response of crowds to the Lord Jesus, even as we sing:

I stand amazed in the presence / Of Jesus the Nazarene,

and . . .

Amazing grace, how sweet the sound / That saves a wretch like me.

As you read the Gospels, it's almost funny to picture these crowds. Everything Jesus said left them slack-jawed and rubbing their eyes. He did something and they were "amazed." Then He said something else, and they were "utterly amazed."

I. **What Amazed the Crowds**

A. **They were amazed at His teaching** (Matt. 7:28–29). Imagine that kind of response from a person's first sermon. Dr. E. Stanley Jones, Methodist missionary statesman, once described his first sermon: "The little church was filled with my relatives and friends, all anxious that the young man should do well. I had prepared for three weeks. . . . I started on rather a high key and after half dozen sentences used a word I had never used before and I have never used since: indifferentism. Whereupon a college girl smiled and put down her head. Her smiling so upset me that when I came back to the thread of my discourse it was gone. My mind was an absolute blank. I stood there clutching for something to say. Finally I blurted out 'I am very sorry, but I have forgotten my sermon,' and I started for my seat in shame and confusion. As I was about to sit down, the Inner Voice said: 'Haven't I done anything for you? If so, couldn't you tell that?' I responded to this suggestion and stepped down in front of the pulpit—I felt I didn't belong behind it— and said, 'Friends, I see I can't preach, but you know what Christ has done for my life, how He has changed me, and though I cannot preach

I shall be His witness the rest of my days.' At the close a youth came up to me and said he wanted what I had found. . . . Today he is a pastor, and his daughter is a missionary in Africa." Most of us have trouble with our first sermon, but the Carpenter of Nazareth left His woodworking shop, hung up His carpenter's apron, and His first public utterance is the greatest sermon the world has ever heard. (Also see Matt. 13: 53–54, 22:15–22.) These are only a few examples. We could find story after story of various groups being amazed at our Lord's teaching ministry.

B. **They were amazed at His miracles.** (See Matt. 9:27–33; 15:29–31; Mark 6:45–51). The Greek word for "amazed" here is εςξιστημι, which comes from the prefix ἐκ—"out of"—and ἵστημι—"to stand"—literally, to stand outside of oneself. It's very similar to our phrase, "he was beside himself," and it has the idea of jumping out of your skin, to be astonished. If Jesus is "God in Flesh Appearing" we *should* be amazed, and the sad thing is that we so easily lose the sense of wonder that is essential to genuine worship. We need to mean it with our hearts when we say, "I stand amazed in the presence of Jesus the Nazarene."

2. **What Amazed Jesus.** Let's shift gears and notice occasions when the tables were turned and it was Christ who was amazed. These are the only two times when this word is applied to the Lord Jesus, for you'd expect it to take a lot to amaze the Amazing One.

A. **He Was Amazed at Faith** (Luke 7:1–10). "I tell you, I have not found such great faith even in Israel."

>>> *sermon continued on following page*

APPROPRIATE HYMNS AND SONGS

My Savior's Love, Charles H. Gabriel; Public Domain.

I Stand Amazed, Dennis Jernigan; © 1991 Shepherd's Heart Music, Inc. (Admin. by Word Music Group, Inc.).

Amazing Grace, John Newton/Edwin Excell/John P. Rees; Public Domain.

Say to the Mountain, Paul Wilbur; © 1997 Integrity's Hosanna! Music.

The Solid Rock, Edward Mote/William B. Bradbury; Public Domain.

B. He Was Amazed at Lack of Faith (Mark 6:1–6). It is *faith* that aston-
ishes Jesus, either its presence or its absence. In one instance, He
found faith where it wasn't expected. In the other, He didn't find it
where it should have been. Both cases amazed Him. Jesus isn't
impressed with status, wealth, power, or abilities, but He's amazed
when we trust Him as we should—and equally amazed when we
don't.

Conclusion: Is the Lord Jesus amazed at your faith today in spite of the difficulties you're facing, or is He amazed at your lack of faith in spite of the
promises He's given? What's bothering you today? Are you trusting Him?
Are you resting in His promises? Trust Him fully today. He'll be amazed, and
so will you.

FOR THE BULLETIN

❂ March 30, 1135, is the birthday of Moses Maimonides, Jewish philosopher,
born in Spain. He is regarded as the foremost intellectual figure of medieval
Judaism. ❂ March 30, 1533, Thomas Cranmer became archbishop of
Canterbury, setting the stage for the English Reformation. ❂ Sicke Freerks,
more commonly known as Sicke the Snyder (Tailor), was condemned on
March 30, 1531, for his views on baptism. The court record reads: ". . . to be executed by the sword; his body shall be laid on the wheel, and his head set on a
stake, because he has been rebaptized and perseveres in that baptism." Freeks
was executed in Leeuwarden, the Netherlands. His martyrdom prompted a
Dutch priest named Menno Simons to begin studying the Scriptures about
baptism. Simons later renounced the Roman Catholic Church and became a
leader of the Anabaptist movement in the Netherlands. ❂ Dr. Thomas Coke
was a zealous young Anglican curate in the Parish Church of South Petherton,
England, who, to the annoyance of his flock, came under the evangelical influence of John Wesley and the Methodists. On Sunday morning, March 30, 1777,
following his sermon, there was an interruption in the service. It was
announced that the vicar had dismissed his curate, forbidding him to preach in
his church again. Suddenly the bells in the old tower burst into a discordant
clanging, so that Dr. Coke was unable to respond. The next Sunday found him
standing in the village marketplace, preaching in the open air. He later became
one of Methodism's greatest leaders.

STATS, STORIES AND MORE

Christ's Voice

How I would have loved to have heard Christ in person! Yet, every day I have that opportunity, as I read His words in the Gospel and as the Holy Spirit serves as the amplifier. He teaches us as one having authority. He gives unto us the words of life. He speaks as one having authority and not as the scribes and Pharisees. And as we study His Word and hear His voice, we stand amazed at the life-changing power of His teaching ministry to our own hearts.—*RJM*

Freedom from Anxiety

In his book, *None of These Diseases,* Dr. S. I. McMillen tells of going on a fishing trip in Canada with his daughter, Linda, and his wife, Alice. They arrived at their cabin around 5 p.m. on Saturday. To catch fish for their Sunday meals, Dr. McMillen and Linda rowed up the treacherous Matawan Rapids while Alice stayed at the cabin to unpack. Eight o'clock came, but there was no sign of father or daughter. It was lunacy to be on the Matawan Rapids past dark, but instead of worrying, Alice recalled the verse of Scripture she had been memorizing, Psalm 34:4. Nine o'clock came, and still no sign of her loved ones. She prayed and rested her trust in the Lord. At ten o'clock, she heard a voice. It was Linda: "Daddy sent me by land. He didn't want to bring me down the rapids in the dark. The fish were slow in biting; but once they started, they bit like a house afire." Still more waiting followed, but her faith gave her power over panic until, at 11 p.m., her husband showed up at the dock. Alice chose faith over fear, trusting in the promise God had given her in Psalm 34:4.

WORSHIP HELPS

Call to Worship:
"As you therefore have received Christ Jesus the Lord, so walk in Him, rooted and built up in Him and established in the faith, as you have been taught, abounding in it with thanksgiving" (Col. 2:6–7).

Scripture Reading Medley:
Now faith is the substance of things hoped for, the evidence of things not seen. For by it the elders obtained a good testimony. He is a shield to all who trust in Him. . . . None of those who trust in Him shall be condemned. . . . He knows those who trust in Him. But without faith it is impossible to please Him, for he who comes to God must believe that He is, and that He is a rewarder of those who diligently seek Him. O God, You are my God; early will I seek You; my soul thirsts for You; my flesh longs for You in a dry and thirsty land where there is no water. Jesus stood and cried out, saying, "If anyone thirsts, let him come to Me and drink. He who believes in Me, as the Scripture has said, out of his heart will flow rivers of living water." So, trust the LORD always, because He is our Rock forever (Ps. 18:30; 34:22; 63:1; Isa. 26:4 NCV; Nahum 1:7; John 7:37–38; Heb. 11:1–2, 6).

Offertory Prayer:
Give us the heart today, O Lord, of the poor widow in the Gospels who would rather give all that she had to You than to squander all that You gave her on herself. In Jesus' name, Amen.

Benediction:
Thank you, Lord, for the songs that have gone out. Thank you for the supplications that have gone up. Thank you for the sermon that has gone forth. Now, O Lord, let us leave to serve until we meet again hence, or in that better world. Amen.

Additional Sermons and Lesson Ideas

Are You in Your Right Mind?
By Kevin Riggs

Date preached:

SCRIPTURE: Matthew 6:19–24

INTRODUCTION: Our priorities determine our state of mind. Right in the middle of His "Sermon on the Mount," Jesus discusses the theme of laying up treasures. These "treasures" are things that are really important to an individual. In this passage, Jesus mentions three types of persons.

1. The Earthly-Minded Individual—"treasures on earth" (v. 19). An earthly-minded person lives for self, seeking pleasure. This type of person is not in his right mind.
2. The Heavenly-Minded Individual—"treasures in heaven" (v. 20). A heavenly-minded person lives life for the glory of God. This type of person is in his right mind.
3. The Double-Minded Individual—"No one can serve two masters" (vv. 22–24). A double-minded person tries to serve God and serve self. This type of person is out of his mind.

CONCLUSION: The key to this passage is verse 21, "For where your treasure is there your heart will be also." Where are your treasures? Which of these three are you?

Hell's Horrors
By Melvin Worthington

Date preached:

SCRIPTURE: Luke 16:19–31

INTRODUCTION: The doctrine of eternal punishment remains one of the strongest incentives for coming to Christ for salvation. Jesus spoke more about hell than about heaven.

1. A Place. The Bible identifies hell as a place (Luke 16:27–28; 2 Pet. 2:4; Rev. 20:13–15). Hell is a place of *punishment, partition,* and *permanence.*
2. A Population. A comprehensive list of the inhabitants in hell is found in 1 Corinthians 6:9–12 and Revelation 21:8.
3. A Portrait. Luke 16:19–31 provides a detailed account of a man in hell. Careful attention should be given to his *dying moment, described misery, desired mercy, disturbing memory, deadly mistake,* and *the divine message.*

CONCLUSION: What about you? Are you a believer? Have you placed your faith in the finished work of Christ for salvation? God has given His Son, the Scriptures, and His Spirit to bring men to Christ. He will give nothing else.

APRIL 6, 2003

SUGGESTED SERMON

The Elder Brother Syndrome

Date preached:

Adapted from a message by Andrew Murray

Scripture: Luke 15:11–32, especially verse 31: And he said to him, "Son, you are always with me, and all that I have is yours."

Introduction: The parable of the Prodigal Son is one of the best-loved of our Lord's stories, but we often neglect the plight of the elder son who complained that though his father had made a feast for the prodigal, he himself had never received so much as a kid that he might make merry with his friends. The father's answer was, "Son, you are always with me, and all that I have is yours." If we're honest, many of us are suffering from the "Elder Son Syndrome." Notice:

I. **The High Privilege of the Children of God.** Verse 31 contains two rich privileges for Christians:
    A. **Unbroken Fellowship with the Father.** "Son, you are always with me." God is always near us; we can dwell every hour of our lives in His presence. In the Old Testament, Enoch and Noah walked with God (Gen. 5:22; 6:9). God told Jacob, "Behold, I am with you" (Gen. 28:15). He told Moses, "My presence will go with you" (Ex. 33:14), and God's presence with Israel distinguished them from other nations. Our Savior promised He would be with us always and that the Father and Son will make Their abode with us. Christians should live every moment in fellowship with God. That presence is with us wherever we go; and in all kinds of trouble, we have undisturbed repose and peace.
    B. **Unlimited Blessings from the Father.** "And all that I have is yours." In Matthew 7:11, Jesus said, "If you then, being evil, know how to give good gifts to your children, how much more will your Father who is in heaven give good things to those who ask Him!" John 1:16 says, "From the fullness of His grace we have all received one blessing after another" (NIV). Ephesians 1:3 says that God "has blessed us with every spiritual blessing in the heavenly places in Christ." (Also see 1 Cor. 1:4, 5 and 3:21–23.) Is not that the meaning of the wonderful promises

given in connection with prayer? Whatever you ask the Father, He will give (John 15:16). Yes, there it is. That is the life of the children of God, as He Himself has pictured it to us—unbroken fellowship and unlimited blessings.

2. **The Low Experience of Too Many of Us.** But he enjoyed neither. The elder son had served his father "these many years," yet he complained that his father had never given him a kid, though the prodigal received a fatted calf. His father gave him everything, yet he never enjoyed it. Is this not the life of many a believer?

3. **The Cause for This Discrepancy Between God's Gifts and Our Low Experience.** Why this discrepancy? Simply because, not believing he would get it, he lived in constant murmuring and dissatisfaction. The elder son thought he was serving his father faithfully in his father's house, but it was in the spirit of bondage and not in the spirit of a child, so that his unbelief blinded him to the conception of his father's love and kindness. He was unable all the time to see that his father was ready, not only to give him a kid, but a hundred, or a thousand, if he would have them. If our experience is similar, it is because of unbelief in the love and power of God. Unbelief made the wilderness experience a wilderness experience for the Israelites, and for many of us. If we really believed in the infinite love of God, His power and promises, what a change it would make!

>>> sermon continued on following page

APPROPRIATE HYMNS AND SONGS

From the Fullness of His Love, Greg Nelson/Bob Farrell; © 1996 Gentle Ben Music/Dayspring Music/BMI/Summerdawn (Admin. by Word Music.).

A Sense of His Presence, Bruce T. Ballinger; © 1988 New Spring Publishing (Admin.by Brentwood-Benson Music Publishing, Inc.).

Abide with Me, Henry F. Lyte/William H. Monk; Public Domain.

I Was Glad, John Chisum/George T. Searcy; © 1990 Ariose Music/Tourmaline Music, Inc. (Admin. by Tourmaline Music, Inc.).

Jesus Lives Through Me, Dennis Jernigan; © 1991 Shepherd's Heart Music (Admin. by Word Music Group, Inc.).

4. **The Way to Restoration.** The younger son "came to himself," (v. 7), that is, he came to his senses and turned his steps toward home. That's also the first step for those who have been living in the Father's house but not trusting His love, enjoying His presence, or claiming His promises. The Father says to us, "You must repent and believe that I love you, that I am always with you, and that all I have is yours."

Conclusion: Many children of God need to confess that though they are His children, they are not willing for God to fill their hearts all day long with His blessed presence or to fill their lives with His blessings. May the Lord God work this conviction in the hearts of all cold believers, so that they may be led into the blessedness of His presence and enjoy the fullness of His power and love.

FOR THE BULLETIN

❂ On April 6, 1415, the Synod of Constance issued what was called "the most revolutionary document in the world"—the *Sacrosancta*—declaring its own authority over popes. In the end, the popes won the dispute, but only after years of struggle. ❂ The artist Raphael died on his 37th birthday, April 6, 1520. ❂ On April 6, 1735, the first Moravians from Europe arrived in America as part of their great missionary advance. Invited by governor James Oglethorpe, ten males of the *Unitas Fratrum* landed in Savannah, Georgia. ❂ Today is the birthday of Edmund Hamilton Sears, author of "It Came Upon A Midnight Clear." He was born in 1810. ❂ On April 6, 1830, Joseph Smith organized the first church of Latter Day Saints in Fayette, New York. ❂ James Augustine Healy, the first black Roman Catholic bishop in America, was born to an Irish planter and a slave on a plantation near Macon, Georgia, on April 6, 1830. ❂ The first modern Olympic Games opened in Athens, Greece, on this day in 1896. ❂ On April 6, 1923, athlete Eric Liddell shared his testimony with a group of about eighty men in Armadale, Scotland. "It wasn't a speech at all," someone later wrote. "It was more of a quiet chat, and in his slow clear words, Eric for the first time in his life told the world what God meant to him." It was his debut in public evangelism. Liddell later became famous as an Olympic champion and as an outspoken Christian missionary who died in 1945 during the Japanese occupation of China.

STATS, STORIES AND MORE

Practicing God's Presence

- "The presence of God (is) a subject which, in my opinion, contains the whole spiritual life; and it seems to me that whoever duly practices it will soon become spiritual."—*Brother Lawrence*

- "Were I a preacher, I should, above all other things, preach the practice of the presence of God."—*Brother Lawrence*

- "'The practice of the presence of God' consists not of projecting an imaginary object from within his own mind and then seeking to realize its presence; it is rather to recognize the real presence of the One whom all sound theology declares to be already there."—*A. W. Tozer*

He Owned It All

In west Texas there is a famous oil field known as the Yates pool. During the depression this field was a sheep ranch, owned by a man named Yates. Mr. Yates was not able to make enough money on his ranching operation to pay the principal and interest on the mortgage, so he was in danger of losing his ranch. With little money for clothes or food, his family, like many others, had to live on a government subsidy. Day after day, as he grazed his sheep over those rolling west Texas hills, he was no doubt greatly troubled about how he would be able to pay his bills.

Then a seismographic crew from an oil company came into the area and told Mr. Yates that there might be oil on his land. They asked permission to drill a wildcat well, and he signed a lease.

At 1,115 feet they struck a huge oil reserve, giving 80,000 barrels a day. In fact, thirty years after the discovery, a government test of one of the wells showed that it still could flow 125,000 barrels of oil a day. And Mr. Yates owned it all. The day he purchased the land he received the oil and mineral rights. Yet, he was living on relief. A multimillionaire living in poverty: What was the problem? He did not know the oil was there. He owned it, but he did not possess it. That is like many Christians today who don't realize how rich they are in Christ.—*Parables, Etc.*

WORSHIP HELPS

Call to Worship:

"Blessed be the God and Father of our Lord Jesus Christ, Who has blessed us with every spiritual blessing in the heavenly places in Christ" (Eph. 1:3).

Pastoral Prayer:

We praise You, Father, Son, and Holy Spirit. Grant us today the Spirit of wisdom and revelation in the knowledge of Christ, the eyes of our understanding being opened; that we may know the hope of Your calling, the riches of the glory of Your inheritance in the saints, and what is the exceeding greatness of Your power toward us who believe. May we not live as paupers in a land of plenty, but show us how rich we are as children of the Most High who, by faith, are receiving one blessing after another.

Responsive Reading:

Leader: Hear, LORD, the voice of Judah, and bring him to his people; Let his hands be sufficient for him, and may You be a help against his enemies.

People: The beloved of the LORD shall dwell in safety by Him, Who shelters him all the day long; And he shall dwell between His shoulders.

Leader: Blessed of the LORD is His land, with the precious things of heaven, with the dew, and the deep lying beneath, with the precious fruits of the sun, with the precious produce of the months, with the best things of the ancient mountains, with the precious things of the everlasting hills, with the precious things of the earth and its fullness, and the favor of Him who dwelt in the bush.

People: The eternal God is your refuge, and underneath are the everlasting arms.

Leader: Happy are you, O Israel! Who is like you, a people saved by the LORD, the shield of your help and the sword of your majesty!

Everyone: Your enemies shall submit to you and you shall tread down their high places.

(Taken from selected verses of Deuteronomy 33)

Additional Sermons and Lesson Ideas

He Leadeth Me

Date preached:

Adapted from an outline by William Evans in the book The 23rd Psalm.

SCRIPTURE: Psalm 23:3

INTRODUCTION: Christians frequently ask, "How can I know the will of God?" Three things indicate clearly the particular will of God concerning decisions, careers, and direction in life.

1. The Infallible Word. As we study the Bible, the Lord gives wisdom in knowing His will, often giving specialized guidance through certain verses He brings to our attention.
2. The Inward Impression. The Holy Spirit within us prompts us in certain ways, and as we grow sensitive to His leadership, we often sense an inner peace about wise decisions and an uneasiness about unwise ones.
3. The Open Door. God's providential ordering of circumstances often directs us in one way or another.

CONCLUSION: Why does He lead us in paths of righteousness? For His name's sake— for His glory. When we find and follow God's will in matters great and small, it glorifies Him.

Accurate Accounting

Date preached:

By Melvin Worthington

SCRIPTURE: Revelation 20:11–15

INTRODUCTION: Have you ever considered how you will act when you stand before the God of the universe? This passage sets forth a sobering scene of God's final judgment.

1. The Awesome Throne (v. 11). John saw a great white throne and one sitting on it. The earth and the heaven fled away and there was found no place for them.
2. The Ashamed Throng (vv. 12, 13). The dead small and great stand before God. The sea gave up the dead in it and death and hell delivered up the dead which were in them.
3. The Accurate Testimony (vv. 12, 13). The books are opened and the dead are judged out of those things written in the books—according to their works. Every individual is judged according to their works.
4. The Awful Truth (vv. 12, 14, 15). Another book is opened which is the Book of Life. Those whose names are not written in the Book of Life are cast into the lake of fire. This is the second death.

CONCLUSION: Is your name written in the Book of Life?

Saint Basil:
The Man Who Knew the Difference Between Fame and Faithfulness

"A celebrity," quipped comedian Fred Allen, "is a person who works all his life to become well-known, then wears dark glasses to avoid being recognized."

Many of us have an inner craving for—well, not fame perhaps, but significance. We want to feel we're doing something that others notice and admire. We want to leave a mark. Is that wrong?

Maybe not, but remember what Babe Ruth once said: "I knew an old minister once. . . . How I envy him. . . . I am listed as a famous home-runner, yet beside that obscure minister, who was so good and so wise, I never got to first base."

It isn't fame, but faithfulness, that scores the winning run.

That brings us to Saint Basil, who was born three centuries after Christ in a wealthy Christian home in Caesarea of Cappadocia (Turkey). His parents named him Basil, meaning Kingly, and his godly grand-mother instilled the richness of the Christian faith into his mind at an early age.

Basil attended the finest schools in Constantinople and Athens, and graduated with honors. He thought highly of himself and returned home dreaming of becoming great in public life. Fame and fortune were virtually insured. But his parents and grandparents loved the Lord, and he had a heritage of Christianity. It was his sister, Macrina, who actually led him to faith in Christ, then she spoke a sentence he never forgot: "It's better to be faithful before God," she insisted, "than famous before men."

Basil took those words to heart and cultivated a quiet life of study, prayer, and writing. He settled along the bank of the Iris River on the family estate, praying, preaching, and helping the poor. He wrote to a friend:

> God has shown me a region which exactly suits my mode of life; it is, in truth, what in our happy jesting we often wished. . . . A high mountain, covered with thick forest, is watered towards the north by fresh perennial streams. At the foot of the mountain a

wide plain spreads out, made fruitful by the vapors which moisten it. The surrounding forest, in which many varieties of trees crowd together, shuts me off like a strong castle. The wilderness is bounded by two deep ravines. On one side the stream, where it rushes foaming down from the mountain, forms a barrier hard to cross; on the other a broad ridge obstructs approach. My hut is so placed upon the summit, that I overlook the broad plain, as well as the whole course of the Iris. . . . Shall I tell of the lovely singing of the birds and the richness of blooming plants? What delights me above all is the silent repose of the place.

His gifts and stature became well-known despite his attempts to withdraw from prominence, and Emperor Julian the Apostate, though a fierce opponent of Christianity, tried to recruit him as advisor. Basil declined. But he couldn't refuse the appeal of his own bishop, Eusebius, who warned that the church faced both imperial attacks from without and dangerous heresy from within. Basil reluctantly left his quiet retreat for public ministry. He championed orthodoxy, preaching, and writing brilliant messages on the nature of Jesus Christ and the composition of the Trinity.

In 370, Basil succeeded Eusebius and proved himself a gifted bishop who organized the ministries of the church. Using his own fortune, Basil founded a hospital, perhaps the first in Christian history, for the care of lepers. He was a kind man, often personally treating the diseased. He ate plainly, dressed simply, and bore his frequent illnesses with patience.

Basil's complex of churches, schools, hospitals, hostels, monasteries, and almshouses outside Caesarea became a town within itself called Basiliad. His rules for monks and monasteries are used to this day in the Greek church. Despite his accomplishment, Basil was always happiest serving the Lord quietly, retreating whenever possible to quiet spots where he could cultivate his soul and enjoy his Lord.

"What is more blessed," he once wrote, "than to imitate the choir of angels at break of day, to rise to prayer and praise the Creator with anthems and songs; then go to labor in the clear radiance of the sun, accompanied everywhere by prayer, seasoning work with praise, as if with salt? Silent solitude is the beginning of purification of the soul, (and in the Scripture is) a store of all medicines, the true remedy for sickness." ✿

APRIL 13, 2003

Have Faith in God

Date preached:

Scripture: Mark 11:20–26, especially verses 21–22: Peter, remembering, said to Him, "Rabbi, look! The fig tree which You cursed has withered away." So Jesus answered and said to them, "Have faith in God."

Introduction: On Palm Sunday, Jesus made a dramatic entrance into Jerusalem amid cries of "Hosanna!" He spent the day there, and Mark 11:11 says, "since it was already late, He went out to Bethany with the Twelve." The next morning, Jesus returned to the city, passing a fig tree along the way. Wanting a breakfast of figs, He was disappointed; the tree was barren. To the disciples' surprise, He cursed it. The next morning—Tuesday of the Passion Week—they found the tree withered. This is our Lord's only "destructive" miracle, but there were two reasons for it. The first was parabolic. The fig tree was a symbol of the Israelites who, despite the loving care of the divine gardener, bore no spiritual fruit but withered spiritually in rejecting the Messiah. The other reason was this: Christ was giving the disciples a lesson in faith so that in coming days they themselves would not wither. On the eve of their greatest trauma, He wanted to teach them to trust God. We have here:

1. **A Command** (v. 22). Four one-syllable, sharp words: *Have Faith in God.* Faith is the answer to our challenges in life.
    A. **What do we do when anxious?** Have faith in God. He promises to work everything together for good.
    B. **When disappointed?** Have faith in God. He promises to bring good out of bad in the lives of His children.
    C. **When angry?** Have faith in God. He promises to settle scores on our behalf.
    D. **When impoverished?** Have faith in God. He promises to meet every need.
    E. **When facing sickness or death?** Have faith in God. He gives eternal life.
    F. **When lonely?** Have faith in God. His presence is near.

2. **A Truth** (v. 23). Jesus then used the occasion to explain faith: "Whoever says to this mountain, 'Be removed and be cast into the sea,' and does not doubt . . . he will have whatever he says." This seems problematic; most of us have never met anyone who literally moved mountains. But remember, it's impossible to trust God for something He does not ordain for us. If it's God's will for us to uproot a mountain, He'll give us faith necessary for the job, but it's hard for us to have faith in that particular task because we can't image God wants us to do exactly that. Jesus was using this as an illustration. Just as the fig tree was a parable, so is the mountain, representing specific challenges in our lives. Faith *does* lay hold of specific blessings and victories, but it operates within two concentric circles: God's will and His Word.

3. **A Procedure** (v. 24). Faith is activated in prayer. "Whatever things you ask when you pray, believe . . . and you will have them." Prayer is the mechanism by which we lay hold of God's provisions by faith. When we pray according to His will and His Word, we're claiming what God has already granted. James spoke of the "prayer of faith," and nothing under heaven is more powerful than people of faith who, on their knees with an open Bible, trust God amid life's impossibilities.

4. **A Hindrance** (vv. 25, 26). Finally, we notice that Christ inserts a negative word: "Whenever you stand praying, if you have anything against anyone, forgive him. . . . But if you do not forgive, neither will your Father in

>>> *sermon continued on following page*

APPROPRIATE HYMNS AND SONGS

Have Faith in God, B.B. McKinney; © 1934 Renewed 1962 Broadman Press (Admin. by Genevox Music Group.).

Have Faith in God, Geoff Bullock; © 1993 Word Music, Inc./Maranatha! Music (Admin. by Word Music Group, Inc.).

In the Name of the Lord; Gloria Gaither/Sandi Patti Helvering/Phil McHugh; © 1986 William J. Gaither, Inc./Sandi's Songs Music/River Oaks Music Company (Admin. by EMI Christian Music Publishing.).

Hosanna, Loud Hosanna, Jenette Threlfall; Public Domain.

All Glory, Laud and Honor, John M. Neale/Melchior Teschner; Public Domain.

heaven forgive your trespasses." The disciples and their Lord were about to be badly abused. Jesus was warning that a cold, unforgiving heart would quench the fire of faith and destroy their effectiveness in prayer. Are you holding a grudge against someone? Do you have feelings of resentment? Those things are fire hoses to faith. Forgive. Release the anger. Remember the Cross where Jesus died to forgive our sins and those of others.

Conclusion: When Jesus said, "Have faith in God," He gave us a command, a promise, a procedure, and a warning. Do you have a distress in your life today? A challenge?

Have faith in God; He's on His throne.

Have faith in God, He watches o'er His own.

He cannot fail; He must prevail.

Have faith in God! Have faith in God!

FOR THE BULLETIN

❋ On April 13, 1525, Reformer Ulrich Zwingli, rejecting the doctrine of transubstantiation, abolished the elaborate rite of the Mass in the Great Minster Church of Zurich in favor of the first evangelical communion service. ❋ On April 13, 1598, King Henry IV of France signed the Edict of Nantes, granting toleration to Protestant Huguenots. ❋ Jeanne Marie Bouvier de la Motte was born on this day in 1648 at Montargis, France, about fifty miles north of Paris. She later became known as Madam Guyon (pronounced Gay-yo), a celebrated French Mystic. ❋ On April 13, 1685, four Scottish women stood before the court at Wigtown accused of rebellion due to their Presbyterian views. They were forced to their knees for sentencing. Margaret MacLachlan, 70, was executed by drowning; Margaret Maxwell, 20, was publicly flogged; Margaret Wilson, 18, was drowned, and her sister Agnes, 13, was fined one hundred pounds. ❋ Handel's *Messiah* was first presented on this day in 1742, in Dublin, Ireland. ❋ Adoniram Judson Gordon, powerful Boston pastor and writer, was born on this day in 1836. Among his books is the moving little autobiographical volume, *When Christ Came to Church.* ❋ The most bitter fight in Charles Spurgeon's life was the "Downgrade Controversy" with the Baptist Union. He felt that some of the Baptist ministers were denying the basic tenets of Scripture. On April 13, 1888, five minutes before a critical session of the Baptist Union, the controversy was defused by a hastily developed plan on the part of Spurgeon's brother, James. It left no one satisfied.

Trust in the Lord and Do Good

A Scottish missionary to China named George Duncan, a friend of Hudson Taylor, found himself stranded without money for an extended period in the region around the city of Nanking. There were two banks there, but one folded and the other closed, leaving no way for the China Inland Mission to get money to Duncan. But as the missionary studied his Bible, the Lord gave him a verse of Scripture—Psalm 37:3: "Trust in the LORD, and do good; so shalt thou dwell in the land, and verily thou shalt be fed" (KJV). That verse came to Duncan so powerfully that he had absolutely no worry about his provision, but his Chinese cook and assistant became agitated. "What shall we do when the money is all gone?" he asked.

"Do?" the missionary responded. "Why, we will trust in the Lord and do good. So shall we dwell in the land and be fed." The China Inland Mission was desperately trying to get money to Duncan, but it was the dry season and the water level was so low on the rivers that travel was difficult. Finally the day came when all the money was gone and the cupboard was bare. Duncan, unruffled, went out to preach that morning as usual, telling his cook, "Let us trust in the Lord and do good. His promise is still the same."

That evening as he returned home, hungry and exhausted, his cook ran out to meet him with the exciting news that a CIM representative had finally arrived with money and the needed provisions were available. Duncan just took it in stride. Putting his hand on the man's shoulder, he said, "Did I not tell you this morning it is always all right to trust in the living God?"

Biblical Definitions of Faith (NIV)

- "The man took Jesus at His word" (John 4:50).
- "Blessed is she who has believed that what the Lord has said to her will be accomplished" (Luke 1:45).
- "I have faith in God that it will happen just as He told me" (Acts 27:25).
- "Being fully persuaded that God has power to do what He has promised" (Rom. 4:21).
- "Now faith is being sure of what we hope for and certain of what we do not see" (Heb. 11:1).

WORSHIP HELPS

Call to Worship:
"Hosanna to the Son of David! 'Blessed is He who comes in the name of the LORD!' Hosanna in the highest!" (Matt. 21:9).

Worship Insight:
The Palm Sunday word "Hosanna" is a transliteration from Hebrew to Greek and from Greek to English. The Hebrew word originally meant, "O, save!" or "Save now" (see Ps. 118:25), but it later came to be used as an exclamation of praise to the Lord who comes to save.

Pastoral Prayer:
O Lord our God, enthroned upon the cherubim, You showed Your power by sending Your only-begotten Son, our Lord Jesus Christ, to save the world through His Cross, burial and Resurrection. Today we remember His entry into Jerusalem, how He was welcomed by the people with branches of trees and palms—the symbol of victory, thus prefiguring His Resurrection. You, O Master, bless us today as in our hearts we wave branches and palms, as we sing forth our "Hosannas." Prepare us to consider anew this week the death of our Lord Jesus and His Resurrection on the third day amid the hymns and spiritual songs of His people, now and ever, and forever. Amen.

(Based on an ancient Palm Sunday prayer used in the Eastern Church)

Kids Talk

Have a box of confetti and some palm-like branches handy. Ask the children if they have ever been to a parade. Tell them about parades in which confetti is tossed (throw some confetti over their heads). Explain that in Jesus' day, people didn't have confetti, so they used palm-branches. It became a symbol of celebration, victory, and triumph. The children on the first Palm Sunday were celebrating the Lord Jesus, just as we can do today.

Additional Sermons and Lesson Ideas

Things Aren't Always as They Appear

Date preached:

By Kevin Riggs

SCRIPTURE: Luke 19:28–44

INTRODUCTION: When Jesus rode into Jerusalem different people had various ideas as to what was going on.

1. Palm Sunday from the eyes of the people
   A. Jesus' disciples. Not understanding (John 12:16). Jesus, who liked anonymity, was making Himself the center of attention (Matt. 21:1–3; Mark. 11:1–7; Luke 19:28–35).
   B. The people in Jerusalem. Misunderstanding. They received Jesus like a triumphant king, but they expected a political kingdom instead of a spiritual one (Matt. 21:8; Mark 11:8; Luke 19:36; John 12:13).
   C. The Pharisees. Only understanding one thing: If Jesus was not stopped, His teachings would destroy their religious systems.
2. Palm Sunday from the eyes of Jesus.
   A. He entered Jerusalem to die—the Passover Lamb.
   B. He entered Jerusalem to fulfill Scripture (Zech. 9:9).
   C. He entered Jerusalem to give people a last chance to accept Him.
   D. He entered Jerusalem weeping (Luke 19:41).

CONCLUSION: At the beginning of Passion Week, the Triumphal Entry brings us face-to-face with our Lord's redemptive suffering and draws forth our Hosannas.

A Hymn Lesson: "All Glory, Laud, and Honor"

Date preached:

SCRIPTURE: Mark 11:1–11

INTRODUCTION: The hymn "All Glory, Laud, and Honor" was written in the eighth century by a man named Theodulph, who was born into the Italian nobility, but decided on a life of Christian service. He was eventually imprisoned in Angiers, and there he reportedly wrote this hymn as he meditated on the Lord's Triumphal Entry. Theodulph pictures several groups as raising their Hosannas to Jesus:

1. "The Lips of Children"
2. "The Company of Angels"
3. "The People of the Hebrews"
4. "Mortal Men and All Things"
5. "Our Melody We Raise"

CONCLUSION: How wonderful to join our voices with all the ages and with all the universe to give our Lord all glory, laud, and honor!

A COMMUNION SERMON

The Tree

Date preached:

Scripture: Exodus 15:22–27

Introduction: The contents of Exodus were so dramatic they were mentioned more than 140 times in the rest of the Old Testament. When Christ came to earth, He repeatedly claimed that the writings of Moses were full of references to Him. In the Book of Acts, more than a third of Stephen's speech, leading to his martyrdom, was devoted to events in the Book of Exodus. The Book of Hebrews shows us how the signs and symbols of Exodus pointed toward Jesus Christ. We also know from church history that there are over 450 references to the Book of Exodus in the extant writings of the early Church Fathers of the first two centuries following the original apostles. All of history has been mesmerized by the dramatic nature of this book—the birth of Moses, the bondage of the Hebrews, the plagues that fell on Egypt, the slaying of the Passover lamb, the deliverance from Egypt, the parting of the Red Sea, the giving of the Ten Commandments, the building of the Tabernacle. And in many of the Exodus events and miracles, we can see Jesus Christ. One commentator wrote: "With regard to God's dealings with Israel between Egypt and Canaan, every miracle He performed on their behalf provided a fresh type of Christ." Today's passage gives us a poignant example of that.

I. **The Test.** In the first part of Exodus 15, the people were rejoicing over their miraculous crossing through the Red Sea. In the last part of the chapter they were again trapped, this time in a waterless desert. Why would God deliver them through parted waters only to allow them to suffer lack of water in the desert? Can you imagine hundreds of thousands of people wandering in the desert for three days with absolutely no water for their animals, their children, or themselves? But it was even worse than that. Just when they thought they were goners, someone near the front shouted, "Water ahead!" With an enfeebled burst of energy the hoards of Israel bolted toward the lake, tongues hanging out, cups ready, children eager to lap up the cool life-sustaining liquid. Imagine their disappointment when the first ones there spewed the water out, faces filled with disgust. The water was brackish, salty, and undrinkable. The disappointment was staggering. Why did God map out such a route? Why would He allow such a terrible disappointment? The answer is hidden away in a little phrase in the last part of verse 25. Notice these four words: "There He tested them." The Bible says that God sometimes tests us. He puts us in difficult or perplexing situations to see if we've learned anything from past experiences. He wants to develop and mature us, to see what we're made of spiritually, to develop our faith (1 Chron. 29:17; Prov. 17:3; Ezek. 21:13).

2. **The Tree.** The people failed the test. Instead of trusting God, they grumbled against the Lord. But when Moses cried out to the Lord, "the Lord showed him a tree. When he cast it into the waters, the waters were made sweet" (verse 25). Why a tree? As missionary Amy Carmichael said, "We all know what the Tree means. Nothing less than the powers of Calvary can turn our bitter waters into sweet waters." The tree in Exodus 15 was a prophecy, a type or symbol of the Cross of Calvary that turns the waters of our lives from bitter to blessed. Acts 5:30 says that Jesus was killed by being hanged on a tree. Galatians 3:13, referring to Christ, says, "Cursed is everyone who is hung on a tree." First Peter 2:24 says, "(He) Himself bore our sins in His own body on the tree, that we, having died to sins, might live for righteousness." The Cross of Christ turns our bitterest moments into blessings. It is the Cross of the Lord Jesus Christ, like a tree thrown into a toxic pool, that transforms the waters of our lives into sweet, optimistic blessings. The Bible says that God gives us beauty for ashes, the oil of gladness instead of mourning, and a garment of praise instead of a spirit of despair (Isa. 61:3).

Conclusion: Perhaps today you need the Cross of Christ in your life. You need the power of the death and Resurrection of the Lord Jesus to transform your bitter ponds. As we observe this commemoration of the Lord's Table, remember that it is the Cross of the Lord Jesus Christ that transforms, that redeems, that turns us from a bitter life to a blessed one.

> *O, can it be, upon a tree,*
> *The Savior died for me?*
> *My soul is thrilled, my heart is filled,*
> *To think He died for me!*
> *—John Newton*

APRIL 20, 2003

SUGGESTED SERMON

Every Day Is Easter!

Date preached:

Scripture: John 20:1–10, especially verse 9: For as yet they did not know the Scripture, that He must rise again from the dead.

Introduction: Many people love Easter for the emotions it engenders. Some have warm memories of coloring Easter eggs, wearing Easter clothes, hearing Irving Berlin's "Easter Parade," and enjoying the feeling of springtime with its tulips, daffodils, and hopping bunnies. Some recall going to church on Easter and singing rousing hymns of Resurrection triumph.

Wouldn't it be great to replicate that joyful mood each day of one's life? The disciples were never the same after that first Easter. It affected how they felt, how they viewed the world, and what they did for the rest of their lives. They never got over it. Its implications are not limited to one day per year.

But often, guilt gets in the way. People who have done shameful things have a harder time sustaining self-image, maintaining harmonious relationships, and keeping their spirits up. The preponderance of entertainment, drugs, and alcohol in our society is caused by people wanting to distract themselves from an entangling sense of failure and guilt. It's time we learn that because He lives, all guilt is gone.

I. **Jesus' Easter Text.** In his account of the first Easter, John (who had a lot to feel guilty about) told of running to the tomb with Peter (who had even more to feel guilty about). Seeing the empty tomb, they suspected Christ was alive. But verse ten says, "As yet they did not know the Scripture, that He must rise again from the dead." Whenever we come across the word "Scripture" in the Gospels, we can substitute, "Old Testament." None of the New Testament books had yet been written. Verse 9, then says, "They still did not understand from the Old Testament that Jesus had to rise from the dead." Later that afternoon, two disciples were walking to Emmaus. Jesus appeared to them, but His identity was withheld. After engaging them in conversation, He "expounded to them in all the *Scriptures* the things concerning Himself" (Luke 24:27). Later they said, "Did not our heart burn within us while He talked with us on the road, and while He opened the *Scriptures* to us?" (v.

32). Later that night, Christ "opened their understanding, that they might comprehend the *Scriptures*" (v. 45). Jesus wanted the disciples to understand *from the Old Testament* that He had risen from the dead. Very probably He quoted Psalm 16.

2. **David's Easter Text** (Ps. 16:5–11). This psalm is clearly messianic. "Because He is at my right hand, I will not be shaken. Therefore my heart is glad and my tongue rejoices; My body also will rest secure, because You will not abandon me to the grave, Nor will you let your Holy One see decay" (NIV). Why do we think this is one of the passages Christ quoted to the disciples on the first Easter? First, because it is a primary Old Testament prophecy about the Resurrection; Second, because of what happened fifty days after Christ arose.

3. **Peter's Text** (Acts 2:25–32). On that great day of Pentecost, Peter preached the first evangelistic sermon in church history. Look at the Old Testament text he highlighted: "Whom God raised up, having loosed the pains of death, because it was not possible that He should be held by it. For David says concerning Him . . ."—and he quoted Psalm 16, applying its truths to the risen Jesus of Nazareth.

4. **Paul's Text** (Acts 13:32–38). This was also Paul's text on the Resurrection. In his first recorded sermon, Paul quoted Psalm 16, explaining: "David, after he had served his own generation by the will of God, fell asleep, was buried with his fathers, and saw corruption; but He whom God raised up

>>> sermon continued on following page

APPROPRIATE HYMNS AND SONGS

Christ Jesus Lay in Death's Strong Bands; Martin Luther; Public Domain.

Christ the Lord Is Risen Today, Charles Wesley; Public Domain.

Sing with All the Sons of Glory, William J. Irons; Public Domain.

Blessing, Honor and Glory, Geoff Bullock/David Reidy; © 1990 Word Music, Inc./Maranatha! Music (Admin. by Word Music Group, Inc.).

Celebrate Jesus, Gary Oliver; © 1988 Integrity's Hosanna! Music (Admin. by Integrity Music, Inc.).

saw no corruption. Therefore let it be known to you, brethren, that through this Man is preached to you the forgiveness of sins."

Conclusion: That, then, is the implication of Easter for you and me. Jesus rose from the dead that our sins might be forgiven, that we might once again feel inwardly clean (Is. 1:18). When we come to the Risen Lord in repentance and faith, He forgives our sin, washes our hearts, and makes us new. That was David's message. That was Christ's message. That was Peter's message. That was Paul's message. And today, after all these years, it is our message. Will you receive it?

FOR THE BULLETIN

❋ In early centuries the church had excommunicated heretics, but most church leaders had opposed physical punishment. But as bureaucracy grew and heresy flourished, attitudes changed. During the 1100s and early 1200s, stronger measures evolved; and on April 20, 1233, Pope Gregory IX delegated the prosecution of heresy to the Dominican order. The Inquisitors roamed the countryside, admonishing heretics to confess. Those who didn't were brought to trial, the Inquisition serving as a special court with broad and frightening powers, including the use of torture. ❋ April 20, 1314, marks the death of Pope Clement V, who moved the papacy to Avignon, France. ❋ April 20, 1718, is the birth date of David Brainerd, colonial American missionary to the Indians of New England. He died from tuberculosis at 29, but his journal influenced hundreds to become missionaries after him. ❋ Women in the churches of Puritan New England helped supply the needs of pastors' families by annual "Spinning Bees." For example, in Newbury, Connecticut on April 20, 1768, young ladies met at the house of the Rev. Mr. Parsons, who preached to them a sermon from Proverbs 31:19. They spun and presented to Mrs. Parsons 270 skeins of good yarn while drinking "liberty tea." ❋ During the War in Vietnam, two missionary nurses, Minka Hanskamp and Margaret Morgan, were working among lepers in the predominately Muslim area of neighboring Thailand. On April 20, 1974, while in the town of Pujub to hold a leprosy clinic, they were kidnapped. Their skeletons were later found in the jungle.

An Angelic Reminder

Charles Spurgeon suggested that when the angel appeared to the Lord Jesus in the Garden of Gethsemane to strengthen Him, he did so by reminding Him of Psalm 16 and its promise of Messianic resurrection and glorification.

As the Seed Is Planted

A recent publication from TransWorld Radio tells about a young Cuban named Miguel who had grown up in a large family, receiving little attention from his parents. His early life was marked by hatred and fighting. At 14, he traveled to Havana for school, then went to the coast and became involved in the drug traffic, planting and cultivating marijuana and cocaine. He had several hectares of coca plants with a team of about forty workers.

On one occasion, Miguel was called on to examine a plot some distance away, and he forgot to take along reading material for the trip. The old lady of the plantation gave him a New Testament, and he began reading about the life, death, and Resurrection of Christ. Miguel was so taken with the story that he actually began a Bible reading group among his employees.

One day Miguel suffered an accident. Being in pain that evening, he turned on the radio to distract his thoughts, and tuned into a gospel program. The speaker talked about how terrible it is to have an empty life, full of guilt, full of sin.

Miguel gave his life to Christ. After recovering from his accident, he cut down his plants, burned his laboratory, and got rid of everything related to drug trafficking. When his workers returned from vacation, he shared his experience with them and explained what they were lacking. Every last one of them received Jesus Christ as Lord and Savior.

"From our little band of cocaine farmers," Miguel wrote, "have come twelve pastors. I, myself, have planted ten churches, and for the last six years have pastored in a little town in the interior. The old lady who gave me the New Testament is the leader of a group in another area, and the other pastors are in other parts of the country."

WORSHIP HELPS

Call to Worship:
"Christ, having been raised from the dead, dies no more. Death no longer has dominion over Him." "Blessed be the name of the Lord from this time forth and forevermore!" (Ps. 113:2; Rom. 6:9).

Pastoral Prayer:
Our Father and our God, You have revealed to the nations Your saving power. You have filled the world with springtime and cast a glow of hope over the ages. You have burst the bonds of death and raised your Son from the tomb. Help us today to more fully comprehend all the word "Alleluia" means as we sing Charles Wesley's great hymn, "Christ the Lord is risen today, Alleluia! Alleluia! Sons of men and angels say 'Alleluia! Alleluia!'" May our hearts be overtaken with praise. May our lives be captivated with the vacuity and victory of the tomb, and may we realize that every day is Easter when we live the new birth and walk in newness of life. Give us hearts that feel Your majesty and voices that sing Your praises every day of the year just as we sing this morning in the name of our Risen Lord. Amen.

Benediction:
Like the disciples at the tomb, we have "come and seen." Now, may we "go and tell." In Jesus' name. Amen.

Kids Talk

Tell the children the story of the Lord's Resurrection, using this series of phrases that spell the word "Easter" in acrostic form: *Early in the morning Angels had Sensational news: "The Tomb is Empty! He is Risen!"*

Additional Sermons and Lesson Ideas

Overcoming the Terror of Death

Date preached:

SCRIPTURE: Hebrews 2:14—3:1

INTRODUCTION: Humanity seems transfixed, terrified, and helpless before the rattling hand of the king of terrors, but Easter has the last word on the subject. Hebrews 3:1 says that we should consider Jesus, but how shall we consider Him?

1. Consider Him our eternal Creator (see Heb. 1, especially v. 2).
2. Consider Him our sacrificial Brother (Heb. 2:10-16).
3. Consider Him our great High Priest (Heb. 2:17—3:1).

CONCLUSION: Through His death and resurrection He destroyed the one having the power of death (the devil), releasing all of us who were in bondage to our fear of death. The fear of death cannot abide the presence of our Lord Jesus Christ. It evaporates forever before the empty tomb.

Hearts Afire!

Date preached:

SCRIPTURE: Luke 24:13–35

INTRODUCTION: Today I'd like for us all to take a walk together on the old road to Emmaus. It's a walk for our hearts as we identify with the two disciples who met the Risen Christ on the afternoon of the first Easter.

1. Broken Hearts (vv. 13–24). It was Easter Sunday, but these two disciples had a heartache instead of a Hallelujah! Perhaps today you're dealing with a burdened heart.
2. Their Burning Hearts (vv. 25–32). As Jesus opened the Scriptures to them, they began to feel differently. Their hearts began burning (v. 32).
3. Their Buoyant Hearts (vv. 33–35). "So they rose up that very hour and returned to Jerusalem . . . saying, 'The Lord is risen indeed!'" (vv. 33–34)

CONCLUSION: Anyone here traveling the Emmaus Road? Jesus turned heaviness into heartburn, and heartburn into Hallelujah! He is risen! He is risen indeed!

APRIL 27, 2003

SUGGESTED SERMON

Our Burdens, Our Battles, and Our Bibles

By Melvin Worthington   *Date preached:*

Scripture: James 1:1–27, especially verse 22: But be doers of the word, and not hearers only, deceiving yourselves.

Introduction: The real test of Christianity, James tells us, is obedience—"being doers of the Word and not hearers only." That's the message of this brother of our Lord who wrote the first of the seven General Epistles in the New Testament. He wanted to correct the Jewish notion that their possession and knowledge of the law of God could justify them even though they disobeyed it. James rightly taught that conversion evidences itself in character—in a changed life. In other words belief affects behavior, creed affects conduct, and doctrine affects deportment. James 1 deals with Christians and their *burdens* (vv. 1–11), their *battles* (vv. 12–18) and their *Bible* (vv. 19–27).

I.   **Christians and Their Burdens—Tested by Trials from Without** (vv. 1–11). James taught that:

A. **Problems enlarge the Christian** (vv. 1–4). A correct understanding of the nature and purpose of trials will enable one to respond and react correctly to them. One needs to understand the *purpose, privilege,* and *provision* for trials. Spiritual maturity is God's goal for the Christian. We must focus on the process and product produced through trials. The pathway to maturity is found in James 1:1–4.

B. **Prayer enlightens the Christian** (vv. 5–8). Christians are exhorted to pray for wisdom (v. 5), and to pray in faith (v. 6). They must exercise believing prayer, expecting God to answer with the wisdom needed for every trouble and trial. Praying in faith expects God to answer (v. 7). The identified enemy of praying in faith for wisdom is double-mindedness (v. 8*)*.

C. **Perception enables the Christian** (vv. 9–11). When we perceive that our trials are directed and designed by God to strengthen and purify us, we can face them with assurance that God is tempering us through our trials. Trials are therefore to be looked upon as a means of blessing and received with joy, that we "may be perfect and entire, lacking in nothing."

2. **Christians and Their Battles—Tested by Temptations from Within** (vv. 12–18). Here James wants us to understand:

   A. **The blessing of endurance** (v. 12). Temptation, as this verse suggests, is an inner battle. The temptations we face are not from God but from within ourselves. Our own hearts prove to be the source of these temptations (Matt. 15:19). Endurance brings happiness, holiness and honor. God guarantees blessings to those who endure temptations.

   B. **The basis of enticement** (vv. 13–15). We must not blame God for our temptations. The essential cause of temptation is the sinful nature within every one of us. We should be aware of the *genesis* of evil, the *growth* of evil, and the *grief* of evil. Temptation begins with desires (lust), continues with deeds (sin), and climaxes in death (doom). But we can resist, persevere, endure, and lean upon God's Word. That brings us to:

3. **Christians and Their Bibles—Tested by Truth that Is Written** (vv. 19–27). James admonishes his readers to *be ready* to hear, to *be reluctant* to speak, and to *be reasonable* in wrath. Christians must guard their disposition and attitude. We must *restrain our passions* and *receive the precepts,* submitting to the Word (vv. 21–22). The engrafted Word is to be received with meekness, for it is able to save one's soul (v. 21). Hearers of the Word must become doers (v. 22). This is the burden of James' message—don't

>>> sermon continued on following page

APPROPRIATE HYMNS AND SONGS

Yield Not to Temptation, Horatio R. Palmer; Public Domain.

I Must Tell Jesus, Elisha A. Hoffman; Public Domain.

Burdens Are Lifted At Calvary, John M. Moore; © 1962 Singspiration Music (Admin. by Brentwood/Benson Music Publishing, Inc.).

Thy Word, Amy Grant/Michael W. Smith; © 1984 Meadowgreen Music Co./Word Music Inc. (Admin. by Word Music Group, Inc.).

Your Word Is a Lamp, Frank Hernandez; © 1990 Birdwind Music (Admin. by EMI Christian Music Publishing).

only hear the Word; do it! How easy it is to hear the Word and to agree with it, but not perform it! It is the Word that is able to bring us into the experience of God's salvation that delivers us from sin's penalty, power, and presence. Those who hear the Word and fail to become doers of the Word are deceiving themselves. The proper disposition when receiving the Word will evidence itself in the proper deeds following that reception. James tells us that the Word of God is inspired (v. 18), implanted (v. 21), and indispensable (v. 25).

Conclusion: God molds, matures, and magnifies His children through their trials and burdens, through their temptations and battles, and through the truth—the Bible. Are we passing God's test as we journey by faith?

FOR THE BULLETIN

❀ Pollio, who lived in Gibalea (modern Vinkovce, Hungary), was hauled before a judge on April 27, 204, and asked if he was a Christian. He replied that he was a Christian and his ministry was to read God's Word at church. He was promptly burned to death. ❀ On April 27, 1537, Geneva's first Protestant catechism was published, based on Calvin's "Institutes." ❀ On April 27, 1564, leaders of Geneva tearfully gathered around the deathbed of John Calvin, who told them: "This I beg of you, again and again, that you will be pleased to excuse me for having performed so little in public and private, compared with what I ought to have done." ❀ On April 27, 1667, John Milton, 58, sold the copyright to his religious epic *Paradise Lost* for ten English pounds (less than $30). ❀ Moravian missionary Peter Bohler, who was instrumental in the conversion of Methodist founder and evangelist, John Wesley, died on this day in 1775. ❀ The modern state of Israel was officially recognized by the British Government on April 27, 1950. ❀ Roy and Gillian Orpin were married on this day in 1961 and settled down to serve Christ in the jungles of Thailand. A year later Roy was shot by robbers and rushed to a government hospital. After asking his wife to quote the hymn "Jesus, I Am Resting, Resting," he quietly said, "How good God is!" He was 26. A few days later little Murray Roy was born.

STATS, STORIES AND MORE

More than Hearing

Be ye doers of the Word, and not hearers only, deceiving your own selves, says St. James; and, to take that example, though some may think they are religious because they read the Scriptures daily, religion does not consist in reading God's Word, nor in going to church to hear it preached, Sabbath by Sabbath. I say nothing against hearing; God forbid. We are not to neglect the assembling of ourselves together. It is well to hear; to pitch our tent where manna falls; to sit by the pool where an angel stirs the waters, and descends to heal; to go up to the mountain of the Lord, that, surmounted by the Cross, and trodden by the feet of saints, has conducted many to the skies; and on which, like mountain ranges that attract the clouds, and are watered by many showers that never fall in the valleys, the blessing most frequently and fully descends—God loveth the gates of Zion more than all the tabernacles of Jacob. But will hearing a discourse on fire warm a man? on meat, feed him? on medicine, cure him? If not, no more will it save us to know all about the Savior. It will no more take a man to heaven than it will take him to France, or Rome, or Jerusalem, that he knows the way. We must go, as well as know—travel, as well as be able to trace out the route.—*Thomas Guthrie*, 19th Century Scottish preacher

Challenges

The magazine *Discipleship Journal* asked its readers to rank the areas of greatest spiritual challenge to them. The results came back in this order:

1. Materialism
2. Pride
3. Self-centeredness
4. Laziness
5. (Tie) Anger/Bitterness and Sexual lust
6. Envy
7. Gluttony
8. Lying

The respondents also noted that temptations were more potent when they had neglected their time with God (81 percent) and when they were physically tired (57 percent). Resisting temptation was accomplished by prayer (84 percent), avoiding compromising situations (76 percent), Bible study (66 percent), and being accountable to someone else (52 percent).

WORSHIP HELPS

Call to Worship:
"Blessed be the God and Father of our Lord Jesus Christ, the
Father of mercies and God of all comfort, who comforts us in all
our tribulation, that we may be able to comfort those who are in
any trouble, with the comfort with which we ourselves are comforted by God" (2 Cor. 1:3–4).

Hymn Story:
Pastor Elisha A. Hoffman's pastime was writing hymns, many of
which were inspired by pastoral incidents. One day while calling on
the destitute of Lebanon, Pennsylvania, he met a woman whose
depression seemed beyond cure. She opened her heart and poured
on him her pent-up sorrows. Wringing her hands, she cried, "What
shall I do? Oh, what shall I do?" He said to the woman, "You cannot
do better than to take all your sorrows to Jesus. You must tell
Jesus."
Suddenly the lady's face lighted up. "Yes!" she cried, "That's it! I
must tell Jesus." Her words echoed in Hoffman's ears, and he
mulled them over as he returned home. He drew out his pen and
started writing,

> *I must tell Jesus! I must tell Jesus!*
> *I cannot bear my burdens alone;*
> *I must tell Jesus! I must tell Jesus!*
> *Jesus can help me, Jesus alone.*

Scripture Reading:
"When all kinds of trials and temptations crowd into your lives, my
brothers, don't resent them as intruders, but welcome them as friends!
Realize that they come to test your faith and to produce in you the quality of endurance. But let the process go on until that endurance is fully
developed, and you will find you have become men of mature character with the right sort of independence" (James 1:2–4 J.B. PHILLIPS).

Benediction:
May we go forth from this place as both hearers and doers of Your
Word, Oh God, in the Name of Your dear Son. Amen.

Additional Sermons and Lesson Ideas

"It's For Your Own Good"

By Drew Wilkerson

Date preached:

SCRIPTURE: Deuteronomy 10:12–13

INTRODUCTION: Atheism isn't popular. We live in a world where people are quick to say they believe in God; but many of those people do not revere the Lord as we are instructed in this passage. When we follow God's counsel we realize that He wants only what is in our best interest. Here is what He desires.

1. Fear God (reverence Him).
2. Follow God (walk in all His ways).
3. Love God.
4. Serve God (with all your heart and soul).
5. Obey God (keep His commandments).

CONCLUSION: Notice the last three words of verse 13: *for your good!* I can't count the number of times I heard my parents tell me to do something, adding, "It's for your own good." You know, it was true. They always had my best interest at heart. So does our Heavenly Father. Trust Him.

The Six Best Places to Be

Date preached:

Based on J. Wilber Chapman's meditations of Psalm 23, published in 1899

SCRIPTURE: Psalm 95:7

INTRODUCTION: When the Lord says that He will be with us, He means it. When we are His in Christ, we find ourselves:

1. In His hand for safety (John 10:28).
2. At His feet to be taught (Luke 8:35).
3. On His shoulder for support (Luke 15:5).
4. At His side for fellowship (John 21:20).
5. In His arms for rest (Deut. 33:27).
6. Beside the still waters of refreshment (Ps. 23:2).

CONCLUSION: Can you think of a better place to be?

Everything for the Cross
An "Interview" with Peter Cartwright
(1785–1872) Frontier Evangelist for 70 Years

Since you're one of America's most successful evangelists, I'd be interested in knowing what type of training you received as you began your ministry in 1802.

We had no course of study prescribed, as at present, but William McKendree, my presiding elder, directed me to a proper course of reading and study. He selected books for me, both literary and theological; and every quarterly visit he made, he examined into my progress and corrected my errors, if I had fallen into any. He delighted to instruct me in English grammar. I believe that if presiding elders would do their duty by young men in this way, it would be more advantageous than all the colleges and biblical institutes in the land.

So you had no formal training?

We early Methodist preachers went from fort to fort, from camp to camp, from tent to tent, from cabin to cabin, with or without road or path. We walked on dirt floors, sat on stools, slept on bear skins before the fire or sometimes on the ground in open air. We crossed large rivers without bridges or ferryboats, often swam them on horseback or crossed on trees that had fallen over or waded in waist deep. The above course of training was the colleges in which we early Methodist preachers graduated and from which we took our diplomas! Here we solved our mathematical problems, declined our nouns and conjugated our verbs, parsed our sentences, and became proficient in the dead languages of the Indian and backwoods dialect.

Do you regret having never gone to seminary?

I would rather have the gift of devil-dislodging than all the college lore or biblical institute knowledge that can be obtained from mortal man.

I suppose your experience is a great encouragement for those who feel uneducated or ill-trained for ministry.

Perhaps, among the thousands of traveling and local preachers employed and engaged in this glorious work of saving souls, and building up the Methodist Church, there were not fifty men that had anything more than a common English education, and scores of them not that; and not one of them was ever trained in a theological school or Bible institute, and yet hundreds of them preached the gospel with more success and had more seals to their ministry than all the sapient, downy D.D.s in modern times. Christ had no literary college or university, nor did He require His first ministers to memorize His saying or sermons, but simply to tarry at Jerusalem till they were endued with power from on high.

Well, what do you think of the Baptists?

The Baptists are exclusive immersionists, and won't commune with any other Christian denomination; and they, on these principles, cannot flourish among an enlightened and intelligent religious community.

What do you think of the Calvinists?

If God decreed all things, He decreed there should be Methodists.

How did you conduct worship services in the local church?

We had no pewed churches, no choirs, no organs; in a word, we had no instrumental music . . . wore no jewelry, no ruffles. The Methodists of that day stood up and faced their preacher when they sung; they kneeled down in the public congregation as well as elsewhere, when the preacher said, "Let us pray." There was no standing among the members in time of prayer, especially the abominable practice of sitting down during that exercise. But oh, how things have changed for the worse in this educational age of the world!

What advice would you give a minister regarding preaching with notes?

Mount a stump or stand in the bed of a wagon, and without note or manuscript, quote, expound, and apply the word of God to the hearts of people. The first Presbyterian minister who came to town had studied theology in some of the Eastern states where they manufacture young preachers like they do lettuce in hot-houses. He brought a number of old manuscript sermons and read them to the people. He did not meet with much encouragement. I told him he must quit reading his old manuscript sermons and learn to speak extemporaneously; that the Western people were born and reared in hard times, and were an outspoken and off-hand people; that if he did not adopt this manner of preaching, the Methodists would set the whole world on fire before he could light a match. He tried it awhile, but became discouraged and left for parts unknown.

How did you protect your speaking voice while preaching three or more times a day in the open air, without amplification, for 70 years?

From the beginning I took time to respire freely between sentences, commanded the modulation and cadence of my voice, avoided singing to fatigue, avoided sudden transitions from heat to cold, and when I left the atmosphere of the church, guarded my breast and throat, and even my mouth, from a sudden and direct contact with the chilling air, or air of any kind, got to my room as quick as possible, slept in no cold rooms if I could help it, bathed my throat and breast every morning with fresh, cold water from the well or spring, (and) wore no tight stocks or cravats. The only medicine I used at all was a little cayenne pepper and table salt dissolved in cold vinegar.

What about vacations and time away from the work?

Leisure time with me is a very rare thing.

Did you always have great crowds when you rose to preach?

About eight or nine miles from Nashville, there was a large meetinghouse. One man came. I rose in the stand, sung and prayed, took my text, and preached as best I could for 45 minutes. My friend professed to think it was one of the greatest sermons he had ever heard in his life. For weeks, my one-man congregation proclaimed and circulated my next appointment, telling the people what a great preacher had come to the circuit; and when I came to my next appointment, the whole hillside was covered with horses and carriages, and the church crowded to overflowing. My heart almost fainted within me, for fear I should not meet the expectations of the people; but the Lord helped me, and we had a mighty shaking among the dry bones, and a blessed revival broke out.

Did you ever feel a sense of failure as a minister?

In Boston I was appointed to preach at Churchstreet Church. I took for the text Hebrews 10:22. We had a large congregation; several preachers present; and supposing that most of my congregation had hardly ever seen or heard of me, and that they were an educated people, and had been used to great preaching, I put on all the gravity that I could well command; I tried to preach one of my best sermons, in a plain, grave, sober manner; and although I never thought myself a great preacher, yet I really thought I had done very near my best that time. Well, when I came down from the pulpit, a brother preacher introduced me to several of the prominent members of the congregation; and as I was introduced to them, they asked me very emphatically, "Is this Peter Cartwright from Illinois, the old Western pioneer?"

I answered them, "Yes I am the very man."

"Well," said several of them, "brother, we are much disappointed; you have fallen very much under our expectations; we expected to hear a much greater sermon than that you preached today."

I tell you this was cold encouragement; I felt great mortification; I hastened to my room and prayed over it awhile. I took but little rest in sleep that night. I constantly asked myself, "Is it so, that I cannot preach? What is the matter?" I underwent a tremendous crucifixion in feeling.

The next day I told Dr. Cummings not to give me any other appointments in Boston, "for," said I, "your people here have not sense enough to know a good sermon when they hear it."

Any last words for ministers?

Rise early, get to bed regularly, eat temperately, avoiding high-seasoned victuals, pickles, and preserves. Drink no spirits of any kind. Keep your feet warm, your head cool, and your bowels well regulated, and there will be no need of your ever breaking down till the wheels of life stop. ✵

(Cartwright's quotes are verbatim, sometimes condensed, and are lifted from passages in his autobiography, first published in 1854.)

MAY 4, 2003

Hurry Up and Wait!

Date preached:

By Timothy Beougher

Scripture: James 5:7–11, especially verses 7–8: "Therefore be patient, brethren, until the coming of the Lord. See how the farmer waits for the precious fruit of the earth, waiting patiently for it until it receives the early and latter rain. You also be patient. Establish your hearts, for the coming of the Lord is at hand."

Introduction: New England preacher Phillips Brooks was known for his poise under pressure, but close friends knew he struggled with impatience. One day a friend, seeing him pacing, asked, "What's the trouble, Dr. Brooks?" The great preacher replied: "The trouble is that I'm in a hurry, but God isn't!"

Waiting is a part of the Christian life, as James points out in this passage. The context involves the problem of injustice. In verses 1–6, James dealt with injustice displayed toward believers from businessmen who were mistreating them. When we're treated unfairly, we want justice, and now! But James advises patience, telling us we're to wait with:

I. **Patient Determination** (vv. 7, 8). Patience means holding one's spirit in check, controlling one's temperament, not allowing people to drive us to rage. It could be translated "long-tempered," the opposite of a short fuse. (See Prov. 14:29 and 29:11.) One commentator said, "Patience is the self-restraint which does not hastily retaliate against a wrong." James uses farmers as an illustration (v. 7). If you're impatient, don't take up farming. It takes time after sowing for the harvest. And farmers are dependent on rain. The "early rain" helps soften the soil and give needed moisture; the latter rains help bring the harvest to maturity. Impatience does farmers no good. Likewise we must be patient, awaiting harvest time, waiting for God's vindication. James sums up this point in verse 8, telling us to "establish" our hearts. This verb carries the idea of making something secure. We must deliberately fix our hearts on the Lord's Coming; that focus gives us stability in the face of difficult circumstances.

> *Lord, please show me every day*
> *As you're teaching me your way*
> *That you'll do just what you say*
> *In your time.*

2. **A Positive Disposition** (v. 9). Grumbling and complaining are common human traits, especially when things are difficult. Trials can cause us to lash out at others. The word "grumble" here conveys the idea of "groaning," and the implication is more internal than external. To phrase it differently, it's possible to grumble against another person without saying anything. We can grumble or groan against them in our heart. James warns that grumbling against others is a reflection of the spirit of judgmentalism already condemned in 4:11–12. If we would keep Christ's return in view, we would not complain and criticize so much. Few of us take grumbling against others very seriously, but God does.

3. **Persevering Dependence** (vv. 10, 11). James proceeds to give us two examples of those who persevered through difficulty.
   A. **The Ancient Prophets.** Take Jeremiah, for example. God called him as a teenager in a small town. After he preached his first sermon, his family attacked him. After preaching in Jerusalem, the religious establishment persecuted him. He was beaten, thrown into prison, and dumped into a muddy cistern to die. Yet Jeremiah endured. The prophets weren't some race of super-men. They were human, yet they learned to accept suffering with a persevering dependence. (See Rom. 15:4.)
   B. **Job.** Job suffered mentally, materially, emotionally, physically, and spiritually. But he persevered. Satan predicted that Job would grow impatient with God and abandon his faith, but that didn't happen. (See Job

>>> sermon continued on following page

APPROPRIATE HYMNS AND SONGS

In His Time, Diane Ball; © 1978 Maranatha! Music.

Come and Behold Him, John Chisum/George T. Searcy; © 1994 Integrity's Hosanna! Music/Integrity's Praise! Music (Admin. by Integrity Music, Inc.).

I Wait for You, Ted Sandquist; © 1981 Lion of Judah Music (Admin. by Brentwood-Benson Music Publishing, Inc.).

If You Will Only Let God Guide You, George Neumark/Catherine Winkworth; Public Domain.

Just a Little While, Eugene M. Bartlett; © 1921 E.M. Bartlett. Renewed 1949 Albert E. Brumley and Sons; (Admin. by Integrated Copyright Group, Inc.).

13:15.) Not all suffering is caused by sin. Sometimes suffering is caused by doing right, by living a godly life; but we must persevere.

Conclusion: There is much injustice in the world today. The Bible tells us that God will not settle all wrongs in the world till Christ returns. Therefore we're to patiently endure. To do that, we must:

- Meditate on the sovereignty of God. Impatience is an implicit denial of the sovereignty of God.
- Meditate on the certainty of Christ's return.
- Reflect on the consequences of impatience.
- If it involves another person, remember that you're of like nature. Reflect on your own weakness; it will make your ability to be patient more effective.

FOR THE BULLETIN

❋ On May 4, 1493, the Spanish Pope Alexander VI issued the *Inter caeterea II*, which divided the known world between Spain and Portugal along a longitudinal line running 250 miles west of the Cape Verde Islands. ❋ Returning from the Diet of Worms, Martin Luther was "kidnapped" for his own protection on May 4, 1521, by the German ruler Frederick the Wise and kept at Wartburg where he translated the Bible into German. ❋ Gulielma Springett was born in London in 1644 and joined the Quaker movement at age 15. On May 4, 1672, she married William Penn and lived on an English estate where the couple assembled with their servants each day for worship and Bible reading. William later fled to America to escape persecution, but his wife died in England. Her last words were: "Let us all prepare, not knowing what hour or watch the Lord cometh. . . . I have cast my care upon the Lord." ❋ On May 4, 1737, evangelist George Whitefield penned a note to Gabriel Harris, describing the response to his open air preaching in areas around Gloucester: "People flock to hear the word of God from the neighboring villages as well as our own. They gladly receive me into their houses and I have not a hindrance to my ministerial business." ❋ May 4, 1784 marks the birth of Carl G. Glaser, German music teacher and writer of the tune for Wesley's "O For a Thousand Tongues."

STATS, STORIES AND MORE

The Magic Word

Even children learn impatience at an early age. A young child at the table demanded, "Pass me the meat." His parent said, "What's the magic word?" "Now!" replied the child.

Reacting to Stress

- In *Is it Worth Dying For?* a cardiologist argued that people react to frustration in two major ways. There are hot reactors who respond with angry stress that constricts their coronary arteries and harms their health. The second type are cool reactors who don't fly off the handle when frustrating circumstances come. Encouraging one to be a "cool reactor" is simply another way of saying, "Be patient."

- You may think you're better off when you tell someone off, but you're not, according to research compiled by psychologist-author Gary Emery. "Although a whole school of thought recommends that you verbally express your hostility," he reports in his book, *Rapid Relief from Emotional Distress,* "a great deal of recent research has found the opposite to be the case. . . . Freely venting your anger corrodes relationships and breeds more anger, not less. In one recent study . . . only one out of three hundred happily married couples reported that they yell at each other."—From *USA Today*

Abraham's Example

"God has His set times. It is not for us to know them. Indeed, we cannot know them. We must wait for them. If God had told Abraham in Haran that he must wait all those years until he pressed the promised child to his bosom, his heart would have failed him. So in gracious love, the length of the weary years was hidden. And only as they were nearly spent and there were only a few more months to wait, God told him, according to the time of life, "Sarah shall have a son." If God told you on the front end how long you would wait to find the fulfillment of your desire or pleasure or dream, you'd lose heart. You'd grow weary in well-doing. So would I. But He doesn't. He just says, "Wait. I keep My word. I'm in no hurry. In the process of time I'm developing you to be ready for the promise."—*F. B. Meyer, Abraham*

WORSHIP HELPS

Call to Worship:
"One thing I have desired of the LORD, that will I seek: That I may dwell in the house of the LORD all the days of my life, to behold the beauty of the LORD, and to inquire in His temple" (Ps. 27:4).

Scripture Medley:
I will wait on the LORD, and I will hope in Him. I would have lost heart, unless I had believed that I would see the goodness of the LORD in the land of the living. Wait on the LORD; be of good courage, and He shall strengthen your heart. I am like a green olive tree in the house of God; I trust in the mercy of God forever and ever. I will praise You forever. I will wait on Your name, for it is good. Have you not heard? The everlasting God, the LORD, the Creator of the ends of the earth, neither faints nor is weary. Even the youths shall faint and be weary, and the young men shall utterly fall, but those who wait on the LORD shall renew their strength; they shall mount up with wings like eagles.
(Ps. 27:13–14; 52:8, 9; and Isa. 8:17; 40:28–31)

Offertory Story:
There was a knock on the door of his hut. Answering, the missionary found one of the native boys holding a large fish in his hands. The boy said, "You taught us what tithing is, so here—I've brought you my tithe." As the missionary gratefully took the fish, he asked the young lad, "If this is your tithe, where are the other nine fish?" At this, the young boy beamed and said, "Oh, they're still in the river. I'm going back to catch them now"
—Author Unknown

If we could see beyond today as God can see,
If all the clouds should roll away, the shadows flee
O'er present griefs we would not fret,
Each sorrow we would soon forget;
For many joys are waiting yet for you and me.
—Author Unknown

Additional Sermons and Lesson Ideas

"Deo Volente"
By Timothy Beougher

Date preached:

SCRIPTURE: James 4:13–17

INTRODUCTION: In earlier centuries, believers ended letters with "D.V."—an abbreviation of the Latin *Deo Volente*, meaning "God willing." In James 4 we find:

1. An Attitude of Presumption (v. 13). There's nothing wrong with making plans or business forecasts, but these merchants were excluding God. Are you making plans without seeking guidance in prayer?
2. An Awareness of Limitations (v. 14). These entrepreneurs were boasting about an entire year without really knowing what would happen the next day. (See Prov. 27:1 and Ps. 139:16.)
3. An Affirmation of Submission (v. 15). The phrase, "if the Lord wills," whether stated verbally or believed quietly, helps maintain a trusting submission to God's will.
4. An Analysis of Sin (vv. 16, 17). These people, having forgotten God, were boasting in themselves.

CONCLUSION: The great Latin phrase, *Deo Volente* should be our watchword as we live in dependence on the providence of a sovereign God.

One Thing

Date preached:

SCRIPTURE: Psalm 27

INTRODUCTION: Psalm 27 is the Bible's great cure for insecurity. The first half of the psalm contains a confident attitude, but it's based on the humble reliance on God we find in the last half of the psalm. David's public boldness toward others was based on private dependence on God.

1. One Thing I Know (vv. 1–3). The psalmist had problems in life, but his insecurities were offset by one giant factor. He knew one thing: that the Lord was his light and salvation, the defense of his life.
2. One Thing I Ask (vv. 4–6). That he might continually dwell in God's presence.
3. One Thing I Need (vv. 7–12). We need prevailing prayer. Our most powerful tool for overcoming insecurity is prayer.
4. One Thing I'll Do (vv. 13, 14). I'll be strong and wait on the Lord.

CONCLUSION: If you're troubled by areas of insecurity in your life, claim Psalm 27. It worked for David; it'll work for you.

MAY 11, 2003

SUGGESTED SERMON

Lasting Love on Mother's Day   *Date preached:*

By Melvin Worthington

Scripture: 1 Corinthians 13:1–13, especially verse 1: "Though I speak with the tongues of men and of angels, but have not love, I have become sounding brass or a clanging cymbal."

Introduction: According to the Knoxville *News-Sentinel*, Police Chief Phil Keith was in the middle of a city council meeting in Knoxville, Tennessee, when his pager beeped. Startled to see that the call was from his mother, he rushed to the press table and phoned her. "Phil Keith, are you chewing gum?" demanded his mom, who had been watching on cable TV. "Yes, ma'am." "Well, it looks awful. Spit it out." Keith dutifully removed the gum and went back to his meeting.

There's no one like mothers! The words "mother" and "love" go together like left and right hands, and on this Mother's Day of 2003, there's no better passage to study than the "Love Chapter" of the Bible which describes the *agape* love of God which is necessary for mothers, fathers, sons, daughters—and for all the rest of us.

1. **The Place of Love** (vv. 1–3). Love is superior to eloquent words (v. 1). Love is the vital principle, and without it all other endowments, including excellence in communication, is vain. Love is superior to wisdom (v. 2). If a person could unlock the mysteries of the entire universe and call forth faith to remove mountains, he would be zero without love. Love is superior to work (v. 3). Albert Barnes notes, "If there is not true piety, there can be no benefit in this to my soul. It will not save me. If I have not true love to God, I must perish, after all. Love therefore, is more valuable and precious than all these endowments. Nothing can supply its place; naught can be connected with salvation without it."

2. **The Portrait of Love** (vv. 4–7). Love is patient (v. 4). It bears injustice without anger or despair. Love may be practiced (v. 4). It is mild under all provocations and ill usage. Love produces good manners and courtesy at all times. Love is pure (v. 4), not jealous or displeased when others are successful. Love

never embarrasses the owner or recipient. Love is peaceful (v. 4). It is not rash. Love takes a back seat and is willing to work behind the scenes. Love does not brag or boast or sing its own praises. Love is polite (v. 5), doing nothing to cause shame. Love prefers others (v. 5). There is no selfishness in the true love. It seeks the good of others. Love is not easily provoked (v. 5). When love holds the reins of the soul, there is little danger of provocation to anger and spiteful action that leads to sin. Love is preclusive (v. 5). It does not condemn on suspicion or without evidence, nor is it malicious nor disposed to find fault. Love exhibits propriety (v. 6). It does not sympathize with evil, nor does it delight in anything that does not conform to the standard of right. Love takes pleasure in truth (v. 6). Love rejoices in the virtues of others, not their vices. Love is pleasant (v. 7). Love maintains a disposition that refuses to make public or to avenge the faults of others. Love is not suspicious. It trusts others. Love brightens all things, bears all things and braves all things.

3. **The Permanence of Love** (vv. 8–13). Love's permanency is suggested by the phrase "love never fails" (v. 8). Love will always abide, may always be exercised, and can be adapted to all circumstances in which we may be placed. Love's pre-eminence is suggested by the phrase "but the greatest of these is love" (v. 13). Love is the greatest of all gifts, for love makes the rest of the gifts graceful. Love is the one needful thing—our priority. We lose our goods or even our good names, but if we truly retain love, we have exchanged the temporary for the eternal. For when the Bible has said all it will say about God, it is contained in the one statement: "God is love."

>>> sermon continued on following page

APPROPRIATE HYMNS AND SONGS

The Love of God, Frederick M. Lehman; Public Domain.

All That I Need, Dan Marks; © 1992 Maranatha Praise, Inc. (Admin. by The Copyright Company.).

Come Christians Join to Sing, Christian Henry Bateman; Public Domain.

For What Earthly Reason, Dottie Rambo; © 1986 New Kingdom Music (Admin. by Rambo-McGuire Music.).

O the Deep, Deep Love of Jesus, Samuel Francis Trevor/Thomas J. Williams; Public Domain.

Conclusion: F. E. Marsh tells of some young pastors who paid a visit to one of the great ministers of the past generation. They found him preparing to go to a meeting where a strong debate was expected. He was reading the 13th chapter of 1 Corinthians and praying that its teaching might guide his conduct. The aged minister felt the need of the restraining hand of divine grace and the calming power of love, lest he should be rash in his speech. This is the kind of love that lasts. May God give us loving moms, loving dads, and may He give all of us loving hearts like that.

FOR THE BULLETIN

✸ In A.D. 324, Emperor Constantine, believing the future lay in the East rather than the West, decided to move his capital from Rome to Byzantium. Before long there was a fabulous hippodrome, a prized university, five imperial palaces, nine palaces for dignitaries, 4,388 mansions, 322 streets, 1,000 shops, 100 places of amusement, splendid baths, magnificent churches, and a swelling population. It was a city that shimmered in the sunshine. The New Rome—Constantinople—was dedicated as capital of the Eastern Empire on May 11, 330. It became the center for Eastern Christianity. ✸ On May 11, 1682, the General Court of Massachusetts repealed two Puritanical laws, one forbade the observance of Christmas, and the second demanded capital punishment for Quakers. ✸ On May 11, 1816, delegates from a number of Christian organizations met in New York City to form the American Bible Society. Today the ABS has scriptures available in over a thousand languages and annually distributes hundreds of millions of low-cost Bibles. ✸ The American Tract Society, the first national tract league in America, was formed in New York City on May 11, 1825. ✸ The first CARE packages arrived in Europe, at Le Havre, France, on this day in 1946. ✸ On May 11, 1949, Israel was admitted into the United Nations as the world body's 59th member.

STATS, STORIES AND MORE

Double the Dose

Evangelist Michael Guido told of a wise physician who once said to a young doctor, "I've been practicing medicine for a long time. I've prescribed many things. But in the long run, I've learned that the best medicine is love."

"What if it doesn't work?" asked the friend.

"Double the dose," he said.

Honored

F. E. Marsh observes, "Love has not an irritating thorn in its hand, nor a jealous look in its eye, nor depreciating words on its lips, nor sore feelings in its heart. Love sees the best in others, and the worst in itself. Love will wash another's feet, and think it is honored by so doing."

In *Footsteps of a Pilgrim,* Ruth Bell Graham began this poem for her mother when she was nineteen—on Mother's Day, 1940, and finished it thirty-four years later—November 8, 1974, the day she died.

As the portrait is unconscious
of the master artist's touch
unaware of growing beauty,
unaware of changing much,
so you have not guessed His working
in your life throughout each year,
have not seen the growing beauty
have not sensed it, Mother dear.
We have seen and marveled greatly
at the Master Artist's skill,
marveled at the lovely picture
daily growing lovelier still;
watched His brush strokes
change each feature
to a likeness of His face,
till in you we see the Master,
feel His presence, glimpse His grace;
pray the fragrance of His presence
may through you seem doubly sweet,
till your years on earth are ended
and the portrait is complete.

Call to Worship:
"Let all those rejoice who put their trust in You; Let them ever shout for joy, because You defend them; Let those also who love Your name be joyful in You" (Ps. 5:11).

A Mother's Day Comment by Chuck Swindoll:
I remember a Mother's Day card I saw that was really cute. It was a great big card written in a little child's printing—little first-grade printing. On the front was a little boy with untied sneakers. He had a wagon, and toys were everywhere. He had a little cut on his face and there were smudges all over this card. It read, "Mom, I remember that little prayer you used to say for me every day," Inside was the prayer: "God help you if you ever do that again."

Pastoral Prayer:
Heavenly Father, You know that mothering, though a wonderful calling, is a demanding task, filled with anxious moments and wearisome days. We ask You will restore and refresh every mother here today. And we also pray for our mothers these words from Paul's letter to the Philippians: That their love may abound still more and more in knowledge and all discernment, that they may approve the things that are excellent, that they may be sincere and without offense till the day of Christ, being filled with the fruits of righteousness which are by Jesus Christ, to the glory and praise of God. Amen.

Benediction:
The grace of the Lord Jesus Christ, and the love of God, and the communion of the Holy Spirit be with you all. Amen (2 Cor. 13:14).

Kids Talk

Have a microphone and ask the children about their moms: What do you like best about your mother? Why is your mother so special? What are you doing for your mom today to honor her on Mother's Day? If you have the capability, you might want to visit a Sunday school class in advance and video tape the responses.

Additional Sermons and Lesson Ideas

Take Heed to Yourselves

Date preached:

SCRIPTURE: Acts 20:28

INTRODUCTION: Paul told the Ephesian elders to first "take heed" to themselves, then to their flocks. That's good advice for mothers and for children's workers.

1. Take a Little Time for Yourself (Mark 6:31). If you don't take care of yourself, how can you take care of the kids?
2. Maintain Your Daily Quiet Time (Prov. 8:34). Sure, you're busy; but if nothing else, keep an open Bible near you and take advantage of a minute here and a moment there.
3. Take Your Ministry to Children Seriously (Matt. 18:1–14). This passage is Christ's sermon to parents and children's workers.
4. Serve the Lord With Gladness (Ps. 100:2). Are your children learning *joy* from you?
5. Trust God With the Results (1 Cor. 15:58).

CONCLUSION: Our great task as moms and dads is to nurture our children into the faith.

Prayer–Wrestling

Date preached:

SCRIPTURE: Colossians 4:12 (NIV)

INTRODUCTION: Epaphras is a role model for us parents in our prayerful concern for our children. Notice these things about him:

1. Why He Prayed. According to Colossians 1:7–8, the church of Colosse was born of his efforts. Now his spiritual children were in danger from heresy (Col. 2:4). Imprisoned with Paul, Epaphras could only pray.
2. How He Prayed. Two words in Colossians 4:12 describe Epaphras' prayers:
   - Continually: "He is *always* wrestling in prayer for you."
   - Ardently: "He is always *wrestling* in prayer." This word is the translation of the Greek *agonizomai,* source of our English *agony.* The root *agon* has reference to both athletic contests and military combat and is similar to the word used of Jesus in Gethsemane (Luke 22:44).
3. What He Prayed: "That you may stand firm in all the will of God, mature and fully assured."

CONCLUSION: Our children have ups and downs; sometimes they even go astray like the prodigal son. But they are powerless against our prayers.

MAY 18, 2003

Joyful Stress

Date preached:

By Drew Wilkerson

Scripture: Philippians 1:18–30, especially verses 18–19: "What then? Only that in every way, whether in pretense or in truth, Christ is preached; and in this I rejoice, yes, and will rejoice. For I know that this will turn out for my deliverance through your prayer and the supply of the Spirit of Jesus Christ."

Introduction: On January 24, 2002, *USA Today* published a survey in which respondents were asked, "How often do you experience stress in your daily life?" The answers: Frequently—42 percent; Sometimes—38 percent; Rarely—18 percent; Never—2 percent. Ninety-eight percent of Americans are dealing with stress in their lives. If you're among that number, I have a question for you: Can our stress result in joy? Can we have joy amidst stress? Are the two mutually exclusive? Philippians is the "Epistle of Joy." Paul uses the words "joy" and "rejoice" 16 times in these four chapters, though he himself was in a stressful environment, in jail in Rome. He refused to let circumstances dictate his responses. With the help of the Holy Spirit and the prayers of his friends (v. 19), he was able to turn stress into joy. We can, too, if we can pick up on his secrets in this passage.

1. **Stay Focused** (v. 19). Though in chains and though opposed by those who were preaching Christ out of "envy and rivalry" (v. 15), Paul refused to feel overwhelmed. He said, "For I know . . ." (v. 19). The Greek indicates watching something intently without being distracted. Some translations say, "For I eagerly expect, I anticipate." Instead of basing his faith on feelings, he remained joyful because he stayed focused. He was confident his present circumstances would result in his deliverance. If we're going to model Christ effectively to others, the time to be joyful is when we experience stress. To do this, we must remain focused on the goal Christ has set before us and on the promises He has given to us.

2. **Remain Faithful** (v. 20). Paul discovered that by staying focused he could remain faithful, and that Christ would be magnified in his body whether by life or by death. He was certain his faith in Christ would enable him

to be bold in the midst of a hostile environment. In stressful times we often allow our emotions to take over. We easily confuse what is truth and what is false. Then instead of faithfully trusting in God's strength, we allow our problems to dominate our minds. Paul refused to give in. With joyful expectation and great courage Paul pressed on. We can too.

3. **Be Fruitful** (vv. 21–26). His focus enabled him to be faithful, and his faithfulness produced fruitful labor (v. 22). In spite of all he was going through, Paul overflowed with the joy of knowing that his situation, though stressful, was full of ministry potential. He saw pressure not as an obstacle but as an opportunity to advance the cause of Christ. Paul knew that whether he lived or died it was all gain. If he died he would be with Christ. If he lived he would be used to be bear fruit and win others to Christ. Too often when we are "stressed out" we shut down and become unproductive. This is not God's design. We can choose to be productive. This was Paul's decision. He was fruitful because he turned stress into motivating, life-changing joy.

4. **Stand Firm** (vv. 27–30). With his own example as exhibit one, Paul now told the Philippians to stand firm and to rejoice. No one else can be responsible for our happiness. Others may add to my happiness, but my

>>> *sermon continued on following page*

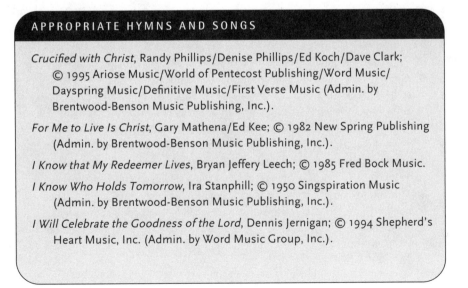

APPROPRIATE HYMNS AND SONGS

Crucified with Christ, Randy Phillips/Denise Phillips/Ed Koch/Dave Clark; © 1995 Ariose Music/World of Pentecost Publishing/Word Music/ Dayspring Music/Definitive Music/First Verse Music (Admin. by Brentwood-Benson Music Publishing, Inc.).

For Me to Live Is Christ, Gary Mathena/Ed Kee; © 1982 New Spring Publishing (Admin. by Brentwood-Benson Music Publishing, Inc.).

I Know that My Redeemer Lives, Bryan Jeffery Leech; © 1985 Fred Bock Music.

I Know Who Holds Tomorrow, Ira Stanphill; © 1950 Singspiration Music (Admin. by Brentwood-Benson Music Publishing, Inc.).

I Will Celebrate the Goodness of the Lord, Dennis Jernigan; © 1994 Shepherd's Heart Music, Inc. (Admin. by Word Music Group, Inc.).

joy is ultimately my decision. This is the approach Paul took with the Philippians. Regardless of what happened to Paul, the Philippians were to conduct their lives in a manner worthy of the gospel. Four words sum up Paul's instruction to the church at Philippi: "Stand firm! Be joyful!" Many Americans suffer the affects of stress, but sometimes the wounds are self-inflicted. Paul tells us that we will suffer for Christ. We are to agonize together, but our pain must bring us closer to one another and serve to testify to our commitment in Christ. Then whatever stress arises, we will be followers full of joy!

Conclusion: Will there always be stress? Yes! The key is not how to avoid it, but how to channel it effectively as a witness for God in a world full of stress. Joy makes all the difference.

FOR THE BULLETIN

❀ On May 18, 1291, the city of Acre fell to invading Moslem armies, signaling the end of a Christian "military presence" in the Middle East during the Crusades. ❀ On May 18, 1593, the Protestant Henry Bourbon of Navarre converted to Catholicism to become France's King Henry IV. Five years later, he issued the Edict of Nantes, granting Huguenots (French Protestants) religious freedom. ❀ Frontier evangelist Sheldon Jackson was born on May 18, 1834. He stood just over five feet tall, but his size, he said, allowed him to sleep anywhere. His bed was a stagecoach floor, a saloon loft, a hollow log, a teepee, a canoe. During 50 years of ministry, he traveled a million miles through the West and North. He oversaw the establishing of 886 churches. ❀ On May 18, 1901, while in Naples, Italy, on a trip to the Holy Land provided by his New York church, Rev. Maltie D. Babcock, 43, suddenly died of "Mediterranean fever." He is best remembered as the author of the hymn "This is My Father's World." ❀ Karol Wojtyla—Pope John Paul II—was born on May 18, 1920. He became the Archbishop of Krakow in 1963, and on October 16, 1978, became the first non-Italian pope since Hadrian VI in the sixteenth century. ❀ On May 18, 1926, popular evangelist Aimee Semple McPherson mysteriously vanished while visiting a beach in Venice, CA. She reappeared a month later, claiming to have been kidnapped. Her story was widely disbelieved. ❀ May 18, 1959 marks the death of pastor and popular author F. W. Boreham.

STATS, STORIES AND MORE

Speaking of Stress . . .

A lot of times we feel like Charlie Brown. Lucy once said to him, "Charlie Brown, life is a lot like a deck chair. Some place it so they can see where they're going. Others place it to see where they've been. And some so they can see where they are at the present."

He replied, "I can't even get mine unfolded."

Six Unforgettable Words

British pastor George Duncan was once invited to preach live from Keswick, England, on the BBC. He choose this text, saying it summed up the "full-orbed and balanced experience" of the Christian in "six unforgettable words, which in English at least are words of one syllable each, and should therefore not be beyond the understanding of the youngest or simplest of us." Victorious Christianity, Duncan said, is something personal—*for me.* It is something practical—*to live.* And it is something possible—*is Christ.*

Bill Wallace

Missionary Bill Wallace of Knoxville, Tennessee, a doctor in China, loved Philippians 1:21. When he was arrested by the Communists and treated brutally, he recalled this verse and its power helped him remain sane. After months of interrogation and abuse, he was found dead. The Communists claimed he had hanged himself, but his body showed signs of having been beaten to death. Defying the Communist authorities, his friends buried him with honor. Over his grave, they inscribed the words they felt described the motivation of his life: "For To Me To Live Is Christ."

Amy Carmichael on Joy

"There is a tremendously uplifting power in joy. Perhaps that is why there is so much about it in the Bible. It may be that if only we live in the power of Psalm 90:14 'all our days,' we shall find at the end that our Lord used the joy that He gave us, to help not only those nearby, but some whom we never met in the flesh, though how that can be I do not know."

WORSHIP HELPS

Call to Worship:
"Sing to Him, sing psalms to Him; Talk of all His wondrous works!
Glory in His holy name; Let the hearts of those rejoice who seek the
LORD!" (1 Chron. 16:9–10).

Responsive Reading:

Leader:	On that day David first delivered this psalm into the hand of Asaph and his brethren, to thank the LORD: Oh, give thanks to the LORD!
People:	Call upon His name;
Leader:	Make known His deeds among the peoples!
People:	Sing to Him, sing psalms to Him;
Leader:	Talk of all His wondrous works!
People:	Glory in His holy name;
Leader:	Let the hearts of those rejoice who seek the LORD!
People:	Let the heavens rejoice, and let the earth be glad; and let them say among the nations, "The LORD reigns."
Leader:	Let the sea roar, and all its fullness; let the field rejoice, and all that is in it.
People:	Then the trees of the woods shall rejoice before the LORD, for He is coming to judge the earth.
All:	Blessed be the LORD God of Israel from everlasting to everlasting!

(1 Chron. 16:7–10, 31–33, 36)

Kids Talk

Ask the children if they would be happy or sad if their goldfish died. Ask them if they would be happy or sad if they won a trip to Disneyland. Then ask them if Jesus loves them and is with them more at one time than the other. Teach the children this maxim and have them say it with you several times: "Happiness depends on happenings, but joy depends on Jesus."

Additional Sermons and Lesson Ideas

While We Wait

By Melvin Worthington

Date preached:

SCRIPTURE: Luke 19:13; John 14:1–3; Acts 1; 1 Corinthians 1:7; 1 Thessalonians 1:10, 4:13–18; Hebrews 9:24–28; 1 John 3.

INTRODUCTION: The Second Coming of Christ is mentioned over 300 times in the Bible. It is a comforting hope, a cleansing hope, a compelling hope, and a certain hope.

1. The Promised Advent. We read the *Almighty's* promise in John 14, the *angelic* promise in Acts 1, and the *apostolic promise* in 1 Thessalonians 4 and 1 John 3.
2. The Prevalent Attitudes. Scoffers have doubted it, skeptics have denied it, sensationalists have distorted it, saints have depended on it, and the Scriptures have disclosed it (2 Pet. 3).
3. The Practical Application. While we wait for the Second Coming of Christ we should *walk circumspectly* (Eph. 5:15), *work consistently* (1 Cor. 15:57, 58), *wait contentedly* (James 5:7), *watch carefully* (Mark 13:32–37), *witness compassionately* (2 Cor. 5:10–21), *warn convincingly* (Acts 20:17–38), and *worship congregationally* (Heb. 10:25).

CONCLUSION: Are you living in light of Christ's Second Coming?

Well-Liked or Off-Key?

Date preached:

SCRIPTURE: 3 John

INTRODUCTION: If we didn't have problems in our relationships, half the publishing industry would go out of business and three-fourths of the talk shows would go off the air. The tiny book of 3 John is about relationships among Christians, and we are introduced to three men.

1. Gaius—A Joy. His name meant "Rejoiced!" and he brought John joy by walking in the truth. Do you lift the spirits of others or depress them?
2. Diotrephes—A Jerk. John wasn't letting himself get tied in knots over Diotrephes, but he was nonetheless honest about the problem.
3. Demetrius—A Jewel. Perhaps the bearer of this letter, Demetrius was well-liked by everyone.

CONCLUSION: Charlie Cello grated on everyone's nerves. He was a constant irritation, off-key, striking a disharmonious cord. That is, until the Master Musician came, turned his strings, and made him a joyful addition to the orchestra. Does your personality need tuning up by the Master? *Come, Thou fount of every blessing, tune my heart. . . .*

Should We Use Notes in the Pulpit?

An "Interview" with R. W. Dale (1829–1895)
Famed Pastor of Carr's Lane Congregational Church,
Birmingham, England
Excerpted from his *Yale Lectures on Preaching*, 1877

Do you take notes into the pulpit when you preach?

It seems to me that the overwhelming weight of the argument is on the side of extemporaneous preaching; but I have very rarely the courage to go into the pulpit without carrying with me the notes of my sermon, and occasionally I read every sentence from the first to the last.

That's not what you've recommended to others, is it?

The contrast between my theory of preaching and my practice is in this respect very glaring. Some of the worst faults, some of the most fatal mistakes which I have entreated you to avoid are the faults and the mistakes which I have found it most difficult to avoid myself.

Does extemporaneous preaching imply lack of specific preparation?

It is not necessary, in order to preach extemporaneously, that we should choose our text as we go into the pulpit, and say what happens to come first. The extemporaneous preacher knows what is he going to say, but does not know how he will say it. Even this definition may require some qualification. A man may be fairly said to preach extemporaneously although he may have in his mind a few strong epigrammatic sentences with which he intends to close and to clinch some passages in his sermon; and who, in thinking over an illustration which requires vivid or delicate treatment, has hit upon the felicitous phrases in which he means to clothe it.

How do extemporaneous preachers develop their thoughts and words in advance?

A friend of mine who was a very effective preacher and speaker used to talk over his sermons and his speeches before he delivered them with any one he happened to meet. How often he has caught me in one of the most crowded streets of Birmingham, or on the steps of the Public Library, and put to me a thought or an argument or an illustration which he meant to use in a sermon on the following Sunday morning. It was his custom to write his sermons and speeches, though he rarely used any notes; but it was my impression that he got not only all his main thoughts, but the very best words he could find for expressing them, before he wrote a line. A member of the House of Commons was telling me a few weeks ago that one of our famous political orators prepares in the same way. Before he makes a great speech he talks over all the points with every man he sees, and if he can talk to nobody else, he will talk to his gardener. Sentence after sentence, one epigram after another gets into shape in this way.

What are the advantages of using notes?

The advantages of writing and reading are obvious. The preacher who goes to church with his sermon in his pocket is sure of having something to say. He escapes the anxiety with which many of the best extemporaneous preachers are tormented every Friday and Saturday.

Do extemporaneous preachers really worry about what they're going to say?

While I was a student, my predecessor, John Angell James, had to preach on a great occasion in connection with the London Missionary Society. He happened to tell me three weeks before the sermon was to be delivered that he intended to read it, and I ventured, rather presumptuously, to remonstrate with him. "Why shouldn't I read?" he asked. "Because you're never so effective when you read," I replied. He gave me an odd look and said, "Well now, I'll tell you how it is. If I preach without reading I shall be miserable for three weeks—miserable until I am in the pulpit; if I read, I shall be quite happy till I begin to preach, though I shall be miserable till I finish." The old man's reason for using his manuscript was not to be answered; and I suppose that there are many preachers who, if they did not read, would soon be worn away by anxiety.

Are there other advantages to writing out one's sermons?

Clearness and precise accuracy in the statement of truth. Language is a difficult instrument to master, and even the ablest speakers cannot always command at the moment the simplest and most transparent expression of their thought.

Any other benefits?

There is one advantage on the side of writing and reading sermons which is rarely mentioned. Extemporaneous sermons spend their whole life in their birth and may have public audience but once. If a man writes and reads, he can preach his old sermons over again.

Do you actually repeat your sermons to the same congregation?

I can see no sufficient reason for not preaching sermons a second or a third time to the same congregation. Indeed, after an interval of seven or eight years, though we may be preaching in the same pulpit, we are not preaching to the same congregation.

But there will be some people there who might remember your having previously preached that sermon.

Some of the people will recognize it as an old sermon, but your congregation will be very remarkable if there are more than a very few persons who will remember the contents of it so perfectly that it will not do them good to hear the sermon again. When you preach an old sermon, be frank about it. There are people who keep a record of our sermons; the margins of their Bibles are enriched with dates and placed against the texts we have preached from. Do not try to cheat these keepers of homiletical chronicles. The old sermon may sometimes require a great deal of revision; you may have to cancel some passages and replace them with others, but do not try to conceal the fact that the sermon is not a new one. Let the old text stand.

Which sermons are best fitted for repetition?

The sermons which we have a right to repeat are sermons to which we have given so much time and strength that they contain the very best that we can say on some great subject.

So you are definitely in favor of preaching with notes or manuscript?

It is certain that there are many able and useful preachers, who, if they did not use their manuscript, would be unable to preach at all. And yet—notwithstanding my own habits—I am compelled to admit that if we can preach without reading we are likely to preach more effectively. ✹

E. Stanley Jones: The Man Who Survived Brain Fatigue

Brain fatigue, nervous exhaustion, near collapse, depression. Those were the terms Methodist missionary Stanley Jones used to describe his deteriorating condition. He had gone to India with visionary passion, but his energy had evaporated amid unbearable heat, hostility, and anxiety. He felt himself unraveling.

His doctor prescribed a year's rest in America, but he collapsed aboard ship while trying to speak at a Sunday morning service at sea and barely made it home. Once there, Jones tried to rest, but his nerves crackled like a short-circuiting electrical connection. He insisted on returning to India a year later, but he no sooner landed in Bombay than he collapsed again and was sent to the mountains for several more months of rest and relaxation. Finally returning to work, Jones quickly used up his meager emotional reserves and was plunged again into depression and debilitation. Friends feared for his life.

It was in this state that Jones traveled to the city of Lucknow to conduct a series of meetings. There one night while praying, he suddenly felt the Lord speaking to him. Though not audible, the Lord's voice almost seemed so. Jones sensed these words: *Are you yourself ready for this work to which I have called you?*

"No, Lord, I am done for," Jones replied. "I have reached the end of my resources." *If you will turn that over to Me and not worry about it, I will take care of it.*

"Lord," Jones said, "I close the bargain right here."

At that moment, E. Stanley Jones later said, a great peace settled into his heart and pervaded his whole being. "I knew it was done! Life—Abundant Life—had taken possession of me. I was so lifted up that I scarcely touched the road as I quietly walked home that night. Every inch was holy ground. For days after that I hardly knew I had a body. I went through the days, working far into the night, and came down to bedtime wondering why in the world I should ever go to bed at all, for there was not the slightest trace of tiredness of any kind. I seemed possessed by life and peace and rest—by Christ Himself."

Jones labored on for decades, serving over forty years in India, preaching around the world, writing a dozen books, and becoming one of the most famous missionaries of his generation. ✺

MAY 25, 2003

When Jesus Tarries

Date preached:

Scripture: Mark 5:21–43, especially verse 35: "While He was still speaking, some came from the ruler of the synagogue's house who said, 'Your daughter is dead. Why trouble the Teacher any further?'"

Introduction: Have you ever raced down a freeway only to pass flashing yellow words that strike fear to every motorist: *Expect Delays*? Occasionally such signs appear on life's freeways, too. Things often take longer than we'd desire, whether beating an illness, finishing school, landing a job, finding a mate, or weathering a crisis. How often we feel like saying, "Hurry up, Lord!" Yet sometimes the Lord tarries. We see this illustrated in Mark 5:21-43:

1. **Verses 21–22.** Jairus was an ἀρχισυνάγωγος (archi-soon-agō-gŏs), from ἀρχων (*archoñ*: ruler, chief) and the Greek word for synagogue. In modern terms we'd call him the local pastor in Capernaum. Jesus was staying nearby at Peter's home, and perhaps Jairus had even turned his pulpit over to the Lord. Can you imagine Christ living near our church and occasionally preaching for us? We know Jesus delivered His sermon on the Bread of Life in the Capernaum synagogue (John 6). So the two men were acquainted, and Jairus evidently was attracted to Jesus. One day, he faced a crisis.

2. **Verses 22–23.** His daughter was twelve, which to the Hebrews was when she became a woman. But she was Jairus' "little girl," and he was in the grip of fear. Fear is an emotion we'll not miss in heaven. It comes in many forms, caused by many things. Sometimes it's rational; other times it isn't. Some people, for various reasons, are especially vulnerable to fear, but there is no fear like the hyperventilating panic that sometimes strikes parents worried about their children.

3. **Verse 24.** How relieved was Jairus when Jesus consented to help. Time was of the essence. When he said in verse 23, "My little girl is dying," it literally says, "My little girl is εσχαρτωσ εαςχει—at the final stage, at the last breath." But now, Jairus faced one delay after another. This was caused at first by the crowds that, according to Luke, nearly crushed them. In the middle of this delay came another.

4. **Verses 25–34.** This "miracle within a miracle" is one of the tenderest stories in the Bible. A desperate woman touching the hem of Christ's garment, virtue flowing from Him into her body, sudden healing, freedom from suffering. It was great for the woman, but not so great for Jairus. This interruption made Jesus late, and it was a fatal delay.

5. **Verse 35.** Jairus' compatriots evidently were unhappy about his flight to Jesus, and they seem almost relieved that the Miracle Worker would not be drawn into the situation.

6. **Verse 36.** Jesus gave Jairus two commands—six words—that made all the difference. This is what Jesus says to us in the middle of our fears. It's our Lord's advice, repeated in various forms throughout the Bible: *Do not be afraid; only believe.* In the former Belgium Congo, 1964 and 1965 were years of martyrdom for Christians. Not since the Boxer Rebellion in China had so many missionaries been killed. One missionary caught in the nightmare was British nurse Margaret Hayes. She was missing seven months; no one knew if she were dead or alive. Later recounting the terror of those months, she said: "Until the last we had expected to be killed any day. The Lord gave me Mark 5:36: 'Do not be afraid, only believe.' I knew that whether I lived or died, the Lord had everything in hand." These are words that make a difference, words we should remember, words we should memorize, claim, and obey. So

>>> sermon continued on following page

APPROPRIATE HYMNS AND SONGS

Praise to the Lord, the Almighty, Joachim Neander/Catherine Winkworth; Public Domain.

O for a Faith that Will Not Shrink, William H. Bathurst/Carl G. Glaser; Public Domain.

They that Wait Upon the Lord, Dale Jackson; © 1975 Scripture in Song (Admin. by Integrity Music, Inc.).

They that Wait, Gary Oliver; © 1991 CMI-HP Publishing (Admin. by Word Music Group, Inc.).

Surely the Presence of the Lord Is in This Place, Lanny Wolfe; © 1977 Lanny Wolfe Music (Admin. by Gaither Copyright Management).

Jairus faced a decision. He could either trust in the face of hopeless odds, or he could yield to fear and grief.

7. **Verses 37–43.** To others, it seemed Christ had arrived too late. But Jesus was keeping His own clock, and His pace was perfect. As one poet put it:

His wisdom is sublime;
His heart profoundly kind;
God never is before His time,
And never is behind.
—*By J. J. Lynch*

Conclusion: If you're impatient today, having to wait on the Lord, passing "Expect Delays" signs, remember that when it seems that the Lord is slow in responding to you, He might be deepening your faith. His advice: "Do not be afraid. Only believe." Our response:

O for a faith that will not shrink,
Tho' pressed by every foe.
That will not tremble on the brink
Of any earthly woe!

FOR THE BULLETIN

✿ May 25, 1085 marks the death of Pope Gregory VII (Hildebrand), one of the greatest popes of the Roman Catholic Church. He had been chosen by the people themselves, and his greatest desire was to reform the Roman Catholic Church. He was driven into exile, however, by Germany's King Henry IV. Gregory died broken-hearted in Salerno. ✿ On May 25, 1793, Rev. Stephen Theodore Badin became the first Roman Catholic priest to be ordained in the United States, in a ceremony in Baltimore. He later became a frontier missionary, and played a key role in establishing Catholicism in Kentucky, Indiana, and Tennessee. ✿ On May 25, 1824, the American Sunday School Union was established. It began as a coalition of local Protestant Sunday school groups, uniting to promote the establishment of Sunday schools and to provide local communities with libraries and materials for religious instruction. ✿ When Billy Bray, a coal-miner in Cornwall, England, was converted, at age 29, he began shouting for joy. He never stopped, becoming a unique Methodist evangelist who danced and shouted his way through a lifetime of ministry. His dying word as he fell asleep on May 25, 1868, was "Glory!" ✿ On May 25, 1949, the Communist forces of Mao Tse-tung entered Shanghai, closing the churches and forever changing the lives of the Christians and pastors living there. One of the pastors later imprisoned was Watchman Nee.

STATS, STORIES AND MORE ·

Hurry Please!
Ruth Graham wrote a little poem during a personal crisis on November 13, 1976, which expresses what Jairus must have been feeling:

> We are told
> To wait on You
> But, Lord,
> There is no time.
> My heart implores
> Upon its knees
> . . . hurry
> . . . please!

Lord, Could You Hurry a Little?
In her book, *Lord, Could You Hurry a Little?*, Ruth Harms Calkin writes:
> *Lord, I know there are countless times*
> *When I must wait patiently for You.*
> *Waiting develops endurance.*
> *It strengthens my faith*
> *And deepens my dependence upon You.*
> *I know You are Sovereign God—*
> *Not an errand boy*
> *Responding to the snap of my finger.*
> *I know Your timing is neatly wrapped*
> *In Your incomparable wisdom.*
> *But, Lord*
> *You have appointed prayer*
> *To obtain answers!*
> *Even David the Psalmist cried*
> *With confident boldness:*
> *"It is time, O Lord, for you to act."*
> *God, on this silent sunless morning*
> *When I am hedged in on every side*
> *I too cry boldly.*
> *You are my Father, and I am Your child.*
> *So, Lord, could You hurry a little?*

Her House
Eusebius, the "Father of Church History" who lived in Caesarea in the 300s, wrote that this woman (Mark 5:25–34) was a Gentile from Caesarea Philippi and that for many years her house was shown to travelers. He also said her townsmen commemorated this miracle by erecting a bronze statue of Jesus which bore a close resemblance to our Lord. Eusebius himself saw this statue. Being a Gentile area, the citizens had no prohibitions (as the Jews did) in making statues or graven images. If this statue had survived, we might have a clearer impression of Jesus' appearance, but it was destroyed by the Romans.

WORSHIP HELPS

Call to Worship:

"Praise ye the Lord, the Almighty, the King of Creation!"

Related Scripture Verses:

- "And the altar shall be most holy. Whatever touches the altar must be holy" (Ex. 39:27).
- "If only I may touch His garment, I shall be made well" (Matt. 9:21).
- "As many as had afflictions pressed about Him to touch Him" (Mark 3:10).
- "Then He came to Bethsaida; and they brought a blind man to Him, and begged Him to touch him" (Mark 8:22).
- "Wherever He entered, into villages, cities, or the country, they laid the sick in the marketplaces, and begged Him that they might just touch the hem of His garment. And as many as touched Him were made well" (Mark 6:56).
- "This Man, if He were a prophet, would know who and what manner of woman *this is* who is touching Him" (Luke 7:39).
- "Then they brought little children to Him, that He might touch them" (Mark 10:13).
- "But Jesus came and touched them and said, 'Arise, and do not be afraid'" (Matt. 17:7).
- "He who has been born of God keeps himself, and the wicked one does not touch him" (1 John 5:18).

Pastoral Prayer:

Today we need the touch of the Master's hand, and we ourselves want to touch the hem of the Master's garment. Some here today need healing. Some need revival in their hearts. Some need restoration in their friendships. Some need forgiveness of their sins. Lord, today we need You. And for those here this morning who wonder if they've been left behind, who fear you've forgotten them, teach them that your delays are not denials. May we wait on You, and may our strength be renewed and our souls be restored. May we this day touch the hem of your garment and receive the healing, the strength, and the answers we need. In Jesus' name. Amen.

Additional Sermons and Lesson Ideas

Real Faith, Real Friends
By Kevin Riggs

Date preached:

SCRIPTURE: Various Proverbs

INTRODUCTION: Living a life of faith will increase our desire to choose the right kinds of friends, and to be the right kind of friend. To help us in that desire, notice these five principles about friendship in the Book of Proverbs:

1. Living a life of faith means choosing your friends carefully (Prov. 13:20).
2. A true friend keeps things in confidence (Prov. 17:9).
3. True friends are there when you need them (Prov. 17:17).
4. A true friend confronts (Prov. 27:5, 6).
5. A true friend strengthens (Prov. 27:17).

CONCLUSION: Perhaps as Solomon wrote these verses, he was thinking of his dad's famous friendship with Jonathan. Remember that the best way to have a friend is to be a friend, and let these maxims from Proverbs strengthen you in your relationships today.

Go, Show Your Love to Your Wife

Date preached:

SCRIPTURE: "Go, show your love to your wife" (Hosea 3:1 NIV).

INTRODUCTION: These seven words can save your marriage. Many men really love their wives, but they do not show it. They aren't good at expressing their love. How can we show our love to our spouse?

1. Time. Plan for more time together, just the two of you.
2. Trips. Have a get-away with your wife.
3. Thoughtfulness. Do things for your wife around the house with no thought of reward.
4. Thankfulness. Have a good attitude at home.
5. Talking. Yes, you can do it. Regular, meaningful conversation is the needle and thread that binds a couple together.
6. Touching. Be affectionate.
7. Togethering. Find a hobby to do together.
8. Trustworthiness. Can your spouse trust you completely?
9. Tenderness. Be sensitive to her needs and she'll be available to meet yours.

CONCLUSION: These seven words and nine ideas can turn around your marriage. You can begin today.

John Calvin's Farewell Address

Drugs and modern medical technology have eased the process of dying, but in so doing they often deprive us of those famous "last words" that were glorious benedictions of the saints of Christian history. John Bunyan of *Pilgrim's Progress* fame, for example, rambled on with such rich and sanctified deathbed ruminations that they were recorded on the spot and published posthumously as *Mr. Bunyan's Dying Sayings*.

One gets the impression that some Christian leaders of past generations rehearsed their final words in advance, at least in their minds. Commentator Matthew Henry selected these words: "You have been used to take notice of the sayings of dying men—this is mine: that a life spent in the service of God and communion with Him is the most pleasant life that anyone can live in this world."

Mrs. Catherine Booth uttered these triumphant words: "The waters are rising, but so am I. I am not going under, but over."

If you've never read a complete account of the passing of evangelist D. L. Moody, just find a good biography, a quiet closet, and an uninterrupted hour—and be prepared to glimpse heaven. "This is no dream, Will," Moody exclaimed to his son. "It is beautiful! It is like a trance! If this is death, it is sweet! God is calling me, and I must go!"

But this article is about John Calvin.

On February 6, 1564, Calvin, 55 years old, stood for the last time in his pulpit at Saint Pierre in Geneva. In mid-sermon, he was seized by a coughing fit and his mouth filled with blood. He slowly forced his way down the circular staircase from the pulpit, his sermon unfinished.

On Easter Sunday, April 2, he was carried back to Saint Pierre's and sat near the pulpit, listening as Theodore Beza preached. At the end of the service, Calvin joined the congregation in singing a final hymn, "Now lettest thou thy servant depart in peace." He was taken to his bed, still working feverishly on his papers. When friends begged him to rest, he replied, "What! Would you have the Lord find me idle when he comes?"

On April 28, he requested that Geneva's ministers pay him a visit. They quietly filed into his bedroom, and he propped himself up to give them this final exhortation, which has challenged many a pastor since:

"Brethren, after I am dead, persist in this work, and be not dispirited; for the Lord will save this Republic and Church from the threats of the enemy.

"Let dissension be far away from you, and embrace each other with mutual love. Think again and again what you owe to this Church in which the Lord has placed you, and let nothing induce you to quit it. It will, indeed, be easy for some who are weary of it to slink away, but they will find, to their experience, that the Lord cannot be deceived.

"When I first came to this city, the Gospel was, indeed, preached, but matters were in the greatest confusion, as if Christianity had consisted in nothing else than the throwing down of images; and there were not a few wicked men from whom I suffered the greatest indignities; but the Lord our God so confirmed me, who am by no means naturally bold (I say what is true), that I succumbed to none of their attempts.

"I afterwards returned thither from Strassburg in obedience to my calling, but with an unwilling mind, because I thought I should prove unfruitful. For not knowing what the Lord had determined, I saw nothing before me but numbers of the greatest difficulties. But proceeding in this work, I at length perceived that the Lord had truly blessed my labors.

"Do you also persist in this vocation, and maintain the established order; at the same time, make it your endeavor to keep the people in obedience to the doctrine; for there are some wicked and obstinate persons. Matters, as you see, are tolerably settled. The more guilty, therefore, will you be before God, if they go to wreck through your indolence.

"But I declare, brethren, that I have lived with you in the closest bonds of true and sincere affection, and now, in like manner, part from you. But if, while under this disease, you have experienced any degree of peevishness from me, I beg your pardon, and heartily thank you that when I was sick you have borne the burden imposed upon you."

Having expended his strength, he shook hands with each one and slumped back into his pillow. Weeping, they sadly exited the room, knowing they would hear the voice of John Calvin no more.

About a month later, when it appeared the end was at hand, a small handful of intimate friends surrounded his bed. Calvin quoted Scripture and prayed until, just as the sun was setting, he quietly passed from one life to another, without gasp or sigh. "On this day with the setting sun," said Beza, "the brightest light in the Church of God on earth was taken to heaven!"

Geneva mourned deeply. Calvin had instructed that his body be laid in a common cemetery with no tombstone. He didn't want his grave becoming a shrine as tombs of earlier saints had become. It didn't—today his grave site is unknown. ✸

JUNE 1, 2003

SUGGESTED SERMON

The Old Lamplighter

Date preached:

By D. James Kennedy

Scripture: Ephesians 5:8: "For you were once darkness, but now you are light in the Lord. Walk as children of light."

Introduction: Sir Harry Lauder, Scottish humorist and comedian of another era, was a Christian. One evening at the Hotel Cecil he told about an incident that might have been spoken from a pulpit. He said: "I was sitting in the gloamin', an' a man passed the window. He was the lamplighter. He pushed his pole into the lamp and lighted it. Then he went to another and another. Now I couldn't see him. But I knew where he was by the lamps as they broke out doon the street, until he had left a beautiful avenue of lights. Ye're a' lamplighters. They'll know where ye've been by the lights [ye have lit]." That is a beautiful description of the Christian life. We are lamplighters. The darkened lamps are the lives and souls of those who sit in a dark world. The flame is the flame of the love of Jesus Christ burning by His Spirit, and the pole is the presentation of the gospel.

1. **Closet Christians.** One of the sociological phenomena of our day is the "emptying of the closet." The closet used to be full in America, but today it's empty. The prostitutes have left the closet and are demanding their rights. The homosexuals are out of the closet and having their own parades. The fornicators have left the closet and have put both names on the mailbox where they cohabit apart from the blessings of marriage. But there behind the coats and scarves, cringing in the corner, clinging to his lamplighter's pole, are those church members who hide their lights and are ashamed to witnesses for their Lord.

2. **Christ's Command.** Jesus, in His last command, said that we are to be witnesses unto Him. He died to purchase eternal life for all who would trust in Him, and we must share the Light of Life. Oh, if we could but see a friend, a loved one, an acquaintance, a business partner, five minutes after their death, we would surely lament if we had not told them of the Light

of Life. Michelangelo once carved several statues out of ice one cold winter day, perhaps to amuse his friends. They were magnificently done and many came to admire them. But, of course, soon the sun rose higher and the statues melted. We would think it foolish for someone to leave a legacy in ice to turn to water and mud. But, my friends, some of you have spent your whole life carving in ice. Making a living. Fixing a house. Making sure your lawn is impeccable. What will it matter 500 years from now?

3. **Making Your Life Count for Eternity.** Those who are truly wise sculpt in human souls and fashion them into the image of Jesus Christ. I urge you to work for the souls of men, and I am not speaking alone. There is a trio of voices speaking to you. I speak God's Word to you, but the Holy Spirit is speaking to you, and so is your own conscience. How many have stood by the grave of a loved one and lamented, "Oh, how I wish I had spoken to this one about Christ."

Conclusion: There are some in this world who will never hear the gospel unless they hear it from you. If every person in this sanctuary today were to become a lamplighter for Jesus Christ, there would be such joy that people would wonder what was going on when they walked into this church. Nothing you can ever do will give you such satisfaction. A businessman had a layover in Dallas. Being a lamplighter, he wondered how he could use the hour-and-twenty-minute wait to good purpose. He had some tracts in his briefcase, so he took them out, inserted a business card in each, and gave one to every man in that particular section of the airport, saying, "Here, this will tell you how to become

>>> sermon continued on following page

APPROPRIATE HYMNS AND SONGS

A Candle in the Darkness, Randy Vader/Jay Rouse; © 1996 PraiseGathering Music (Admin. by Gaither Copyright Administration.).

O Master, Let Me Walk with Thee, Washington Gladden/Henry Percy Smith; Public Domain.

Candle in the Dark, Rob Bryceson; © 1989 Little Peach Music.

Find Us Faithful, Jon Mohr; © 1987 Jonathan Mark Music/Birdwing Music (Admin. by EMI Christian Music Publishing.).

He Keeps Me Singing, Luther B. Bridgers; Public Domain.

a Christian. If you would like to know more, I'll be sitting right over there until my plane leaves in an hour and twenty minutes. Or, if you would like to write me, here is my business card." What do you think happened? Before his plane left, men were standing four deep around his seat trying to find out more about how to become a Christian. And for weeks he was answering letters from those who had inquired. Yes, we are all lamplighters, and they will know where we've been by the lights we have lit.

FOR THE BULLETIN

✸ One day in the second century, Justin Martyr, about 30, met an old man who told him about Christ. He was saved and immediately began telling everyone that Christ can satisfy both mind and heart. He eventually became one of the church's first apologists, and was condemned, flogged, and beheaded for his faith. His life is remembered every year on his feast day, June 1. ✸ James Guthrie, a Scottish Covenanters, was hanged for his faith on this day in 1661, after which his head was affixed on Netherbow Port. In coming months his little son William, sneaking away to steal glances at his father's decaying head, would run home crying, "I've seen my father's head! I've seen my father's head!" ✸ On June 1, 1792, at the Baptist Associational Meeting in Nottingham, England, a motion passed that "a plan be prepared against the next Ministers' Meeting at Kettering, for forming a Baptist Society for propagating the gospel among the heathens." It set the stage for the missionary endeavors of William Carey and has been called the "birthday of modern missions." ✸ On June 1, 1793, Henry Lyle wrote the hymn "Abide with Me." ✸ On June 1, 1859, Philip and Lucy Bliss were married. They were later to perish in a terrible train wreck, but not before Philip had written such popular hymns as *Man of Sorrows—What a Name!; Jesus Loves Even Me; The Light of the World Is Jesus!; Almost Persuaded;* and *Wonderful Words of Life.* ✸ June 1, 1972 marks the death of Chinese Christian Watchman Nee, who died in a Chinese prison for his faith in Christ.

STATS, STORIES AND MORE

A Story from D. James Kennedy

Said one businessman to his friend, "How long have we known each other?"

"About fifteen years."

"And you believe, I understand, that no man can go to heaven except through faith in Jesus Christ. Is that correct?"

"Oh, yes, I believe that very definitely."

"Do you really care for me?"

"Indeed I do."

"Sir, I beg to differ with you. You actually do not care for me at all, for in fifteen years I have heard you talk about hundreds of subjects, but you have never yet once talked to me about Christ."

"You Forget My Soul": a poem used by Dr. D. James Kennedy in his message, "The Old Lamplighter"

You lived next door to me for years;
We shared our dreams, our joys, our tears,
A friend to me you were indeed,
A friend who helped me in my need.

My faith in you was strong and sure;
We had such trust as should endure.
No spats between us e'er arose;
Our friends were like—and so, our foes.

What sadness then, my friend, to find
That after all, you weren't so kind.
That day my life on earth did end,
I found you weren't a faithful friend.

For all those years we spent on earth
You never talked of second birth.
You never spoke of my lost soul
And of the Christ who'd make me whole.

I plead today from hell's cruel fire
And tell you now my last desire.
You cannot do a thing for me;
No words today my bonds to free.

But do not err, my friend, again—
Do all you can for souls of men.
Plead with them now quite earnestly,
Lest they be cast in hell with me.

WORSHIP HELPS

Call to Worship:
"This is the message which we have heard from Him and declare to you, that God is light and in Him is no darkness at all" (1 John 1:5).

Hymn Story:
Washington Gladden was a New England pastor who grew very discouraged with the apparent fruitlessness of his work. One day, downhearted, he climbed up to the church belfry to think. From his high perch, it seemed tempting to jump off, and had he been an unconverted man, he might have considered it, so low were his spirits. Instead he poured out his heart to God, and from that experience wrote out a prayer which later became a powerful hymn: "O Master, let me walk with Thee / In lowly paths of service free; / Tell me Thy secret; help me bear / The strain of toil, the fret of care."

Benediction:
And now, Heavenly Father, may we leave this place to give light to those who sit in darkness and in the shadow of death, and to guide their feet in the way of peace. Amen.

Kids Talk

Today's suggested sermon is easy to illustrate for children, using a set of candles. Light all but one—Candice the Candle—then tell the children that this candle is perfectly made, strong and straight, and is even in church. But there is one thing Candice the Candle isn't doing. She isn't doing the one thing she was made to do—letting her light shine. Talk about the importance of sharing Christ, and end by striking a match to "Candice" and quoting Matthew 5:16.

Additional Sermons and Lesson Ideas

The Original and the Forgery

Date preached:

SCRIPTURE: Galatians 1:3–4

INTRODUCTION: The best way to spot a forgery is to intimately know the original. In Galatians, Paul exposes a forgery. Some Galatians were embracing a false gospel. Before addressing that, Paul reminded them of the original by summarizing the true gospel in the first paragraph. We can isolate six elements that make the gospel an original.

1. A Savior. "Grace to you and peace from our Lord Jesus Christ." *Lord* implies His authority. *Jesus* speaks of His mission (Deliverer), and *Christ* denotes His Messianic anointing.
2. A Sacrifice. "Who gave Himself." We like novels in which the protagonist survives to fight another day, but in real life the hero sometimes perishes. A plaque at a makeshift memorial at the World Trade Center read, "All gave some. Some gave all." Jesus gave all of Himself for us.
3. A Problem. "For our sins."
4. A Purpose. "That He might deliver us from this present evil age."
5. A Design. "According to the will of our God." God designed our salvation from the foundation of the world.
6. A Doxology. "To whom be glory forever and ever."

CONCLUSION: Don't be misled by a forgery. Only the original saves our souls.

Oh Yes, He Cares

Date preached:

SCRIPTURE: Selected Verses from the New International Version

INTRODUCTION: There's an old song that says, "Does Jesus Care?" Well, does He?

1. "No one cares" (Ps. 142:4). Sometimes we feel abandoned.
2. "The LORD your God cares" (Deut. 11:12).
3. "He cares for those who trust in Him" (Nahum 1:7).
4. "After all, no one ever hated his own body, but he feeds and cares for it, just as Christ does the church" (Eph. 5:20).
5. "Cast all your anxiety on Him because He cares" (1 Pet. 5:6-7).
6. "Cast your cares on the LORD and He will sustain you" (Ps. 55:22).

CONCLUSION: "Oh, yes, He cares! I know He cares."

JUNE 8, 2003

Symbols of the Holy Spirit
By Jack W. Hayford

Date preached:

Scripture: Mark 1:1–11, especially verses 9, 10: "It came to pass in those days that Jesus came from Nazareth of Galilee, and was baptized by John in the Jordan. And immediately, coming up from the water, He saw the heavens parting and the Spirit descending upon Him like a dove."

Introduction: Like a Master Teacher, the Lord uses object lessons and symbols to help us visualize the reality of His truth. When it comes to God Himself, symbols were never intended to be little artistic ideas about Him, but ways in which the reality of the invisible might penetrate the visible, helping us see and know Him better. This morning, in looking at seven biblical symbols of the Holy Spirit, the purpose is not just to study objective theology, but also to allow Him to subjectively penetrate our hearts. In other words, when we say that the Holy Spirit is like rain, the purpose isn't thinking, "Oh! The Spirit is like rain." The purpose is to get wet! The Spirit's main job is to glorify Christ—to help us see Christ more, obey better, and to love Him more deeply.

1. **The Holy Spirit Comes as Rain.** Refreshing us where there has been dryness and barrenness (Joel 2:23–29) and restoring us where there has been loss (Isa. 28:11–12). The "pouring out" Peter refers to at Pentecost (Acts 2:17) is not an abstract use of the word; it has to do with "latter rain" that brought about the hastening of the harvest and fruitful crops. When the lawn goes through a long hot day, it dries up and needs refreshing rain. The Spirit comes to bring refreshing and restoration.

2. **The Holy Spirit Comes as Rivers.** Rivers are channels or conduits to places where refreshing water is needed. In John 7:37–39, Jesus promised the Holy Spirit would flow as "rivers of living water" after His Ascension. The Lord wants you to become an overflowing tributary of His Spirit's fullness to others.

3. **The Holy Spirit Comes as Wind.** The Spirit, coming as wind, depicts His power and guidance. When Jesus told Nicodemus about the new birth (John 3:8), He told him that the work of the Spirit in a person's life was

like a gentle wisp of a breeze. You can't see where it comes from or where it goes, but we can attest to times when God has come and dealt with us, and no human being knew how it happened.

4. **The Holy Spirit Comes as Oil.** The anointing, the oil of Scripture, is directly related to the Spirit's work in our life (2 Cor. 1:21–22). The Holy Spirit's anointing makes us sensitive (1 John 2:20) and gives us wisdom in the practicals of everyday life. All the primary offices of Scripture involve anointing:

   A. **Prophets:** We are to speak the Word of the Lord, and the Spirit gives us words of comfort, exhortation, and counsel for others.

   B. **Priests:** The Lord wants to anoint us so that our worship doesn't become stale, habitual, or formal.

   C. **Kings:** It takes fresh anointing from the Spirit for the authority of His life to happen through us so we can move in confidence in ruling and managing our homes, business, and relationships. The Lord also wants to anoint us with the oil of rejoicing when we have been overcome by the spirit of mourning.

5. **The Holy Spirit Comes as Wine.** We are not disallowed from enjoying a number of things in life, but you can find out how much we're living the Jesus-life by how much we need the stimulants of the world. God has given the Spirit as wine (Eph. 5:18). In the Gospels, Jesus described the new work of God, conveyed by the Spirit, as new wine coming into old vessels.

>>> sermon continued on following page

APPROPRIATE HYMNS AND SONGS

Wind of the Spirit, Russ Rosen/Sandy Rosen/Mike Oshiro; © 1989 Rise Up Music (Admin. by Big Tree Music.).

There's a River of Joy, Taran Ash/James Mott/Matthew Pryce; © 1997 King'sway Thankyou Music (Admin. by EMI Christian Music Publishing.).

Spirit of the Living God, Daniel Iverson; © 1935. Renewed 1963 Birdwing Music (Admin. by EMI Christian Music Publishing.).

Spirit Holy Wind, Patti Ridings; © 1990 Ariose Music (Admin. by EMI Christian Music Publishing.).

Send a Great Revival, B.B. McKinney; © 1925. Renewed 1952 Broadman Press (Admin. by Genevox Music Group.).

6. **The Holy Spirit Comes as Fire.** The Holy Spirit comes as fire to probe the inner recesses of life and to refine us as gold is refined in the fire (Isa. 4). He wants to enflame us with a passion for His work (Acts 2:3).

7. **The Holy Spirit Comes as a Dove.** The dove is gentle and a symbol of peace. The Spirit wants to rest upon you—not just sweeping throughout the world as a tidal wave of revival, but He wants to come to you personally.

Conclusion: For the next week, take one symbol of the Holy Spirit each day and invite Him to minister the richness of the Spirit to you. Ask Him to:
- Pour **rain** on you.
- Open **rivers** in you.
- Breathe **wind** in your life.
- Anoint you with **oil.**
- Fill you with holy **wine.**
- Refine and temper you with **fire.**
- Send the Holy Spirit to **come** to you as a dove.

FOR THE BULLETIN

❂ On June 8, 328, Athanasius was named Bishop of Alexandria, the highest ecclesiastical office in the East. During his 46 years as bishop, he combated heresy and fearlessly proclaimed the gospel. He was banished four times from his church and spent a total of 20 years in exile. ❂ The founder of Islam, Mohammed, died on this day in 632. He did not rise again. ❂ John Huss, the Bohemian Reformer, was sentenced to death on June 8, 1415. The night before he had suffered from toothache, vomiting, and headache, yet he defended himself using the example of St. Paul as his model. He was burned on July 6th. ❂ On June 8, 1794, a disciple of Rousseau named Robespierre and the French National Convention formally inaugurated a new religion. It was a form of deism, the belief that there is a God who, having created the universe, more or less disappeared. ❂ The German composer Robert A. Schumann was born on this day in 1819. He wrote the tune Canonbury, which became the setting for the hymn, "Lord Speak to Me That I May Speak." ❂ President Andrew Jackson died on this day in 1845. After resisting the witness of his wife Rachel for many years, Jackson became a Christian after her death. To a friend he said: "I have full confidence in the goodness and mercy of God. The Bible is true. Upon that sacred volume I rest my hope for eternal salvation, through the merits and blood of our blessed Lord and Savior Jesus Christ."

Burned Ropes

When the three Hebrew children were thrown into the furnace, not only were their lives spared, their clothes didn't burn. But the ropes holding them in bondage burned. By the "spirit of judgment"—or deliverance—"and burning" the Holy Spirit burns away the binding things that the enemy has imposed on us.

—*Jack Hayford*

The Theology of the Spirit

The Father is made of none, neither created nor begotten. The Son is of the Father alone, not made, nor created, but begotten. The Holy Spirit is of the Father and the Son: not made, nor created, nor begotten, but proceeding.

—*The Athanasian Creed*

God Is Light

God is light and in Him is no darkness at all. We know the Godhead consists of Three Persons: the Father, the Son, and the Holy Spirit. The Father corresponds to the chemical rays of sunlight; No man hath seen God at any time. The Son, who is the light of the world, corresponds to the light rays, the One whom we can see but not feel. The Holy Spirit corresponds to the heat rays, since He is felt in the lives of believers but never seen.

—*M. R. DeHaan*, in *The Chemistry of the Blood*

Spotlight

In his book, *Life in the Spirit,* Robertson McQuilkin writes: "Imagine the following: the President of the United States comes to speak at your local high school auditorium. The band strikes up, "Hail to the Chief" as the president strides to the microphone. The spotlight follows his every step. Suddenly the crowd, as one, rises and—what's this? They turn their backs to the stage and, pointing to the balcony, erupt in applause for the fine performance of the spotlight operator! Absurd? Of course, but it illustrates a truth about the Spirit. The Spirit glorifies—shines the spotlight on—the Son."

WORSHIP HELPS

Call to Worship:

"Do you not know that you are the temple of God and that the Spirit of God dwells in you? For you were bought with a price; therefore, glorify God!" (1 Cor. 3:16; 6:20).

Pastoral Prayer:

For today's pastoral prayer, try reciting in prayer (or singing) all four stanzas of "Come, Thou Almighty King." You may know this hymn by heart in its entirety. The verses begin:

- Come, Thou Almighty King, Help us Thy name to sing. . .
- Come, Thou Incarnate Word, Gird on Thy mighty sword. . .
- Come, Holy Comforter, Thy sacred witness bear. . .
- To Thee, great One in Three, Eternal praises be. . .

Responsive Reading:

Leader: Therefore, brethren, we are debtors—not to the flesh, to live according to the flesh.

People: For if you live according to the flesh you will die; but if by the Spirit you put to death the deeds of the body, you will live.

Leader: For as many as are led by the Spirit of God, these are sons of God. For you did not receive the spirit of bondage again to fear, but you received the Spirit of adoption by whom we cry out, "Abba, Father."

People: The Spirit Himself bears witness with our spirit that we are children of God;

Leader: and if children, then heirs—heirs of God and joint heirs with Christ, if indeed we suffer with Him, that we may also be glorified together.

(Taken from Romans 8:12–17)

Additional Sermons and Lesson Ideas

God's Prayer Requests

Date preached:

SCRIPTURE: Various passages

INTRODUCTION: If the Lord Himself spoke audibly at one of our meetings, what prayer requests would He share? Scripture gives several, but somehow these are the requests we often neglect.

1. "Pray for the peace of Jerusalem" (Ps. 122:6). We must pray for a resolution of the conflict in the Middle East.
2. "For all men, for kings and all who are in authority" (1 Tim. 2:1–4). The apostles evangelized during the *Pax Roma*, a time of peace that allowed the gospel to spread quickly. Paul wanted those conditions to continue. We must pray that the gospel will be unhindered by war and conflict.
3. "Pray for those who spitefully use you and persecute you" (Matt. 5:44). We must pray for our enemies, for those persecuting the church today.
4. "Pray the Lord of the harvest to send out laborers into His harvest" (Matt. 9:37, 38).
5. "Pray for one another, that you may be healed" (James 5:15).

CONCLUSION: God forbid that we should pray about everything except what He Himself has commanded us to remember.

"Give It a Rest"

Date preached:

By Drew Wilkerson

SCRIPTURE: Exodus 31:12–13

INTRODUCTION: Keeping the Sabbath holy seems old fashioned as it becomes increasingly hard to take time to rest one day out of the week. Why should we still honor God with a Sabbath day of rest? The Bible gives us three great reasons.

1. It is a Commandment. God told us to do it. We should respect His wisdom.
2. It is a Covenant. God loves us. He doesn't want us to forget what He has done.
3. It is a Commitment. God is responsible for us. He wants us to become holy.

CONCLUSION: Keeping the Sabbath holy seems outdated to us, but it isn't to God. It is a teaching that is worth revisiting. It is a conviction worth implementing.

Table Talk in the Pastor's Home: Toxic or Terrific?

Mike, 36, had grown up in parsonages where his spirit was eventually poisoned toward church. As we discussed his PK years, he sounded embittered, wanting little to do with the Lord. "Not after the way my dad was treated," he said. "Every night I'd hear something else that someone had said or done, and I saw how it hurt my folks."

I understand how he feels. My own experiences in ministry have been positive, but every pastoral family lives in a fishbowl, and sometimes the eyes peering through the water can be piercing. How can we keep a wholesome atmosphere as church-talk flies through the air, day-by-day, year after year?

Attitudes are contagious as smallpox. My negative emotions can infect my family like a plague. On the other hand, if I love my congregation and keep an enthusiastic attitude, it filters into my family's hearts, too. Sharing shoptalk at home requires more wisdom than rules, but here are some checks and balances which have worked for us.

For starters, I never break confidences, and neither does my wife. If someone comes to either of us for counsel, we don't share that information, even with each another. I tell Katrina *who* I've been counseling, but not *why*. While it occasionally makes her curious, she's mature enough to just drop it in her To-Pray-About File.

We do, however, discuss almost everything else that happens. I've found that Katrina feels overlooked if I clam up about church matters, for we're in this work together. Furthermore, her advice is invaluable, particularly if she has hesitations about my goals or plans. Her instincts are almost always right.

In any case, it's the tone of our discussion that is all important. I try to major on the positives while minimizing negatives. Regarding criticism, for example, I've generally been able to take it in stride, but my wife and children tend to react defensively on my behalf, so I'm cautious in discussing such things. A few years ago, I heard grumblings around the church that I was gone too much, away from office and pulpit. "Actually, they're right," I admitted as Katrina and I discussed it. "I *have* accepted too many speaking engagements." Instead of reacting to the criticism, our conversation centered on how I could reduce the outside demands on my time.

I've also learned I can lower my family's esteem for parishioners by relaying incidents better kept to myself. Recently I had a leader who lost his temper and erupted in a lava flow of language. Needing to get it off my chest, I almost shared it with my wife and children, but I knew it would leave them disappointed in someone I wanted them to respect. So I kept silent.

When there are victories in the ministry, I share those. It boosts our morale to know we've helped a teenager in jail or a family who needed milk or medicines for their baby. When someone compliments us, I try to noise it around the house, too. Recently I received a note commending my youngest child about how she had welcomed a guest at church. It pleased her when I told her. On another occasion, I told my middle daughter, "There are a lot of people in this church who love you." Her response: "I know, Dad. It makes me feel good to know people are praying for me."

It makes me feel good, too. Yet occasionally, when I'm tired and frustrated, my attitude will nosedive and I'll stalk through the house calling down the Imprecatory Psalms on an unfortunate church member. It fills my home with toxic fumes. In those cases, I revisit the issue quickly, apologizing and offering healthier insights into the situation. I may gingerly defend the people who provoked me. When I can help my family view difficult people empathetically, it's like opening the windows to dispel the poisonous gas.

The deepest hurts I trust with God alone. Here my journal helps, and my little desk against the wall where I can pray. Somehow He always repairs my morale and restores my soul. When my own cup "runneth over," my family gets the overflow, and in return I sometimes hear them say, "I just love our church, Dad. It's the greatest!"

Those are words I wish Mike's dad could have heard him say, too.

JUNE 15, 2003

Faithful Fathering

Date preached:

By Timothy Beougher

Scripture: Ephesians 6:4: "And you, fathers, do not provoke your children to wrath, but bring them up in the training and admonition of the Lord."

Introduction: Today is Father's Day, a day to honor Dad for his special role in the family. Someone described a father like this: "When you're small, a father has two huge hands that lift you onto his shoulders and that put worms on hooks better than any other hands in the world. A father is the man who sits at the head of the table and gets two lamb chops when you get one. He is nice to be near when there's thunder and lightning—or trouble. A father understands when you think you're too old to be kissed good night. He's the one who teaches you how to tie your tie, who buys your first razor, who gives you permission to take the car, and who comforts mom when you aren't home on time. Sometimes he helps you fail algebra. A father spends most of his life reaching in his pocket for money to give someone for something. And his favorite words are, 'Now when I was your age . . .'" Today we're going to examine what it means to be a successful father, but this message is for mothers, too. The immediate context of Ephesians 6:1–4 refers to both parents. Successful parenting is attempting to raise our children in the fear of God, a three-step process:

I. **Do Not Provoke Your Children.** This instruction, which presupposes the fact of parental authority, tells parents not to use that authority to abuse or put down their child. Parents abuse their authority by making irritating or unreasonable demands on their children, or by making no allowance for the inexperience and immaturity of children. See Colossians 3:21. Dan Benson, in his book *The Total Man,* surveyed a number of families and found that for every *positive* statement made in the homes there were ten *negative* ones. We men have an amazing capacity to be critical. We need to learn to see the positive in our children and to frequently praise their strengths rather than continually harping on their weaknesses.

2. **Bring Them Up in the Training of the Lord.** The phrase, "bring them up" contains the idea of nurturing or nourishing. This involves:
   A. **Prayer.** Praying for your children, especially "praying Scripture."
   B. **Modeling.** Values are more caught than taught. While children may not be good at listening to their parents, they never fail to imitate them.
   C. **Time.** Our children need our presence more than our presents. In a study by Cornell University, it was found that the average dad spends about 37 seconds a day with his small children.
   D. **Discipline.** Not just punishment, but retraining. (See Heb. 12:6 and Prov. 13:24.)

3. **Bring Them Up in the Instruction of the Lord.** A consistent life is not enough; we must provide verbal instruction and biblical teachings for our children. The phrase "of the Lord" indicates that the instruction is given by the parents, but it proceeds from the Lord. The suggestion is that the Lord nurtures the child through the parents. We must recognize that God has given us the responsibility to provide for our children in a physical, an emotional, *and* a spiritual sense. According to Deuteronomy 6, one of the best ways to do this is by spontaneously sharing Bible verses with your children as the occasion demands, as you sit at home and as you drive down the road, when you get up and when you go to bed.

Conclusion: Here's the way someone paraphrased 1 Corinthians 13 for parents: "If I speak to my children with remarkable words of wisdom and have no love, I'm a two-year-old banging on a dishpan. If I spend all of my salary

>>> sermon continued on following page

APPROPRIATE HYMNS AND SONGS

A Christian Home, Barbara Hart/Jean Sibelius; © 1965, 1986 Singspiration Music (Admin. by Brentwood-Benson Music Publishing, Inc.).

Family Song, Mary Lang; © 1981 Maranatha Music!

In Our Households Heavenly Father, Marie J. Post/Dale Grutenhuis; © 1987 CRC Publications.

In the Circle of Each Home, Bryan Jeffrey Leech; © Fred Boch Music Company.

Silent Strength, Steve Millikan/Ray Boltz; © 1989 Shepherd Boy Music.

providing the best for them, but have not love, I gain nothing. Love waits with incredible patience for children to develop self-discipline. Love does not puff up in arrogance and pride when an adolescent daughter tests the limits of her newfound independence. Love does not resort to violence when a teenage son talks back. It does not overreact when a child fails to listen or resent the rebellious youth who refuses to accept the message or the messenger. Love does not laugh contemptuously when the child gets what he deserves, but glows with contentment at every small accomplishment. It carries its own burden yet stoops to pick up a tired child. It believes the best about each child, hopes the best for that child, and endures the pain inflicted by the child. Love simply never quits."

FOR THE BULLETIN

❁ On June 15, 1215, King John put his seal on the Magna Carta at Runnymede, which had been heavily influenced by Archbishop Stephen Langton. ❁ On June 15, 1520, Pope Leo X issued his famous *Exsurge Domine*, which began "Arise, O Lord . . . a wild boar has invaded your vineyard." The wild boar was Martin Luther who was threatened with excommunication if he would not recant his beliefs. ❁ On June 15, 1551, Theodore Beza took sick while at Lausanne during the plague. His worried friend, John Calvin, wrote: "I am concerned about the loss the church would suffer if in the midst of his career he should suddenly be removed by death. I hope . . . that he will be given back to us in answer to our prayers." Calvin's prayers were answered. Beza had yet a half-century to minister. ❁ Samuel J. Mills was dedicated to foreign missions by his mother before his birth in 1783. He was converted to Christ at age 17, and was a participant in the famous 1806 "Haystack Prayer Meeting" that helped launch America's first foreign missionary program. He died at age 35 on this day in 1818 while returning from a missionary trip to Africa. ❁ On June 15, 1951, missionary William C. Easton was leading a youth service in Columbia, South America. The police burst in and seized him and four young men. They were clubbed, whipped, dunked in cold water, stripped, and forced to roll in hot ashes. The next morning upon his release, Rev. Easton told the police, "I forgive you in the name of Jesus Christ."

STATS, STORIES AND MORE

Praying for Our Children

- Once after I had earnestly prayed for my child about a certain matter involving a phone call, the Lord allowed the exact opposite of what I had requested. I was bewildered and angry. But that morning's Bible reading took me to Psalm 18, and I was struck by verse 30: "As for God, His way is perfect." Later in the day I came across this quote by Ruth Graham: "How often has God said no to my earnest prayers that He might answer my deepest longings, give me something more, something better."
  —*Robert J. Morgan*

- "But Thou, taking Thy own secret counsel and noting the real point of her desire, didst not grant what she was then asking in order to grant to her the thing that she had always been asking"—*Augustine*, about his mother Monica, who prayed earnestly that her son would not sail to Italy, for she feared the bad influences on him there. Despite her prayers, Augustine *did* go to Italy—and there found Christ.

- "When we pray for our children, we are asking God to make His presence a part of their lives and work powerfully in their behalf. That doesn't mean there will always be an *immediate* response. Sometimes it can take days, weeks, or even years. But our prayers are never lost or meaningless. If we are praying, something is happening, whether we see it or not."
  —*Stormie Omartian* in *The Power of a Praying Parent*

- "Patience frees the Lord to answer prayer in His way and in His time. God never is in a rush, even though we usually are. Waiting on God allows Him to provide the best answer."
  —*T. W. Hunt* and *Claude King* in *The Mind of Christ*

- "God wants us to trust Him, no matter what He does. There is a heavenly carelessness that leaves it all with Jesus and doesn't become upset when He does things contrary to what we expected."
  —*Vance Havner*

WORSHIP HELPS

Call to Worship:
"Sing to the LORD a new song, And His praise from the ends of the earth. . . . Let the wilderness and its cities lift up their voice. . . . Let them shout from the top of the mountains. Let them give glory to the LORD, and declare His praise in the coastlands" (Is. 42:10–12).

Scripture Reading Medley:
The father shall make known your truth to the children. Only take heed to yourself, and diligently keep yourself, lest you forget the things your eyes have seen, and lest they depart from your heart all the days of your life. And teach them to your children and your grandchildren. I will utter sayings of old, which our fathers have told us. We will not hide them from their children, telling to the generation to come the praises of the LORD, and His strength and His wonderful works that He has done. But you must continue in the things which you have learned and been assured of, knowing from whom you have learned them, and that from childhood you have known the Holy Scriptures, which are able to make you wise for salvation through faith which is in Christ Jesus. Hear, my children, the instruction of a father, and give attention to know understanding; for I give you good doctrine. But as for me and my house, we will serve the LORD. (Taken from Deut. 6:9; Josh. 24:15; Ps. 78:2–4; Prov. 4:1, 2; Isa. 38:19; 2 Tim. 3:14, 15.)

Offertory Prayer:
Our Father, how can we say thanks for the things You have done for us. Things so undeserved. Blessings so unceasing. Grace so freely given. Please accept our tithes and offerings today as tokens of our appreciation and gratitude. We love you, dear Lord, and from this love we return to You a portion of Your bounty to us. In Jesus' name, Amen.

Additional Sermons and Lesson Ideas

Old Advice for New Fathers

Date preached:

SCRIPTURE: Miscellaneous Passages in Deuteronomy

INTRODUCTION: Deuteronomy, Moses' last message to Israel, repeatedly stresses the importance of passing the mercy and the message of God on to the next generation.

1. Deuteronomy 4:6, 9. Take heed to God's truth, keep yourself, and teach your children and grandchildren.
2. Deuteronomy 6:6–9. These words shall be in your heart and you shall teach them to your children when you sit at home and walk along the way.
3. Deuteronomy 11:18–21. Lay up these words, teaching them to your children.
4. Deuteronomy 29:29. The things that are revealed belong to us and to our children forever.
5. Deuteronomy 31:12, 13. Gather the people together that the children might hear and learn to fear the Lord.

CONCLUSION: The responsibility of teaching children about the Lord and His Word is not primarily given to the church (though we have a part)—but of the home and of the father.

Living Your Faith in the Workplace
By Kevin Riggs

Date preached:

SCRIPTURE: Colossians 3:22–25

INTRODUCTION: God created work to give us a sense of dignity, to teach us responsibility, and to give our lives accomplishment. What difference will your faith make on the job site? Paul mentions four distinguishing marks of those who live out their faith at work.

1. Submission (v. 22). Obedience and submission in the work place is how you show "reverence" to your Lord.
2. Diligence (v. 23). When you look at your job as "working for men" you can get angry, depressed, dissatisfied, apathetic. When you look at it as "working for the Lord" you will be grateful and diligent.
3. Excellence (v. 24). Our reward is not our paycheck, but what the Lord will give us, and He has the best retirement plan around.
4. Honesty (v. 25). If you realize you are really working for God, then you will know that when you are dishonest, you are cheating God as well as men.

CONCLUSION: The Christian's ultimate employer is the Lord. We work for Him with all our heart, and from Him comes our reward.

A MISSIONS SERMON

From Here to Timbuktu

Scripture: Acts 1:8: But you shall receive power when the Holy Spirit has come upon you; and you shall be witnesses to Me in Jerusalem, and in all Judea and Samaria, and to the end of the earth.

Introduction: Almost everyone loves to travel, but few people have ever been to Timbuktu. This city of about 20,000, known locally as Tombouctou, is located in west central Africa, in the country of Mali. Somehow through the years, Timbuktu has gotten the reputation of being the most remote and inaccessible place on earth. That isn't true, but one thing we know—the Lord wants to bring the gospel to the primarily-Islamic people of Timbuktu. From here to Timbuktu, the Lord intends for His word to be proclaimed across all the earth. There is no nation, no tribe, no hamlet on the face of the globe that He does not want the gospel to go. Jesus said, "You shall receive power when the Holy Spirit has come upon you; and you shall be witnesses to Me in Jerusalem, and in all Judea and Samaria, and to the end of the earth." In other words, "You will be my witnesses from here to Timbuktu. You will be my witnesses to the last place on earth." What could compel us to leave hearth and homeland to go to the regions beyond? What would cause us to give our money, our means, our young people, our children, our very lives in this effort? There are three unquenchable motives:

1. **The Character of God.** Missions was throbbing in God's heart when He sent Jesus Christ to die for all the world. As someone said, "Missions didn't really begin with "Go ye into all the world. . . ." It began with "For God so loved the world. . . ." The first two letters of the words *God* and *gospel* are the same: GO! God loves His creation, and He is not willing for any to perish. Before the foundation of the world, He devised a plan of redemption, and we are His ambassadors in its proclamation.

2. **The Commandment of Christ.** Each of the four Gospels contains the Great Commission (Matt. 28:18–20; Mark 16:15; Luke 24:45–49; John 20:21). So often, when we tell our children to do something, we preface it with that word "Go!" It is a word of commandment and commission.

It's a word that frequently occurs throughout the Bible. In Matthew's Gospel, for example, the word "go" occurs 70 times:

A. Go your way; and as you have believed, so let it be done for you (8:13).
B. Go rather to the lost sheep of the house of Israel (10:6).
C. Go and tell John the things which you hear and see (11:4).
D. Go into the highways, and as many as you find, invite (22:9).
E. Go quickly and tell His disciples that He is risen from the dead (28:7).
F. Go therefore and make disciples of all the nations (28:19).

3. **The Condition of the Lost.** One of the most eloquent pleas for missions in the Bible comes from the lips of a dead man—the rich man in hell who lifted up his voice pleading for someone to go to his brothers and warn them of the coming wrath (Luke 16:27–28). There are currently 6.1 billion people on earth, and more than 5 billion of them are lost. The best calculations of missiologists tell us that about 600 million people claim a personal, saving relationship with Jesus Christ. There are an additional 1.4 billion "cultural Christians" who are associated in some way with the Christian religion. Another 2.5 billion people are non-Christian, but have some access to the gospel message. But more than 1.6 billion people have virtually no access to the gospel.

Conclusion: The Lord expects us to go, to pray, to give, and to be globally-minded Christians. In his book, *The Great Omission,* Robertson McQuilkin points out that in the days before William Carey, the father of the modern Protestant missionary movement, the Moravians from Herrnhut considered a support base of four adequate to keep one missionary at the front. Using that formula, America's forty million evangelicals could support ten million overseas workers. Instead, there are currently about 33,000 fully-supported Christian workers from America serving overseas for more than four years. "The truth is," says McQuilkin, "less than one percent of full-time Christian workers are engaged in evangelistic ministry among the unevangelized of the world. Is this the way the Commander-in-Chief would assign His troops? Or is someone not listening?"

JUNE 22, 2003

SUGGESTED SERMON

Jonah's Journey

Date preached:

By Melvin Worthington

Scripture: Jonah 1–4, especially Jonah 1:1–3: "Now the word of the LORD came to Jonah the son of Amittai, saying, 'Arise, go to Nineveh, that great city, and cry out against it; for their wickedness has come up before Me.' But Jonah arose to flee to Tarshish from the presence of the LORD."

Introduction: The Book of Jonah differs from other minor prophets. It is a narrative, biographical rather than prophetic. It's the story of a servant, a storm, and a sovereign God. Jonah is God-called but disobedient; the storm is God-appointed and God-controlled, and God's powerful attributes are evident throughout the story. Jonah himself is a strange paradox: a prophet of God, and yet fleeing from God; thrown into the sea, yet alive; a preacher of repentance, yet needing repentance. He is pictured as sanctified in spots, self-willed, godly, courageous, prayerful, obedient after chastisement, bigoted, concerned with his own reputation, zealous for the Lord. As if this was not enough, Jonah is a great missionary book, and Jonah himself a great evangelist.

I. **The Rebellious Prophet** (ch. 1).
   A. **The Word Heard** (vv. 1, 2). God spoke to Jonah and instructed him to go to the wicked city of Nineveh and cry against it because of its wickedness. This word from God was a definite word, a disturbing word, a distinct word, and a disobeyed word.
   B. **The Will Hardened** (v. 3). Jonah *understood* God's Word and yet he was *uncomfortable* with God's Word and *unwilling* to obey God's Word. He acted as people often do who don't like God's commands— he rebelled and ran away, thus removing himself as far as possible from being under the influence of God.
   C. **The Wrath Hurled** (vv. 4–16). The truths embedded in these verses include the *directed storm* (v. 4), the *discovered sin* (vv. 5–13), and the *devoted sailors* (vv. 14–16).
   D. **The Whale Handy** (v. 17). The sailors cast Jonah into the sea and a huge fish swallowed him. Jonah was in the belly of the fish three days

and three nights. Truths found in this verse include the *prepared fish*, the *providential fact*, the *prophetic figure,* and the *prophet's fate*.

2. **The Repentant Prophet** (ch. 2).
    A. **The Servant Speaks** (vv. 1–9). These verses record Jonah's *supplication* (v. 1), *suffering* (v. 2), *statement* (vv. 3–6), *submission* (vv. 7–8), and *singing* (v. 9). Jonah's prayer reveals a note of triumph. He prayed out of the belly of the fish but with an absolute confidence in God and in His deliverance. He had disobeyed God and God had disciplined him and now he abandoned his disobedience and vowed to be obedient—obey God's Word.
    B. **The Sovereign Speaks** (v. 10). This verse reminds us of the *faithfulness* of Jehovah, the *freedom* of Jonah, and the *focus* on Jehovah and Jonah. God caused the fish to vomit Jonah up on dry land. God hears and heeds the prayers of His people.

3. **The Re-commissioned Prophet** (ch. 3).
    A. **The Willing Prophet** (vv. 1–4). *The Renewed Commission (vv. 1–2).* God is a God of second chances. Illustrations abound that confirm this—Peter, Thomas, John Mark, and Samson. God disciplines Jonah for his rebellion, Jonah repents, and the word of the Lord comes a second time. This time Jonah is ready to obey God's word. He recognized that this second chance was undeserved, unexpected, unparalleled, unique, and unequivocal. God did not change the task but changed His man. *The Ready Compliance (vv. 3–4).* Jonah is as ready to obey now as he was to disobey in the beginning.

>>> *sermon continued on following page*

APPROPRIATE HYMNS AND SONGS

Trust and Obey, Rev. John H. Sammis/Daniel B. Towner; Public Domain.

A Man with a Perfect Heart, Jack Hayford; © 1995 Annamarie Music (Admin. by Maranatha! Music.).

Blessed Are the Broken, David Baroni; © 1994 Integrity's Praise! Music.

Jonah, Ron Hamiliton; © 1981 Musical Ministries (Admin. by Majesty Music, Inc.).

Where He Leads Me, E.W. Blandy/John S. Norris; Public Domain.

B. **The Wicked People** (vv. 5–9). The people of Nineveh responded to the message of Jonah. They *believed* (v. 5). It affected their *behavior* (v. 5). The repentance *began* with the leaders and extended to the people (vv. 6–7). They *beseeched* God for mercy (vv. 8–9).

C. **The Wondrous Pardon** (v. 10). God saw their conduct and spared the city. Divine judgment was averted.

4. **The Raging Prophet** (ch. 4). Jonah was filled with rage when God spared the city.

A. **The Grieved Prophet** (vv. 1–5). His *grief* (v. 1) in light of God's action reveals his shortsightedness, selfishness, stubbornness, and superficiality. His *grip* (v. 2) indicated that he knew this would be God's response to the repentance of the people of Nineveh and he didn't want God to withhold judgment. His *groaning* (v. 3). Jonah wanted to die. His *grace* (v. 4). God responded to Jonah's attitude and actions with gentle, gracious grace. His *grudge* (v. 5). He went out of the city and made a booth and sat in its shadow waiting to see what God would do.

B. **The Gracious Provision** (vv. 6–11). God dealt with Jonah by using: the *plant* (v. 6), the *pest* (v. 7), the *passion* (v. 8), and the *principle* (vv. 9–11).

Conclusion: The love of God in our hearts will constrain us to that full commitment which God sought from Jonah and which he received so joyfully from Paul. To be an effective servant of the Lord one must, like Jonah, die to the lusts, the attractions, allurements, and rewards which man has to offer and be content with the compensation which God gives. We must be worldwide witness. We must hear God's call to a solemn, sacred stewardship of life and possessions.

FOR THE BULLETIN

❊ The Third General Council of the church convened in Ephesus on June 22, 431, primarily to deal with the Nestorian heresy. ❊ Queen Elizabeth's Prayer Book was published on this day in 1559. ❊ America's first "Blue Laws" requiring church attendance in Virginia were enacted on June 22, 1611. Everyone was required, morning and afternoon, to attend services on the Sabbath. Penalty for the first offense was economic sanction; second offenders were whipped. ❊ Commentator Matthew Henry died on June 22, 1714. ❊ On this day in 1750, Jonathan Edwards was dismissed from his pulpit in Northampton, Massachusetts by popular vote, after serving there 23 years.

STATS, STORIES AND MORE

Is Jonah Historical?

"It is a mistake (based in part on the difficulty some readers have in coming to terms with the miraculous character of the story line) to assume that the events and actions of the book are not historical in nature. While the story line is unusual, it is presented as normal history. Further, Jesus used the story of Jonah as an analogy of His own impending death and resurrection (Matt. 12:39–41). Jesus' analogy depends on the recognition of two historical realities: (1) the historical experience of Jonah in the belly of the great fish, and (2) the historical experience of the repentance of the people of Nineveh based on the preaching of Jonah (Luke 11:29–32). Indeed, the phrase 'the sign of the prophet Jonah' must have been a recurring phrase in the teaching of Christ, for it is found on more than one occasion in Matthew's account of Christ's ministry (Matt. 16:4). Thus any view of the Book of Jonah that does not assume it describes historical events is obliged to explain away the clear words of Jesus to the contrary."—From *Nelson's New Illustrated Bible Commentary,* edited by *Earl Radmacher, Ronald B. Allen,* and *H. Wayne House.*

Obedience

A missionary translator was endeavoring to find a word for "obedience" in the native language. This was a virtue seldom practiced among the people into whose language he wanted to translate the New Testament. As he returned home from the village one day, he whistled for his dog and it came running at full speed. An old man, seeing this, said, admiringly in the native tongue, "Your dog is all ear." Immediately the missionary knew he had his word for obedience.—from *Encyclopedia of 7700 Illustrations* by *Paul Lee Tan.*

WORSHIP HELPS

Call to Worship:
"Come we that love the Lord, and let our joys be known. Join in a song with accord and thus surround the throne"—*Isaac Watts*

Pastoral Prayer:
We are distracted today, O Father, many of us. We have heavy loads, multiplied burdens, busy lives, and short attention spans. Please forgive our scattered thoughts, and teach us now to "stay" our minds on You. Lord, we would see Jesus today. Lord, we would cast our cares on You. Lord, we would rest ourselves in Your mercy. Give us today a wondrous sense of Your magnificent presence, and in the light of Your glory may our perspective be healed and helped. We pray in Jesus' name. Amen.

Scripture Reading Medley:
Your ears shall hear a word behind you, saying, "This is the way, walk in it," whenever you turn to the right hand or whenever you turn to the left. I will instruct you and teach you in the way you should go; I will guide you with My eye. Do not be like the horse or like the mule, which have no understanding, which must be harnessed with bit and bridle, else they will not come near you. Trust in the LORD with all your heart, and lean not on your own understanding; in all your ways acknowledge Him, and He shall direct your paths. (*Taken from Ps. 32:8; Prov. 3:5–6; Isa. 30:21.*)

Kids Talk

Have a fish bowl. Describe the fish to the children and talk God's creative genius. He is able to create funny little creatures that live under the water and move by wagging their tails. Ask: "If God can make a *little* fish, don't you think He could make a *big* one? Jonah 1:17 says, 'The Lord had prepared a great fish to swallow Jonah.' Some people don't believe that, but I do. After all, the real miracle is that God could make something as complex and wonderful as fish to begin with. The size, large or small, is just a detail."

Additional Sermons and Lesson Ideas

God's Three Great Abilities

Date preached:

SCRIPTURE: Ezra 1:1

INTRODUCTION: The phrase "God is able," which occurs five times in the New King James Version of the Bible, is a truth found throughout the Bible. Even here in the first verse of this oft-neglected book, we find that God is able:

1. To Keep His Promises. "That the word of the LORD by the mouth of Jeremiah might be fulfilled." (See Jer. 25:14 and 29:10. Also see Num. 23:19; Josh. 23:14, 1 Kings 8:56; and 1 Thess. 5:24.)
2. To Move Hearts. "The LORD stirred up the spirit of Cyrus king of Persia" ("moved the hearts"—NIV). (See verse 5. Also Prov. 21:1.)
3. To Guide History. "So that he made a proclamation throughout all his kingdom." Benjamin Franklin once addressed the Second Continental Congress, saying: "I have lived, Sir, a long time, and the longer I live, the more convincing proofs I see of this truth—that God governs in the affairs of men. And if a sparrow cannot fall to the ground without His notice, is it probable that an empire can rise without His aid?"

CONCLUSION: "And God is able to make all grace abound toward you" (2 Cor. 9:8).

Doing Something for God

Date preached:

SCRIPTURE: Ezra 7

INTRODUCTION: The last half of the Book of Ezra (chs. 7–10), tell us of the ministry of one of Israel's greatest rabbis. We, too, can be 'great' for God if we have:

1. The Word of God Within Us (vv. 1–10). The NIV says Ezra was "well-versed in the law."
2. The Mission of God Before Us (vv. 11–26). The letter from Artaxerxes detailed Ezra's mission.
3. The Hand of God Upon Us (vv. 27, 28). Phrases like "the hand of God was on us" (see v. 28) are frequent in these chapters.

CONCLUSION: If the Word is within us, the Lord will show us His mission, and we can know His hand of blessing on our work.

Green Leaf in Drought Time
By Isobel Kuhn

Meet Isobel Kuhn, dancer turned missionary, agnostic turned devotional writer, whose small collection of books are classics of honesty and insight.

Isobel was born in Toronto, Canada, just before Christmas in 1901. She grew up in a conservative Presbyterian home, but abandoned her faith at the University of British Columbia, plunging into endless rounds of theaters and parties. Her personality was vivacious, and she was an excellent dancer. These were the "Roaring Twenties," and Isobel danced away the nights and slept away the days.

By lengths, however, the Lord won back Isobel's heart, directed her to Moody Bible Institute, and brought her under the influence of the great missionary, J. O. Fraser, who was working among the Lisu of Southwest China. On October 11, 1928, Isobel sailed for China, where she and her soon-to-be husband, John Kuhn, worked among the Lisu until escaping from the Communists in 1950 by a daring trek over the 11,000-foot-high Pien Ma Pass into Burma.

Shortly afterward Isobel contracted breast cancer. Before her death in 1957, she said, "When I get to Heaven they aren't going to see much of me but my heels, for I'll be hanging over the golden wall keeping an eye on the Lisu Church."

It was Ruth Bell Graham who introduced me to Isobel Kuhn's books nearly thirty years ago. *Green Leaf in Drought Time* is my favorite. It's the story of Arthur and Wilda Matthews, among the last missionaries to leave China after the Communist Revolution. *Green Leaf* could be called a "devotionalized biography" in the tradition of Mrs. Howard Taylor, Amy Carmichael, and Elizabeth Elliot, in which dramatic biographical events become a classroom for teaching the reader the deeper truths of the Victorious Christian Life.

As it relates to the Matthews, for example, and their harrowing experiences within Communist China, Isobel writes, "And yet as trial piled upon trial; as the ground (their human comforts) grew so parched with drought that it threatened to crack open, their leaf was still green."

Isobel relates that during the darkest days of their detainment in China, Wilda daily heard gunfire from the nearby execution range where the Marxists were killing townspeople in mass numbers. She wondered when her own time would come, and she shuddered at what would happen to their little girl, Lilah, if she and Arthur should perish. They were near starvation, but the Communists wouldn't release their funds or issue exit visas. They were trapped, and every day seemed their last.

What good could possibly come out of such prolonged anxiety? Isobel points out that having explained the message of the Victorious Christian Life to the Chinese, the Matthews now had an even deeper, more lasting ministry. "There was an unseen Source of secret nourishment, which the Communists could not find and from which they could not cut them off. . . . The message above all others which the Chinese church needed was to see that truth lived out under circumstances equally harrowing as their own."

That is the theme of *Green Leaf.* God allows suffering, but provides a secret source of inward strength—what Isobel Kuhn calls "spiritual vigor." In a sense, this book is a vivid, extended illustration of the reality of Jeremiah 17:8: "He shall be as a tree planted by the waters, and that spreadeth out her roots by the river, and shall not see when heat cometh, but her leaf shall be green, and shall not be careful in the year of drought, neither shall cease from yielding fruit."

To save time and money, I'd suggest ordering several copies of *Green Leaf in Drought Time,* because after reading it, you'll want to pass it along to others.

While you're at it, you might as well order Isobel's other books. You'll be hooked. ❀

Other Books By Isobel Kuhn

- *By Searching: My Journey Through Doubt Into Faith* (Moody Press). The first half of Isobel's autobiography telling of her upbringing in Canada, her university years, her broken engagement, her turning to Christ, and her experiences at Moody Bible Institute.

- *In the Arena* (OMF Books). The second half of Isobel's autobiography which traces her years as a missionary in China and ends with her battle with the cancer that was to take her life.

- *Stones of Fire* (OMF Books). The true story of Mary, a young Lisu tribeswoman.

- *Nests Above the Abyss* (OMF Books). Classic stories of the power of the Holy Spirit to transform lives that are otherwise beyond hope.

- *Earthen Jar* (OMF Books)

- *Second Mile People* (OMF Books)

JUNE 29, 2003

The Upside-down Kingdom of Jesus

By Ed Dobson   *Date preached:*

Scripture: Mark 10:35–45, especially verses 44–45: "Whoever of you desires to be first shall be slave of all. For even the Son of Man did not come to be served, but to serve, and to give His life a ransom for many."

Introduction: This is our Lord's personal mission statement. If I'm to be an authentic follower of Christ, what marked His life ought to mark mine, and my personal mission statement ought to be "serving and giving." The opposite of that, of course, is to be served and to receive. I can live life with a passion to be served and to receive, or I can live with a passion to give and serve. Set your Bible down a moment and hold your hands in front of you. Clench one of your hands into a fist and leave the other open. This is the choice being a follower of Christ. Am I going to live with a clenched fist expecting others to serve me, receiving, accumulating, and getting? Or am I going to live with an open hand, giving and serving?

1. **Verse 35.** This statement is actually Christ's conclusion to a conversation with two of his disciples, which begin with a request: "Teacher, we want You to do for us whatever we ask." What an incredible request! Their view of following Jesus was not, "How can I serve Jesus?" but "What can Jesus do for me?" The root problem was selfishness.

2. **Verse 36.** Jesus responded with a question: "What do you want Me to do for you?" Matthew 20:21 adds, "in your kingdom." They believed Jesus was going to establish an earthly political kingdom, and they wanted to be Number 1 and Number 2 in that kingdom. What began as selfishness moved into pride. They wanted to be above the rest of the disciples. Where did this selfish, prideful attitude come from? You'd think that some of Jesus would have rubbed off on them. Three factors may have contributed to their attitude:

    A. They had a mother with great ambitions for her sons (see Matt. 20:20).

B. James and John were part of the inner circle and had been privy to some incredible spiritual moments, such as in Mark 9:1–13. We have to be careful with the spiritual moments God gives us that we don't allow spiritual knowledge and experience to build pride in our lives.

C. Their upper class status. Mark 1:20 speaks of their owning a business and overseeing employees. There were few fishing families in Galilee with the wealth to actually hire people to fish for them. Zebedee was a cut above the rest of the fishermen.

3. **Verse 37.** "Grant that we may sit on Your right hand and on Your left." We instinctively want everyone else and everything to meet our needs.

4. **Verses 38–44.** Jesus, saying "You do not know what you ask," offers two principles in response. First, the Cost of Leadership: "Are you able to drink the cup that I drink?" The path to glory and greatness always takes us through suffering and difficulty. Second, the Call to Leadership: His is an upside down kingdom. In the world, greatness is determined by how many people serve you. In Christ's kingdom greatness is determined by how many we serve. It's not a matter of authority and control but of humility and service.

5. **Verse 45.** Jesus concluded by saying He Himself exemplifies these principles. Obeying them is a process of becoming like Him.

>>> *sermon continued on following page*

APPROPRIATE HYMNS AND SONGS

Great Creator God, Jane Parker Huber/Henry Smart; © 1986 Jane Parker Huber (Admin. by Westminster John Knox Press.).

I Wonder Have I Done My Best for Jesus, Ensign Edwin Young/Harry Storrs; © 1924. Renewed Harry N. Storrs (Admin. by Brentwood-Benson Music Publishing, Inc.).

Jesu, Jesu, Tom Calvin; © 1969, 1989 Hope Publishing Company.

Make Me Your Servant, Russell Fragar; © 1993 Russell Fragar/Hillsong (Admin. by Integrity Music, Inc.).

May the Words of My Mouth, Terry Butler; © 1995 Mercy/Vineyard Publishing.

Conclusion: Am I living my life expecting others to serve me? My spouse? My children? The people at work? Or do I view those around me and my circumstances as opportunities to serve both Christ and others? Am I closed-fisted or open-handed? I don't mean we will never receive and that we should never be served—there are times when that happens—but I'm talking about the passion of our life. Receiving or giving? There are also church implications. This morning many of us are in the receiving mode, but have you also come with a passion to give? To worship? To serve? Much of our culture is designed to make us feel good. The radical message of Jesus counteracts that. The greater message this morning is, "Who's in control of my life? Why am I following Christ? What am I doing for Christ?" May the Lord Jesus take our lives and let them be consecrated, Lord, to Thee.

FOR THE BULLETIN

❋ On June 29, 48 B.C., Julius Caesar defeated Pompey at Pharsalus, becoming sole dictator of Rome. ❋ This is the traditional date for the crucifixion of St. Peter, who was reportedly executed upside down on June 29, A.D. 64. It is also the traditional date for the execution of the Apostle Paul who is said to have been executed on this day, perhaps in the year A.D. 67. ❋ Hildebrand was consecrated Pope Gregory VII on this day in 1073. He became one of the greatest popes in Christian history, a tireless advocate and reformer of the papacy. ❋ On June 29, 1685, the great English Puritan Richard Baxter was found guilty of unauthorized preaching and was confined to the Tower of London where he remained for eighteen months, during which time he continued writing. An early biographer wrote, "He continued his imprisonment nearly two years, during which he enjoyed more quietness than he had done for many years before." ❋ The first American Missionary society was organized on June 29, 1810—the American Board of Commissioners for Foreign Missions, in Bradford, Massachusetts, by the Congregationalists. ❋ On June 29, 1875, the first session of the famous Keswick Convention (pronounced Kes'-ick) convened in Keswick, England. The annual summer conference, still going on today, emphasized the Victorious Christian Life, the indwelling and fullness of the Holy Spirit, and the priority of global missions.

Pride

- Pride is the only disease known to man that makes everyone sick except the person who has it.
- A man wrapped up in himself makes a mighty small package.

Do Not Expect Reward

"When you serve God, do not expect a reward. Be prepared instead to be misunderstood, suspected, and abused. An evil world cannot speak well of holy lives. The sweetest fruit is most pecked at by the birds. The tallest mountains are most battered by the storms. The loveliest character is the most assailed. If you succeed in bringing many to Christ, you will be charged with self-seeking, or popularity hunting, or some such crime. You will be misrepresented, belied, caricatured, and counted as a fool by the ungodly world. If you serve God, the probabilities are that the crown you win in this world will contain more spikes than sapphires, more briers than emeralds. When it is put on your head, pray for grace to wear it, and count it all joy to be like your Lord. Say in your heart, 'I feel no dishonor in this dishonor. The world may attribute shameful things to me, but I am not ashamed. People may degrade me, but I am not degraded. They may look on me with contempt, but I am not contemptible.'"
—*Charles Spurgeon*

From *Spiritual Leadership* by J. Oswald Sanders

When Robert Louis Stevenson arrived in Samoa, he was invited by the head of the Malau Institute for training native pastors to address the students. He willingly consented. His address was based on the Mohammedan story of the veiled prophet. This prophet, a burning and shining light among the teachers of his people, wore a veil over his face because, he said, the glory of his countenance was so great that no one could bear the sight. But at last the veil grew old and fell into decay. Then the people discovered that he was only an ugly old man trying to hide his own ugliness. Stevenson went on to enforce the need for sincerity on the ground that, however high the truths the teacher taught, however skillfully he might excuse blemishes of character, the time comes when the veil falls away, and a man is seen by people as he really is. It is seen whether beneath the veil is the ugly face of unmortified egotism or the transformed glory of Christlike character.

WORSHIP HELPS

Call to Worship:
Then a voice came from the throne, saying, "Praise our God, all you His servants and those who fear Him, both small and great!" And I heard, as it were, the voice of a great multitude, as the sound of many waters and as the sound of mighty thunderings, saying, "Alleluia! For the Lord God Omnipotent reigns!" (Rev. 19:5, 6).

Pastoral Prayer:
Almighty God, may our hearts join the angelic song today, crying, "Alleluia! The Lord God Omnipotent reigns!" May we gladly submit to Your rule in our own lives, and may we learn to be givers, servants, and those whose hearts are humble and eager to do Your will. Forgive this incessant, insistent selfishness that expects our husbands, wives, children, church, and friends to serve *us*. Remind us that even the Lord Himself came not to be served, but to serve and to give His life as a ransom for many. Lord, in this church we need nursery workers, musicians, teachers, and those who will wash floors and mow grass. We need some to go as missionaries, and others to finance Your mission. Make us willing workers, generous givers, and selfless servants for Jesus' sake. Amen.

Kids Talk

Have a box filled with toys. Tell the children you have a question for them. Open the box and toss the toys hither thither, then ask, "Which is easier? To take our toys out and play with them, or to put them back when we're done?" Talk to the children about the importance of picking up their things so that someone else doesn't have to clean up after them. Let the children help you gather the toys and carefully return them to the box.

Additional Sermons and Lesson Ideas

Love in Your Home
Date preached:
By D. James Kennedy

SCRIPTURE: Ephesians 5:25

INTRODUCTION: Our homes were designed by God to be a little foretaste of heaven. Unfortunately, many have discovered them to be a foretaste of hell. Most probably find them somewhere in between. I would like to talk to you about making yours a triple—a marriage.

1. Acceptance. Rejection is a painful part of life, but we should be accepting of one another in marriage. Matthew 7:1 says, in the Greek form of the verb: "Do not be continually judging others or finding fault with others."
2. Affection. There is a feeling of love that comes when we are doing the things the Bible commands us to do for one another.
3. Appreciation. Philippians 4:8 tells us to think on good things. Consider the good things about your spouse, and tell him or her. Express your appreciation.

CONCLUSION: Determine right now to put acceptance, affection, and appreciation into your home and you will find that it can be a little taste of heaven.

Are You Listening?
Date preached:
By Drew Wilkerson

SCRIPTURE: 1 Samuel 3:1–10

INTRODUCTION: Some people question whether or not God really speaks. In this familiar Old Testament story we are reminded that God speaks to anyone who is willing to listen. The key is knowing how to tune into God's voice. The boy Samuel shows us how.

1. Believe God wants to speak. We can't hear God if we don't have faith.
2. Believe God wants to speak to you. God desires a personal relationship with us.
3. Believe God wants a response. It is overwhelming but true. God wants to use us.

CONCLUSION: God's voice is not dead. It's our hearing that we need to work on. God is always looking for people, children and adults, who are willing to say, "Speak, Lord, for your servant is listening."

Churches Without Boundaries:
Mobilizing and Globalizing Your Ministry

Discouragement among pastors is an Anthrax-like spore that weakens our effectiveness and spreads quickly in settings dominated by me-mine-and-ours. It has little to do with the size of our churches, and everything to do with the size of our vision. Without global optics, we limit ourselves to a lean harvest on small acreage, regardless of the size of Sunday's crowd.

Somewhere in the world a great harvest is occurring—and when a church figures out how to mobilize and globalize, it enters a realm of unlimited borders—a Jabez-like ministry expanding beyond church walls and city limits. How thrilling to retire at night knowing that across the globe someone is beginning a new day in the Lord's work, supported by our church! How comforting—knowing that our greatest fruitfulness may occur through our overseas enterprises, that we'll meet souls in heaven who were saved through our international endeavors.

How, then, can we develop churches without boundaries? Here's a tool chest of ideas:

1. **Preach the Victorious Christian Life.** In the "Keswick" tradition, the Victorious Life message declares that sin can rob Christians of daily joy, but Calvary provides victory, not just over the penalty, but over the power of sin. The indwelling Holy Spirit applies that victory to trusting, yielded souls. As the Christ-life flows through us, consistent victory becomes possible, and our Lord's burden for lost humanity burns within us. Our hearts go with Christ to the ends of the earth. This message, faithfully modeled and preached, provides fertile soil for a Great Commission church.

2. **Ask God to Send Missionaries from Your Church.** The Great Commission assumes a flesh-and-blood character when God flings someone we know into a cross-cultural ministry. In our church, we have several serving in Africa, Brazil, and, soon, among Muslims in southern France. Our church knows their names, sees their pictures, provides their income, remembers their prayer requests, and shares their victories. Ask the Lord of the harvest to raise up some of your members as international harvesters. Of course, this means you'll "lose" some of your best workers, but God will replace them. Some of your children will be called overseas, some of your retirees

will spend their golden years as short-termers, and some of your budget will be invested elsewhere. But that's great! Don't grieve over things you should rejoice about. When the church at Antioch sent Paul and Barnabas to the "regions beyond," the whole congregation went with them in spirit.

3. **"Adopt" a Missionary.** If there's no immediate missionary candidate in your church, find one in a nearby church who needs backing. In our denomination, there are always missionaries needing financial and prayer support. Contact the foreign missions office and schedule a missionary to visit your church. Learn all you can about them and their field of labor, then help underwrite their needs, share their passion, and send them on their way in a manner worthy of God (3 John 6).

4. **Send Short-Term Workers.** The fastest way to generate passion for the field is to get your people there. There's a cross-cultural opportunity for almost every member of your church, from teenagers to young-at-hearts. Some short-term assignments last for days, some for years. Information on such opportunities is available from mission agencies, or from sources such as the annual magazine *Into All The World: The Annual Great Commission Opportunities Handbook.*[1]

5. **Travel Yourself.** I recently read the autobiography of aviator Charles Lindbergh, written in 1927, just after his famous flight in the *Spirit of St. Louis.* In his early days, Lindbergh kept a parachute with him. When his plane got into trouble he would crawl from the cockpit and jump off the wing. Aviation was primitive, its future uncertain. "Trans-Atlantic service is still in the future," wrote Lindbergh. "Multi-motored flying boats (airplanes) with stations along the route will eventually make trans-oceanic airlines practical." How times have changed! Now we can board a jetliner in America at bedtime and have breakfast in Paris. By shopping carefully, we can do it relatively inexpensively. There's little reason for a pastor not to save his dollars and occasionally vacation overseas with a special eye on the spiritual conditions of the land being visited. Spending a few days in another culture, perhaps among the missionaries you support, is worth a semester's work in missionary school.

6. **Listen to CNN World News**, and read the overseas news in the *New York Times, The Washington Post,* and, when abroad, *The International Herald Tribune.* Keep a world atlas close at hand.

7. **Make Friends with an International.** There's probably a cross-cultural friendship right around the corner from where you live, just waiting to be made.

8. **Draw Sermon Illustrations from Missionary Biographies and Magazines.** Where could you find a better story, for example, than when Dick Hillis and his family were trapped between the Chinese Nationalists and the Communist forces of Mao Tse-tung. The bombing reached a crescendo one night as each shell dropped closer to the Hillis' home. The family huddled in the corner as explosions sent dirt, glass, and bricks through windows and walls. The children screamed, and the family prepared for death as best it could. But the shelling abruptly stopped, and the Hillises finally emerged from their corner. The room was filled with debris, but no one was hurt. By and by, as Dick tucked each child into bed, he knelt beside little Margaret Anne and noticed a dirty scrap of paper stuffed under her pillow. On it was printed in big, childlike letters: "God is our refuge and strength, a very present help in trouble" (Ps. 46:1).[2] That little girl was resting on a big promise from a faithful God. Using stories like that helps the church see biblical truth through missionary eyes and helps them become accustomed to thinking in missionary terms.

9. **Revive Faith-Promise Support.** Ever since Andrew Fuller and William Carey passed a snuffbox and took up history's first collection for organized Protestant missions, pastors have been seeking ways to fund missions. For most of the 20th century, the old "faith-promise" card proved useful. Individual Christians were asked to trust God for a certain amount of money each month (above and beyond their regular tithes) toward the support of a particular missionary. At our church, we're still doing this. Each fall on Missions Sunday, we pass out a "MEGO" Card (My Enlistment in Global Outreach) on which individuals can make a number of commitments, including:
   • Financially supporting a missionary
   • Praying daily for a missionary
   • Memorizing a "missionary text" in the Bible

- Subscribing to missions periodicals
- Taking a missions course offered by the church
- Participating in an overseas short-term project
- Reading a book on missions

These are completed in duplicate, collected, and tallied; they represent our church's commitment toward missions for the next twelve months.[3]

10. **Include Missionary Support in the Church's General Fund Budget.** Several years ago, we realized not everyone would fill out a MEGO card, yet everyone in the church should be a part of Christ's commission. At the time we were giving little of our general fund budget to outside ministries. We began increasing the amount by a half-percent per year, and now we are at tithe-level—10 percent—and counting. This goes directly to missionary accounts, other overseas ministries, and joint denominational projects. It provides a consistent monthly "floor" for missionary support, one that grows each year as our church grows.

11. **Develop a Global Outreach Committee.** Certain people in your church are more missions-minded than others. Find them, and develop a task force that meets each month to brainstorm and implement ways in which missions can become a greater force in your church.[4]

12. **Plan an Annual Global Sunday.** International Outreach should be a 52-week-a-year emphasis, woven into the fabric of the church's thinking as reflected in every service. But it helps us to set apart an annual Sunday to focus on missions, to hear from missionaries, to preach, pray, and sing about missions, and receive our annual MEGO commitments.

13. **Host the "Perspectives on the World Christian Movement"** course in your church. This in-depth study fuels a passion for missions as it covers the biblical, historical, cultural, and strategic aspects of God's plan to reach the nations.[5]

14. **Pray.** God's church is a house of prayer for all nations. I once visited All Soul's Church in London, and I was impressed by the global sweep of the pastoral prayer. He led us in prayer for elections in Mexico, India, and New Zealand; for rioting in Indonesia;

for the refugee crisis in Somalia; for missionaries in South Africa; for the persecuted church in China and Chad; and so on. It was a literal, unhurried intercessory tour of global events. J. O. Fraser was a missionary to China in the early 1900s. He credited the conversion of hundreds of Lisu families to the prayers of his very earnest little prayer group back in England. He said, "Christians at home can do as much for foreign missions as those actually on the field. It will only be known on the Last Day how much has been accomplished in missionary work by the prayers of earnest believers at home."[6]

15. **Envision Your Church in Global Terms.** Having done these things, you'll find that your church will begin thinking of itself as a world-class church, one that is known around the world for its global impact. In our church, we've adopted this attitude into our purpose statement—"to extend and strengthen the Kingdom for Christ and His glory"—and in our "marketing" slogan—"Reaching around the world . . . Reaching out to you." Those statements represent who we are. A church of 10,000 people without a global vision is a little church, too small to pastor. A church of fifty whose resources reach around the world is bigger than it knows, and it does more good than it realizes. It has a ministry without boundaries, with fruit that will last throughout eternity. ❖

[1] www.aboutmissions.com

[2] This story comes from Jan Winebrenner, *Steel in His Soul: The Dick Hillis Story* (Mukilteo, WA: OC International, 1996). Unfortunately, not many missionary biographies are currently published due to declining interest among readers. My favorite source of missionary biographical material is from OMF Publishers, located on the web at <www.us.omf.org>.

[3] Special "AMEGO" cards are designed for the children.

[4] Check out <www.acmc.org> for excellent resources for advancing churches in missions commitment.

[5] For information, see <www.perspectives.org>.

[6] I keep a copy of J. O. Fraser's biography by my desk all the time and refer to it often. Geraldine Taylor, *Behind the Ranges: The Life-Changing Story of J. O. Fraser* (Singapore: OMF Books International, 1998).

Quotes for the Pastor's Wall

❝ It's very simple. All you've got to do is pour a
bucket of kerosene over yourself and set yourself
on fire, and people will come to watch you burn. **❞**

—Charles Haddon Spurgeon,
when asked, "How can I communicate like you do?

❝ I would say that a "dull preacher" is a contradiction in terms; if he is dull he is not a preacher. He
may stand in the pulpit and talk, but he is certainly not a preacher. With the grand theme and
message of the Bible dullness is impossible. **❞**

—Martyn Lloyd-Jones

JULY 6, 2003

The Great Physician's Upper Room Clinic

Date preached:

Scripture: John 14:28–31, especially verse 29: I have told you before it comes, that when it does come to pass, you may believe.

Introduction: On March 28, 2002, the Canadian *National Post* ran this headline: "Worshipping God Can Keep You Sane." The article by Tracey Tong said, "Regular religious worship can relieve the severity of mental health problems and shorten the hospital stays of psychiatric patients. . . . 'Religious commitment has a significant impact on depressive symptoms, satisfaction with life, hospital use, and alcohol use,' says the study, which is being published today in the *Canadian Journal of Psychiatry*." It's no surprise that prayer, Bible study, and church attendance help people stay mentally healthy. God created the psyche, and Christianity is uniquely designed to meet our inner needs. In John 14, Jesus and His disciples were under duress. A cloud of anxiety hung over the Upper Room, yet the words Jesus spoke that night have calmed more distraught souls than virtually any other words ever spoken (See John 14:1–3, 13, 15–16, 27.) This wonderful chapter ends with Jesus giving His disciples a prescription for joy, faith, and obedience.

1. **His Position: A Basis for Joy** (v. 28). Our Lord had frequently told the twelve that He was going away, then returning. Have you noticed how there is sadness when people separate, but the greater sadness is borne by those left behind? When a student leaves for college, he may experience tinges of grief, but it's offset by the excitement of new adventure. His parents, however, watching him drive off, return to an empty nest. Jesus was going to return to heaven. For Him it was a restoration of glory, and He told His heavyhearted disciples they should be glad for His sake. It's important to understand this verse correctly, because those who deny the deity of Christ use the last part of verse 28 to bolster their claims: "For My Father is greater than I." But note the context. He wasn't speaking of His divine nature but of His current circumstances. Jesus was saying something like this: "In this present state of humility and sacrifice, the Father

is greater than I in terms of honor, for I have laid aside My glory to be crucified. But shortly I'll resume My place of highest majesty, and you should be glad about that." We should be happy in our hearts that Jesus returned to the heavenly throne, keeping watch over His own. It's a basis for joy.

2. **His Prediction: A Basis for Faith** (v. 29). Jesus continued: "And now I have told you before it comes, that when it does come to pass, you may believe." He had explained repeatedly and in advance that He was going to be betrayed, arrested, killed, and resurrected. The disciples later recalled these things, and it bolstered their faith. This is one of the reasons we teach children Bible verses, though at the time they may not fully understand them. If we can get these verses into their brains—and into ours—the Holy Spirit will bring them to mind later and use them as a basis for a healthy faith.

3. **His Passion: A Basis for Obedience** (vv. 30–31). Jesus then spoke of His passion. "I will no longer talk much with you, for the ruler of this world is coming, and he has nothing on Me." This phrase implies that Satan has no leverage over Jesus, could not charge Him with sin, could not hold Him in the tomb. The accuser of the brethren can accuse you and me before the throne (Job 1; Zech. 3), and we can never redeem the human race, because Satan can bring charges against us. But against Christ, He has nothing to say. Jesus continued, "But that the world may know that I love the Father, and as the Father gave Me commandment, so I do." Two

>>> *sermon continued on following page*

APPROPRIATE HYMNS AND SONGS

Jesus, I My Cross Have Taken, Ralph E. Hudson; Public Domain.

A Pure Heart, Ronald E. Gollner; © 1990 Discovery House Music.

Center of My Joy, Gloria Gaither/William J. Gaither/Richard Smallwood; © 1987 William J. Gaither/Century Oak Publishing/Richwood Music (Admin. by Copyright Management, Inc.).

God Can Do It Again, Don Moen; © 1976 Integrity's Hosanna! Music.

Take Time to Be Holy, William D. Longstaff/George C. Stebbins; Public Domain.

reasons are given why Christ was going to the Cross: He loved the Father, and He was obedient. Jesus is our example.

Conclusion: The chapter ends with, "Arise, let us go from here." These were our Lord's last words in the Upper Room. Leaving that hallowed spot, they trudged toward the Garden of Gethsemane, and the rest of the "Upper Room Discourse" was uttered en route. But this final paragraph of chapter 14 gives us a basis for mental and spiritual health, a basis for sanity, as we "go from here." We can be joyful, trusting, and obedient because of our Lord's position, predictions, and passion.

FOR THE BULLETIN

❂ On July 6, 1415, Bohemian Reformer John Huss, refusing to recant his beliefs before the Council of Constance, was found guilty of heresy, condemned, and taken to the outskirts of the city to be burned. His last words: "God is my witness that the evidence against me is false. I have never thought nor preached except with the one intention of winning men, if possible, from their sins. In the truth of the gospel I have written, taught, and preached; today I will gladly die." ❂ July 6, 1535 also marks the execution of Sir Thomas More, lord chancellor of England. He was beheaded in the Tower of London for refusing to recognize Henry VIII as supreme head of the Church of England following the king's split with Rome. ❂ The death of England's King Edward VI (Protestant son of Henry VIII) on this day in 1553 put the Protestant movement at risk. His half-sister, Mary Tudor, rose to the throne, intent on reestablishing Catholicism throughout the land. Known to history as "Bloody Mary," she unleashed a terrible persecution against Protestants, which was later chronicled by John Foxe in his *Book of Martyrs*. Over 300 Protestant leaders were burned at the stake, including Thomas Cranmer, Hugh Latimer, and Nicholas Ridley. ❂ July 6 is the birthday of William M'Kendree (1757), first American-born bishop of the Methodist Church, and of John Sammis (1846), author of "Trust and Obey" ❂ Francis and Edith Schaeffer were married on this day in 1935.

STATS, STORIES AND MORE

Jesus, I My Cross Have Taken

Pioneer radio evangelist Michael Guido of Metter, Georgia, grew up in a home in which his mother was a Christian but his father was violently opposed to the faith. Shortly after Michael was converted, a friend told him that his voice was good enough to sing Gospel songs for the Lord. He was invited to sing for a Friday night evangelistic service. At the supper table that Friday, Michael mentioned that after supper he was going to sing at a little Methodist church out in the country. His father jumped to his feet, his face turning red with rage, and shouted, "Tonight you must decide between your father and your new faith. Which will it be?" Michael turned to his mother and asked, "Ma, shall I go?" She replied, "Son, put Jesus before your mother and father; put Him first in your life." With that, her husband struck her and she fell to the floor bleeding. Michael tried to step forward to help her, but his father prevented him. "Tonight," said the older man, "you must make that decision. If you go and sing, you can't ever come home again. What is your decision?" Putting on his coat, Michael started to sing, "Jesus, I my cross have taken." His father cursed him, slammed the door behind him, shouting, "You can't come home tonight!" As he left the house, Michael was heartbroken, but the song he was singing became the theme of his life.

> Jesus, I my cross have taken,
> All to leave and follow Thee;
> Destitute, despised, forsaken,
> Thou, from hence, my all shall be.
> Perish every fond ambition,
> All I've sought, and hoped, and known;
> Yet how rich is my condition,
> God and heaven are still my own.

Biblical Definitions of Faith

- The man took Jesus at His word . . . —John 4:50 (NIV).
- Blessed is she who has believed that what the Lord has said to her will be accomplished—Luke 1:45 (NIV).
- I have faith in God that it will happen just as He told me—Acts 27:25 (NIV).
- . . . being fully persuaded that God has power to do what He has promised—Romans 4:21 (NIV).
- Now faith is being sure of what we hope for and certain of what we do not see—Hebrews 11:1 (NIV).

WORSHIP HELPS

Call to Worship:
"If you love Me, keep My commandments. And I will pray the Father, and He will give you another Helper, that He may abide with you forever—the Spirit of truth, whom the world cannot receive, because it neither sees Him nor knows Him; but you know Him, for He dwells with you and will be in you" (John 14:15–17).

Readers' Theater (may be adapted as Scripture reading or responsive reading):

Reader 1:   Then Joab said to Amasa, "Are you in health, my brother?" Can these bones live?

Reader 2:   Beloved, I pray that you may prosper in all things and be in health, just as your soul prospers.

Reader 1:   Therefore all those who devour you shall be devoured; and all your adversaries, every one of them, shall go into captivity; those who plunder you shall become plunder, and all who prey upon you I will make a prey. For I will restore health to you and heal you of your wounds,' says the LORD.

Both: But He was wounded for our transgressions, He was bruised for our iniquities; the chastisement for our peace was upon Him, and by His stripes we are healed.

Reader 1:   I can count all My bones. They look and stare at Me. They divide My garments among them, and for My clothing, they cast lots.

Reader 2:   Do not be wise in your own eyes; fear the LORD and depart from evil. It will be health to your flesh, and strength to your bones.

Reader 1:   Those who wait on the LORD shall renew their strength; they shall mount up with wings like eagles, they shall run and not be weary, they shall walk and not faint.

Both   Go in peace, and be healed of your affliction."

(Taken from 2 Sam. 20:9; Ezek. 37:3; 3 John 2; Jer. 30:16–17; Isa. 53:5; Ps. 22:17–18; Prov. 3:7–8; Isa. 40:31; Mark 5:34)

Additional Sermons and Lesson Ideas

A Mood-altering Prayer

Date preached:

SCRIPTURE: 1 Samuel 1

INTRODUCTION: Too many of us are victims of our moods. We suffer from low spirits, anger, depression, or anxiety, often brought on by difficult circumstances. We need to practice "mood-altering" prayers. One of the Bible's best examples is Hannah, the mother of Samuel.

1. Difficult Conditions (vv. 1–7).
2. Depressed Spirits (v. 8). According to David Hazard, 43 percent of Americans suffer adverse health effects due to stress. One million Americans miss work each day due to stress, and 75-90 percent of doctor visits are stress-related complaints.
3. Earnest Prayer (vv. 9–16).
4. Shared Burden (v. 17). Eli's response helped Hannah realize that God was sharing her burden.
5. Changed Attitude (v. 18). Hannah's circumstances had not changed, but her frame of mind was completely different.
6. Heaven's Answer (vv. 19–20).

CONCLUSION: Cast your burden on the Lord, and He will sustain your spirits.

Weighed and Wanting
By Melvin Worthington

Date preached:

SCRIPTURE: Daniel 5:1–31

INTRODUCTION: Disrespect and defiance of God are dangerous, as this chapter shows.

1. The Feast (vv. 1–4). Belshazzar made a great feast for his lords. He drank wine from the vessels Nebuchadnezzar had taken from the temple of God in Jerusalem.
2. The Fingers (vv. 5–9). During the feast, the fingers of a hand wrote on the wall and the king's countenance changed, his thoughts troubling him. He sought someone to read the writing.
3. The Forecast (vv. 10–29). The queen suggested Daniel be called. His interpretation included: (1) God has numbered the kingdom and finished it, (2) You are weighed in the balances and found wanting and (3) Your kingdom is divided and given to the Medes and Persians.
4. The Fate (vv. 30–31). That night Belshazzar was slain and Darius the Mede took over the kingdom.

CONCLUSION: Will you be weighed and found wanting before the God of the universe?

JULY 13, 2003

Integrity in Doctrine

Date preached:

By Ed Dobson

Scripture: Titus 1:5–9, especially verse 9: ...holding fast the faithful word as he has been taught, that he may be able, by sound doctrine, both to exhort and convict those who contradict.

Introduction: This passage has to do with the qualifications for church leaders, and the overall requirement is blamelessness. Elders must be blameless in family life (v. 6), personal character (vv. 7–8) and doctrine (v. 9).

1. **Leaders Must Be Committed to Sound Doctrine—** *"Holding fast the faithful word. . . ."* The same verb was used in Luke 16:13 where Jesus said we cannot be *devoted* to two masters. An elder must be exclusively devoted to the faithful word. The Greek for "faithful word" is πιστοῦ λόγου (*pistoo-logoo*) the faithful word or trustworthy saying. This phrase is unique to the writings of Paul and specifically to the Pastoral Epistles. (See 1 Tim. 1:15; 3:1; 4:9; 2 Tim. 2:11; Titus 3:7–8.) Paul and the apostles had provided authority for the early church, but they were growing old. In future years where could the church turn for authority? Paul was saying, "When I'm no longer here, you still have the authority—it is the authority of the word of God. Hold it firmly."

2. **Leaders Must Be Committed to Public Proclamation of Sound Doctrine—** *. . . as he has been taught, that he may be able, by sound doctrine, both to exhort and convict.* The public proclamation of the word of God is a central focus of the church. This is one of the major themes of the Pastoral Epistles. (See 1 Tim. 3:2; 4:13; 5:17; 2 Tim. 2:1–2; 2:15; 2:25; 4:1–2.)

3. **Leaders Must Make Practical Application of Sound Doctrine—** *. . . both to exhort and convict those who contradict.*
    A. The leader must exhort and encourage by sound teaching. The word encourage is the word παρακαλέω (*para-ka-lĕ-ō*). The preposition *para* means "along side of something," the stem means "to call." Teaching and preaching is not merely the dissemination of theological truth or the passing out of information. We are to communicate God's truth so

as to call people along side of the truth of God. How does God's Word apply to our lives?

B.   **The Leader Must Convict by Sound Doctrine.** We are to refute those who oppose the truth. The word "refute" means to bring to light, to expose, to set forth, or to convince and convict. We must teach God's Word clearly enough to expose error and to allow the Holy Spirit to convince and convict those who oppose it.

Conclusion: Let me suggest, by way of application, that there are three dimensions or categories to our doctrine:

- There is absolute truth—the truth that draws a line between believers and non-believers. These are essential doctrines necessary for salvation, such as the person of Christ, the power of His shed blood for the remission of sins, His bodily resurrection, etc. We adhere to these truths because we accept the authority of inspired Scripture.

- There are convictions, which do not have to be accepted in order to go to heaven. These are our beliefs about things such as details about baptism, the gifts of the Spirit, or the return of Christ.

- There are preferences. Different Christians and different churches enjoy different styles of worship or types of music, for example.

>>> sermon continued on following page

APPROPRIATE HYMNS AND SONGS

All Creation Worships You, Kirk Dearman/Jim Mills; © 1988 Integrity's Hosanna! Music.

All I Once Held Dear, Graham Kendrick; © 1993 Way Make Music (Admin. by Music Services.).

I Will Sing the Wondrous Story, Francis H. Rowly/Peter P. Pilhorn; Public Domain.

Jesus, I Believe, Bill Batstone; 1992 Maranatha Praise, Inc. (Admin. by The Copyright Company.).

Lead On, O King Eternal, Ernest W. Shurtleff/Henry Smart; Public Domain.

There are three dangers in the area of absolutes, convictions, and preferences. Number one is to take everything you believe and elevate it to an absolute. A second danger is to so focus on one of the convictions to the exclusion of all the others. Danger number three is saying, "We just believe in Jesus. Doctrine is really not all that important. After all, doctrine divides and love unites." May I suggest that *lack* of doctrine divides. When everyone believes whatever they want without a commitment to doctrine, then you have division. As pastor of this church I have a personal commitment to doctrine, to publicly proclaiming it, and to applying it to my life and, hopefully, to the lives of our attenders. I'm also committed to our heritage here of absolutes, convictions, and preferences. That is who we are. It is incumbent upon leadership to keep these things in balance while at the same time loving those outside our congregation who are brothers and sisters in Jesus who differ with us in our convictions and in our preferences.

FOR THE BULLETIN

✺ On Wednesday evening, July 13, 1099, the Crusaders attacked the Muslim-held city of Jerusalem with shouts of "God wills it!" After two days of furious fighting, the city fell, and Crusaders rushed through the city, killing and looting. ✺ On July 13, 1234, St. Dominic, founder of the Dominicans, was canonized. ✺ On this day in 1587, Manteo became the first Native American baptized as a Protestant. He was declared to be Lord of Roanoke. One week later, Virginia Dare became the first white child to be born and baptized in North America. Shortly thereafter, the entire colony disappeared in one of American history's greatest mysteries. ✺ Scottish Puritan Samuel Rutherford, exiled to the city of Aberdeen for his preaching, wrote to his congregation in Anwoth on July 13, 1637, describing how he felt at being removed from his pulpit: "Next to Christ, I had but one joy, the apple of the eye of my delights, to preach Christ my Lord; and they have violently plucked that away from me. It was to me like the poor man's one eye; and they have put out that eye, and quenched my light in the inheritance of the Lord." ✺ Irish Episcopal clergyman, Thomas Kelly, was born on July 13, 1769. He wrote 765 hymns, the best known being "Praise the Savior, Ye Who Know Him." ✺ On July 13, 1960, the wife of C. S. Lewis, Joy, died. Lewis later wrote about this in *A Grief Observed*.

STATS, STORIES AND MORE

Between Two Worlds

John R. W. Stott wrote a book several years ago about preaching entitled, *Between Two Worlds.* His thesis was that preaching or teaching involves two worlds, the world of biblical truth and the world of human reality. Preaching or teaching the Bible is the process of building a bridge from the world of biblical truth into the world of human experience so that we apply the truth of God to daily life.—*Ed Dobson*

Quotables:

- Great saints have always been dogmatic.—*A. W. Tozer*
- There can be no spiritual health without doctrinal knowledge. —*J. I. Packer*
- We cannot have the benefits of Christianity if we shed its doctrines. —*D. Martyn Lloyd-Jones*
- The truth is, no preacher ever had any strong power that was not the preaching of doctrine.—*Phillips Brooks*
- The time will come when they will not endure sound doctrine. —*2 Timothy 4:3*
- Contend earnestly for the faith.—*Jude, verse 3*
- Theology means "the science of God," and I think any man who wants to think about God at all would like to have the clearest and most accurate ideas about Him that are available.—*C. S. Lewis*
- Some pastors preach "longhorn sermons," a point here, a point there, and a lot of bull in between.—*Anonymous*

Statistics from George Barna on America's Theology

- 60 percent of all adults agree that "the Bible is totally accurate in all of its teachings." (2001)
- Nearly three out of five adults (58 percent) say that the devil, or Satan, is not a living being but is a symbol of evil. (2001)
- Half of all adults (51 percent) believe that if a person is generally good, or does enough good things for others during their life, they will earn a place in heaven. (2001)
- More than two out of every five adults (43 percent) believe that when Jesus Christ lived on earth He committed sins. Conversely, 41 percent of Americans believe that Jesus lived a sinless life on earth. (2001)

WORSHIP HELPS

Call to Worship:
But you stand here awhile, that I may announce to you the word of God (1 Sam. 9:27).

Offertory Comments:
John Wesley had three rules about money: "Make all you can. Save all you can. And give all you can." We realize that many people are no longer willing to give to a church simply because it is a church. They want to know their donation will make a difference and leave a mark on the world. I'd like to take a moment today to tell you how your contributions *are* making a difference. (Briefly describe to your congregation one of the ministries of your church, then say:) This is only one of the ministries made possible by our generously given dollars. Today as you give, ask the Lord to bless and use that gift to extend and strengthen the kingdom for Christ and His glory.

Benediction:
Father, we are thankful for your word and I pray that in all of our preferences and choices and our convictions that we would never lose sight of the absolutes—the centrality of Jesus Christ and His finished work on the Cross. Grant us that we might be in balance and be committed to Your Word and most of all to applying Your Word to our lives. In Jesus' name I pray. Amen.—*Ed Dobson*

Kids Talk

Sing with the children the old chorus "The B-I-B-L-E," then sing it again putting the name of one of the children in it: "The B-I-B-L-E! Yes, that's the book for Jill. She stands upon the Word of God. The B-I-B-L-E!" Do this with several children, then have them all sing it, saying, "The B-I-B-L-E! Yes, that's the book for us. We stand upon the Word of God . . ."

Additional Sermons and Lesson Ideas

Lord, Teach Us to Pray
By Andrew Murray

Date preached:

SCRIPTURE: Luke 11:1

INTRODUCTION: The disciples had learned that Jesus was a Master at the art of prayer, so they asked Him, "Lord, teach us to pray." Shall we, too, not enroll our names in Christ's School of Prayer?

1. Lord, Teach Us *To Pray.*—Though prayer is so simple that the feeblest child can pray, it is also the highest and holiest work to which we can rise. True prayer takes hold of God's strength and avails much.
2. Lord, Teach *Us* To Pray.—We have read in His Word with what power the believing people of old used to pray and what mighty wonders were done in answer to their prayers. If this took place under the Old Covenant, how much more will He not now give His people the privilege and power of prayer?
3. Lord, *Teach* Us To Pray.—At first no work appears so simple; later, none proves more difficult.
4. *Lord,* Teach Us To Pray.—A pupil needs a teacher who has the gift of teaching, who in patience and love will descend to the pupil's needs. Jesus is all that and more.

CONCLUSION: Jesus never taught His disciples how to preach, but how to pray. Not power with others, but power with God is the first thing. Jesus loves to Teach Us To Pray.

Overcoming Shyness

Date preached:

SCRIPTURE: 2 Timothy 1:5-7

INTRODUCTION: If you struggle with shyness and timidity, I'd like to introduce you to Timothy. He did the same, and Paul frequently exhorted him about it, saying things like: "God has not given you the spirit of timidity. . . . Let no one look down on you. . . . Don't be ashamed. . . . Be strong. . . . Be a good soldier." Three verses in particular help us:

1. Not I, but Christ—2 Timothy 1:5. Shyness is basically a problem of self-centeredness. Be Christ-centered instead.
2. Not a Hopeless Klutz, but a Gifted Christian—2 Timothy 1:6.
3. Not a Spirit of Timidity, but a Spirit of Power—2 Timothy 1:7.

CONCLUSION: As you grow in Christ and reflect more and more on His qualities, it frees you up to be yourself in Christ and to let His character flow through you.

JULY 20, 2003

The Barnabas Secrets

Date preached:

By Stuart Briscoe

Scripture: Acts 11:24: For he (Barnabas) was a good man, full of the Holy Spirit and of faith.

Introduction: If we were to ask, "What should we look for in a leader?" some would say, "Well, a leader is someone who has the ability to identify what needs to be done, the ability to communicate vision, mobilize people, and get the project done." But others would point out that leadership is more than getting projects done. It is leading people to where they need to be in the formation of their character and in the development of their lives. That's what we see in the life of Barnabas. The wonderful thing about Barnabas is that he was not a Peter and he wasn't a Paul, nor are most of us. He moved quietly in the shadows and exerted a tremendous influence, and we can all do that.

I. **He Was a Good Man.**—Acts 11:24 says that Barnabas was a "good man." One day the Lord Jesus was confronted by a young ruler asking, "Good Master, how can I have eternal life?" Jesus replied, "Why do you call me good? There is none good, but one, and that is God." In Romans, Paul quoted approvingly of what Isaiah said, "There is none good." Yet here Barnabas is called "good." Is that a contradiction? When Barnabas is described as a good man, it means he was a man of solid moral and ethical principle. When it speaks of God alone being good, the Bible is referring to perfection. When it says that Barnabas was a good man, it doesn't mean he was perfect or sinless, but that he was a moral and ethical man who lived consistently by his principles. It is possible for an ordinary fallen human being who is less than perfect to learn how to develop a moral and ethical principle, and to live consistently according to it. Now, we know that Barnabas was a Levite, which means he was thoroughly familiar with the Old Testament. So his moral and ethical principles were biblically based. They originated from God's self-revelations, from God's character. So Barnabas was a good man in the sense that his life reflected the moral and ethical principles of God.

2. **He Was Full of the Holy Spirit.**—Verse 24 also says he was full of the Holy Spirit. Scripture gives us a very succinct statement about being filled with the Holy Spirit in Ephesians 5:18, when it tells us not to be drunk with wine, but to be filled with the Spirit. There's an obvious rhythm there. We are not to be captivated and motivated and activated by alcohol, but we are to be captivated and motivated and activated by the Holy Spirit. It's one thing to be a moral and ethical person. It is an entirely different thing to be a moral and ethical person empowered by the Holy Spirit. By implication, Barnabas exercised his spiritual gift, and he exhibited the fruit of the Spirit as described in Galatians 5:22-23. What kind of leader, then, should you be becoming? An ethical and moral person, high-principled, exercising your gifts and attitudes in the power of the Holy Spirit.

3. **He Was Full of Faith.**—He was also full of faith. That means two things. First, his mind was fixed on certain truths he had heard, evaluated, and embraced wholeheartedly. Second, his actions were based on those beliefs. For him, it wasn't just a cognitive belief but a daily experience. He lived in conscious enjoyment of the truths his mind had embraced.

Conclusion: These qualities so impressed people that they called Barnabas the "Son of Encouragement." His name was not really Barnabas, it was Joseph. But there was a fragrance about his life. He was an upbuilder. He was an uplifter. He was a renewer. He was a refresher. When he moved through an area, people would look at each other and say, "Wasn't it good to have him around!" So his friends said, "We're not going to call you Joseph any more,

>>> sermon continued on following page

APPROPRIATE HYMNS AND SONGS

Here Is My Life, Ed Seabough/Gene Bartlett; © 1969 Broadman Press (Admin. by Genevox Music Group.).

Brighten the Corner Where You Are, Ina Duley Ogdon/Charles H. Gabriel; Public Domain.

I'll Do My Best, Jeremy Dalton; © 1983 Word Music, Inc.

Living for Jesus, Thomas O. Chisholm/Harold C. Lowden; Public Domain.

The Heart of a Servant, Michael Puryear; © 1994 Careers-BMG Music, Inc.

but Barnabas—the Son of Encouragement." That's the kind of person God wants us to be. We may not have the limelight, but we can walk and work quietly in the shadows, uplifting and encouraging others. We may not produce many Peters here, or many Pauls. But I would love to think that this church is a breeding ground for "Barnabi."

FOR THE BULLETIN

✸ During the first millennium of Christianity, two centers of gravity emerged—Rome and Constantinople. In the mid-eleventh century, Michael Cerularius became patriarch of Constantinople, and Pope Leo IX, head of the Church of Rome. Leo sent Humbert to Constantinople, where he excommunicated Michael Cerularius. Four days later, on July 20, 1054, Cerularius responded by excommunicating the pope and his followers. This became the Great Schism, separating the Western Church (Catholic and Protestant) and the Eastern Church (Orthodox). ✸ Peter Lombard, Latin theologian and intellectual, died on July 20, 1164. ✸ On July 20, 1648, the Westminster Larger Catechism was adopted by the General Assembly of the Church of Scotland at Edinburgh. ✸ Jonathan Edwards and Sarah Pierpont were married on this day in 1726. ✸ Rev. Samuel Langdon, noted pastor in Portsmouth, New Hampshire, resigned from his pulpit to become a chaplain to patriot troops during the American Revolution. His journal for July 20, 1775, says: "This has been one of the most important and trying days of my life. I have taken leave of my people for the present and shall at once proceed to the American camp at Boston and offer my services as chaplain in the army. . . . The scene in the house of God today has tried me sorely. How silent, how solemn, was the congregation, and when they sang the 61st Psalm—commencing, "When overwhelm'd with grief / My heart within me dies"—sobs were heard in every part of the building." ✸ Hymn writer Charles Tindley died on this day in 1933. He is the author of "We Shall Overcome," and "Stand By Me."

STATS, STORIES AND MORE

Stuart Briscoe's Encourager

On my first trip to America in my early thirties, I spoke in Grand Rapids, Michigan, and a man came up to me. I had no idea who he was. Rather brusquely, he said, "That was a good talk, young man. I want it and eleven others like it in manuscript form on my desk in three months, and we'll publish it." He thrust a card into my hands; it said, "Pat J. Zondervan, Manager-Director, Zondervan Publishing Company." In those days Pat Zondervan was called "Mr. Christian Publisher."

Years later, I got a call from Pat Zondervan, and he said, "Stuart, I'm about to retire, and I'm spending my last few weeks traveling around the country saying goodbye to the authors I've introduced to Christian publishing, and you and Jill are two of them. Can I come and have dinner with you?" Now, Pat had written to me every month in the intervening years. A very brief letter each month, three paragraphs, and in the last paragraph he would always say, "As I was reading my Bible this morning, I thought of you and this is what I prayed for you." Every month for years, I got a letter like that from Pat Zondervan.

While we were having dinner, I said, "You have the most wonderful gift of encouragement, Pat." He looked startled and said, "What did you say?" I repeated, "You have the most wonderful gift of encouragement." His eyes filled with tears and he said, "Do you really think so? I don't know. No one ever told me!" There was a man about to retire who had spent his life in public ministry, and nobody ever encouraged him, the greatest encourager I ever knew. Can you think of what it would mean in people's lives if we actually got around to encouraging them?

Someone Said . . .

Everybody can be great . . . because anybody can serve. You don't have to have a college degree to serve. You don't have to make your subject and verb agree to serve. You only need a heart full of grace, a soul generated by love.
—*Martin Luther King, Jr.*

WORSHIP HELPS

Call to Worship:
Lift up your heads, O you gates! Lift up, you everlasting doors! And the King of glory shall come in. Who is this King of glory? The LORD of hosts, He *is* the King of glory (Ps. 24:9-10).

Word of Welcome:
I've found a web site that tells us how to say "Good Morning" in 250 languages. Everyone on earth has a way of saying *Good Morning*, whether it is *Bonjour* (French), *Guten Morgen* (German), or *Buenos dias* (Spanish). But you'll not find a warmer and more sincere Good Morning than we want to extend here at (name of church). May God bless you for being with us today.

Selections on Encouragement for Scripture Reading:
- 2 Chronicles 30:21–27
- Romans 1:8–12
- Colossians 2:1–7
- Hebrews 10:19–25

Hymn Story: "Brighten the Corner Where You Are"
The old gospel song "Brighten the Corner Where You Are" was written in 1913 by Ina D. Ogdon, who was born in 1872. In her earlier years, she had planned on a missionary tour in which she would be proclaiming the gospel on the Chautauqua circuit. Her plans were dashed, however, by her father's illness, and she abandoned her evangelistic dreams to care for him at his home. Out of this experience, she wrote this song to show the importance and joy of serving the Lord in whatever place we find ourselves.
> *Do not wait until some deed of greatness you may do,*
> *Do not wait to shed your light afar,*
> *To the many duties ever near you now be true,*
> *Brighten the corner where you are.*

Benediction: We sometimes look at the people in the Bible and put them on pedestals. Thank you, Lord, for Barnabas—a man who is all about character, reputation, and attitude. As we leave here, we ask you to make us more and more members of the church of Saint Barnabas. We pray this in Christ's name, Amen.

Additional Sermons and Lesson Ideas

Sons of Encouragement
By Stuart Briscoe

Date preached:

SCRIPTURE: Acts 4:36

INTRODUCTION: Character is what God knows you are. Reputation is what people think you are. There can be an enormous gap between these two, particularly in our culture where so much emphasis is placed on "image." The great thing about Barnabas is that his character and his reputation were very much in step. We see his influence in:

1. Encouraging the Church—Acts 4:32–37. There was a generous spirit about Barnabas. It's relatively easy to be a "taker," but what a joy to find a "giver."
2. Encouraging Someone Ostracized—Acts 9:26-32 and 11:25–30. Barnabas said, "Let's reach out to this guy, Saul of Tarsus, and love him into the kingdom."
3. Encouraging Someone Who Failed—Acts 15:36–31. Barnabas gave up traveling with the great apostle Paul in order to pour his life into this wobbly kid Mark.

CONCLUSION: If it hadn't been for Barnabas, we wouldn't have had Mark's Gospel or Paul's Epistles. Who can you encourage this week?

The Power of Temptation
By Kevin Riggs

Date preached:

SCRIPTURE: Judges 16:1–21

INTRODUCTION: When we are overcome by the power of temptation, we lose our spiritual strength. From the story of Samson and Delilah, we can learn ten principles about overcoming temptation.

1. Temptation is a process.
2. Temptation comes from the enemy.
3. Temptation comes in beautiful packages.
4. Temptation hits us where we are weak.
5. Temptation blinds us from reality.
6. Temptation builds us up before knocking us down.
7. Temptation plays on our emotions.
8. Temptation, when given into, separates us from God.
9. Temptation, when given into, makes us its slave.
10. Temptation has a way of escape.

CONCLUSION: Samson's story is given as a warning. We can be overcomers—more than conquerors through Him who loves us.

JULY 27, 2003

Easter in July

Date preached:

Scripture: Romans 6:4: Just as Christ was raised from the dead by the glory of the Father, even so we also should walk in newness of life.
Phillips Version: "Just as He was raised from the dead by that splendid revelation of the Father's power so we too might rise to live life on a new plane altogether."

Introduction: The research organization Public Agenda recently found that 79 percent of us say that lack of respect and courtesy is a serious problem, and 61 percent feel things have gotten worse in recent years. People everywhere are grumpy, irritable, and rude—in stark contrast to the kind of life the Bible describes as one of joy and rejoicing. The Bible insists we're to live on a new plane, as though every day were Easter. The Christian life is joy all year long.

1. **Easter Brought Joy to Jesus.** Prior to the Cross, our Lord was troubled (John 12:27; Matt. 26:38). But what was His attitude when He rose from the dead? In Psalm 16, a messianic Psalm that foretells the resurrection, Jesus is quoted in advance as saying: "Therefore my heart . . . rejoices. . . . In your presence is fullness of joy." We read in Hebrews 12:2 that He endured the Cross because of the joy set before Him. When the sun rose on that premier Easter, when the lightning of resurrection struck Him and the voltage of glorification surged through His body, when the tomb unsealed itself and the stone rolled away and the Risen Christ emerged into the freshness of that new day, He was infused and enthused with joy unspeakable and full of glory.

2. **Easter Brought Joy to His Followers.**
   A. **Matthew 28:8.** The women hurried from the tomb "with fear and great joy." Our hearts are big enough to hold more than one attitude or emotion at the same time. We can be afraid, yet filled with joy. We can be hurting, yet filled with joy. We can be grief-stricken, yet filled with joy.
   B. **Luke 24:40.** When Jesus revealed Himself to the disciples they could hardly believe it, because of joy and amazement. In verse 52, they returned to Jerusalem in great (Greek: mega-) joy.
   C. **John 20:19–20.** The disciples were glad (NIV: overjoyed) when they saw the Lord—not their circumstances, but the Lord.

3. **Easter Brings Joy to Us—John 16:19–22.** Jesus implied that in all of human history, the devil has had but three days of joy. This ungodly world had a three-day period of jubilation. While the body of Jesus was in the borrowed tomb, Satan was ecstatic. Likewise, in human history there has only been three days of soul-sinking despair for believers—while the body of Jesus was in that tomb. Jesus said, "For a few hours, the world will rejoice and you will weep and mourn. But suddenly your mourning will turn to joy, and the world's joy will turn to grief." Imagine the sudden reversal of emotions on Easter Sunday. The devil's exaltation was turned inside out, and the disciple's grief became unmitigated joy. Today we who know the risen King, should live a life of sustained, unbroken joy. The king of a particular country traveled often, but one day a man living near the place remarked, "Well, it looks like the king is home tonight." "How do you know?" asked his friend. "Because the castle is all lit up," the man said.

Conclusion: Have you lost the joy of salvation? Billy Sunday said, "If you have no joy in your religion, there's a leak in your Christianity somewhere." How can we turn the lights back on? How can we plug the leak?

- Confess your lack of joy as sin. The Bible says, "Be joyful! Be glad! Be of good cheer!" Tell God you're sorry you haven't been exhibiting those qualities.

>>> sermon continued on following page

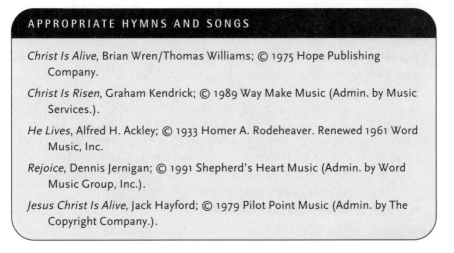

APPROPRIATE HYMNS AND SONGS

Christ Is Alive, Brian Wren/Thomas Williams; © 1975 Hope Publishing Company.

Christ Is Risen, Graham Kendrick; © 1989 Way Make Music (Admin. by Music Services.).

He Lives, Alfred H. Ackley; © 1933 Homer A. Rodeheaver. Renewed 1961 Word Music, Inc.

Rejoice, Dennis Jernigan; © 1991 Shepherd's Heart Music (Admin. by Word Music Group, Inc.).

Jesus Christ Is Alive, Jack Hayford; © 1979 Pilot Point Music (Admin. by The Copyright Company.).

- Focus on the Lord Himself. Rededicate yourself to Him. Our joy flows from our fellowship with Him. Spend time with Him each day in Bible study and prayer. Bring your burdens to Him.

- Make up your mind to be joyful. Abraham Lincoln said that a person is about as happy as he makes up his mind to be. Sometimes we have to be joyful by faith (James 1:2).

- Internalize some of the Bible's great verses about joy—Nehemiah 8:10; John 20:20, James 1:2, Philippians 4:4, and Psalm 118:24. The word "joy" occurs 158 times in the Bible (NKJV), and the word "Rejoice" another 287 times.

- Live as though every day were Easter—because it is!

Joyful, joyful, we adore Thee, God of glory, Lord of love;
Hearts unfold like flowers before Thee, opening to the sun above.

FOR THE BULLETIN

❋ Today marks the death of Pope St. Celestine I in A.D. 432. He fought heresy, supported Augustine of Hippo, and perhaps sent St. Patrick to Ireland. ❋ Donald Cargill was a powerful Scottish Presbyterian preacher when such were outlawed. On July 10, 1681, Scottish troops burst into the house where Cargill, James Boig, and Walter Smith were sleeping. The men were rousted from bed and taken to prison. Soon, two others joined them. All were condemned. At the scaffold Cargill put his foot on the ladder, turned, blessed the Lord with uplifted hands, and said, "The Lord knows I go up this ladder with less fear, confusion, or perturbation of mind than ever I entered a pulpit to preach." Five good men were martyred in Edinburgh on "that never-to-be-forgotten bloody day—July 27, 1681." ❋ On July 27, 1926, British Methodist leader William Sangster was ordained at Wesley Chapel in York. In 1939, Sangster assumed leadership of London's Westminster Central Hall. During his first worship service he announced to his stunned congregation that Britain and Germany were officially at war. He quickly converted the church basement into an air raid shelter, and for 1,688 nights Sangster ministered to the various needs of all kinds of people. ❋ The parents of German Christian Dietrich Bonhoeffer, who was killed by the Nazis at Flossenberg Prison, heard of their son's death while listening to a radio broadcast of a memorial service from London on this day in 1945. The speaker said, "We are gathered here in the presence of God to make thankful remembrance of the life and work of his servant Dietrich Bonhoeffer, who gave his life in faith and obedience."

Tears, Yet Joy

While missionaries L. Nelson and Virginia Bell were in China, their little baby boy contracted a fever and died. As they left the cemetery, Virginia said to Nelson, "I have a song in my heart, but it is hard to keep the tears from my eyes." The next morning, Dr. Bell sat at his rollup desk for his usual devotional hour. He wrote, "His going has left an ache in our hearts, and our arms feel empty, but, oh, the joy of knowing he is safe. It has but drawn us closer to Him and given us a new tie and joy to look forward to in Heaven."

The Underground River

In middle Tennessee, there is a river that runs through an area known as the Savage Gulf. Sometimes it disappears into an underground channel. If you put your ear to the ground, you can hear it, but it is out of visible sight. A little further along, it reappears. Then again, it disappears and flows underground awhile. I think that's the way it is with joy. Sometimes it is above ground and obvious. Sometimes it runs beneath the surface of our lives. But it is always there, deep inside us, flowing with a rich current and fresh waters. There's an old song that says, "I've got joy like a river in my soul."

An Old Hymn

There's an old hymn from the fourth century that says:

Joy dawned again on Easter Day,
The sun shone out with fairer ray,
When, to their longing eyes restored
Th'Apostles saw their risen Lord.

That's John 20:20, and it seems to me that this describes the Christian with 20/20 vision, the Christian who sees life clearly, the Christian who sees life in the light of the Resurrection of Christ. Because Christ is alive, we live a life of overflowing joy.

Sherwood Wirt once said:

"Joy is the enjoyment of God and the good things that come from the hand of God. If our new freedom in Christ is a piece of angel food cake, joy is the frosting. If the Bible gives us the wonderful words of life, joy supplies the music."

WORSHIP HELPS

Call to Worship:
"My heart is glad, and my glory rejoices. . . . You will show me the path of life; in Your presence is fullness of joy; at Your right hand are pleasures forevermore (Ps. 16:9–11).

Scripture Reading Medley:
Then it came to pass on the third day . . . that there were thunderings and lightnings, and a thick cloud on the mountain; and the sound of the trumpet was very loud. . . . And Moses brought the people out of the camp to meet with God, and they stood at the foot of the mountain. He who touches the dead body of anyone . . . shall purify himself with the water on the third day. "Return and tell Hezekiah . . . 'Thus says the LORD, the God of David your father: "I have heard your prayer, I have seen your tears; surely I will heal you. On the third day you shall go up to the house of the LORD. Come, and let us return to the LORD; for He has torn, but He will heal us; He has stricken, but He will bind us up. After two days He will revive us; on the third day He will raise us up, that we may live in His sight. And He said to them, "Go, tell that fox, 'Behold, I cast out demons and perform cures today and tomorrow, and the third day I shall be perfected.'" From that time Jesus began to show to His disciples that He must go to Jerusalem, and suffer many things from the elders and chief priests and scribes, and be killed, and be raised the third day. Then He said to them, "Thus it is written, and thus it was necessary for the Christ to suffer and to rise from the dead the third day, and that repentance and remission of sins should be preached in His name to all nations, beginning at Jerusalem. And you are witnesses of these things." *(Taken from Ex. 19:16–17; Num. 19:11; 2 Kings 20:5; Hosea 6:1–2; Luke 13:32; Matt. 16:21; Luke 24:46.)*

Additional Sermons and Lesson Ideas

The Joy of the Lord

Date preached:

Based on a devotional by Charles Haddon Spurgeon

SCRIPTURE: Nehemiah 8:10

INTRODUCTION: There is a bottomless well of delight for every Christian who fellowships with God. When we habitually walk with God, our joy is like the Jordan at harvest; our banks overflow.

    1. Enoch's Joy: to Walk with God—Genesis 5:22
    2. Mary's Joy: to Sit at Jesus' Feet—Luke 10:39
    3. John's Joy: to Lean on the Savior's Bosom—John 13:23
    4. Our Joy: Fellowship with Him—John 15:4

CONCLUSION: Fellowship with the Lord is not mere talk. We've known this fellowship in affliction. We've known this fellowship in the solitude of many nights of broken rest. We've known this fellowship beneath discouragement, under sorrow, and in all sorts of ills. We reckon that one drop of Christ's fellowship is enough to sweeten an ocean of trials. Just to know that He is near, to enjoy His presence and to see His gleaming eye, would transform even hell into heaven. The habit of fellowship is the life of happiness.

The Sequence of Salvation

Date preached:

By Melvin Worthington

SCRIPTURE: 2 Kings 5:1–19

INTRODUCTION: Salvation is an instantaneous event that culminates a sequential process. This process includes the facts we embrace, the feelings we experience, the faith we exercise, and the fruit we exhibit. The story of Naaman serves as illustration of the sequential process that leads to an instantaneous conversion.

    1. Naaman's Condition (vv. 1–7). Naaman's character, condition, captive, and communication are recorded.
    2. Naaman's Cure (vv. 8–10). God's *man* gave God's *message* to Naaman.
    3. Naaman's Choice (vv. 11–14). Naaman was *filled with wrath* at the message of the prophet. He *fully weighed* his options. He *finally willingly* obeyed the prophet's word.
    4. Naaman's Cleansing (vv. 14–19). Naaman's obedience to God's message resulted in complete cleansing.

CONCLUSION: Intellectually, emotionally, and volitionally we respond to God's message. The proper response brings instant cleansing.

The Deeper Christian Life
A Classic by Andrew Murray

The first and chief need of our Christian life is *Fellowship with God.* The Divine life within us comes from God, and is entirely dependent upon Him. As I need every moment fresh air to breathe, as the sun every moment afresh sends down its light, so it is only in direct living communication with God that my soul can be strong.

The manna of one day was corrupt when the next day came. I must every day have fresh grace from heaven, and I obtain it only in direct waiting upon God Himself. Begin each day by tarrying before God, and letting Him touch you. Take time to meet God.

To this end, let your first act in your devotion be a setting yourself still before God. In prayer, or worship, everything depends upon God taking the chief place. I must bow quietly before Him in humble faith and adoration, speaking thus within my heart: "God is. God is near. God is love, longing to communicate Himself to me. God the Almighty One, Who worketh all in all, is even now waiting to work in me, and make Himself known." Take time, till you know God is very near.

When you have given God His place of honor, glory, and power, take your place of deepest lowliness, and seek to be filled with the Spirit of humility. As a creature, it is your blessedness to be nothing, that God may be all in you. As a sinner you are not worthy to look up to God; bow in self-abasement. As a saint, let God's love overwhelm you, and bow you still lower down. Sink down before Him in humility, meekness, patience, and surrender to His goodness and mercy. He will exalt you. Oh! take time, to get very low before God.

Then accept and value your place in Christ Jesus. God delights in nothing but His beloved Son, and can be satisfied with nothing else in those who draw nigh to Him. Enter deep into God's holy presence in the boldness which the blood gives, and in the assurance that in Christ you are most well-pleasing. In Christ you are within the veil. You have access into the very heart and love of the Father. This is the great object of fellowship with God, that I may have more of God in my life, and that God may see Christ formed in me. Be silent before God and let Him bless you.

This Christ is a living Person. He loves you with a personal love, and He looks every day for the personal response of your love. Look into His face with trust, till His love really shines into your heart. Make His heart glad by telling Him that you do love Him. He offers Himself to you as a personal Savior and Keeper from the power of sin. Do not ask, can I be kept from sinning, if I keep close to Him? but ask, can I be kept from sinning, *if He always keeps close to me?* and you see at once how safe it is to trust Him.

Christ's Likeness

We have not only Christ's *life* in us as a power, and His *presence* with us as a person, but we have His *likeness* to be wrought into us. He is to be formed in us, so that His form or figure, His likeness, can be seen in us. Bow before God until you get some sense of the greatness and blessedness of the work to be carried on by God in you this day. Say to God, "Father, here am I for Thee to give as much in me of Christ's likeness as I can receive." And wait to hear Him say, "My child, I give thee as much of Christ as thy heart is open to receive." The God who revealed Jesus in the flesh and perfected Him, will reveal Him in thee and perfect thee in Him. The Father loves the Son, and delights to work out His image and likeness in thee. Count upon it that this blessed work will be done in thee as thou waitest on thy God, and holdest fellowship with Him.

The likeness to Christ consists chiefly in two things—the likeness of His death and Resurrection, (Rom. 6:5). The death of Christ was the consummation of His humility and obedience, the entire giving up of His life to God. In Him we are dead to sin. As we sink down in humility and dependence and entire surrender to God, the power of His death works in us, and we are made conformable to His death. And so we know Him in the power of His Resurrection, in the victory over sin, and all the joy and power of the risen life. Therefore every morning, "present yourselves unto God as those that are alive from the dead." He will maintain the life He gave, and bestow the grace to live as risen ones.

All this can only be in the power of the Holy Spirit, who dwells in you. Count upon Him to glorify Christ in you. Count upon Christ to increase in you the inflowing of His Spirit. As you wait before God to realize His presence, remember that the Spirit is in you to reveal the things of God. Seek in God's presence to have the anointing of the Spirit of Christ so truly that your whole life may every moment be spiritual.

As you meditate on this wondrous salvation and seek full fellowship with the great and holy God, and wait on Him to reveal Christ in you, you will feel how needful the giving up of all is to receive Him. Seek grace to know what it means to live as wholly for God as Christ did. Only the Holy Spirit Himself can teach you what an entire yielding of the whole life to God can mean. Wait on God to show you in this what you do not know. Let every approach to God, and every request for fellowship with Him be accompanied by a new, very definite, and entire surrender to Him to work in you.

"By faith" must here, as through all Scripture, and all the spiritual life, be the keynote. As you tarry before God, let it be in a deep quiet faith in Him, the Invisible One, who is so near, so holy, so mighty, so loving. In a deep, restful faith too, that all the blessings and powers of the heavenly life are around you, and in you. Just yield yourself in the faith of a perfect trust to the Ever Blessed Holy Trinity to work out all God's purpose in you. Begin each day thus in fellowship with God, and God will be all in all to you. ✹

Quotes for the Pastor's Wall

❝ The great work of the Christian preacher is not to be an orator but an interpreter, to teach the people how to read and use the Word of God. ❞

–Dr. John Ker

Quotes for the Pastor's Wall

" Some Bible texts are more difficult to preach on

than others. I've often said if you give a preacher

five minutes, he can complicate or confuse any

passage of Scripture in the whole Bible. **"**

–Chuck Swindoll

AUGUST 3, 2003

SUGGESTED MESSAGE

When Satan Attacks You   *Date preached:*

(A Sermon Classic, originally titled "Satan Considering the Saints," preached April 9, 1865)

By Charles Haddon Spurgeon

Scripture: Job 1:1–12, especially verse 8: Then the LORD said to Satan, "Have you considered My servant Job?"

Introduction: How foolish to lay up treasures anywhere except in heaven! Job's prosperity appeared to give him much stability in life. He had around him a large household of servants. He had accumulated a kind of wealth that does not suddenly depreciate. His children were numerous enough to promise a long line of descendants. Yet beyond the clouds where no human could see, the spirit of evil stood before God, and an extraordinary conversation took place. Satan challenged God over Job, and the Lord gave permission to remove Job's supports and see whether the tower would stand in its own inherent strength. The Lord said to Satan, "Have you considered my servant Job?"

1. **How Does Satan Consider Us?**
   A. **He considers us a marvel.** When Satan finds Christians faithful to God, he considers it a phenomenon.
   B. **He considers us to detect any flaw in us.** How he chuckles over our secret sins. Each sin born in the believer's heart cries to him, "My father! My father!" and, seeing his foul offspring, he feels something like the joy of fatherhood.
   C. **He considers us barriers to the progress of his kingdom.** He's aware that mournful Christians often dishonor the faithfulness of God by mistrusting it, and he thinks if he can worry us until we doubt the goodness of the Lord, he will have robbed God of His praise.

2. **What Does Satan Consider About Us?** Satan isn't omniscient, but after thousands of years dealing with fallen humanity, he has acquired vast experience. He knows what the springs of human action are, and how to play on them.

A. **Satan considers our peculiar infirmities.** He looks us up and down like a horse-dealer, reckoning us heel to head, so that he will say of one, "His infirmity is lust," or of another, "She has a quick temper," or, "He is proud," or, "She is lazy."

B. **He considers our state of mind.** The devil knows when we're most vulnerable, and we're often overtaken through an unwatchful frame of mind.

C. **He considers our friends.** Among some people I can scarcely sin; among others I can scarcely remain pure. Satan knows this and tempts us accordingly.

D. **He considers our condition in the world.** He has different temptations for various people. I don't suppose the Queen's temptations ever likely annoy Mary, the kitchen-maid. On the other hand, Mary's temptations may never trouble me. Our position, capabilities, education, or standing in society may all be doors through which he attacks.

E. **He considers our objects of affection.** By blowing down the house where his children were feasting, Satan sought to derange Job's mind; he later used Job's wife.

3. **A Higher Consideration Overrode Satan's Consideration.** Satan was mining, and he intended to light the fuse to blow up God's building. All the time God was *under*mining him, planning to blow up Satan's mine before he could do any mischief. The devil is the greatest of all fools. He has more knowledge but less wisdom than any other creature. He didn't know that while he was tempting Job, he was answering God's purpose.

>>> sermon continued on following page

APPROPRIATE HYMNS AND SONGS

Trading My Sorrows, Darrell Evans; © 1998 Integrity's Hosanna! Music.

When the Battle's Over, Isaac Watts/Harriette Waters/A.E. Lind; Public Domain.

The Victory Is the Lords, Kevin Prosch; © 1987 Mercy/Vineyard Publishing.

Teach Us to War, George T. Searcy/John Chisum; © 1989 Tourmaline Music/Ariose Music (Admin. by EMI Christian Music Publishing.).

Soldiers of Christ Arise, Charles Wesley/George J. Elvey; Public Domain.

A. **The Lord considered exactly how far to let Satan go.** God says, "Thus far, and no farther."

B. **The Lord considered how to sustain His servant under trial.** God poured secret oil upon Job's fire of grace while the devil was throwing buckets of water on it.

C. **The Lord considered how to sanctify Job by this trial.** Job was a better man at the end of the story than at the beginning, and God gave him twice the property he had before. He made him a more famous man, whose name will ring through the ages. Instead of influencing a handful in one neighborhood, Job has touched all of history. The devil went to the forge and worked away with all his might—to make Job illustrious! Foolish devil! When he attacks us, he's piling up a pedestal on which God will set us as displays of His grace to all ages.

Conclusion: If you want to make the devil angry, throw the story of Job at him. Oh, how many saints have been comforted by this history of patience! Let us commit ourselves in faith to the care and keeping of God—come poverty, sickness, or death. Through Jesus Christ's blood we will be conquerors, and more than conquerors. May those who have not trusted Jesus be led to begin this very morning, and God shall have all the praise in us all, evermore.

FOR THE BULLETIN

✸ On Friday, August 3, 1492, Columbus and his 52-member flagship *Santa Maria* crew weigh anchor for a voyage from Palos, Spain, seeking passage to "India." Two smaller ships, the *Nina* and the *Pinta,* accompany him. ✸ Holy Roman Emperor Charles V convened a church council in Augsburg in 1530 to address the Catholic-Protestant conflict that was tearing apart his empire. This proved to be the last Protestant attempt for acceptance by the church. They presented a statement of their beliefs which became known as the Augsburg Confession. On August 3, 1530, the Catholics issued their own statement, the *Confutio,* in response to the Augsburg Confession. ✸ On August 3, 1553, Mary, daughter of Catherine of Aragon entered London to begin a harsh five-year reign in which hundreds of Protestants were burned at the stake. ✸ August 3, 1858, marks the birth of Maltbie D. Babcock, American Presbyterian clergyman, remembered as author of the "This Is My Father's World." ✸ On August 3, 1966, Ernie Fowler, missionary to Columbia, South America, was vacationing with his family in the high mountains near the Venezuelan border. While hiking, he was shot and killed by bandits in front of his children.

STATS, STORIES AND MORE

Quotes from Spurgeon's actual sermon:

- Where he cannot destroy, there is no doubt that Satan's object is to worry. He does not like to see God's people happy. Martin Luther used to say, "Let us sing psalms and spite the devil," and I have no doubt Martin Luther was pretty nearly right; for that lover of discord hates harmonious, joyous praise.

- Oh may God grant us grace as a church to stand against the wiles of Satan and his attacks, that having done his worst he may gain no advantage over us, and after having considered, and considered again, and counted well our towers and bulwarks, he may be compelled to retire because his battering rams cannot jar so much as a stone from our ramparts, and his slings cannot slay one single soldier on the walls.

- As the worker in metals knows that one metal is to be worked at such a heat, and another at a different temperature; as those who have to deal with chemicals know that at a certain heat one fluid will boil, while another reaches the boiling-point much earlier, so Satan knows exactly the temperature at which to work us to his purpose. Small pots boil directly when they are put on the fire, and so little men of quick temper are soon in a passion; larger vessels require more time and coal before they will boil, but when they do boil, it is a boil indeed, not soon forgotten or abated. The enemy, like a fisherman, watches his fish, adapts his bait to his prey; and knows in what seasons and times the fish are most likely to bite.

Satan Is OK, but Jesus Isn't

According to Charisma news service, Kaimuki High School in Honolulu has dropped a ban on clothing and accessories that promote Satanism after a protest from a member of the staff who belongs to the Church of Satan. Students are now free to wear t-shirts that promote the devil. But a crucifix got Kimberly Draper in trouble in Logan County, Kentucky. She was fired for continuing to wear a cross necklace to her job at the local library, despite warnings she was violating a dress code banning religious decoration.

WORSHIP HELPS

Call to Worship:
We are more than conquerors through Him who loved us. For I am persuaded that neither death nor life, nor angels nor principalities nor powers, nor things present nor things to come, nor height nor depth, nor any other created thing, shall be able to separate us from the love of God which is in Christ Jesus our Lord (Rom. 8:37–39).

Pastoral Prayer:
Almighty Father, as we assemble this morning, we bring a large assortment of failures and weaknesses to Your throne, pleading for Your forgiveness, and confessing them as sins to be plunged into the fountain filled with blood. We recognize we have a strong enemy who accuses us day and night. But we have a stronger advocate—Jesus Christ, the righteous One, Himself the propitiation for our sins, and not for ours only but also for the whole world. So forgive us our sins as we forgive those who sin against us. And having forgiven us, Lord, renew the joy of our salvation, restore our enthusiasm for life, revive our spirits, and refresh us this day with the thirst-quenching waters of worship and praise. We ask in Jesus' name. Amen.

Possible Scripture Readings:
- 1 Peter 5:5–11
- Zechariah 3:1–5
- Matthew 4:1–11

Kids Talk

A little boy once went to his father, troubled about something. He asked, "Dad, is the devil bigger than I am?"

The father said, "Yes, he is."

"Is he bigger than you are?"

"Well, yes, he is," replied the father.

The little boy thought a moment, then asked, "Is he bigger than Jesus?"

Now, what do you think the father said? He replied, "Oh, no. Of course not. Jesus is bigger, and we are more than conquerors through Him."

Additional Sermons and Lesson Ideas

Five Reasons to Be Filled with the Holy Spirit
Date preached:
By Jack Hayford

SCRIPTURE: Ephesians 5:18

INTRODUCTION: The indwelling of the Spirit is given to us at the time we receive Jesus. The overflow of the Holy Spirit happens when we receive the Holy Spirit at the dimension that He comes from Jesus with power. Being filled with the Holy Spirit is not automatic; we open up to it. Literally translated, this text says, "Be filled with the Spirit—and keep on being filled." Why should we be filled with the Spirit?

1. Because Jesus promised the "Comforter" to come beside us and complete God's purpose for us by His power in us.
2. Because Jesus wants to replicate His life in each of us by this means.
3. Because the fullness of the Holy Spirit overflows into the empty places of our spiritual capacities and expels the unworthy influences of the world's spirit.
4. Because the power of the Holy Spirit births a passion to reach the unsaved.
5. Because spiritual fullness begets ceaseless praise and prayer that exalts Christ, breaks evil bonds, and builds up believers.

CONCLUSION: We're living in tough times, but there's a reservoir in heaven with enough for every person forever. We need to tap in and keep on being filled with the Spirit.

The Making of a Prophet
Date preached:

SCRIPTURE: 1 Samuel 3

INTRODUCTION: God wants to use each person, and when we bring our children to Jesus and to church, He has a head start, as we see with the boy Samuel. In this chapter, we see:

1. A Boy Who Ministered Before the Lord (v. 1). What did he do? Simple tasks, such as opening the gates of the tabernacle (v. 15). But he learned in childhood to be faithful in little things.
2. A Youth Who Listened to the Lord (v. 10). Eli taught him a vital prayer: "Speak, Lord, for your servant hears."
3. A Man Who Spoke for the Lord (vv. 19-21). God let none of his words "fall to the ground."

CONCLUSION: The Lord can use us, beginning right where we are.

Pilgrim's Progress
By John Bunyan

A literary classic, according to Mark Twain, is "a book which people praise and don't read."

A book, in other words, like *Pilgrim's Progress*. It's a sad, safe bet that only a few of us have actually read *Pilgrim's Progress*, but in the days before fiction was so frothy and non-fiction so specialized, Christians regularly read *Pilgrim's Progress* alongside their Bibles, finding the former a light on their pathway and the latter a roadmap for their journey. It sold more than 100,000 copies during Bunyan's lifetime, and millions of copies since.

The Tinker of Bedford

The author of *Pilgrim's Progress* was an unlikely prospect for greatness. John Bunyan (1628–1688) was born and raised with little education in the village of Bedford, England. He grew up wild and course, lying, blaspheming, drinking, gambling, and punctuating every sentence with profanity. He became a tinker by profession, a mender of pots and pans. But one day, passing some women in the street, he overheard them talking of the things of God and was seized by conviction. After a period of anguish, he found Christ as his Savior and joined the local Baptist church.

On November 12, 1660, Bunyan arrived at a farmhouse to conduct a service only to learn that a warrant had been issued for his arrest on charges of unauthorized preaching. His friends urged him to flee, but he refused. The service was disrupted by the local constable, and Bunyan managed only a few parting words before being arrested. He spent the next twelve years in a dank prison, during which time his wife and children lived in bitter poverty. For a while Bunyan supported his family by making laces in prison; but shortly he discovered a hidden gift—the ability to write. His fame as an imprisoned writer fueled sales of his books, and he eventually wrote 60 volumes, one for every year he lived.

Two Scenes

Pilgrim's Progress, written during the final years of his incarceration, is an allegory in which Bunyan describes the Christian life in terms of a pilgrim's traveling from the City of Destruction to the Celestial City.

Two scenes from the book are favorites of mine. The first is at the beginning of the story, when pilgrim realized his guilt and lostness. Saddled to his back was a heavy burden of sin and shame. "I fear that this burden upon my back will sink me lower than the grave," he said, staggering under its weight. But then he approached a hill called Calvary.

Up this way, therefore, did burdened Christian run, but not without great difficulty, because of the load on his back. He ran thus till he came to a place somewhat ascending; and upon that place stood a cross, and a little below, in the bottom, a sepulchre. So I saw in my dream, that just as Christian came up with the cross, his burden loosed from his shoulders, and fell from off his back, and began to tumble, and so continued to do till it came to the mouth of the sepulchre, where it fell in, and I saw it no more.

In another memorable scene near the end of the book, Christian, taking a wrong turn, was captured by Giant Despair, who imprisoned him in the dungeon of Doubting Castle with its grim battlements and thick, black walls. Christian tried to sing, but couldn't. His mood was dungeon-dark. Giant Despair beat him mercilessly, and he grew weaker each day. At length he found in his cell a rope, a knife, and a bottle, and for a moment he was tempted to end his misery.

But one evening about midnight he began to pray, and "a little before day, good Christian, as one half amazed, brake out into this passionate speech: What a fool am I, thus to lie in a stinking dungeon, when I may as well walk at liberty! I have a key in my bosom, called Promise, that will, I am sure, open any lock in Doubting Castle."

It did. Using the key of God's promises, Christian escaped, never again to fall into the clutches of Giant Despair.

Those two scenes illustrate the vividness of Bunyan's grip on the Christian life. Every stage of pilgrim's journey illustrates some aspect of our spiritual experience, and Bunyan portrays Christian living with remarkable insight, clarity, and hopefulness.

If you've never read *Pilgrim's Progress,* try wading through the original—it isn't all that difficult—or pick up a version in which the language and format have been updated, making it easier to follow. You can purchase a new copy, or, even better, search out a sturdy old volume in a used book store. In either case, you'll find *Pilgrim's Progress* a marvelous map for your journey and a classic worth reading. ❈

AUGUST 10, 2003

SUGGESTED SERMON

And the Walls Fell Down Flat *Date preached:*

Scripture: Joshua 6:1–27, especially verse 1: Now Jericho was securely shut up because of the children of Israel; none went out, and none came in.

Introduction: Americans are having problems sleeping well. A poll released last year by the National Sleep Foundation showed that 74 percent of respondents suffered symptoms of a sleep disorder a few nights a week or more. The number was up significantly from 62 percent in 1999. Those symptoms include difficulty falling asleep, waking up a lot during the night, waking up too early and not being able to go back to sleep, and waking up unrefreshed. The problem is that we have more to worry about nowadays. Most of us are experiencing various levels of stress due to problems in life. This chapter in Joshua tells us what to do with those stubborn problems that are like a city "securely shut up."

Background: Joshua and the children of Israel had finished their forty-year trek in the wilderness, had crossed the Jordan River, and were ready to sweep into the long-awaited Promised Land. But they faced a great obstacle, the city of Jericho. It was an unsolvable problem—vast, powerful, directly in their path, and undefeatable. Do you have any problems like that? For the Israelites, the Lord's solution was strange. He told them to march around the city one time a day for six days, then to march around the city seven times on the seventh day. Afterward they were to blow the trumpets, to shout with a great shout, and the walls would fall down flat—and that's what happened. What is the lesson for us? When we face an unsolvable problem, one like a city securely shut up, we must realize that God alone can solve it. But He expects us to encompass the problem as He directs:

1. **Encircle the Problem with Prayer.** How often in the Bible did the Lord's people, facing an unsolvable problem, encompass it with prayer, beseeching the Lord to do what no human power could do. Examples: Abraham's servant praying for a bride for Isaac in Genesis 24; the Israelites praying for deliverance at the Red Sea in Exodus 14; Hezekiah facing the invasion of Assyria in 2 Kings 19; the church praying for Peter's deliverance in Acts

12. In *The Kneeling Christian,* the anonymous author gives this advice to those burdened for loved ones who, despite our pleading, are tightly "shut up" against the Lord: "They may not listen to us when we plead with them, but they cannot hold out if we pray for them. . . . Tell God, and then trust God."

2. **Encircle the Problem with Praise.** On the seventh day, Joshua said, "Shout, for the Lord has given you the city!" The ability to praise the Lord in the midst of impossibility is a powerful secret. Satan can't abide the presence of godly praise and worship. An old hymn, translated from the German, says: "Does sadness fill my mind? A solace here I find, May Jesus Christ be praised! / Or fades my earthly bliss? My comfort still is this, May Jesus Christ be praised! / The night becomes as day, when from the heart we say, May Jesus Christ be praised! / The powers of darkness fear when this sweet chant they hear, May Jesus Christ be praised!"

3. **Encircle the Problem with Faith.** What an act of faith for Joshua and the Israelites! They had no organized army, no weapons, nothing but sheer obedience to an odd command while going against a powerful enemy. Hebrews 11:30 says, "By faith the walls of Jericho fell down after they were encircled for seven days." When we have those unsolvable problems, we encompass them by prayer and praise, then we continue walking around them by faith until the walls fall and the Lord sends His deliverance.

>>> *sermon continued on following page*

APPROPRIATE HYMNS AND SONGS

'Tis So Sweet to Trust in Jesus, Louisa M.R. Stead; Public Domain.

Faith, Geoff Bullock; © 1994 Word Music, Inc./Maranatha! Music; © Admin. by Word Music Group, Inc.

God Is in Control, Twila Paris; © 1993 Ariose Music/Mountain Spring Music (Admin. by EMI Christian Music Publishing.).

God Will Make a Way, Don Moen; © 1990 Integrity's Hosanna! Music (Admin. by Integrity Music, Inc.).

I Believe in Miracles, Carlton C. Buck/John W. Peterson; © 1956 Singspiration Music (Admin. by Brentwood-Benson Music Publishing, Inc.).

4. **Encompass the Problem with Perseverance.** Notice that the successful result was not achieved in a day or two. It took day after day of encompassing the city. The Israelites must have grown weary, but they didn't give up. It may take time for the Lord to break through and achieve the victory in your situation, but don't give up!

Conclusion: If you're worried about a particular problem today, one that is "securely shut up," one that is robbing you of sound sleep at night, try the Jericho pattern. Encircle the situation with prayer, praise, faith, and perseverance. Don't give up, and in due time the walls will fall down flat.

FOR THE BULLETIN

❋ The Roman siege of Jerusalem began in April, A.D. 70, immediately after the Passover, when Jerusalem was filled with strangers. Captured Jews were crucified at a rate of 500 a day, crosses encircling the city. Daily temple sacrifices ceased July 17, all hands being needed for defense. The Romans, using catapults and battering rams, finally broke through the walls. The Jews fled to the temple for refuge. Titus had reportedly wanted to spare the edifice, but his soldiers would not be restrained. A firebrand was hurled through the golden gate and exploded like a bomb. The temple became an ocean of fire. It was August 10, the same day of the year, it was said, in which Solomon's earlier temple had been destroyed by Babylon. ❋ Laurentius of Rome, a deacon, was slowly roasted to death for his faith on this day in A.D. 258. ❋ A German churchman, Poppo, bishop of Brixen, was elected as Pope Damasus II, but died 23 days later, perhaps by poison, on August 10, 1048. ❋ Alexander VI was elected pope on this day in 1492. He was one of history's worst. ❋ Halley's comet appeared in the August skies in 1531, and the Swiss Reformer, Ulrich Zwingli, saw it as a sign of war and of his own death. While walking in a graveyard on August 10, 1531, he told a friend, "It will cost the life of many an honorable man and my own. The truth and the Church will suffer, but Christ will never suffer." ❋ On August 10, 1854, Charles Spurgeon's sermons began being published weekly. ❋ Missionary Robert Moffat died on this day in 1883.

STATS, STORIES AND MORE

Joy Ridderhof, born in 1903, started an organization called Gospel Recordings, Inc. to record the gospel for every language group on earth. It is now approaching 5,000 languages, and millions around the world have heard of Christ through GR recordings.

But it wasn't easy. Joy, a single career woman, faced loneliness, sickness, dangerous travels, foreign intrigue, and financial crises at every step. One year, Gospel Recordings badly needed more room at its Los Angeles base. Joy and her staff prayed about it for months, and suddenly a large site became available. It seemed ideal, and the board authorized a $6,000 deposit. The property cost ten times that much, but Joy refused to publicly appeal for funds.

She was in Wheaton, Illinois, as the deadline approached. If $60,000 didn't materialize within a week, the property would be lost along with the $6,000 deposit. Only half the amount was on hand, and Joy's staff called her in crisis. Her laconic instructions were to claim Joshua 3:5 and to "follow the Jericho pattern for the remaining seven days. And cable the branch offices to join us." No other explanation was given, but none was needed. The staff understood. Cables flew around the world: BUILDING DEADLINE OCTOBER NINTH FOLLOW JERICHO PATTERN NEXT SEVEN DAYS JOSHUA 3:5.

The walls of Jericho had fallen after the Israelites had circled them for seven days. In the same way, the staff of Gospel Recordings encircled the problem with prayer, two hours a day for seven days.

The walls fell. In an overseas call from London, a British GR staffer announced an unexpected legacy had just arrived for the ministry, and it was exactly enough to complete the building's purchase. The home staff burst into the Doxology, and Joy Ridderhof continued her speaking tour through Illinois with a new story of God's faithfulness.

Kids Talk

For today's children's sermon, why not introduce them to the old spiritual, "Joshua Fit the Battle of Jericho." Black spirituals were created by African Americans who were enslaved in this country in its earlier years. Though often forbidden to read or write or gather in groups, they could sing. They loved singing the stories of the Bible. In this way, they passed down the Word of God to their children. Sing this song for, then with, the children (using the minister of music if necessary), and end with singing it as a congregational song.

Call to Worship:
Praise the Lord! Praise God in His sanctuary; Praise Him in His mighty firmament! Praise Him for His mighty acts; Praise Him according to His excellent greatness! Let everything that has breath praise the Lord. Praise the Lord! (Ps. 150:1–2, 6).

Suggested Scripture Readings:
- Deuteronomy 20:1–4
- 2 Kings 6:15–17
- 2 Chronicles 32:6–8
- Hebrews 11:30–38a

Offertory Comments:
George Barna wrote, "When people show their full faith in God, He responds. Often we face financial challenges; often those challenges are tests of our will and behavior. God is always looking for an excuse to bless us; when we give Him a reasonable chance, He invariably out-blesses us." Sometimes we must give *by faith;* but when we do, we tap into God's abundance. As is often said, we cannot out-give God.

Word of Welcome:
In Numbers 10:29, Moses gave this invitation to a relative: "Come with us, and we will treat you well; for the Lord has promised good things to (His people)." I would say the same to our guests today. We want to treat you well and to share with you the love and joy God has given us this morning. Thank you for being here.

Benediction:
Dismiss us, Father, with a victorious heart. Send us on our way as more than conquerors. Give us this week a spirit of triumph. In Jesus' name, Amen.

Additional Sermons and Lesson Ideas

Beyond Rubies

Date preached:

SCRIPTURE: Proverbs 3:15

INTRODUCTION: Rubies are almost as hard as diamonds, much more colorful, and more rare and expensive. The most famous source of fine rubies is Burma (Myanmar). The ruby mines of Myanmar are older than history, and rubies from this area have a pure red color, described as "pigeon's-blood." In antiquity, rubies were called the "King of Precious Stones." Solomon imported rubies into his kingdom, along with vast amounts of gold, silver, and precious stones. When he wrote Proverbs, he used rubies as the standard for comparing the value of other things. In his estimation, there are three things more precious than rubies.

1. Wisdom—Proverbs 3:15 and 8:11
2. The Ability to Speak with Sense—Proverbs 20:15
3. A Wife of Noble Character—Proverbs 30:10

CONCLUSION: These may be our most undervalued assets, and those who possess them are the richest people on earth.

"Speak Up!"

Date preached:

By Drew Wilkerson

SCRIPTURE: Matthew 7:28

INTRODUCTION: Jesus spoke with authority, amazing the crowds because His words were life-changing. God has called us to be His messengers. Often our words seem feeble and we feel inadequate, but Jesus models the ingredients we need to be effective communicators.

1. The Right Voice—We must speak on God's behalf. When we do He empowers us.
2. With the Right Words—We must trust God's Word. It is life itself.
3. Spoken with the Right Tone—We must speak with gentleness and respect.
4. For the Right Reason: Changing Lives—We must believe that every time we speak we can make a difference.

CONCLUSION: We are ambassadors of Christ, and when we speak in His stead we speak with His authority (2 Corinthians 5:20). So speak up! God will use us, often to our own amazement. It is not what impresses the crowd that is important to God. Authority grounded in humility is the formula for effective communication.

AUGUST 17, 2003

SUGGESTED SERMON   *Date preached:*

Growing, Guarding, and Glorifying

By Melvin Worthington

Scripture: 2 Peter 3:17–18: "You therefore, beloved, since you know this beforehand, beware lest you also fall from your own steadfastness, being led away with the error of the wicked; but grow in the grace and knowledge of our Lord and Savior Jesus Christ. To Him be the glory both now and forever. Amen."

Introduction: All our problems can be divided into two realms—inside and outside. Some are within our own hearts, and others are found in our circumstances. Likewise, the church of Jesus Christ has always faced problems both inside and outside. Simon Peter, in his two letters near the end of the Bible, addressed both realms. His first epistle deals with pressures Christians were facing outside the church, specifically persecution. His second epistle deals with problems inside the church. In this letter, written shortly before his death, Peter wanted to leave his churches with an assurance of the veracity and validity of the truths of the gospel (1:13–14). After a warm salutation, he wrote three chapters, emphasizing the importance of: Growing (ch. 1), Guarding (ch. 2), and Glorifying God (ch. 3). In his conclusion, he summarized the whole, saying, "You therefore, beloved, since you know this beforehand, beware lest you also fall from your own steadfastness, being led away with the error of the wicked; but grow in the grace and knowledge of our Lord and Savior Jesus Christ. To Him be the glory both now and forever. Amen."

1. **Foundational Truths—Growing (ch. 1).** We have here:
    A. The *Exhortation to Grow* (vv. 1–11). Included is Peter's *prayer* for the Christians, the *provision* God had given for growth (vv. 2b–4), including His incredible *promises*.
    B. The *Encouragement to Grow* (vv. 12–21). Here Peter speaks personally of the divine origin of Scripture and of his desire to see his disciples "heed as a light that shines in a dark place, until the day dawns and the morning star rises in your hearts" (v. 19).

2. **False Teachers—Guarding (ch. 2).** False teachers and their damnable doctrines were a threat to these believers. They were a threat to holiness. Peter

reminded his readers that they needed discernment and discipline regarding false teachers and their teaching. They were to be on guard—vigilance was necessary. We have here:

A. *The Presence of False Teachers* (vv. 1–3a). In these brief verses, Peter clearly sets forth the truth, teaching, tactics, and throngs that characterized false teachers. They would have a multitude of adherents and money in abundance. He addresses the deeds, damage, and doom of false teachers.

B. *The Punishment of False Teachers* (vv. 3b–9).

C. *The Portrait of False Teachers* (vv. 10–22). Here we have the *deeds* that characterize them (vv. 10–11), the *damage* they cause (vv. 17–18), and the *destiny* that awaits them (vv. 20–22).

3. **Future Things—Glorifying (ch. 3).** Last year, the hands of the "Doomsday Clock"—that symbolic timepiece at the University of Chicago designed to gauge the threat of nuclear war—was moved ahead for the first time in four years, largely as a result of the outbreak of global terrorism. Second Peter 3 deals with the end of time, and with the solemn duty of Christians to glorify God as the ages draw to a close. Peter begins this chapter with:

A. *The Truth of His Coming* (vv. 1–7). Peter writes to stir up their pure minds by way of remembrance and to warn them of the coming of scoffers who will not believe the doctrine of the Second Coming of Christ. He reminds them (and us) to wait patiently until God's time.

>>> *sermon continued on following page*

APPROPRIATE HYMNS AND SONGS

Close to Thee, Fanny Crosby/Silas J. Vail; Public Domain.

Come, Come Ye Saints, Avis B. Christiansen/William Clayton; © 1966 Hope Publishing Co.

Day by Day, Steve Mills/Timothy Jones/Craig Bidondo; © 1990 Little Peach Music.

He Has Showed You O Man, Graham Kendrick; © 1987 Make Way Music (Admin. by Music Services.).

I Want to Be Like Jesus, Handt Hanson; © 1991 Changing Church Forum, Inc.

B. ***The Time of His Coming*** (vv. 8–13). The Lord's Coming may seem slow to us, but He is patient, not wanting any to perish but all to come to repentance. We must exhibit diligence, recognize danger, show discernment, and be steady. The Second Coming should comfort our hearts, cleanse our habits, and compel holiness.

Conclusion: Growth in grace is necessary in order to continue in the faith (ch. 1). Guarding is necessary in order not to be led astray by false teachers (ch. 2). Glorifying God is to be the consuming passion of Christians in light of the Second Coming (ch. 3). Peter had a balanced perspective of the Christian life, and these three words comprise our assignment in the end times. We must continually *grow* in the grace and knowledge of Jesus Christ. Christians should *guard* against false teachers and teaching. Christians must be *glorifying* the Lord Jesus Christ in our daily lives as we patiently await His Coming.

FOR THE BULLETIN

❂ The Second Nicea Council, convoked by the Empress Irene to end the Iconoclastic Controversy, met on this day in the church of the Holy Apostles at Constantinople, but was immediately broken up by iconoclastic soldiers. ❂ Pope Julius II, who laid the cornerstone of St. Peter's Basilica, was seized by violent illness on this day in 1511. For three days he hovered near death, but as his successor was about to be chosen he surprised (and disappointed) his cardinals by recovering. ❂ On August 17, 1635, Richard Mather arrived in Boston. An English Puritan and staunch defender of congregational church government, he is remembered as the father of Increase Mather and the grandfather of Cotton Mather. ❂ When the British monarchy was reinstated in 1660, a series of new laws stifled religious liberty. The Act of Uniformity, for example, required ministers to use *The Book of Common Prayer* as a format for worship. Many non-Anglicans refused, and in August 17, 1662, over 2,000 of England's finest ministers preached their "farewell sermons" and were ejected from their pulpits. ❂ August 17, 1761, is the birthday of William Carey, "Father of Modern Missions." ❂ August 17, 1780, is the birthday of George Croly, author of "Spirit of God, Descend Upon My Heart." ❂ On August 17, 1809, Thomas Campbell founded the Disciples of Christ Church. ❂ Radio Bible teacher Theodore Epp was converted on this day in 1927 after listening to a sermon from Ephesians 1.

STATS, STORIES AND MORE

Reading Second Peter

A Dr. Congdon once approached Bible teacher R. A. Torrey, complaining he could get nothing out of his Bible study. "Please tell me how to study it so that it will mean something to me."

"Read it," replied Dr. Torrey.

"I *do* read it."

"Read it some more."

"How?"

"Take some book and read it twelve times a day for a month." Torrey recommended Second Peter.

Dr. Congdon later said, "My wife and I read 2 Peter three or four times in the morning, two or three times at noon, and two or three times at dinner. Soon I was talking 2 Peter to everyone I met. It seemed as though the stars in the heavens were singing the story of 2 Peter. I read 2 Peter on my knees, marking passages. Teardrops mingled with the crayon colors, and I said to my wife, "See how I have ruined this part of my Bible."

"Yes," she said, "but as the pages have been getting black, your life has been getting white."

God's Precious Promises

Corrie ten Boom and her family had a special secret that helped them get through their difficult days under Hitler's regime. The family members would quietly ask each other, "What do you have in your shoe, Mama?" "What do you have in your shoe, Daddy? "What do you have in your shoe, Betsy?" The answer—precious portions of Scripture that they had torn from their Bible. They were literally standing on the promises of God!—from *Turning Points Magazine*

False Teaching

"We are living in a time when . . . philosophically, you can believe anything, so long as you do not claim it to be true. Morally, you can practice anything, so long as you do not claim that it is a 'better' way. Religiously, you can hold to anything, so long as you do not bring Jesus Christ into it."—*Ravi Zacharias*, in the introduction of his book, *Jesus Among Other Gods*.

WORSHIP HELPS

Call to Worship:
But grow in the grace and knowledge of our Lord and Savior Jesus Christ. To Him be the glory both now and forever. Amen (2 Pet. 3:18).

Daily Light
Here is today's Scripture from the famous classic, *Daily Light*. Use today's Bible reading to acquaint your church with this wonderful old resource developed by Jonathan Bagster, which is the inspiration for the "Scripture Medleys" in this volume. *Daily Light* is still available in book form, or on the internet.

As for man, his days are as grass: as a flower of the field, so he flourisheth. For the wind passeth over it, and it is gone; and the place thereof shall know it no more. O teach us to number our days, that we may apply our hearts unto wisdom. What shall it profit a man, if he shall gain the whole world, and lose his own soul? Surely the people are grass. The grass withereth, the flower fadeth: but the word of our God shall stand forever. The world passeth away, and the lust thereof: but he that doeth the will of God abideth for ever. Behold, now is the accepted time; behold, now is the day of salvation. Use this world, as not abusing it: for the fashion of this world passeth away. Let us consider one another to provoke unto love and to good works: not forsaking the assembling of ourselves together, as the manner of some is; but exhorting one another: and so much the more, as ye see the day approaching. (*From Ps. 103:15–16; 91:12; Mark 8:36; Isa. 40:7–8; 1 John 2:17; 2 Cor. 6:2; 1 Cor. 7:31; Heb. 10:24–25.*)

Offertory Verse:
"Bring to the storehouse a full tenth of what you earn so there will be food in my house. Test me in this," says the LORD All-Powerful. "I will open the windows of heaven for you and pour out all the blessings you need" (Mal. 3:10 NCV).

Benediction:
To Him be all glory and honor, both now and forevermore. Amen (2 Pet. 3:18 NLT).

Additional Sermons and Lesson Ideas

The C's of Guidance

Date preached:

SCRIPTURE: John 10:4

INTRODUCTION: The psalmist said, "He leads me in the right paths" (paraphrase). Sheep don't have good eyesight and can't see very far ahead. They need someone to guide them, and Jesus said in John 10 that His sheep follow Him because they know His voice. Here are the six C's of Divine Guidance.

1. *Commit* your decision to the Lord in prayer.
2. Open the *covers* of the Bible and seek Scriptural direction.
3. Ask for the *counsel* of those who know more about the matter than you do (Prov. 11:14).
4. What do the *circumstances* indicate?
5. Inner *conviction* will begin to develop. The Holy Spirit helps us instinctively know what to do.
6. *Contemplate* the issue. Think it through. God gave each of us a brain, and He expects us to use it.

CONCLUSION: "Savior, like a Shepherd, lead us."

"Harvest Time"

Date preached:

By Drew Wilkerson

SCRIPTURE: Matthew 9:35–38

INTRODUCTION: Jesus came to save the lost. His concern for people never diminished. Ours shouldn't either. If we are disciples of Christ, we must be willing to reach out to those in need. Jesus models the three steps it takes to touch the world.

Step #1: Be willing to go. Jesus went out among the people. It is easy to stay in our comfort zones, but God said go!

Step #2: Be willing to see. Ignorance is not bliss. We must be willing to open our eyes to the needs surrounding us and respond with compassion.

Step #3: Be willing to ask. The Lord of the harvest is ready to help us if we will ask. There is nothing more important than to reach out to people who are hurting and lost.

CONCLUSION: "A ship in harbor is safe, but that is not what ships are built for" (William Shedd). It's harvest time!

Through a Cracked Door . . .

Passing the partially opened door of my pastor's bedroom one evening, I saw a sight I've never forgotten. I was a teenager at the time, and since I was to accompany Rev. Floyd on a trip the next morning, I'd been invited to spend the night in the parsonage. That evening, through the cracked door, I saw him and his wife on their knees by their bed, pouring out their hearts to the Lord for their congregation. It was the private side of a successful public ministry in our mountain town, and I was deeply moved.

Such scenes are rare in today's frantic world of ministry. Many couples seldom pray together, and it's more than oversight. Some families race past the Throne of Grace like speeders through a school zone, their schedules too full, their lives too busy. Others don't realize how powerfully their joint prayers can affect both marriage and ministry. And some men don't pray with their wives for the same reason they fail in ordinary conversation. It takes them outside their masculine comfort zone, making them feel too vulnerable.

But think of the benefits!

Praying together blesses our marriages. Arkansas Pastor Doug Little observes, "When so much of the ministry tends to pull couples apart, praying is what pulls us back together." Numbers of ministerial marriages are troubled today, often because of busyness. Two paychecks. Schedules aflutter. Kids running everywhere. Phone calls and meetings, e-mail and breaking news. But there is a spiritual dynamic in praying together that echoes through the interiors of a marriage and slows things down. It's an intimate exercise. The spiritual, the emotional, and the physical are all interrelated. An intimate prayer-union adorns the other dimensions of both life and love, enriching the whole.

It also has self-esteem ramifications for the spouse. "Praying together has drawn me into Henry's ministry," said Virginia Van Kluyve, pastor's wife in coastal Beaufort, North Carolina. "Sometimes the spouse of a pastor feels excluded from her husband's world. But when we pray together about the needs of the church, it gives me a sense of involvement in the ministry. It becomes 'our' work, not just 'his.'"

Praying together blesses our ministries. Dave and Marilyn Tosi of First Baptist Church of Asbury Park, New Jersey, credit prayer with the success they've had in growing an interracial church. "Many ethnic groups populate our area," explains Dave. "Each has its own church. Ours is the only nearby congregation where Puerto Ricans, Cubans, Blacks, Whites, and Filipinos worship side-by-side. I think the reason is because every evening after supper, Marilyn and I earnestly ask the Lord to bring into our church those He wishes to save. We bathe our church in prayer. We don't actually have a door-to-door visitation program, though we seek ways to reach people. But the Lord can draw people to Himself; as we've prayed, people from many backgrounds have showed up."

Praying together blesses our Master. Jesus said, "If two of you on earth agree about anything you ask for, it will be done for you by my Father in heaven. For where two or three come together in my name, there am I with them" (Matt. 18:19–20 NIV). When we pray together, Jesus enters our marriages and ministries in a special way. While it's a blessing to us, it's surely a joy to Him.

But how can the two of us agree on anything in prayer if there's no time for it? Well, if we're too busy to pray, our schedules have excluded the Spirit. Samuel told Israel, "As for me, far be it from me that I should sin against the LORD by failing to pray for you" (1 Sam. 12:23). The apostles devoted themselves to "prayer and the ministry of the word" by relinquishing other seemingly important activities (Acts 6:4).

Dave Tosi explained to me that he's blessed with lots of energy, but Marilyn suffers from fatigue due to diabetes. He's usually up earlier and later than she is, and praying in the mornings and evenings didn't work for them. So they decided to join hearts after supper each night. "We made a specific time," Dave said. "Sometimes we don't even clear away the dishes. We just push them aside, read from the Scripture, and pray together."

The Van Kluyves don't have a regimented routine, but they frequently pray together during the day. "It might be when I'm leaving the house," said Henry, who celebrates his 50th anniversary in the ministry this year. "We'll embrace at the door and ask God's blessing on our activities that day. We often pray at bedtime and at meals, and always before trips."

Wally and Donna Schoon, missionaries and educators in Sweden, have found that prayer over the miles keeps them together. Wally travels extensively through Eastern Europe and is often away from home. "Every day when I pray for Donna I remember that she, too, is praying for me. It brings us closer. It is a spiritual connection point."

In my own marriage, my wife, Katrina, has been a refreshing prayer partner. Often when we pray, I'll try to choose my words carefully, praying just the right thing about a situation, thinking pastorally, and sometimes a little sermonicly. But Katrina's prayers are simple and sensible, and I come away saying, "Yes, Lord! That's what we really need!"

Katrina and I began praying together before we were married, but it has been the trials and troubles of the past twenty-five years that have deepened our prayer-dependence on each other—the addictions of a close friend, the ups-and-downs of our children, the deaths of our parents, the onset of a crippling disease. We join hands at the Throne and there find His grace sufficient. We pray at meals and at bedtime, on trips, and whenever a need arises. Often I'll come home troubled about something and unable to relax. We've learned to stop and pray, giving it to the Lord. Such times become little turning points for me, enabling me to rest and enjoy the evening.

Praying together isn't a substitute—but a supplement—to personal devotions. Each morning I arrive early in my office for a period of private Bible study and prayer. Katrina, taking a cup of tea to her desk in the bedroom, does the same. But there are times when, despite my most earnest prayers, I need another to come alongside, to bear the burden, to amplify the prayer and send it to heaven with doubled force. That's when I thank God I married my prayer partner.

Maybe it's time to lay aside this book, call your spouse, and say, "Honey, I've been thinking. . . ." ✺

David Brainerd and the Power of Prayer

David Brainerd was a frail young man, tubercular, sickly, and easily depressed. He longed to reach the Indians of Colonial America, but his first venture to a tribe in Massachusetts was fraught with danger. Unknown to him, his every move was monitored by warriors intent on killing him. But as they raised their bows, they saw a rattlesnake slithering alongside him, lifting its head, flicking its tongue, preparing to strike. Suddenly the snake uncoiled and glided away. The warriors attributed Brainerd's safety to the "Great Spirit."

But the incident didn't lead to sustained evangelistic fruitfulness, and Brainerd's missionary work in 1743 saw little success. His despondency increased during Christmas. He wrote, "I was very fatigued with my journey, wherein I underwent great hardships; much exposed and very wet by falling into the river." The next year was no better; he grew even more depressed.

On January 3, 1745, Brainerd set aside the entire day for fasting and prayer, pleading for an outpouring of spiritual power. He claimed the promise in John 7:38: "He who believes in Me, as the Scripture has said, out of his heart will flow rivers of living water."

That passage took hold in Brainerd's heart, and he began preaching repeatedly from it. The unfolding year proved the most fruitful of his ministry. His interpreter, an alcoholic named Tattamy, was converted. An immediate change seemed to transform Tattamy's life and his translating of Brainerd's sermons. Scores of Indians were saved and baptized.

Brainerd grew weaker, and in 1747, he died at age 29 in the home of Jonathan Edwards. But his story moved his generation—Henry Martyn, William Carey, Adoniram Judson—toward missions. His diary became one of the most powerful Christian books in early American history, containing such entries as this one: "Here am I, send me; send me to the ends of the earth; send me to the rough, the savage pagans of the wilderness; send me from all that is called comfort on earth; send me even to death itself, if it be but in Thy service and to promote Thy kingdom." ✿

AUGUST 24, 2003

How to Iron Out Your Differences Without Being Burned

Date preached:

Scripture: Romans 12:16–18: Be of the same mind toward one another. . . . If it is possible, as much as depends on you, live peaceably with all men.

Introduction: One translation says: "Live in harmony with each other." Our English word *arm* comes from the same Greek root as *h-a-r-m-o-n-y*. The stem word is *harmos,* which means *joint.* Your arm is attached to your shoulder at its joint. In the same way, when you have a soprano, tenor, base, and alto, all singing the proper notes, their voices *join* together to create one sound, one song. If everyone sang the same notes, we'd have boring unison without any fuller, more harmonious sound. In a marriage, you have a bass and an alto. That is, you have a two people with different backgrounds and different ways of looking at things. One is in a man's body, the other in a woman's. One has the mind of a man, the other the mind of a woman. There will never be boring unison, but neither should there be continual discord. There are three ways of responding to disagreements.

1. **Clamming Up.** See King Ahab in 1 Kings 21, who, not getting his way, went about sullen and silent. Sometimes we engage in this kind of game with each other, sending a barrage of non-verbal signals, hoping our partner will get the message. We sulk or mope around, wanting our spouse to feel guilty and to come and ask us about it, drawing us out, and eventually giving in.

2. **Blowing Up.** See Jezebel in 1 Kings 19. Elijah wasn't the first or last man to run away from an angry woman. Blowing up—loud, angry arguments—are almost always destructive. They can torpedo a marriage faster than anything else. When we lose our tempers and say more than we should, we inflict wounds on the other person and on the marriage.

3. **Wising Up.** See Solomon in 1 Kings 3 as he pleads with God for wisdom to handle disputes. Out of this wisdom, Solomon wrote the Book of Proverbs. Here are two verses to clamp onto your refrigerator and memorize as personal rules for marriage: Proverbs 12:18 and Proverbs 15:18.

Application: How then can we learn to live in harmony? Here are eight suggestions:

A. Make a conscious decision to keep your anger under control (see Prov. 29:11 NIV).

B. Learn to call a cease-fire. An escalating argument quickly reaches a point of diminishing returns, and we're better off saying, "I've got to cool down before I say something damaging. Let's go out to dinner Saturday night and try to talk through this with civility, and let's ask the Lord to give us the sense and the patience to work through it."

C. Apologize. When you do go too far and say too much, apologize as quickly as possible.

D. Don't let problems simmer. Be mature enough to sit down and talk through things openly, with a minimum of excess emotion. Ephesians 4 tells us to speak truthfully to each other. It's harder on the front end to deal with problems forthrightly, but it's much easier in the long run.

E. Remember you don't have to say everything you think. Proverbs 29:11 in the King James Version reads, "A fool uttereth all his mind." Elizabeth Elliot advises, "Never pass up an opportunity to keep your mouth shut."

F. Be willing to agree to disagree. If two people agree on everything, they double their chances of being wrong.

>>> sermon continued on following page

APPROPRIATE HYMNS AND SONGS

Bind Us Together, Bob Gillman; © 1977 Kingsway's Thank You Music (Admin. by EMI Christian Music Publishing Co.).

Family Song, Steve Hampton; © 1978, 1985 Scripture in Song (Admin. by Integrity Music, Inc.).

In Our Households Heavenly Father, Marie J. Post/Dale Grotenhuis; © 1987 CRC Publications.

Lord, Make Our Homes, Bob Burroughs/Esther Burroughs; © 1982 Broadman Press (Admin. by Genevox Music Group.).

Quiet Please, Brent Lamb/Laurie Lamb; © 1985 Singspiration Music (Admin. by Brentwood-Benson Music Publishing, Inc.).

G. Pick up a good book on marriage. Christian bookstores have a wide assortment of books on marriage, and it's surprising how they can help. Or attend a marriage retreat, or sign up for some simple marriage counseling from a Christian counselor.

H. Keep tight accounts with the Lord. Many conflicts with other people are not fundamentally horizontal but vertical. In other words, if my heart isn't right with the Lord, it probably isn't going to be positive toward my mate. The reason Ahab was bitter toward Naboth, and Jezebel was furious with Elijah, was that their own hearts were out of fellowship with God. If I become irritable or out-of-sorts with my spouse it's often because my heart is out of tune with the Lord in some way.

Conclusion: We're either going to harm or harm*onize*. If we're going to enjoy healthy relationships, we can't clam up or blow up. We've got to wise up, which

---

FOR THE BULLETIN

❁ Mt. Vesuvius erupted on August 24, A.D. 79, burying the Italian towns of Pompeii and Herculaneum. ❁ On August 24, 410, Barbarian invaders stampeded across Europe, trampling everything in their path. Roman legions, unable to defend their 10,000-mile frontier, collapsed; the intruders penetrated Italy to the gates of Rome itself. The Eternal City fell to Alaric and his swarms. For three days Rome was plundered. This represented the fall of the western Roman Empire. ❁ The second volume of the Gutenberg Bible was bound on this day in 1456, making the Bible the first full-length book to be printed using movable type. ❁ Today is the birthday of the Countess of Huntingdon, born Selina Shirley Hastings in 1707. She became a great benefactor and supporter of the Wesleys and of George Whitefield, selling her jewels to help promote the gospel. ❁ Isaac Backus, American Baptist minister and champion of freedom of religion, was born on August 24, 1741; and William Wilberforce, evangelical leader who led the crusade against slavery in the British Empire, was born on August 24, 1759. ❁ On August 24, 1891, Thomas Edison patented his motion picture camera. ❁ Pastor and devotional writer, E. M. Bounds, died on August 24, 1913, at his home in Washington, Georgia, at age 78. He is chiefly remembered for his powerful volumes on prayer. He wrote, "Prayer is no fitful, short-lived thing. It is no voice crying unheard or unheeded in the silence. It is a voice which goes into God's ear, and it lives as long as God's ear is open to holy pleas, as long as God's heart is alive to holy things."

STATS, STORIES AND MORE

Scott Stanley is part of a research team at the University of Denver that has identified factors that accurately predict whether a marriage will survive or fail. Two of them are especially dangerous. The first is *escalation*. Escalation occurs when a person says something negative and his or her spouse responds in kind, with an even harsher statement. This leads to an argument that spirals to greater levels of anger and frustration. In some ways, this is very natural for us. Whenever we're criticized, our first impulse is to defend ourselves by turning the tables on the one attacking us. We lash back, and our words can be harsh. It's especially dangerous when one of the partners says something like, "If that's the way you feel, maybe I should just move out." The other might respond with: "Don't let me stand in your way!"

Stanley refers to one couple he counseled who began discussing household chores, but in no time they were threatening divorce. He said, "They made the mistake of threatening their very commitment to the relationship—a very common and very destructive battle strategy. No matter how angry you become or how much pain you're feeling, it's never appropriate to punish your mate by threatening divorce. Rather than helping your spouse see things your way, it only causes him or her to question your commitment to the relationship."

The second deadly factor in a marriage, according to Dr. Scott Stanley, is *invalidation*. In simplest terms, this means putting each other down, calling one another names, or making personal comments or insults about the other. It includes ridiculing one another and being sarcastic. You invalidate the other person. You belittle them and attack their self-worth. This is no way to deal with conflict; it only hurts the marriage and the mate. Instead of clamming up and blowing up, I'd like to recommend a third response to problems in your marriage: Wising up.

Kids Talk

For today's children sermon, photocopy some little cards bearing the words of Romans 12:18 (use an easy-to-read translation). This is the verse about getting along with others. Ask the children if they sometimes argue or fight with others. Ask them to think of someone that they may not like very well. Tell them that God has a wonderful verse to help us in such times. Give out the cards, read the verse together, and suggest they post this verse somewhere at home where they can see it often and learn it.

WORSHIP HELPS

Call to Worship:

Come, behold the works of the Lord. . . . (He) will be exalted among the nations, (He) will be exalted in the earth! The Lord of hosts is with us, the God of Jacob is our refuge (Ps. 46:8–11).

Responsive Reading from Song of Solomon 2:10–14:

Leader: My beloved spoke, and said to me: "Rise up, my love, my fair one, and come away. For lo, the winter is past, the rain is over and gone.

People: "The flowers appear on the earth; the time of singing has come, and the voice of the turtledove is heard in our land.

Leader: "The fig tree puts forth her green figs, and the vines with the tender grapes give a good smell. Rise up, my love, my fair one, and come away!

People: "O my dove, in the clefts of the rock, in the secret places of the cliff, let me see your face, let me hear your voice; for your voice is sweet, and your face is lovely."

Pastoral Prayer:

Our Lord and the Lover of our souls, we do want to see Your face. We want to hear Your voice, for it is sweet and Your face is lovely. Help us to see You more clearly, love You more dearly, and follow You more nearly. And for those who are married, may this Scripture describe their love for each other. Help and heal our homes, Oh Lord, and give us the ability to nurture wholeness and harmony in our homes. Keep us from distance and divorce, and work within us what is pleasing to You. We ask in Jesus' name. Amen.

allows us to iron out our differences without being burned. If we learn to live in harmony with each other, we can make beautiful music together all our lives.

Additional Sermons and Lesson Ideas

Party People
By Kevin Riggs

Date preached:

SCRIPTURE: John 12:1–11

INTRODUCTION: John 12 begins the last week of Jesus' life. On His way to Jerusalem, Jesus stops in Bethany to attend a party or reception in His honor. At the meal are four individuals whose lives are testimony of their relationship with Jesus.

1. Martha (v. 2), a working Christian. In Luke 10:38–41, Martha complained about Mary not helping. Here, there is no complaint. She had learned that service to Christ was a joy and privilege.
2. Mary (vv. 3–8), a worshiping Christian. Mary anoints Jesus as a real act of worship. What she did was a spontaneous reaction to her love for Christ.
3. Judas (vv. 4–6), a worldly Christian. Judas, the treasurer for Jesus and His disciples, was concerned with worldly, material things.
4. Lazarus (vv. 9–11), a witnessing Christian. Jesus had raised Lazarus from the dead. As a result, Lazarus became a mighty witness of the grace of God. Many people believed because of Lazarus.

CONCLUSION: The question is, "What kind of Christian are you? How you live your life will be a testimony to your relationship with Jesus Christ.

"Choose Your Attitude Carefully!"
By Timothy Beougher

Date preached:

SCRIPTURE: James 4:7–10

INTRODUCTION: James sets forth four attitudes we must cultivate to overcome worldliness.

1. Submission (v. 7). The world tell us to assert ourselves, but the Word says "Submit yourself." Submission is saying, "Not my will but Thy will be done."
2. Repentance (v. 8). This exhortation contains a veiled reference to the Old Testament sacrificial system. The phrase "come near" was used to describe the high priest's entering God's presence. Cleansing the hands and purifying the heart refer to the ceremonial cleansing that was a prerequisite for approaching God in the Levitical system.
3. Contrition (v. 9). James isn't saying we should go around as if we have been sucking on a lemon. He was writing to people whose worldliness had brought harm to the body of Christ.
4. Humility (v. 10). He has now come full circle in his argument.

CONCLUSION: "The true way to be humble," Phillips Brooks said, "is not to stoop until you are smaller than yourself, but to stand at your real height against some higher nature."

AUGUST 31, 2003

Water to Wine

Date preached:

By Peter Grainger

Scripture: John 2:1–11, especially verse 11: This beginning of signs Jesus did in Cana of Galilee, and manifested His glory; and His disciples believed in Him.

Introduction: This was a "first"—our Lord's first miracle. John calls it, "the beginning of signs." But what did it signify? Many implausible theories have been propounded. Augustine, for example, suggested the water-pots represented six successive ages from Adam to Christ. Some modern writers have construed here a license to attend parties with uninhibited consumption of alcohol. But verse 11 explains the point of the miracle: By it Christ revealed His glory, and His disciples trusted Him. The purpose of the miracle was to show who Jesus is—the first clue to His true identity. The occasion is a marriage, but the focus is on a miracle. We know nothing of the bride or groom, not even their names—the spotlight is on Jesus.

I.   **The Request of Mary.** Perhaps Mary was related to the bride or groom, or she may have just been catering the arrangements. Wine was the common and safest drink in those days, usually diluted so it was only mildly alcoholic, enough to preserve it from degeneration in a hot climate. Running out of wine was a serious breach of protocol, and Mary quietly informed Jesus. His reply to her, "Woman . . . ," was not as abrupt as it sounds, but it is significant that Jesus addressed her like this and not as "Mother." The priority of Jesus now is His relationship with His heavenly Father, not His earthly mother. Yet He doesn't ignore her request, for there is a pressing need. Human resources have run dry. In His ministry, Jesus constantly met with people whose resources had run dry—sick people, sad people, lonely people, lost people, even those who had "everything," yet something was missing, like the rich young ruler to whom Jesus said, "One thing you lack." Even the joy and fulfilment of love between a man and a woman which culminates in marriage is not enough. Sooner or later the wine will run out. Maybe that's your experience. You have everything life has to offer, but something is missing.

2. **The Obedience of the Servants.** When people acknowledge their need, they often seek help from "religion." But mere religion is an outer shell with no inner life, symbolised here by the water jars standing nearby, used for ceremonial washing. They were empty, like the religion they represented. The water had been used, and the guests were externally clean but still inwardly defiled. Jesus told the servants, "Fill the jars with water," so they filled them to the brim. They obeyed with enthusiasm, and the divine part was done by Him. It was a miracle of transformation by which the ordinary became extraordinary, and that which was insipid became full of life.

3. **The Surprise of the Host.** The chief steward was surprised as he tasted this wine. "You've saved the best till last," he said, and therein lies another wonderful lesson. Bishop J. C. Ryle wrote: "The world gives its best things, like the best wine, first, and its worst things last. The longer we serve the world, the more disappointing, unsatisfactory, and unsavoury will its gifts prove. Christ, on the other hand, gives His servants their best things last. They have first the cross, the race, the battle, and then the rest, the glory, and the crown."

4. **The Faith of the Disciples.** Ordinary water became wine, for Jesus was no ordinary man, and, seeing that, the disciples placed their faith in Him. That was the purpose of the miracle for them—and for us. Are you trusting Him to bring about the needed transformations in your life?

>>> sermon continued on following page

APPROPRIATE HYMNS AND SONGS

Above All Others, Craig Musseau; © 1990 Mercy/Vineyard Publishing.

Let the Weight of Your Glory Fall, Steve Merkel; © 1999 Integrity's Hosanna! Music (Admin. by Integrity Music, Inc.).

Let Go and Let God Have His Way, Harry D. Clarke; © 1937, 1965 Singspiration Music (Admin. by Brentwood-Benson Music Publishing, Inc.).

Here I Am, Bill Batstone; © 1996 Maranatha Praise, Inc. (Admin. by The Copyright Company.).

Christ, We Do All Adore Thee, Theodore Dubois/Theodore Baker; Public Domain.

5. **The Glory of Jesus.** "Glory" describes God's divine nature. According to John 20:30–31, John recorded these "signs" that we, too, may see who Jesus really is and believe. When you put your trust in Him, He'll do a miracle of transformation in your life, allowing you to see His glory, to believe, and to experience His miraculous power in your own life.

Conclusion: Christ offers us, as it were, new wine, new life. God's presence within us fills us with indescribable joy. It is not external religion but inner reality. It is not produced by alcohol or other stimulants but by the Spirit (see Eph. 5:18). Is that your experience? Jesus said that the kingdom of heaven is like a wedding banquet, prepared by the king for his son (Matt. 22: 1–14). The invitations are going out. The messengers are combing the highways and byways to invite all they find. Today the invitation is extended. Everything is ready. Come to the banquet. For the Spirit and the Bride say "Come," and let whosoever will come and take of the water of life freely.

FOR THE BULLETIN

❊ On August 31, 1688, John Bunyan, author of *Pilgrim's Progress,* died. On his deathbed, battling high fever, Bunyan rambled in tortured, fractured words; but even these were collected and published as *Mr. Bunyan's Dying Sayings.*

❊ August 31, 1820, marks the birth of Anna Bartlett Warner, author of the children's hymn, "Jesus Loves Me." ❊ Missionary Sarah Judson, second wife of missionary Adoniram Judson, was a devout Christian, a hymnist, and the mother of eleven children. She and Adoniram (whose first wife, Ann, had died in 1826) were married in 1834. She went to work translating Christian works into the Burmese language. Suffering from exhaustion, she and Adoniram left for America in June, 1845. Sarah died en route on August 31, 1845. ❊ August 31, 1861, is the birthday of Jesse Brown Pounds, author of the hymns, "Anywhere with Jesus," "I Know that My Redeemer Liveth," and "The Way of the Cross Leads Home." ❊ Evangelist J. H. Sullivan was holding a revival service at Pine Log Methodist Church in Pine Log, Georgia, but the response to the meetings was disappointing. During the last service, Sunday night, August 31, 1886, Sullivan prayed, "Lord, If it takes it to move the hearts of these people, shake the ground on which this old building stands!" Almost immediately, the building shook perceptibly. Many of those present rushed to the altar to pray for repentance. This became known as the "Earthquake Revival." It was later learned that the tremors they had felt were marginal shock waves from the great earthquake which demolished much of Charleston and the coastal area of South Carolina." ❊ On August 31, 1937, missionary Isabel Kuhn set sail for China.

STATS, STORIES AND MORE

Everything, Yet Empty

- "To the outside world, I was mother of two beautiful kids, a wife to Rod, and a successful model without any financial worries, but, inside, I was in torment."—*Rachel Hunter*, on why she divorced rock legend Rod Stewart

- "Everybody basically has an empty hole inside of them that they try to fill with money, drugs, alcohol, power—and none of the material stuff works."—*Robert F. Kennedy, Jr.*

- The great Israeli statesman, Abba Eban, wrote in his autobiography about a conversation he once had with Edmund Hillary, the first man to climb Mount Everest. Eban asked Hillary what exactly he felt when he reached the peak. He replied that the first sentiment was one of ecstatic accomplishment. But then there came a sense of desolation. What was there now left to do?

- *USA Today* recently (September 27, 2001) ran an article about the great, great grandson of Charles Darwin, a man named Matthew Chapman, who is devoted to the teachings and reputation of his great, great grand-father. But in the article, Chapman described himself as "up to now, a more or less cheerful and defiant atheist, suddenly overwhelmed by an inexplicable sense of spiritual emptiness."

Quotes for the Pastor's Wall

❝ Preach The Word 20 Minutes

Then People Will Not Sleep or Muse or Go Away ❞

—For many years, this notice sat behind the old walnut pulpit at the Pacific Garden Mission of Chicago, visible to the speakers.

WORSHIP HELPS

Call to Worship:
To Him who loved us and washed us from our sins in His own blood . . . to Him be glory and dominion forever and ever. Amen (Rev. 1:5–6).

Scripture Medley:
I beseech you therefore, brethren, by the mercies of God, that you present your bodies a living sacrifice, holy, acceptable to God, which is your reasonable service. And do not be conformed to this world, but be transformed. . . . When the master of the feast had tasted the water that was made wine, and did not know where it came from . . . he said . . . , "Every man at the beginning sets out the good wine, and when the guests have well drunk, then the inferior. You have kept the good wine until now!" Just think how much more surely the blood of Christ will transform our lives and hearts. Now . . . we all, with unveiled face, beholding as in a mirror the glory of the Lord, are being transformed into the same image from glory to glory, just as by the Spirit of the Lord. *(From Rom. 12:1–2; John 2:9–10; Heb. 9:14 TLB; 2 Cor. 3:17–18.)*

Kids Talk

Are any of you children having a birthday today? I know someone who is! Her name is Anna Warner, and she is in heaven now. She was born on this day, August 31, in the year 1860, in Long Island, New York. Her father was a wealthy lawyer in New York City, but a terrible time came and he lost his wealth. Anna started writing stories and verses to make money. Can anyone guess what her most famous poem was? It was turned into a children's song, and I wonder if you would sing it with me in honor of Anna Warner's 143rd birthday? It is, "Jesus loves me, this I know, for the Bible tells me so."

Additional Sermons and Lesson Ideas

Let Me Introduce Myself

Date preached:

SCRIPTURE: Romans 1:1–7

INTRODUCTION: When you're called on to introduce yourself, what do you say? Paul introduced himself at the beginning of each of his epistles, but his longest introduction is at the beginning of Romans. Interestingly, in introducing himself, he says little about himself. He talks instead about:

1. His Calling (v. 1). We are all called to be Christians (v. 6), but there is another calling, that of service. Just as Paul was called to be an apostle, we are all called to some area of service.
2. His Gospel (v. 2). Promised beforehand in the Old Testament.
3. His Saviour (vv. 3–4).
   - Christ's Humanity (v. 3).
   - Christ's Deity (v. 4).
4. His Task (v. 5). This is the missionary mandate.
5. His Resources (vv. 6–7). Grace and peace to you.

CONCLUSION: Our self-image is brightest and healthiest when it is in the background, and instead of being all wrapped up in ourselves, we are wrapped up in the calling, the message, the Master, the job, and the resources from God our Father and our Lord Jesus Christ.

The Church in Revival

Date preached:

SCRIPTURE: Acts 5:12–21a, 42

INTRODUCTION: Here we have a description of a church in revival. Ananias and Sapphira were out of the way, the church had been cleansed of sin, and after judgement comes revival—not a momentary euphoria, but an abiding enthusiasm for the things of the Lord.

1. Their Miracles (vv. 12, 15, 16). Miracles in the Bible occurred in "spurts"—during the Exodus, the ministries of Elijah and Elisha, and with Christ and the early church. God can and does, on occasion, perform miracles today, but the bottom-line miracle is the supernatural presence of Christ abiding by His Spirit in a congregation or Christian.
2. Their Meetings (v. 12b). They were all with one accord.
3. Their Magnification (v. 13). They were held in esteem.
4. Their Multitudes (vv. 14–16a)
5. Their Message (vv. 17–21).

CONCLUSION: Revival occurs when a group of Christians experience the miracle of the indwelling Christ coming upon them, filling them, binding them together in one accord, and radiating such a joy that others say, "That's for me. Lord, I want to be a Christian, too."

SEPTEMBER 7, 2003

SUGGESTED SERMON

Facing Up to a Challenge

Date preached:

By Timothy Beougher

Scripture: Nehemiah 1:1–4, especially verse 4: When I heard these words, . . . I sat down and wept, and mourned for many days.

Introduction: Green Bay Coach Vince Lombardi used to say, "When the going gets tough, the tough get going." That may inspire football players, but most of us don't respond as heroically to challenges. We shrink back and feel overwhelmed. The action-packed Book of Nehemiah can help us. The first six chapters deal with rebuilding the walls of Jerusalem, and the final seven chapters deal with rebuilding the lives of the people within the walls. Both are vitally important. Both presented a great challenge for this royal cupbearer. Nehemiah's example shows us that God can take anyone, regardless of background, education, and training, and use that person in powerful ways to accomplish divine purposes.

1. **Recognizing the Need** (vv. 1–3). Nehemiah was cupbearer to the king, a combination of advisor and bodyguard. He would taste the king's food to insure it wasn't poisoned. He would guard the king during the day and secure his sleeping quarters at night. It was a position of responsibility, equivalent to the head of our Secret Service. As this account begins, Nehemiah learned that the walls of his beloved Jerusalem were rubble, leaving the city without protection. This condition dated from the destruction of Jerusalem in 586 B.C. Nehemiah didn't have his head in the sand. He sought to get the facts about the reality of the situation and he faced up to it. We have a tendency to go to one of two extremes with our problems. Sometimes we ignore them, hoping they'll go away. Other times we become so overwhelmed we fall into despair and do nothing. Nehemiah took a balanced approach, being deeply concerned, but not in despair.

2. **Accepting Personal Responsibility** (v. 4). Hearing the news, Nehemiah sat down and wept. He wasn't like the bumper sticker that says: "Apathy is rampant in America—but who cares?" God cares, and He wants us to care. In our culture we've been told that real men don't show emotion, but

Ecclesiastes 3 says there's a time to weep. Nehemiah wept and mourned. The need became a personal burden for him. He knew this was a God-issue. God's honor was at stake, as well as the condition of his country-men. Jerusalem should have been a city on a hill, a place where God's activity could be seen by the pagan nations. Now it was in shambles. The other nations mocked Judah and her God. Nehemiah could have offered excuses ("I haven't been trained for this; I haven't even seen Jerusalem; Jerusalem is a thousand miles away). He could have been critical ("Why hasn't this been taken care of already?"). But as he prayed, he realized God wanted him to accept personal responsibility. Many things in life will catch your eye, but only a few things will catch your heart. Pursue them. This need caught Nehemiah's heart.

3. **Seeking God for the Solution** (v. 4). Nehemiah had never faced a challenge like this, and initially the solution wasn't obvious to him, so he fasted and prayed before the God of heaven. Someone asked Elisabeth Elliot, "What do you do when you don't know what to do?" She said, "When you don't know what to do, do what you know to do." Nehemiah didn't know what to do, but he knew who *did* know what to do. For four months he poured out his heart to God until he got an answer. We must do this regarding:

A. **The parent's challenge of raising godly children.** In Babylonia without the temple, religious training had to take place in the home. Nehemiah's very name ("God Comforts") reflects his parents' faith. They would have been pressured to give him a pagan name, but they

>>> sermon continued on following page

APPROPRIATE HYMNS AND SONGS

Your Ways Are Right, Dan Adler; © 1997 Heart of the City Music.

Christ Is Made the Sure Foundation, John Mason Neale/Henry T. Smart; Public Domain.

Take Up Your Tambourines, Kirk Dearman/Jim Mills; © 1992 Maranatha! Music.

Take My Life, Scott Underwood; © 1994 Mercy/Vineyard Publishing.

Sanctuary, John W. Thomson/Randy Scruggs; © 1982 Whole Armor Music/ Full Armor Publishing (Admin. by The Kruger Organization.).

unashamedly gave him a Hebrew name. They were serious about raising a godly son. I'm grateful to the opportunities we have for children at our church, but the home must be central.

B. **The Christian's challenge to personal holiness.** Nehemiah shows us it's possible to be godly even in a pagan culture.

C. **The worker's challenge to obey God's call.** A need is not a call, but a need is a call to pray about the call. Nehemiah was prepared when God's call came.

Conclusion: Are you facing challenges in your life? Learn from Nehemiah. A. W. Tozer wrote, "God is looking for people through whom He can do the impossible. What a pity that we plan only the things we can do by ourselves."

FOR THE BULLETIN

❋ Roman troops overran Jerusalem on September 7, A.D. 70, destroying the Jewish temple which had been completed only six years before. The retaining wall, left standing, is today called the "Wailing Wall." ❋ On September 7, 1159, Cardinal Orlando Roland was proclaimed Pope Alexander III, but he wasn't well received by Holy Roman Emperor Frederick II, who immediately named a rival pope, Octavian, who moved into the Vatican, leading to a war among European powers. ❋ Queen Elizabeth I was born on September 7, 1533, to King Henry VIII and Anne Boleyn (who was beheaded three years later). ❋ Count Nicolaus von Zinzendorf was a devout believer who helped launch the Moravian missionary advance of the 18th century. As a young man, he carefully studied what the Bible said about marriage, and after much prayer, he proposed to the young Countess Erdmuth Dorothea von Reuss. The two were married on September 7, 1722. ❋ On September 7, 1785, Robert Raikes helped found the Sunday School Society of London. ❋ On Sunday, September 7, 1807, Robert Morrison, 25, became the first Protestant missionary to arrive in China. ❋ Arthur F. Tylee, a brilliant missionary to Brazil from Worcester, Massachusetts, and his wife Ethel, set out to evangelize the warlike Nhambiquaras. On October 27, 1930, their little mission station was attacked. Arthur and baby Marian were killed. Ethel returned to the United States to spend the rest of her life telling her story in churches and colleges, appealing for more workers for the unreached. She passed away on this day in 1955.

STATS, STORIES AND MORE

Nehemiah is introduced as the son of Hacaliah. We don't know anything about his father, but it seems that Hacaliah had been taken into captivity and carried off to Babylon when Jerusalem had fallen to the Babylonian army. Nehemiah would have been born in captivity and grown up in a pagan culture. The month Chislev is late November and early December, and the twentieth year means the twentieth year of the reign of King Artaxerxes. Historians place this in 445 or 446 B.C. Susa was the location of the winter palace of the ancient Persian Empire, located in modern-day Iran, not far from the Iraqi border.
—*Timothy Beougher*

Gene Warr is a Christian businessman in Oklahoma. I worked with him in setting up a foundation board, and we ran into numerous problems along the way. Mr. Warr told me one day, "Tim, these are not problems, but opportunities to trust God. Don't call me and tell me we have a problem, tell me we have an opportunity." The next week I called him and said, "We have a very significant opportunity in front of us." Whether we see challenges as problems or opportunities, the first step in facing up to a challenge is to recognize the need.
—*Timothy Beougher*

Eileen Egan, who worked with Mother Teresa and with the Missionaries of Charity for thirty years, described Mother Teresa's outlook like this: "One day, after my conversation had been filled with a litany of problems, Mother Teresa remarked, 'Everything is a *problem*. Why not use the word *gift*?' With that began a shift in vocabulary. Shortly thereafter, we were to fly from Vancouver to New York City. I was dismayed to learn that the trip had to be broken enroute, with a long delay, and was about to inform her of the *problem*. Then I caught myself and said, 'Mother, I have to tell you about a gift. We have to wait four hours here, and you won't arrive at the convent until very late.' Mother Teresa settled down in the airport to read a book of meditations, a favorite of hers. "From that time on, items that presented disappointments or difficulties would be introduced with 'We have a small gift here,' or 'Today we have an especially big gift.'"

WORSHIP HELPS

Call to Worship:
Be still, for the day is holy; do not be grieved. . . . for this day is holy to our Lord. Do not sorrow, for the joy of the LORD is your strength (Neh. 8:11, 10).

Pastoral Prayer:
O great and awesome God, Lord God of heaven, You who keep Your promises, You who extend Your mercy to those who love and obey You, please let Your ear be attentive and Your eyes open to us today. Hear our prayer as we confess to You that we are unworthy and sinful. Our forefathers have sinned, and we have acted corruptly against You, and have not kept the commandments, the statutes, nor the ordinances which You have commanded. Forgive our sins, O Lord. Search every heart here, and convict us and convert us. May we return to You. May we keep Your commandments and do them. May we be pleasing to You, for we are Your people whom You have redeemed by Your great power, and by Your strong hand. O Lord, I pray, please let Your ear be attentive to the prayer of Your servant, and to the prayer of Your servants who desire to fear Your name; and let us prosper this day, I pray, on our work and in our worship. In Jesus' name, Amen. *(Based on Neh. 1:5–11.)*

Word of Welcome:
Jesus said that all the world would know that we are His disciples by our love for one another. We hope that you can sense the love that is in this church today, and that you experience it, soak it in, and then pass it on. God bless you for being here.

Benediction:
Remind us, Lord, as we face this week's set of problems, that they are opportunities, and that none of them are bigger than You. In Jesus' name, Amen.

Additional Sermons and Lesson Ideas

Secrets to a Happy Life
By Kevin Riggs

Date preached:

SCRIPTURE: Ecclesiastes 11:1–6

INTRODUCTION: King Solomon searched high and low for happiness in this world apart from God. He could not find it. He discovered that happiness is found in a relationship with God, living life God's way. In this passage, there are four keys to happiness:

1. Give of yourself to others (v. 1). Give of yourself to others and one day you will be repaid. A truly happy person is selfless.
2. Give of yourself generously and often (v. 2). The idea is to sacrificially give to others, and give often. Success is not measured by the size of your house, or the size of your pocketbook. It is measured by the size of your heart.
3. Be active and stay active (vv. 3–4). The picture here is of a person sitting around, doing nothing. Enjoy life, don't just watch the weather. Don't retire from living.
4. Trust God for the results (vv. 5–6). Some things in life we'll never understand. Happiness is found in trusting God, no matter what the results.

CONCLUSION: Give God control. He will take care of you.

Just Great!
By Drew Wilkerson

Date preached:

SCRIPTURE: Mark 9:33–35

INTRODUCTION: Martin Luther said, "Until a man is nothing, God can make nothing out of him." Many people are too concerned about their position in life. The Twelve had the same problem, but Jesus refused to let their wrong thinking go unchecked. Look at the insights we find in this passage.

1. Jesus knows our thoughts. The Bible tells us that God sees and hears what is done in secret.
2. Jesus cares about our motives. We should do nothing out of selfish ambition.
3. Jesus determines our position by our attitude. A servant's heart is the key to character.

CONCLUSION: Jesus never taught the expected. His was always a teaching of the ironic or the unthinkable. This was true of our position in life. "If anyone wants to be first, he must be the very last." If we don't like the teaching, we know little of greatness.

SEPTEMBER 14, 2003

Go, Stand, and Speak

Date preached:

Scripture: Acts 5:17–33, especially verse 20: "Go, stand in the temple and speak to the people all the words of this life."

Introduction: This little story is simple, yet so profound. It tells of deliverance and revival, of deep courage and high goals, of world-changers inflamed for Christ. In the early days of the church, revival fires were setting Jerusalem aflame. Thousands were embracing the Nazarene; the number of disciples was multiplying. No sector of the city was untouched. The streets, markets, schools, and homes were buzzing with the latest news. In Acts 4, the high priest called an urgent meeting of the Sanhedrin, Israel's seventy religious politicians. This council functioned both as a Senate and a Supreme Court. They met in a chamber somewhere in the temple complex, sitting in a semi-circle with the high priest, Annas, serving as moderator. He hated the church. Peter and John were censured and forbidden to preach. But in chapter 5, they are preaching anyway, and it was becoming clear that Christianity was not a passing fad, but a permanent faith. In fury, Annas sent the temple police to arrest all twelve apostles and to put them in the common prison. The Jerusalem jail must have been filthy. The rattle of chains and the moans of prisoners reverberated in the darkness. But suddenly the chains fell from their wrists, the angel of the Lord opened the door, and the disciples were delivered. An old song says: 'Tis the grandest theme through the ages rung. . . . Our God is able to deliver Thee." God is in the delivering business. He delivers from sadness, sorrow, and sin. He can deliver you from addictions and afflictions. He can deliver you from guilt and shame:

- The Lord your God walks in the midst of your camp, to deliver you (Deut. 23:14).

- He shall deliver you in six troubles, yes, in seven no evil shall touch you (Job 5:19).

- The Lord shall help them and deliver them; He shall deliver them from the wicked, and save them, because they trust in Him (Ps. 37:40).

- Call upon Me in the day of trouble; I will deliver you, and you shall glorify Me (Ps. 50:15).

- Do not lead us into temptation, but deliver us from the evil one (Luke 11:4).

Charles Wesley said: "My chains fell off! My heart was free! I rose, went forth, and followed Thee!" What, then, are we to do after we've been delivered? What are our instructions? The angel's words are short and sweet: "Go, stand in the temple and speak to the people all the words of this life."

1. **Go.** These are the first letters of the "gospel." It was one of Jesus' favorite words. He told the missionaries in Matthew 10 to GO to the lost sheep of Israel. He told John's disciples to GO and tell John what they had heard and seen. He told the demonic to GO home and tell his friends what Christ had done. He told the seventy in Luke 10 to GO as lambs among wolves. He told the wedding servants to GO into the highways and byways, inviting others to the banquet. He told those at the tomb to GO with the news. He tells us to GO into all the world. Where does Christ want you to go with the gospel?

2. **Stand.** This is a favorite New Testament word, occurring 47 times. We're to stand firm in the faith, to stand against the schemes of the devil, to stand fast in the liberty with which Christ has set us free, to stand girded with truth, to stand fast in one spirit—and having done all, to stand. The

>>> sermon continued on following page

APPROPRIATE HYMNS AND SONGS

He Is Able to Deliver Thee, William A. Ogden; Public Domain.

We Are Strong in the Lord, Dennis Jernigan; © 1989 Shepherd's Heart Music (Admin. by Dayspring Music, Inc.).

Arise, O Lord, Paul Wilbur; © 1997 Integrity's Hosanna! Music (Admin. by Integrity Music, Inc.).

Firm Foundation, Nancy Gordan/Jamie Harvill; © 1994 Integrity's Hosanna! Music/Integrity's Praise! Music (Admin. by Integrity Music, Inc.).

God Is Able, Chris Machen/Robert Sterling; © 1988 Word Music, Inc./Desert North Music/Two Fine Boys Music (Admin. by Word Music Group, Inc.).

angel meant: "Plant your feet, your shoulders back, your head high, your jaw set. Don't be intimidated, but take a stand."

3. **Speak.** We live amid unprecedented communications technology, but the most effective way of spreading the gospel is still one teenager sharing with another, one homemaker with another, one golfing partner telling another about Christ. Have you shared your message with anyone recently?

Conclusion: These twelve escaped convicts walked, leaped, and praised God through the pre-dawn Jerusalem streets. As the sun rose, they were back in the temple, preaching Jesus crucified and risen. They were arrested and whipped for it, but nothing could stop them. Do you need to be delivered? From anxiety? From addiction? From a messed-up life? Jesus is the great Deliverer. Come to Him. Have you been delivered? Then go, stand, and speak to the people all the words of this life. Tell them, "Our God is able to deliver you."

FOR THE BULLETIN

❋ Cyprian was a pagan rhetorician who became a Christian in approximately A.D. 246. He gave himself to diligent Bible study, and two years later was appointed bishop of the city of Carthage in North Africa. He fled Carthage during the Decian persecution, but continued pastoring the people through his epistles. He returned in 251. During the persecution of Emperor Valerian, however, he was arrested. On September 14, 258, he was beheaded. ❋ Jerusalem's Church of the Holy Sepulcher was consecrated on this day in A.D. 335. ❋ One of the greatest preachers in Christian history died on this day in A.D. 407. He was John of Antioch, known as Chrysostom, which means "Golden-mouthed." ❋ On September 14, 1224, Francis of Assisi, while on spiritual retreat, has a mystical experience that leaves him with the "Stigmata"—the marks of Christ on his hands, feet, and side. ❋ Dante Alighieri, author of *The Divine Comedy*, died on September 14, 1321. ❋ On September 14, 1741, German composer George Frederick Handel, 56, finished composing "The Messiah." He wrote the score, start-to-finish, in only 24 days. ❋ September 14, 1735 is the birthday of Robert Raikes, founder of the Sunday school. ❋ Georgetown attorney, evangelical Christian, and Sunday school leader Francis Scott Key was inspired to write "The Star Spangled Banner" on September 14, 1814, after it became clear that that American forces at Fort McHenry had withstood a 25-hour bombardment by the British. ❋ On September 14, 1927, Bob Jones University opened in South Carolina with 88 students.

STATS, STORIES AND MORE

The Indian Christian, Sundar Singh (pronounced Sing), served the Lord in the ancient land of Tibet. On one occasion, by order of the chief of the village, he was thrown into a dry well, the lid of which was securely locked. His crime? Preaching the gospel in the marketplace. He was left in the well to die like others before him, whose bones and rotting flesh lay nearby. On the third night, when he had been crying to God in prayer, he heard someone unlocking the lid of the well and removing the cover. A voice spoke and told him to take hold of the rope being lowered. He found a loop at the bottom in which he could place his foot, and he was drawn up. The lid was replaced and locked. When he looked around him to thank his rescuer, he could find no trace of anyone. The fresh air revived him, and when morning came he returned to the city and began preaching again. News reached the chief that the man who had been thrown in the well for preaching was free and back to his evangelistic activity. Singh was hauled before the chief and questioned. The chief declared that someone must have gotten the key and let him out. But when the search was made the key was found attached to the chief's own belt. Villagers afterward assumed that their evangelist had been delivered by an angel, perhaps the one that delivered the apostles in Acts 5.

Delivered

"I was not a sinner because I was shooting heroin. I was shooting heroin because I was a sinner. Sin takes on many forms. But in God's sight, all of us are sinners. Following Jesus and getting into a right relationship with God meant I had to turn away from my sins. . . . By the end of 1971, I was a new man! The heavenly Father intervened in my affairs, making me to know that I was guilty in His sight, exposing the corruption of my heart, and showing me a new and better way"—From the testimony of *Dr. Michael L. Brown* of INC Ministries of Pensacola, Florida, formerly a teenage "heroin-shooting, LSD-using Jewish rock drummer."

WORSHIP HELPS

Call to Worship:

Praise God from whom all blessing flow! Praise Him all creatures here below! Praise Him above ye heavenly hosts! Praise Father, Son, and Holy Ghost.

Reader's Theater (may be used as Scripture reading or responsive reading):

Reader 1: Son of man, I have made you a watchman for the house of Israel; so hear the word I speak and give them warning from Me.

Reader 2: When I say to a wicked man, "You will surely die," and you do not warn him or speak out to dissuade him from his evil ways in order to save his life, that wicked man will die for his sin, and I will hold you accountable for his blood.

Reader 1: But if you do warn the wicked man and he does not turn from his wickedness or from his evil ways, he will die for his sin; but you will have saved yourself.

Reader 2: The fruit of the righteous is a tree of life, and he who wins souls is wise.

Reader 1: Therefore those who were scattered went everywhere preaching the word.

Both: Preach the Word.

(From Ezek. 3:17–19; Prov. 11:30; Acts 8:4; 2 Tim. 4:2.)

Pastoral Prayer:

This prayer is adapted from an Army and Navy chaplain's handbook, used during World War II, and taken originally from the Book of Common Prayer: Eternal God, Who commits to us the swift and solemn trust of life; since we know not what a day may bring forth, but only that the hour of serving You is always present, may we be alert to the instant claims of Your holy will. Consecrate with Your presence the way our feet may go; and lift us above unrighteous anger and mistrust into faith and hope and love. In all things draw us to the mind of Christ, that Your lost image may be traced again in us, to the glory of Your holy name. Amen.

Additional Sermons and Lesson Ideas

Obedience: Our Obligation

Date preached:

By Melvin Worthington

SCRIPTURE: John 14:15

INTRODUCTION: The vocabulary of Christians is often void of terms such as duty, obligation, commitment, sacrifice, obedience, and discipline. Jesus declared that those who loved Him would keep His commandments and live obedient lives.

1. Regarding Our Wealth. Christians have an obligation to use their wealth for the glory of God. Jesus commends giving (Matt. 23:23). God desires the tithe, deserves the offering, defends saving, and directs spending.
2. Regarding Our Words. We must guard our tongue. We have a sacred obligation to speak words that edify, enlighten, and encourage others (Col. 4:4, 6; Eph. 4:29).
3. Regarding Our Walk. Christians have an obligation to walk worthy of their vocation (1 Thess. 4:1, 1 John 2:6).
4. Regarding Our Work. Jesus addressed this in John 13 when He washed the disciples' feet. We are called to serve one another (John 13:12–15).
5. Regarding Our Worship. We are to worship the Lord in spirit and truth. Worship is not an option but an obligation (1 Tim. 3:15).

CONCLUSION: Do we love the Lord Jesus? Such love evidences itself in loyal obedience.

God's Gardens

Date preached:

SCRIPTURE: Hosea 14:1–9

INTRODUCTION: Have you ever "messed up"? The people of Hosea's time had "messed up," but God was calling them back. If they returned, He said, they would be His:

1. Lilies (v. 5).
2. Cedars of Lebanon (v. 5 NIV).
3. Olive Trees (vv. 5–6). Also see Psalm 52:8.
4. Wheat (v. 7). "They shall be revived like grain."
5. Grapes (v. 7). "They shall . . . grow like a vine. Their scent shall be like the wine of Lebanon." Also see John 14:1–5.
6. Cyprus Trees (v. 8).

CONCLUSION: Jesus said in John 15:1, "My Father is the Gardener" (NIV). You are God's plantings; we are His garden.

A BAPTISM SERMON

No Other Name

Scripture: Acts 4:8–13

Introduction: Baptism is our way of announcing to all the world that we are followers of Jesus Christ. It is a public declaration of our private decision. It's something about which we cannot keep silent, even as Peter could not help but speak of what he had seen and heard. In the Gospels, Peter was wobbly, sometimes bold as a lion and other times as timid as a mouse. He is an arrow full of quivers, as unreliable as a tottering fence and as impulsive as a thief. But after the Resurrection, inflamed by the Holy Spirit, he became an evangelistic powerhouse, preaching sermon after sermon to hostile crowds in the lion's den of Jerusalem. In this sermon in Acts 4, he preaches something that has become very controversial in our own day: "Nor is there salvation in any other, for there is no other name under heaven given among men by which we must be saved." Our modern culture claims that there are many ways to God, just as there are many roads to the top of a mountain. But Peter disputed that in Acts 4:12. When we are baptized and announce to the world that we are followers of Christ, we are going down a unique and narrow road. When our friends accuse us of holding an exclusive faith, we can say four things:

1. **It Is Factual.** This is one accusation about Christians that is true—we believe that Christ is the only way to God. The Christian message *is* dogmatic and exclusive; and while Christians may not, in general, be narrow-minded people, we are narrow-minded in this.

2. **It Is Scriptural.** The narrowness of the Gospel is Scriptural. Let's take a little tour of the New Testament to see how consistently and insistently the Bible teaches the truth of Acts 4:12. We live in such a tolerant and accommodating age, that even we Christians get caught up in it, and we're sometimes surprised ourselves to see how plain-spoken the Bible is on this subject.
   A. Matthew 5:20
   B. Matthew 7:13–14
   C. Matthew 7:21–22
   D. John 8:24
   E. John 14:6

F. Romans 3:10, 21–26
G. 1 Corinthians 3:11
H. 1 Timothy 2:5–6
I. Hebrews 2:3

3. **It Is Logical.** What would you think of someone who said, "Mathematics cannot be true because it is too narrow-minded, too restrictive, and too dogmatic. It claims that two plus two equal four, and never three or five. It claims that its laws are universally true. It claims absolute precision. I refuse to believe anything that is so dogmatic, narrow-minded, and exclusive. Therefore mathematics must be false." Dave Hunt, a Christian professor, says, "The very nature of reality demands that there be unchangeable absolutes. Without definite and predictable physical laws, this universe could not function. Is it not reasonable that spiritual reality should be just as definitely defined?" Hunt continued, "Everyone knows that to fly an airplane or practice medicine or even bake a cake, one must follow specific procedures. One can't even play a game without rules. Then why attempt to avoid the rules which God has set in the realm of the spirit? Sincerity won't get astronauts to the moon, nor will it prevent arsenic from killing the person who ingested it by mistake. . . . What folly it would be to refuse to follow a map because maps are so restrictive, and to insist that any road in any direction will do! How much greater is the folly of insisting that any road sincerely followed will take one to heaven!"

4. **It Is Profitable.** A woman in California was picked up for speeding. She was ticketed and taken before the judge. The judge read off the citation and said, "Guilty or not guilty?" She said, "Guilty," and the judge banged his gavel and fined her $100. But then, standing up, he removed his robe, walked down around to the front, stood beside the woman, and took out his billfold. He removed $100 and paid the fine. The judge was her father. He was a just judge, yet he loved his daughter and paid her penalty. That is what God did for us. We've broken His standards of morality and behavior, and the Bible says, "The wages of sin is death." God bangs down His omnipotent gavel and says, "Death!" But He left His heavenly throne, laying aside His glory. And by dying on the Cross, He took our punishment in our place.

Conclusion: And so we follow Him, living for the One who died for us and who alone can take us to heaven. Here at these baptism waters, we dedicate ourselves to Him who is the Way, the Truth, and the Life. There is no other name, given among men under heaven, whereby we must be saved. We live for Him alone.

SEPTEMBER 21, 2003

SUGGESTED SERMON

A Look at the Hereafter

By D. James Kennedy

Date preached:

Scripture: Matthew 7:13–14, especially verse 14: Narrow is the gate and difficult is the way which leads to life, and there are few who find it.

Introduction: Years ago, I heard someone pejoratively described as a man that was "so heavenly minded that he was no earthly good." Well, today, for every person who is so heavenly minded he's no earthly good, there are 10,000 people who are so worldly minded they're of no heavenly good. We live in a secular age. The word "secular" comes from the Latin "saecularis," which means, "time perceived without any concept of eternity." It is like a smoked glass dome placed over the secular city so that one can see neither up to God nor out to eternity. It wasn't always that way. In earlier days, there were thousands of volumes of prose and poetry written about heaven. But, of course, in those days, sex was taboo. Today, you can't turn on the television without seeing some program about sex. But death and eternity have become the taboos of our age.

1. **Unbelievers Face Death.** When Professor T. H. Huxley, the father of agnosticism, came to the end of life, the nurse attending him said that as he lay dying, the great skeptic suddenly looked up at some sight invisible to mortal eyes, and staring a while, whispered at last, "So it is true." And he died. I wonder how many young people in college who are being taught about agnosticism are taught that? According to Svetlana Stalin, when her father, Joseph Stalin, was dying, he was lying with his eyes closed. At the very last moment, he suddenly opened his eyes and looked at the people in the room. It was a look of unutterable horror and anguish. Then he lifted his left hand, as though pointing to something, and dropped it and died. I wonder how many budding Communists are told how Stalin left the world.

2. **Christians Face Death.** The departure of Christians is far different and our destination is many light years away. Dwight L. Moody said as he was

dying, "This is my coronation day! It is glorious!" The great Puritan, John Owen, having come to the end of life, dictated from his deathbed a final letter to a friend, saying: "I am yet in the land of the dying, but I hope soon to be in the land of the living." So it is, that those of us who trust in Christ will be more alive at our death than we have ever been before, for we go to a far better place than we have ever known before; a place the Bible calls heaven; the city that comes down from God (Rev. 21:1–4).

3. **Two Destinations.** The Bible makes it clear there are two different destinations after death—heaven and hell. Hell is a place of eternal death, eternal torment, eternal punishment. Many people act as if somehow modern skepticism has evaporated hell. But it has not changed at all, as many in the last moment of the cold clammy sweat of their death agonies have discovered to their unutterable horror. Jesus called it "Gehenna," the valley of Hinnom which was outside Jerusalem. It was a dump where all manner of garbage burned continually and the smoke of its burning went up everlastingly (Mark 9:44; Rev. 22:15; 1 Cor. 6:9b–10). I say to you, with heavy heart, that there are some here in this sanctuary who will never see the inside of Paradise. They have deceived themselves into supposing all is well, yet they know in their hearts they've never truly repented of their sins or surrendered themselves to Christ. Perhaps they're waiting for "someday." But remember what Christ said to the man in Luke 12:20: "Fool! This night your soul will be required of you." God offers you freely the gift of eternal life, paid for at infinite cost by Jesus Christ. It is a

>>> sermon continued on following page

APPROPRIATE HYMNS AND SONGS

O Lord, the Clouds Are Gathering, Graham Kendrick; © 1987 Make Way Music (Admin. by Music Services.).

At the Name of Jesus, Caroline Maria Noel/Ronn Huff; © 1986 Word Music (Admin. by Word Music Group, Inc.).

Father's House Lament, Brian Doerkson; © 1994 Mercy/Vineyard Publishing.

Jesus Is Tenderly Calling, Fanny Crosby/George C. Stebbins; Public Domain.

You Must Open the Door, Ina Duley Ogden/Homer A. Rodeheaver; © 1934. Renewed 1962 Word Music, Inc. (Admin. by Word Music Group, Inc.).

straight and narrow way. The portal to Paradise is as narrow as the Cross. There on the blackened hill of Golgotha, Jesus Christ took our sin upon Himself.

Conclusion: Many people spend more time preparing for a two-week vacation than for where they will spend eternity! Do you know you have eternal life? Do you know you're on your way to heaven? The Scripture says, "These things I have written to you who believe in the name of the Son of God, that you may know that you have eternal life." Oh, Jesus, I come. I come.

FOR THE BULLETIN

❋ September 21, 1452, is the birthday of Girolamo Savonarola, Florentine preacher and Italian reformer, who was martyred in 1498. ❋ Martin Luther published his German translation of the New Testament on this day in 1522. ❋ John Coleridge Patteson, great-nephew of poet Samuel T. Coleridge, was an Oxford athlete and scholar who became an Anglican missionary in the South Pacific. On September 21, 1871, he anchored alongside an island, saying, "Any one of us might be asked to give up his life for God, just as Stephen in the Bible. . . . It might happen today." Closing his Bible, he went ashore and was met by a barrage of arrows. He was in his mid-forties. ❋ Ancel Allen, graduate of Moody Bible Institute, began working with a missions organization called "Air Mail from God," which dropped Christian literature from low-flying airplanes to unreached tribes in Mexico. On September 21, 1956, his plane disappeared. It was later found with his body inside, riddled with bullets. ❋ According to the Far East Broadcasting Company, political terrorists invaded FEBC's radio station in Zamboanga, the Philippines, on September 21, 1992, and shot three people to death. The executions were carried out after numerous threats had been made to the station about continued broadcasts to the Tausug-speaking people. The dead were: Greg Hapalla, himself a Tausug, was a Christian pastor with the Christian and Missionary Alliance. Greg Bacabis was one of the radio technician-operators. A third person, Ambri Asari, was a local fisherman who was there to tape a public service announcement.

STATS, STORIES AND MORE

Half of all adults (51 percent) believe that if a person is generally good, or does enough good things for others during their life, they will earn a place in heaven.—*George Barna* in 2001 Survey

I remember one time being in a building and when ready to leave, I opened a door thinking that it was an exit, only to discover that I had stepped into a tiny broom closet! Of course I stepped out instantly and closed the door. I probably was in there only one or two seconds at most. Now, wouldn't it be extraordinarily odd if I were to spend the rest of my life talking about that little closet? Since it is without doubt that we will spend 99.99+ percent of our lives in heaven, or wherever it is we are going, then why do we spend all our time talking about this "little closet" which will be but a moment's fleeting passing in the prospect of eternity?
—*D. James Kennedy*

Two men struck gold in the wilderness during the great Klondike Gold Rush. Each day they could hardly wait to get out of their bunks to continue their search for gold. They found more and more each day. They were so busy they didn't noticed that summer had passed and that fall was upon them. They didn't notice the chill in the air because they were so eager to get more and more of the glittering yellow gold. One morning they awoke to find themselves in the midst of a howling snowstorm that lasted four days. When it was over, they discovered they were snowbound. The winter months had come, and within a few weeks, their food supply was exhausted. Several years later, the prospectors' cabin was discovered. All that remained of them were their skeletons. On a rough-hewn table, next to bags of gold, was found a note describing what had happened to them, of how they had not noticed that winter was coming, and they were caught unprepared.
—*D. James Kennedy*

WORSHIP HELPS

Call to Worship:
Then the Spirit lifted me up, and I heard behind me a loud rushing sound—May the glory of the LORD be praised in his dwelling place! (Ezek. 3:12 NIV).

Scripture:
See, I have set before you today life and good, death and evil, in that I command you today to love the LORD your God, to walk in His ways, and to keep His commandments, His statutes, and His judgments, that you may live and multiply; and the LORD your God will bless you in the land which you go to possess. But if your heart turns away so that you do not hear, and are drawn away, and worship other gods and serve them, I announce to you today that you shall surely perish. . . . I call heaven and earth as witnesses today against you, that I have set before you life and death, blessing and cursing; therefore choose life, that both you and your descendants may live; that you may love the LORD your God, that you may obey His voice, and that you may cling to Him, for He is your life and the length of your days; and that you may dwell in the land which the LORD swore to your fathers, to Abraham, Isaac, and Jacob, to give them" (Deut. 30:15–20).

Kids Talk

(Adapt to your own experience.) The other day I was driving into the city, and there were six lanes of inbound traffic. Even though the road was very wide, it was clogged with cars, and I got stuck in a traffic jam. On the other hand, I know a path in the mountains that is very narrow. It goes through a beautiful forest up a tall mountain to an overlook. There aren't many people on it. Which path is the most popular? Which goes to the most beautiful place? Jesus said that following Him was like being on that narrow path. Not many people take that path, but it leads to a more beautiful place.

Additional Sermons and Lesson Ideas

A Sick Son Healed
By Peter Granger

Date preached:

SCRIPTURE: John 4:43–54

INTRODUCTION: If you've ever had a sick child, you can identify with this story. Here was a man whose child was sick, but who found his own superficial faith developed into genuine faith in the power of the Lord Jesus Christ.

1. A Crisis—faith in the reputation of Jesus. Notice the father's desperation (despite his status) and his persistence (despite a rebuke). Such faith is rewarded (Heb. 11:6).
2. A Command. The response of Jesus shows His love (He is willing to help) and His power (He is able to help).
3. A Commitment. The nobleman's faith is extended to the person of Jesus, and it spreads to his household.

CONCLUSION: The word of Jesus is enough.

Empowered!

Date preached:

SCRIPTURE: Acts 1–3

INTRODUCTION: According to CNN, 24-year-old Katina Shaddix was kidnapped by a truck driver and kept against her will for over a year. She left more than 100 messages in truck stop restrooms all over the country, saying, "Won't let me out. Beating me, this is no joke!" While cleaning a restroom in Tennessee, maintenance worker Binford Aycock saw the message and called authorities who, using a global positioning system, traced the truck, arrested the driver, and set her free. People everywhere are sending out pleas for help, but we usually miss them. Acts 1, 2, and 3 shows us the sequence that empowers us to hear the pleas and help:

1. The Lord Went Up (Acts 1). This chapter tells of the ascension of Christ, His return to the throne of Glory.
2. The Spirit Came Down (Acts 2). This chapter tells how the Lord Jesus sent the promised Holy Spirit upon His people.
3. The Church Went Forth (Acts 3). Here we have the healing of the lame man, Peter's sermon, heated opposition, and overcoming courage.

CONCLUSION: In a world in which Satan is holding so many people hostage, we must "go forth," having the Lord as our Master and the Spirit in our hearts.

SEPTEMBER 28, 2003

SUGGESTED SERMON

Like Peter

Date preached:

By Stuart Briscoe

Scripture: John 6:1–68, especially verse 68: Simon Peter answered Him, "Lord, to whom shall we go? You have the words of eternal life.

Introduction: There is so much we can say about Simon Peter. It reminds me of a preacher who went to talk to a group of students. He said, "I have so many things to tell you, I just don't know where to begin." One of the students said helpfully, "Why don't you begin near the end?" Well, I can't begin near the end as far as Simon Peter is concerned, but I will select three incidents in his life that, I think, will give us some helpful lessons.

1. **The Challenge of Vision** (vv. 1–15). It all started when Jesus and His disciples got the news that John the Baptist had been murdered. Jesus was troubled by this, and He wanted to retreat to a deserted area. But word spread, and 5,000 families showed up. When He saw the multitude, Jesus put His own grief aside and set about meeting needs. That's a startling response on His part. There is a tendency for us to feel that when we're dealing with our own problems, we really don't have time or energy to deal with anyone else's problems, when in fact the best therapy for our problems is very often to get involved in the needs of others. Jesus became so absorbed in dealing with these people that He allowed time to get by, and the disciples became concerned about how the masses would be fed. Imagine their consternation when Jesus said, "You feed them!" When all they could come up with was a lad's lunch, Jesus took that lunch, gave thanks, and began to break it and distribute it among the people. It was a noteworthy miracle, but Peter and the other disciples missed its significance, which is: Human resources, however limited, willingly offered, divinely empowered are more than adequate to achieve divine ends. Do we look at the enormity of human need confronting the church today and say, "Send them away, they are not our problem! Our resources are abysmally limited. What can we do among so many?" Our vision must be broad enough to embrace the principle of this miracle. That was the lesson Jesus wanted Peter to learn.

2. **The Challenge of Faith** (vv. 15–24). Jesus, still wanting time by Himself, compelled the disciples to sail off. They got into the boat, and Jesus went up the mountainside. Later He went to them, walking on the water. The disciples thought it was a ghost, but Jesus shouted to them, "Take courage. It is I. Don't be afraid." The reason He could make the first and last statements is because of the middle one: "It is I!" It's pointless to say "Be of good courage," and "do not fear," without the middle bit. Peter, catching a glimmer of this truth, asked to join Christ on the water. Jesus didn't seem too enthusiastic, but said in a monosyllable, "Come!" When Peter began to sink, Jesus rescued him, then gave him a talk. "You were doing very well, Peter, while you kept your eyes on Me, but when you began concentrating on your circumstances and doubted, you ran into problems." The challenge this time was not about Peter's vision, but about his faith. Is your faith strong enough to walk over the things that sink other people?

3. **The Challenge of Commitment** (John 6:25–68). Arriving on the other side of the lake, the Lord met some critics who said, "When the Messiah comes," they said, "He will be greater than Moses. Moses fed a million people every day for 40 years with bread from heaven. You only provided one miraculous meal." Jesus conceded the point. "You are quite right, but I want to tell you something. *I am* the bread from heaven. I have come to a world populated by millions of people living in a spiritual desert, and I am the Source and Substance of Life for them. I am all they will need." Some of His disciples thought this was going too far, and they walked

>>> sermon continued on following page

APPROPRIATE HYMNS AND SONGS

Yes, Lord, I Believe, Paul Baloche/Ed Kerr; © 1994 Integrity's Hosanna! Music (Admin. by Integrity Music, Inc.).

We've Come This Far by Faith, Albert A. Goodson; © 1963 Manna Music, Inc.

Trusting Jesus, Edgar Page Stites/Ira D. Sankey; Public Domain.

O For a Faith That Will Not Shrink, William H. Bathurst/Carl G. Glaser; Public Domain.

Nobody Else But You, Bill Cantos; © 1992 Doulos Publishing/Sausage Bread Music (Admin. by Maranatha! Music.).

away. Turning to Peter, Jesus said, "Are you going to leave, too?" Peter replied, "Master, where can we go. You have the words of eternal life." The challenge here is the challenge to commitment.

Conclusion: In the end, Peter became a man of vision, faith, and commitment—a disciple of Jesus Christ. The challenges are still the same. Is your vision broad enough to embrace the principle that human resources, however limited, willing offered, divinely empowered are more than adequate to achieve divine ends? Is your faith strong enough to walk across what sinks other people? Is your commitment deep enough to allow you, regardless of where He leads you, to keep on?

FOR THE BULLETIN

❋ Today marks the murder of good King Wenceslaus, subject of the famous Christmas Carol. Wenceslaus, who received a good Christian education from his grandmother, ruled Czechoslovakia (Bohemia) in the 10th century. His brief reign was marked by peacemaking and concern for the poor. He was assassinated by his mother and brother, who fiercely opposed Christianity.

❋ Lemuel Haynes, Congregationalist preacher and the first known black pastor of a white congregation in America, passed away on this day in 1833. His tombstone reads: "Here lies the dust of a poor hell-deserving sinner, who ventured into eternity trusting wholly on the merits of Christ for salvation."

❋ On September 28, 1884, Joseph Parker announced to his London congregation that he was planning to preach straight through the Bible. ❋ In Atlanta on this day in 1895, three Baptist groups merged to form the National Baptist Convention, today the largest African-American denomination in the world. ❋ Evangelistic song-leader and personal evangelist, Charles M. Alexander, conducted his last service, a Young People's meeting in Birmingham, England, on Tuesday, September 28, 1920. He was promoting the Pocket Testament League which had been started by his wife, Helen Cadbury, of Cadbury Chocolate fame. Alexander broke new ground in evangelical music with the inclusion of the improvisational piano style during his evangelistic meetings. At the same time, Alexander was sanctifying the piano for use in church. He led the singing for the evangelistic crusades of D. L. Moody, R. A. Torrey, and J. Wilber Chapman. He died of a heart attack.

❋ C. S. Lewis was converted on September 28, 1931. ❋ On September 28, 1938, evangelist John R. Rice began publishing *The Sword of the Lord*.

STATS, STORIES AND MORE

"One of the evangelists recording this story uses a very interesting word. He said, 'Jesus compelled them to get into the boat.' That's a very significant word. They sensed the weather patterns, and they didn't think it wise to launch onto the Galilee that evening. But Jesus *compelled* them to do something they didn't want to do. There's a little lesson here, and it is simply this: Once in a while Jesus, who is Lord of heaven and earth, tells people to do what they don't want to do. The Lord Jesus is the one in whom ultimate authority resides, and sometimes He puts His foot in His voice, and He says, 'DO THIS!' A question that I ask myself occasionally is this: 'What have I done recently that I didn't want to do for no other reason than He told me to do it.'"—*Stuart Briscoe*

Elva Minette Martin routinely experienced severe panic attacks before her dentist appointments. One week shortly before a routine visit, Elva was preparing to teach her Sunday school class from John 6. Just as the disciples' panic reached its worst, Jesus came walking on the water, saying, "It is I; do not be afraid." As she studied, Elva was convicted about her own fears. She later wrote in *Decision* Magazine, "Acknowledging his Lordship in my life, I finally gave up my hold on fear. I prayed, 'Lord even when I go to the dentist, I will remember your promise.' As she headed toward her appointment, Elva was nervous yet excited, sensing the Lord would give her a breakthrough. "He calmed me," she wrote, "even relieved my grasp on the arms of the dentist's chair. Each time I began to worry, I remembered His promise: 'It is I; do not be afraid.' What a joyous time! I had never thought that I could ever say that going to the dentist was a wonderful experience—but it was. Not because of what went on around me or what happened to me, but because of what was in my heart."

Kids Talk

Can you name something little? Look at the lunch in this bag—five fish sandwiches. If this were all we had to serve over 5,000 people, would it seem too small? Yes, but not to Jesus. A boy once gave him a lunch like this, and Jesus thanked God for it, broke it into pieces, and fed 5,000. It was a miracle, and it teaches us that every gift we sincerely give to God is big in His eyes. You might not be able to give Him a hundred dollars, but do you put your dimes and quarters and dollar bills in the offering plate? You might not be able to change the world, but can you take out the trash for your mom? Whatever we do for the Lord is big in His eyes.

WORSHIP HELPS

Call to Worship:
Fear not, for I am with you; be not dismayed, for I am your God. I will strengthen you, Yes, I will help you, I will uphold you with My righteous right hand (Isa. 41:10).

Closing Prayer:
Lord, we do recognize that sometimes our commitment is volatile, that sometimes You tell us to do things we don't want to do, and we suddenly become desperately uncommitted. Sometimes You tell us to go where we've no intention of going, and we head off in the opposite direction, like Jonah. We would ask ourselves a very searching question, and it is this: Where else can we go to find forgiveness of sins? Where else can we go to find the hope of eternal life? Where else can we go to find meaning and direction and empowerment for life? Where else can we go? And the answer is "Nowhere else." Help us, then, to recognize that the only thing to do is to be utterly committed to You. Help us to examine our vision, and our faith, and our commitment, and may You be glorified in what we discover, for we pray in Christ's name. Amen!
—*Stuart Briscoe*

Additional Sermons and Lesson Ideas

Taming the Tongue
Date preached:
By Timothy Beougher

SCRIPTURE: James 3:7–12

INTRODUCTION: This passage deals with one of our greatest problems.

1. The Uncontrollable Character of the Tongue (vv. 7–8). The tongue makes a mockery of our professed wisdom and self-control.
2. The Revealing Nature of the Tongue (vv. 9–10). Whether lifting up or cutting down others, the tongue reveals what is in our heart.
3. The Spiritual Cure for the Tongue.
   - Admit the problem (James 1:26; Isa. 6:5).
   - Focus on your heart (Matt. 12:34; 2 Cor. 5:17; Ps. 51:10).
   - Ask God for help (Prov. 4:23; Ps. 19:4 and 141:3).
   - Talk less (James 1:19; Prov. 10:19 and 29:20).
   - Cultivate positive speech (Col. 4:6; Eph. 4:29).

CONCLUSION: A young lady once said to John Wesley, "I think I know what my talent is. It's to speak my mind." He replied, "I don't think God would mind if you bury that talent."

Communicating Christianity
Date preached:
By Melvin Worthington

SCRIPTURE: 2 Corinthians 5:17–21

INTRODUCTION: Christians are God's ambassadors in this world. They have been given the *message* of reconciliation, *ministry* of reconciliation, and are the *models* of reconciliation. As Christians we communicate Christianity by:

1. Our Lives. Conversion produces a radical change in the character, conduct, and career of one who believes.
2. Our Lips. Changed lives cause those around us to ask what happened to us. We respond by sharing our conversion experience.
3. Our Loyalty. Daniel, Joseph, Moses, Paul, and the three Hebrew boys illustrate this principle.
4. Our Love. Jesus told His disciples that all men would know they belonged to Him because of their love for one another.
5. Our Labor. Christians are to maintain good works and to always abound in the work of the Lord.

CONCLUSION: Are you a Christian communicator?

The Craft of Preaching
An Interview with Rev. David Jackman
Director of Proclamation Trust and of
Cornhill Training Course in London

What is the role of a preacher's quiet time or daily devotions in sermon preparation?

I don't make a big division between the two because all my study of Scripture needs to be both devotional and theological. I need to understand it and apply it to my own life before I teach and apply it to others. It's important that we don't just study the Bible to find sermons, but that we study the Bible for ourselves. I often study in my own personal devotion life the very books or passages I'll be preaching later, and I find that helpful because the things that impact me often prove to be helpful for other people in the preaching context. It's got to be internalized before it can be proclaimed.

That brings up your recommended pulpit style, which is to preach through books. Why do you think that is a preferred method?

It's got a huge number of advantages. The first is this—that's the way God has put the Bible together, all these different books with different authors, related to different problems and situations, all with their own theme-tunes and melodic lines. When we are working with books of the Bible we are cutting *with* the grain of Scripture. We are working with the way God has put it together. Also the busy preacher knows what the next passage is. Once you've decided to preach through the book, you don't have to spend all week trying to find the right passage. You can go step-by-step through the whole book, for all Scripture is profitable.

What do you do when you come to a passage that just doesn't seem to yield anything for a sermon?

You pray. Pray that the Lord will give you insight. I often pray for a sort of key. The two things I pray for are (1) a key to understanding the message of a passage, and (2) clarity in expressing it. Very often the key comes by reading and reading and reading again. Also by setting this particular text in its context. I ask, "What has gone before? What has come after? How does the message of this unit relate to the theme-tune of the whole book?" That approach will often suggest a key that unlocks the message within a passage. Every passage of Scripture has a message that must be preached from it, and we will do it different ways at different times in our ministerial careers. It takes prayer, hard work—and a good pot of coffee.

Anything else?

Yes. After you've studied a text for awhile, just leave it. Get up and do something else—go visiting, walk the dog, play with the kids, whatever. Then come back to it with a fresh mind.

What length of passage works best for you as a preaching unit?

I try to work with whatever I think is the natural unit of the passage. If it is a prayer, like Philippians 1:9–11, that would be a natural unit to work with, and I'd probably preach one sermon on that section. In Old Testament narrative, that might be a couple of chapters.

How do you preach through a longer book, such as Isaiah?

The only way I have preached it is in sections. I have preached through it all, but not consecutively. So I have done chapters 1–12, then in another series later, I preached through chapters 40–55, then later through chapters 56–66. Chapters 13–27 I covered in just three or four sermons because of the similarity of the prophecies against the nations. So I spread out my preaching through the longer books, off-and-on over a period of years.

Where do you study and how should a pastor's study be laid out?

I'm very fortunate because I have both a study at home and an office at work. But when I had only one office, I tried to use two surfaces, one for study and one for administration. I kept all the administrative tools at one desk and all the study tools at another. It just helped me to make the break, because I found when I am sitting down to study, all the administrative needs would come floating into my mind unless my study desk was exclusively the place where I had my Bible and materials.

How do you schedule your study time?

Well, I'm best in the mornings. I think you have to find your own best working time. For me from 8:30 through lunchtime is my most productive time. Obviously you've got to be available for exceptional circumstances, a bereavement, a funeral, things like that. But normally, people know that I'm in my study working on Sunday's sermons, and I ask them in the church not to ring me during that time, or to ring and leave a message on the answering machine.

How would you advise bi-vocational pastors who just don't have time for all the preparation they feel is necessary for their sermons?

We could all do with more preparation time. I would say don't despair about that at all. Come in your own mind to what you think is a reasonable amount of time in terms of the pressures on your life and put that into your diary on a regular basis. So if, for example, it's going to be two evenings a week, then know what those two evenings are, book them in, and don't change them. I think you've got to be realistic. We can't do a perfect job at any of this, however much time we have, but we can do the best job that God enables us to do within the time constraints. I'd also say that it's better to preach less often and better, rather than more frequently and more poorly.

What do you do when a sermon seems to have "flopped"?

We think the preacher has to do the work, but it's the Word that does the work. The preacher is only the channel of the Word. He's got to be a clean channel, he's got to be a dedicated, effective channel. But ultimately, it's the Lord who does the work through His Word by His Spirit. So my job is to stand back and give the Bible to the people. Don't have too much confidence in the preacher, in the sermon, in the stories we tell, in the illustrations we use, in the way we structure it. All of those things matter, but it's the Word itself that actually changes lives. We may not see it all, but God is doing His work through His Word. ✹

Ten Commandments for a Healthy Voice

Preachers must keep their voices healthy to communicate effectively. Professional actors and vocalists go to great lengths to preserve and protect their voice quality, but most preachers never bother to consider the importance of voice maintenance. Here are some simple rules every public speaker should follow:

1. Drink lots and lots of water. Have a bottle of water available before and after the sermon, and drink several glasses per day for several days before and after a preaching event.

2. Relax your hands during sermon delivery. When your body is tense, your voice muscles are also tense, and strain results. It's difficult for your body to remain tense when you consciously attempt to relax your hands.

3. Get plenty of sleep before preaching. Since your throat and voice are part of the human body, they will be just as rested or fatigued as the rest of the body, and strain could result from the preaching endeavor. A good night of sleep keeps the throat relaxed and refreshed for its work.

4. Exercise several times a week with a vigorous workout that opens the lungs.

5. Drink lots and lots of water. One easy way of drinking three extra glasses of water is to develop the habit of drinking a glass every time you finish brushing your teeth.

6. Wash your hands often. Upper respiratory infections often involve the vocal cords, leading to hoarseness. Good and frequent hand-washing can reduce these infections.

7. When you do get a cough and cold, avoid coughing loudly. Learn the "silent cough" technique, as harsh coughing can damage already-swollen vocal cords. Also avoid "clearing" your throat.

8. Warm your voice up before preaching by quoting Scripture softly, then at conversational pitch. Consciously breath deeply, letting the words flow out on the exhale.

9. Avoid all voice abuse, such as yelling, screaming, and loud crying.

10. Drink lots and lots of water. ✿

OCTOBER 5, 2003

SUGGESTED SERMON

Don't Give Up on Believing Prayer

By David Jackman   *Date preached:*

Scripture: Luke 18:1–8, especially verse 1: Then He spoke a parable to them, that men always ought to pray and not lose heart.

Introduction: Verse 8 asks a strange and troubling question: "When the Son of Man comes, will He really find faith on the earth?" In other words, when Jesus returns, will He find His people eager to greet Him and full of faith? Or will that kind of faith have evaporated from the world? Perhaps your faith is wavering and you're struggling in your own particular situation. You've tried so hard and prayed so long about your family or friends, yet there still seems to be as much resistance as ever. It becomes very demoralizing. That's a challenge most Christians face at one time or another.

Background: But here Christ spoke a parable, saying we must pray and not give up. Give up on what? On praying, yes. But the verse has a wider application than that, and the context is the indication of that's being so. This unit opens in Luke 17:20 by the Pharisees asking Jesus about the coming of the kingdom. He responded by talking about His Second Coming (vv. 22–26), then He told this parable, ending with the question, "When the Son of Man comes, will He find faith on the earth?" This parable is therefore the climax of Jesus' teaching about how His people are to live in the expectation of His return. We're to keep on praying and trusting, basing our everyday lives on the great certainty that Jesus will come again in power and glory. How do we keep our faith strong and steadfast till then? By praying. Praying and giving up are mutually exclusive; so, Jesus said, we should always pray and not give up. Hence, this parable.

1. **What Seems So Obvious.** These two characters, the judge and the widow, were carefully drawn by Jesus at polar opposites. The phrase "who neither feared God nor cared about men" was used in the first century to mean someone who was thoroughly corrupt. By contrast, the widow was a picture of vulnerability. Her case seems hopeless.

2. **What We Overlook.** What we easily overlook is what was going on inside the judge's mind. It was unseen, so the tendency is to overlook it and view the case as hopeless. Inwardly, however, a dialogue is occurring in the judge's mind. Nothing in his mind changed toward God or man, or even toward the widow. He was still totally self-consumed, but it was that very priority that changed his behavior. "Though I don't fear God or care about men, I will see that she gets justice so that she doesn't wear me out." The powerless widow, then, wins her case by sheer persistence. In verse 6, the Lord said, "Hear what the unjust judge said." Clearly the contrast between the unjust judge and God is the point of the story; so to get the force of the application, we must reverse our two points.

3. **What We Overlook.** There is something we overlooked in the application, and that is, of course, the character of the unseen God. This parable is based on some unspoken questions of the heart: Does God really care? As the times draw toward the end and the days become more perilous, will He really keep His word? Jesus brings us back to the unseen character of our God in verse 7, moving us from the unjust judge to the faithful Father. If the unjust judge behaves like that, how much more will God respond, who is loving, merciful, compassionate, and deeply committed to His children. There's another contrast here, too—between a downtrodden widow and God's elect (verse 7) who cry to Him day and night. Whenever we're up against our adversaries, the elect of God come to Him, whether day or

>>> sermon continued on following page

APPROPRIATE HYMNS AND SONGS

Does Jesus Care, Frank E. Graeff/J. Lincoln Hall; Public Domain.

Answer Us, Andy Park; © 1995 Mercy/Vineyard Publishing.

Ask, Seek, Knock, Dale Garratt; ©1970 Scripture in Song (Admin. by Integrity Music, Inc.).

We Have Called on You, O Lord, Stuart Garrard; © 1992 Kingsway's Thankyou Music (Admin. by EMI Christian Music Publishing.).

Beautiful Garden of Prayer, Eleanor Allen Schroll/James H. Fillmore; Public Domain.

night. Their continual coming is not wearisome to Him. He cares about every detail of our lives, for we are His chosen ones.

4. **What Seems Obvious.** From this perspective, what we almost overlooked now seems so obvious—verse 8: "I tell you that He will avenge them speedily." If we are His elect (v. 7), we can be very secure in God's choice and in His preserving grace, and He is not going to abandon us along the way though at times we may be very hardpressed.

Conclusion: Persistent prayer is therefore the way we express steadfast faith. The only way to keep trusting is to keep praying, day and night, never off duty, right up till the end. Shall we give up appealing to God and thus make Him out to be more unfeeling and unjust than the unjust judge himself? No! Whatever our burden, we must always pray, and not give up.

FOR THE BULLETIN

❋ On October 5, A.D. 59, Saint Paul celebrated the Jewish Day of Atonement while sailing into dangerous waters as a prisoner headed to Rome (Acts 27:9). Shortly afterward he warned the ship's crew they were headed toward disaster. ❋ October 5, 1056, marks the death of Holy Roman Emperor Henry III, a deeply religious man who supported reform of the church throughout his empire. When he died, he left the throne to his six-year-old son. ❋ Another Holy Roman emperor, Charles V, came to power in the middle of the Protestant revolution. He vigorously sought to resolve the differences between Catholics and evangelicals, calling the Diet of Augsburg in 1530, and spending the next 15 years seeking peace between the groups. On this day in 1556, he retired, frail and depressed, to the monastery of Yuste, where he quietly passed the last two years of his life. ❋ October 5, 1600, is the birthday of Puritan Thomas Goodwin, English Nonconformist preacher. ❋ John Gerard, a Catholic who was tortured for his faith in the Tower of London during the reign of Queen Elizabeth I, climbed through a hole in the roof of Cradle Tower on October 5, 1597, threw a rope over the side, and slid down it, mutilating his hands. He labored secretly in England, then in Rome until he passed away at age 73. He is one of an elite handful of people who outwitted the Tower of London. ❋ October 5, 1703, is the birthday of Jonathan Edwards. ❋ On October 5, 1744, David Brainard began his work among the Indians. ❋ William Carey was baptized on October 5, 1783.

STATS, STORIES AND MORE

- "True prayer does not require eloquence but earnestness."
  —*Anonymous*
- "Our prayers should be persistent. God's delays are not denials. Each day brings the answers to our prayers nearer."
  —*Cameron V. Thompson*
- "I never prayed sincerely for anything but it came, at some time, somehow, in some shape."
  —*Adoniram Judson*

The popular author of the "Simple Sermons" series of books, W. Herschel Ford, once told of an experience that happened in his first pastorate, which was in Atlanta. They asked him to conduct a revival in the little church, a two-week meeting. During the first week, several people were saved. Mid-way through the meeting, some of the church members felt burdened to have a late-night prayer meeting in one of the member's homes. Rev. Ford went to that home and everyone sat in a circle in the living room. They prayed around the circle, and the burden of the prayer was for a young man from the church who had gone deep into sin. They didn't know where he was, but they prayed that the Lord would bring him home and save him before the meetings ended. To their great delight and astonishment, he came home on the Saturday before the meetings closed on Sunday. He surprised them by promising to go to church with them on Sunday night. That night the little church was packed with people and he had to sit in an open window at the rear of the church. After the message, when the invitation was given, this young man came weeping down the aisle to give his heart to the Savior. Ford later wrote, "He was gloriously converted. He had been away in another state, but some unseen force, which he could not understand, impelled him to come back home. I believe that God, in answer to those earnest prayers, brought him home and brought him to Jesus."
—*Herschel Ford*, in *Simple Sermons on Prayer*

WORSHIP HELPS

Call to Worship:
Those who regard worthless idols forsake their own mercy. But I will sacrifice to You with the voice of thanksgiving; I will pay what I have vowed. Salvation is of the LORD
(Jonah 2:8–9).

Pastoral Prayer:
Hear our prayer, O Lord, and let our cry come to You. Do not hide Your face from us in the day of trouble; incline Your ear to us. In the day we call, answer us speedily. Lord, incline our hearts to Yourself, to walk in all Your ways, and to keep Your command-ments and Your statutes and Your judgments. Incline our hearts to perform Your statutes forever, to the very end. Let not our hearts be inclined to any evil thing, to practice wicked works with those who work iniquity. But cause us to put away foreign gods and to incline our hearts toward the Lord our God. Incline our minds to wisdom, our ears to the words of Your mouth, and our hearts to Your testi-monies and not to covetousness. In Jesus' name, Amen. *(Based on Ps. 102:1–2; 1 Kings 8:58; Ps. 119:12; 141:4; Josh. 24:23; Prov. 2:2; Ps. 78:1; 119:36.)*

Offertory Comments:
According to Christian pollster George Barna, Americans remain among the most generous people on earth. In 2001, four out of five adults (80 percent) donated money to one or more non-profit orga-nizations. Sixty-two percent of all Americans donated money to churches. Here at our church, we thank God for those who are faithful supporters of our ministries. We couldn't get along without you.

Benediction:
Bless us now as we depart, O Lord, for Thine is the kingdom, the power, and the glory forever. Amen.

Additional Sermons and Lesson Ideas

Glimpse of Glory

Date preached:

SCRIPTURE: Ezekiel 1

INTRODUCTION: A. W. Tozer suggested that the modern church suffers from the loss of the concept of the majesty of God. "If we would bring back spiritual power to our lives," he wrote, "we must begin to think of God more nearly as He is." The prophet Ezekiel opens his book with a powerful vision of the glory of God, and in so doing he finds himself in two places:

1. Among the Captives by the River (vv. 1–28a). In a refugee camp in Babylon, Ezekiel's eyes are opened, and he saw:
   A. A Whirlwind of Fire (v. 4). (Compare with Job 37.)
   B. The Cherubim of God (vv. 5–25). Mysterious angels that surround the Lord.
   C. The Throne of Heaven (vv. 26–28). Similar to John's vision in Revelation 1.
2. Among the Worshipers before the Throne (v. 28b). When he saw these things, Ezekiel fell on his face and heard a voice of One speaking.

CONCLUSION: May God open our eyes to His glory, whether it be in church, in your closet, on an airplane, or even in a refugee camp.

Pool of Healing
By Peter Grainger

Date preached:

SCRIPTURE: John 5:1–30

INTRODUCTION: We are physical people, and we pay great attention to the needs and conditions of our bodies. Jesus, however, had a broader perspective:

1. There Is Something Far Worse than Sickness. Jesus spoke to this man twice, both times addressing different needs in his life.
   A. "Get up." And the man's immediate need was met.
   B. "Stop sinning." The man's long-term welfare was threatened by judgment and condemnation (v. 29).
2. There Is Something Far Greater than Healing. Jesus challenged His accusers in verses 16–30. He told them He only did what the Father showed Him. He has authority from the Father to:
   A. Give eternal life.
   B. Execute final judgment.

CONCLUSION: We must honor the Son (v. 23) and hear and believe (v. 24).

OCTOBER 12, 2003

Moving from Pain to Praise

Date preached:

Scripture: 2 Corinthians 1:8–11, especially verse 8: For we do not want you to be ignorant, brethren, of our trouble which came to us in Asia: that we were burdened beyond measure, above strength, so that we despaired even of life.

Introduction: Sometimes you can get inside another person's soul by asking a little question. It's very personal, but quite revealing: "What is the most painful thing you've ever experienced?" Some people tell of a broken arm in childhood, and we realize they've not yet encountered much pain in life. Others have endured more pain than we can imagine—not just physically, but life-pain. Such pain changes us, either for better or worse. In this passage, Paul talked about his most painful experience, and I'd like to show you how it changed him.

1. **What We Faced** (v. 8). Paul used stark language here. "We do not want you to be ignorant, brethren, of our trouble." The word *trouble* is often translated *tribulation*. The root idea is that of pressure. What kind of pressure? "We were burdened beyond measure." He was saying, "I've had difficulties in the past, but I've been able to measure them. When I was chained, that was a *five* on the pain-scale. When I was beaten with rods, that was *seven*. When I was shipwrecked in the deep, that was *eight*. When I was stoned, that was *nine*. When I was flogged, that was *ten*. But this pressure and pain was off the chart. It was: "above strength." He didn't have the inner reserves to deal with it. It was crushing. "I despaired even of life." Here the great advocate and example of resilience and hope used the word *despair*. What experience in the apostle's life is he referring to? The older commentators felt it was something that happened in Ephesus in Acts 19, but recent scholars point out that nothing in the Book of Acts equals what Paul described here. By not knowing the specifics, we can better relate it to our own experiences.

2. **What We Learned** (v. 9). When in pain, we often ask *Why?* But Paul didn't ask it—he answered it. "We had the sentence of death in ourselves, that we should not trust in ourselves, but in God who raises the dead." The

Lord brought him to the edge of the grave to teach him to trust the One who can work all things for good even when it seems too late. Our most accelerated times of spiritual growth have been during difficult periods of life. Perhaps if you are in considerable pain today, it's because God wants to develop your faith in order to accomplish a wonderful result.

3. **What We Experienced** (v. 10). Having taught him that lesson, the Lord gave Paul a threefold deliverance: *(He) delivered us . . . and does deliver us . . . and He will still deliver us.* The verb "to deliver" occurs here in the past, present, and future tenses. He did and He does and He will deliver. In 2 Timothy 4:17–18, his last extant writing, Paul similarly wrote: "Also I was delivered out of the mouth of the lion. And the Lord will deliver me from every evil work and preserve me for His heavenly kingdom." Then having written this, Paul was promptly beheaded! Isn't that interesting? That tells us something about God's perspective on deliverance. He delivers us all along the way, but one day He's going to snatch us out of all our pain and pressures and problems.

4. **Why We're Thankful** (v. 11). There is something that helps the process along—the prayers of God's people. "You also helping together in prayer for us, that thanks may be given by many persons on our behalf for the gift granted to us through many." Have you ever wondered why God provides for prayer? If He has delivered, is delivering, and will yet deliver, why pray? So we'll have a part in what He's doing. When we pray about a situation, we

>>> sermon continued on following page

APPROPRIATE HYMNS AND SONGS

Thank You, Lord, Dennis Jernigan; © 1991 Shepherd's Heart Music, Inc. (Admin. by Word Music Group, Inc.).

Everlasting Hope, Chrissy Cymbala; © 1991 Word Music, Inc. (Admin. by Word Music Group, Inc.).

Praise Him! Praise Him!, Fanny Crosby/Chester G. Allen; Public Domain.

Praise the Lord, the King of Glory, W. Hines Sims/Delma B. Reno; © 1964 Broadman Press (Admin. by Genevox Music Group.).

Your People Sing Praises, Russell Fragar; © 1995 Russell Fragar (Hillsong) (Admin. by Integrity Music, Inc.).

gain a sense of ownership for it, and when the deliverance comes, our thanksgiving rises up to God.

Conclusion: If there is pressure or pain in your life today, take it to the Lord Jesus and learn afresh to lay it at the feet of the One who can raise the dead. If you know someone in pain, come alongside as an invisible ally, praying earnestly for them and rejoicing when the deliverance comes. As the old hymn says:

> 'Tis the grandest theme through the ages rung;
> 'Tis the grandest theme for a mortal tongue;
> 'Tis the grandest theme that the world e'er sung,
> "Our God is able to deliver thee."

FOR THE BULLETIN

❋ On October 12, 539 B.C., King Cyrus launched an invasion against Babylon, leading to the fall of the Babylonian Empire as recorded in the fifth chapter of Daniel. ❋ Claudius became Roman emperor in A.D. 41 at age 50, as is referred to in Scripture. He lowered taxes, extended the empire into Britain and Mauritania, and refused to be worshiped as a god. But the latter years of Claudius were marred by intrigue, much of it centered around his wife, Agrippina, who wanted to secure the throne for her son, Nero. On October 12 of A.D. 54 she fed Claudius mushrooms with a potent pinch of poison. He suffered 12 agonizing hours before dying. ❋ On October 12, 1285, 180 Jews were set on fire for refusing baptism in Munich, Germany. ❋ At 2 a.m. on October 12, 1492, Christopher Columbus discovered the new world. ❋ Edward VI was born at Hampton Court to King Henry VIII and Jane Seymour on this day in 1537. He inherited the throne from his father at age 10, and tilted the nation toward the Protestant cause. He was a sickly young man, and died in his teens from consumption or perhaps from over-medication. The throne passed to the Catholic Mary I ("Bloody Mary"), under whose reign 300 Protestants were slain. ❋ October 12, 1845, marks the death of Elizabeth Fry, a Quaker, famous as a prison reformer in Britain. ❋ After a torrential morning rain, the sun broke out and 2,400 Roman Catholic bishops began a long procession toward the Basilica of St. Peter's to open the Second Vatican Council on October 12, 1962.

STATS, STORIES AND MORE

In her autobiography, *Evidence Not Seen,* Missionary Darlene Deblier Rose tells of being interred in a Japanese death camp during World War II. At length she began to doubt God's goodness and she lost a sense of His presence. As fear engulfed her, her heart went to various Scriptures she had previously memorized, and she realized that only her faith would get her through this ordeal. Then this verse suddenly flashed into her mind—2 Corinthians 1:10: "Who delivered . . . and does deliver . . . and will deliver." "Yes, Lord," she said, "I know that I've been delivered from sin. I'm free from the law of sin and death." But she couldn't get those words *and will deliver* out of her mind. She later wrote, "My mind began to explore the possibility that the Lord might be trying to make me understand that He was yet to deliver me from Kempeitai prison."

The next morning, she rose early, fixed her hair as best she could, and unexpectedly a guard came and escorted her from her cell. She was taken to another prison and finally liberated on September 19, 1945, after four years of unspeakable suffering. She was 28, and she went on to fulfill a lifetime of fruitful service for the "gracious God Who alone could help me to understand the mysteries of deep pain and suffering."

"It is not certain what particular troubles in Asia are here referred to. . . . This, however, is evident, that they were great tribulations. They were pushed out of measure, to a very extraordinary degree, above the common strength of men or of ordinary Christians, to bear up under them. . . . What they did in their distress: They trusted in God. And they were brought to this extremity in order that they should not trust in themselves but in God (Who) often brings His people into great straits, that they may apprehend their own insufficiency to help themselves, and may be induced to place their trust and hope in His all-sufficiency. Our extremity is God's opportunity."—*Matthew Henry*

WORSHIP HELPS

Call to Worship:

Sacrifice thank offerings to God, fulfill your vows to the Most High, and call upon Me in the day of trouble; I will deliver you, and you will honor Me" (Ps. 50:14–15).

A Hymn to Quote:

John Newton was a prodigal son and a slave trader in the 18th century. His whole life was changed through an encounter with the Lord Jesus Christ, and he is now best known for his hymn, "Amazing Grace." But he wrote many hymns, most of which have fallen into disuse. Here is one that goes along perfectly with today's message:

I asked the Lord that I might grow
In faith, and love, and every grace;
Might more of His salvation know,
And seek, more earnestly, His face.

'Twas He who taught me thus to pray,
And He, I trust, has answered prayer!
But it has been in such a way,
As almost drove me to despair.

I hoped that in some favored hour,
At once He'd answer my request;
And by His love's constraining pow'r,
Subdue my sins, and give me rest.

Instead of this, He made me feel
The hidden evils of my heart;
And let the angry pow'rs of hell
Assault my soul in every part.

Yea more, with His own hand He seemed
Intent to aggravate my woe;
Crossed all the fair designs I schemed,
Blasted my gourds, and laid me low.

Lord, why is this, I trembling cried,
Wilt thou pursue thy worm to death?
"'Tis in this way," the Lord replied,
"I answer prayer for grace and faith.

"These inward trials I employ,
From self, and pride, to set thee free;

Benediction:

"Help us, O God of our salvation, for the glory of Your name; and deliver us, and provide atonement for our sins, for Your name's sake" (Ps. 79:9).

Additional Sermons and Lesson Ideas

Perfection
By Charles Haddon Spurgeon

Date preached:

SCRIPTURE: Hebrews 12:23

INTRODUCTION: There are two kinds of perfection the Christian needs:

1. The Perfection of Justification in the Person of Jesus. Believers in Christ receive the gift of justification, a fruit produced not in the future but right now. Justification is the result of faith, and it is given the moment you accept Christ as your all in all. We are now, even now, pardoned. Even now our sins are put away. Even now we stand in the sight of God accepted as though we had never been guilty.

2. The Perfection of Sanctification Worked by the Holy Spirit. At present, corruption remains in the heart of the regenerate, as experience teaches. Within us are lusts and evil imaginations. Do not let your hope of perfection in heaven make you content with imperfection now. A good hope is a purifying thing. Let us pray to be filled with the Spirit, that we may bring forth increasingly the fruits of righteousness.

CONCLUSION: When I cross the Jordan, the work of sanctification will be finished, and not until that moment shall I even claim perfection. In heaven there will not be an angel purer than I. With a double sense, I will be able to say, "I am clean through the blood of Jesus and through the work of the Spirit."

Be Passionate!
By Drew Wilkerson

Date preached:

SCRIPTURE: Acts 26:19–23

INTRODUCTION: As Paul spoke boldly before King Agrippa, he never lost sight of his heavenly vision. As leaders, we often become overwhelmed with ministry, but we do not need to burn out. Paul models the passion of fulfilling a God-given dream. Here are three questions we can ask ourselves when the flame of passion for our ministry needs to be rekindled.

Question #1: What has God called me to do specifically for Him?

Question #2: Am I being faithful to share the Word of God to those entrusted to me?

Question #3: Do I ask for God's help daily to achieve the impossible task set before me?

CONCLUSION: What are we waiting for? Let's go and change the world in the name of Christ!

Robinson Crusoe
By Daniel Defoe

For a rich source of sermon illustrations, or just for some good, sanctified entertainment, try spending a little time with Robinson Crusoe—not the movie, the book. Long before Frank Peretti plucked at his keyboard, there was Daniel Defoe. And before the *Left Behind* novels, there was *Robinson Crusoe*—a masterpiece of Christian fiction.

Everyone thinks they've read Defoe's *Robinson Crusoe*, but most of us haven't. Perhaps we've heard it discussed in English Lit, seen the movie, or confused it with *Gilligan's Island* or *Castaway*.

But if you like Christian fiction, this is a Must Read.

Robinson Crusoe is considered the first novel in the English language. True, *Pilgrim's Progress* was published when Defoe was a boy, but *Pilgrim's Progress* is more an allegory than a novel. As one scholar put it, "Daniel Defoe's novel *Robinson Crusoe* is a European literary classic and the prototype of the novelistic genre."

The first English novel was, therefore, a Christian work, written by a thoroughly evangelical man.

Defoe was a Dissenter; that is, he was a believer who preferred the Puritans and Baptists to the Anglicans. A journalist by trade, Defoe one day read a fascinating account of Alexander Selkirk, a sailor abandoned on a deserted island who survived by his wits. Defoe pondered the story and from it invented Robinson Crusoe.

As the novel begins we meet Robinson Crusoe, eighteen years old and headstrong, rejecting his godly father's pleas and leaving home like an impulsive prodigal bound for the far country. He quickly encounters a series of life-threatening adventures, and finally ends up in Brazil, where he purchases a sugar plantation. By and by his neighbors persuade him to sail to Africa for slaves, but the voyage is ill-fated. Blown along by a raging storm, the ship is wrecked; Robinson, the sole survivor, washes ashore on a Caribbean island, more dead than alive.

As his strength returns, Robinson salvages food, clothes, and tools from the wreckage of the ship; and in a chest he discovers three Bibles. Putting the Bibles aside, he begins building shelter, gathering food, and crafting the necessities of life. He starts a journal in which he converses with himself, making the best of his lonely exile.

Robinson's thoughts are drawn to God only when he contracts a deadly fever. In dire distress and expecting to die, he retrieves one of his Bibles and it falls open to the words, "Call on Me in the day of trouble, and I will deliver, and thou shalt glorify Me."

That verse—Psalm 50:15—makes a deep impression on his mind, and before bed "I did what I never had done in all my life; I kneeled down, and prayed to God to fulfil the promise to me, that if I called upon Him in the day of trouble, He will deliver me."

A few days later, Robinson pens in his diary: "In the morning I took the Bible; and beginning in the New Testament, I began seriously to read it, and imposed upon myself to read awhile every morning and every night, not tying myself to the number of chapters, but as long as my thought should engage me. It was not long after I set seriously to this work, but I found my heart more deeply and sincerely affected with the wickedness of my past life."

He begins asking God to give him a sense of repentance, and when he comes to Acts 5:31 ("He is exalted a Prince and a Savior, to give repentance, and to give remission"), "I threw down the book; and with my heart as well as my hands lifted up to heaven, in a kind of ecstasy of joy, I cried out aloud, 'Jesus, Thou son of David! Jesus, Thou exalted Prince and Savior, give me repentance!'"

Crusoe's island becomes a sort of sanctuary where he converses with God and grows in grace. His productivity increases as he plants crops, raises animals, explores, and pits himself against the forces of nature.

Years pass, and one day Crusoe is jolted to see a man's footprint in the sand. He "stood there like one thunderstruck," and for nights afterward he cannot sleep, his mind tormented with thoughts of cannibals.

"Thus my fear banished all my religious hope. All that former confidence in God, which was founded upon such wonderful experience as I had had of His goodness, now vanished."

As the novel unfolds, Robinson repents of his anxiety and slowly strengthens himself in faith, eventually learning the great lesson of faltering Christians: The things we most fear are likely, in the providence of God, to be most used for our good.

This novel is frequently criticized for touting an attitude of Western colonialism and imperialism. It was, after all, published in England in 1719, and it reflects the tenor of its time. But I can nonetheless relate to Robinson Crusoe, his prodigal ways, his self-caused disasters, his repentance, his struggles with loneliness and anxiety. Robinson Crusoe is the story of a man's conversion to Jesus Christ, his struggles to grow in grace, and his subsequent passion to evangelize others.

And best of all, this novel—just like the Christian life—ends well. ✸

OCTOBER 19, 2003

The Intelligent Designer

Date preached:

Scripture: Genesis 1:1: In the beginning God created the heavens and the earth.

Introduction: Dr. Paul Gentuso, a physician in Nashville, Tennessee, was a budding evolutionist until he studied the human hand in medical school. "In anatomy class, we dissected a human hand. I first removed the skin, then isolated the individual tendons and muscles as I worked my way to the bones. The tendons of the hand are aligned in tendon sheaths, like self-lubricating pulleys, allowing the hand to work in tireless, noiseless, almost effortless fashion. It was perfectly designed to carry out the work it was called to do, from lifting a small object to lugging a tree trunk." Till then, Paul had entertained serious doubts about God's existence. "Now," he said, "it became obvious to me that there was a Creator who had intelligently designed and created the human hand. It was the first time in my adult life I could say with assurance that a Creator existed." Today increasing numbers of scientists are confessing they cannot explain the wonders of the universe without acknowledging the existence of an intelligent designer. Genesis 1 tells us that in the beginning God created the heavens and the earth. We can detect the Creator in:

1. **The Existence of the Universe.** Anyone wanting to deny the existence of Almighty God has to provide an answer to one supreme question: Where did the universe come from? Dr. R. C. Sproul wrote: "For something to come from nothing it must, in effect, create itself. Self-creation is a logical and rational impossibility. For something to create itself it must be able to transcend Hamlet's dilemma, 'To be or not to be.' Hamlet's question assumed sound science. He understood that something (himself) could not both be and not be at the same time and in the same relationship. For something to create itself, it must have the ability to be and not be at the same time and in the same relationship. For something to create itself, it must be before it is. This is impossible." Scientists have been unable to dispute the simple truth that nothing comes from nothing.

2. **The Complexity of the Universe.** Suppose I told you there was an explosion the other day at a junkyard, and all the bits and pieces of debris just happened to fall together by accident to produce my automobile. Or suppose I told you I had set a monkey at my typewriter, and by sheer accident he had created a brilliant play. Well, the universe is billions of times more complex than an automobile or a play. What makes us think it could possibly have fallen into place by accident? Dr. Fred Hoyle once said that nothing had shaken his faith in his atheism as much as his discoveries involving the complexity of the carbon atom. He began to suspect that "some supercalculating intellect must have designed the properties of the carbon atom, otherwise the chance of my finding such an atom through the blind forces of nature would be utterly minuscule. . . . A common sense interpretation of the facts suggests that a superintellect has monkeyed with physics, as well as with chemistry and biology, and that there are no blind forces worth speaking about in nature. The numbers one calculates from the facts seem to me so overwhelming as to put this conclusion almost beyond question."

3. **The Beauty of the Universe.** Have you ever snorkeled off the coast of a tropical island? Have you peered into the saltwater aquarium of the local pet store? Ever visit a botanical garden or stood on the ledge of a vast canyon? Seen the midnight sky spangled with a billion stars? Is this all-encompassing splendor the blind produce of random accidents? If we visited an art museum to view a painting of a beautiful landscape with trees and a river, fluffy while clouds and a pasture dotted by flowers, would you

>>> sermon continued on following page

APPROPRIATE HYMNS AND SONGS

Ah, Lord God, Kay Chance; © 1976 Kay Chance.

All Things Bright and Beautiful, Cecil Francis Alexander; © Territorial Copyright.

Father of Creation, Robert Eastwood; © 1995, 1996 Robert Eastwood (Hillsong) (Admin. by Integrity Music, Inc.).

It Took a Miracle, John W. Peterson; © 1948. Renewed 1976 John W. Peterson Music Company.

Psalm 8, John Barnett; © 1998 Mercy/Vineyard Publishing.

assume that the artwork was an accident, that a delivery truck wrecked, spilling cans of paint onto a canvas? Or would you assume that an artist of fabulous skill had created the beauty and signed his name at the bottom? The beauty of the universe is God's signature (Ps. 19:1).

Conclusion: God has given us the heavens as a natural revelation of His grandeur. He has given us the Scriptures as the special revelation of His grace. In the latter, He bids us come to the Cross and meet for ourselves the gracious Creator of heaven and earth.

FOR THE BULLETIN

❋ George Abbot was born on this day in 1562. He became an Oxford scholar whose Puritan leanings brought him into conflict with others at the university. In 1604, he was named as one of the translators of the King James Bible, and in 1611, he became Archbishop of Canterbury. ❋ Jacob Arminius, the theologian who sought to soften the stronger points of Calvinism, died at age 49 on October 19, 1609. ❋ On Saturday, October 19, 1698, the Christian and mathematician, Blaise Pascal, by conducting experiments at the French volcanic mountain, Puy-de-Dome, determined that atmosphere has definite weight, and that the level of mercury varies in different altitudes and in different weather. His conclusions virtually invented the barometer. ❋ On Sunday night, October 19, 1856, 12,000 people streamed into London's Surrey Hall and an additional 10,000 overflowed into the surrounding gardens to hear Charles Spurgeon preach. The services started, but as Spurgeon rose to pray, someone shouted "Fire! Fire! The galleries are giving way!" There was no fire, but the crowd bolted in panic, and in the resulting stampede seven people were trampled to death. Twenty-eight more were hospitalized. The young preacher, reeling in shock, was literally carried from the pulpit to a friend's house where he remained in seclusion for weeks. ❋ October 19, 1912, marks the death of Mrs. A. R. M'Farland, first missionary to Alaska. Her husband, a Presbyterian home missionary, had died in May, 1876, while church-planting among the Nez Perces Indians in Idaho. Moving to Portland, Oregon, Mrs. M'Farland heard of explorations in Alaska. She sensed God's calling her there, and labored there from 1877 to 1897. ❋ October 19, 1921, is the birthday of Bill Bright, founder of Campus Crusade for Christ.

STATS, STORIES AND MORE

- The universe is not a chaos but a cosmos.
  —*Anonymous*

- This most beautiful system of the sun, planets, and comets could only proceed from the counsel and domain of an intelligent and powerful Being.
  —*Sir Isaac Newton*

- The more I study physics, the more I am drawn toward metaphysics.
  —*Dr. Albert Einstein*

- The existence of the universe requires me to conclude that God exists.
  —*Robert A. Naumann*, professor of chemistry and physics at Princeton University

- Can you tell me anything we know about evolution, any one thing . . . that is true? I tried that question on the geology staff at the Field Museum of Natural History and the only answer I got was silence. I tried it on the members of the Evolutionary Morphology seminar in the University of Chicago, a very prestigious body of evolutionists, and all I got there was silence for a long time and eventually one person said, "I do know one thing—it ought not to be taught in high school."
  —*Colin Patterson*, senior paleontologist at the British Natural History Museum and the author of the museum's general text on evolution, in a lecture at the American Museum of Natural History

- Ultimately the Darwinian theory of evolution is no more nor less than the great cosmogenic myth of the twentieth century.
  —Molecular biologist and medical doctor *Michael Denton*

- Evolution is a fairy tale for grown-ups.
  —*Dr. Louis Bounoure*, Director of Research at the National Center of Scientific Research in France

- The only possible answers are religious. . . . I find a need for God in the universe and in my own life.
  —*Arthur L. Schawlow*, winner of the Nobel Prize for Physics.

- (Evolution is) the key philosophical concept that has allowed the athe-ists and agnostics to dominate the whole intellectual world and govern-ment world (leading to) the complete marginalization of theism (in those realms).
  —*Dr. Phillip Johnson*

- It is becoming increasingly apparent that evolutionism is not even a good scientific theory.
  —*Dr. Willem J. Ouweneel*, Research Associate in Developmental Genetics, Ultrech, Netherlands

WORSHIP HELPS

Call to Worship:

O LORD, our Lord, How excellent is Your name in all the earth, Who have set Your glory above the heavens! (Ps. 8:1).

Scripture Medley:

Gideon said to Him, "If the LORD is with us, why then has all this happened to us? And where are all His miracles which our fathers told us about?" "Men of Israel, hear these words: Jesus of Nazareth (was) a Man attested by God to you by miracles, wonders, and signs which God did through Him in your midst, as you yourselves also know." If they were written one by one, I suppose that even the world itself could not contain the books that would be written. For You formed my inward parts; You covered me in my mother's womb. I will praise You, for I am fearfully and wonderfully made; marvelous are Your works. When I consider Your heavens, the work of Your fingers, the moon and the stars, which You have ordained, what is man that You are mindful of him, and the son of man that You visit him? O Lord, our Lord, how excellent is Your name in all the earth. *(From Num. 6:13; Acts 2:22; John 21:25; Ps. 139:13–14; 8:3–4, 8:1.)*

Kids Talk

How much money do you have in your pockets? Do you know that every time you stick your hand into your pocket and feel your coins, it reminds you to trust God. Here is a Lincoln penny, and just above Abraham Lincoln's head are the words "In God We Trust." On this nickel is a picture of Thomas Jefferson, and right in front of his nose are the words "In God We Trust." It's right under Roosevelt's chin on this dime, behind Washington's pigtail on the quarter, along Kennedy's neck on the half dollar, and right over the baby's head in the Sacagawea dollar. This reminds us that we must trust the Lord with our money, with our lives, and all our hearts, not leaning on our own understanding (Prov. 3:5).

Additional Sermons and Lesson Ideas

Don't Give Up Sowing to the Spirit
By David Jackman

Date preached:

SCRIPTURE: Galatians 6:1–10

INTRODUCTION: Many start a new diet, but later quit. That happens in our overall Christian life. We try it, but grow discouraged. Paul addressed that problem here, telling us not to grow weary of sowing to the Spirit.

1. What Does Sowing to the Spirit Look Like? It means doing good to everyone, especially to fellow Christians (vv. 9–10; also 5:14). It's demanding, selfless, the lifestyle of Calvary; we shouldn't be surprised when it's hard. But if we stop sowing in the Spirit, we'll begin sowing to the flesh.
2. What Alternatives Might We Fall For? Sowing in the flesh might mean open rebellion (5:19–21), or outward religion (5:1–6).
3. What Then Will Keep Us Keeping On? Sowing to the Spirit. That's how we're changed, by the Spirit. That's the theme that runs through chapters 5 and 6.

CONCLUSION: Only when the Cross is at the center of my life can I be sure I'm not sowing to the flesh. It is only through faith in a crucified Jesus that I can be accepted before God, and only through the power of the Holy Spirit can we persevere in faith. Come to Jesus Christ day by day and say, "Lord, I can't live this Christian life for one moment within my own stength. You come and live Your life through me."

Searching for a Servant
By Melvin Worthington

Date preached:

SCRIPTURE: Ezekiel 22:1–31

INTRODUCTION: Jerusalem and Judah were corrupt, as is our world today. God wanted to address this issue before pouring out His judgment. He deals with the rebellious gently, graciously, and gradually.

1. The Sinfulness of Jerusalem (vv. 1–12). God needed a man to address the sinful practices in Jerusalem and the entire land of Judah.
2. The Surety of Judgment (vv. 13–22). God decreed judgment was *imminent, inevitable,* and *indescribable.*
3. The Search of Jehovah (vv. 23–31). The Lord sought for a man among the prophets, priests, princes, and people, yet did not find a single man that He could use.

CONCLUSION: God still needs those willing to serve Him and stand in the gap—people of character, courage, compassion, and commitment.

Preaching: Nothing Can Ever Take Its Place

By Phillips Brooks (1835–1893)

Excerpted from the *Yale Lectures on Preaching*

What, then, is preaching? It is not hard to find a definition. Preaching is the communication of truth by man to men. It has in it two essential elements, truth and personality. Neither of those can it spare and still be preaching. The truest truth, the most authoritative statement of God's will, communicated in any other way than through the personality of brother man to men is not preached truth. Suppose it is written on the sky, suppose it embodied in a book which has been so long held in reverence as the direct utterance of God that the vivid personality of the men who wrote its pages has well-nigh faded out of it; in neither of these cases is there any preaching.

And on the other hand, if men speak to other men that which they do not claim for truth, if they use their powers of persuasion or of entertainment to make other men listen to their speculations, or do their will, or applaud their cleverness, that is not preaching either. The first lacks personality. The second lacks truth. And preaching is the bringing of truth through personality. It must have both elements . . . .

If we go back to the beginning of the Christian ministry we can see how distinctly and deliberately Jesus chose this method of extending the knowledge of Himself throughout the world. Other methods no doubt were open to Him, but He deliberately selected this. He taught His truth to a few men and then He said, "Now go and tell the truth to other men."

Both elements were there, in John the Baptist who prepared the way for Him, in the seventy whom He sent out before His face, and in the little company who started from the chamber of the Pentecost to proclaim the new salvation to the world.

This was the method by which Christ chose that His Gospels should be spread through the world. It was a method that might have been applied to the dissemination of any truth, but we can see why it was especially adapted to the truth of Christianity. For that truth is preeminently personal. However the Gospel may be capable of statement in dogmatic form, its truest statement we know is not in dogma but in personal life. Christianity is Christ; and we can easily understand how a truth which is of such peculiar character that a person can stand forth and say of it, "I am the Truth," must always be best conveyed through, must indeed be almost incapable of being perfectly conveyed except through personality.

And so some form of preaching must be essential to the prevalence and spread of the knowledge of Christ among men. There seems to be some such meaning as this in the words of Jesus when He said to His disciples, "As the Father has sent me into the world even so have I sent you into the world." It was the continuation, out to the minutest ramifications of the new system of influence, of that personal method which the Incarnation itself had involved.

If this be true, then, it establishes the first of all principles concerning the truth and preparation for the ministry. Truth through Personality is our description of real preaching. The truth must come really through the person and not merely over his lips, not merely into his understanding and out through his pen. It must come through his character, his affections, his whole intellectual and moral being. It must come genuinely through him.

The preparation for the ministry . . . must be nothing less than the making of a man. It cannot be the mere training to certain tricks. It cannot be even the furnishing with abundant knowledge. It must be nothing less than the kneading and tempering of a man's nature till it becomes of such a consistency and quality as to be capable of transmission. . . .

It is not for me, standing here or anywhere, to depreciate the work which our theological schools do. It is certainly not my place to undervalue the usefulness of lectures on preaching, or books on clerical manners. But none of these things make a preacher. You are surprised, when you read the biographies of the most successful ministers, to see how small a part of their culture came from their professional schools. It is a real part, but it is a small part. Everything that opens their lives towards God and towards man makes part of their education. . . . The whole world is the school that makes them. . . .

If we look at preaching only, it must still be true that nothing can ever take its place because of the personal element that is in it. No multiplication of books can ever supersede the human voice. . . .

Let a man be a true preacher, really uttering the truth through his own personality, and it is strange how men will gather to listen to him. ❁

OCTOBER 26, 2003

SUGGESTED SERMON *Date preached:*

Falling Down, Standing Up, Going Forth

Scripture: Ezekiel 1:28b–2:3a, especially 2:1: Then the Spirit entered me when He spoke to me, and set me on my feet; and I heard Him who spoke to me.

Introduction: Numerous sources are warning of a serious shortage of those going into the ministry. We also know that within churches themselves, there is a shortage of workers. The proportion of those genuinely committed to Christ's kingdom seems to be growing smaller. The prophet Ezekiel has something for us on this subject.

Background: Ezekiel 1 begins: "Now it came to pass in the thirtieth year . . . I as among the captives by the River Chebar." He was 30 years old and a priest. Priests were supposed to begin their service at 30. But Ezekiel wasn't among the worshipers at the temple in Jerusalem, but among the exiles by the Chebar River. He'd been caught in Nebuchadnezzar's invasion, and at the moment he should have entered priestly service, he was exiled 900 miles away in a refugee camp with no altars, no sacrifices, no temple. His life's training seemed wasted. Then three things happened to him in rapid succession, and from that moment he became one of the most effective men God ever planted on earth. The Lord wants to do the very same three things to us.

1. **God Knocks Us on Our Faces** (v. 28b). "So when I saw it, I fell on my face." The vision in chapter 1 is one of the strangest in the Bible, but the point is reasonably clear: Ezekiel was getting a glimpse of the Sovereign Throne of Almighty God. We have a description of the whirlwind and the cherubim who guard the throne, but the main point is the majesty and grandeur of Almighty God who is in total control of His creation. (See Ezek. 1:26–28.) One moment Ezekiel's face was downcast, and the next he fell facedown in worship. One of the reasons so few today are going into the ministry is because we have lost the sense of the majesty and the grandeur of God. If we don't have a vision of who He is, it's difficult to acquire a vision of what He wants us to do. If we would serve God as we should, we must see Him as He is.

2. **God Stands Us on Our Feet** (v. 2:1a). Ezekiel didn't stay on his face very long, for the Lord told him to get up, for He had something to say to him. The Spirit entered Ezekiel, and he stood on his feet to listen. At the end of chapter 2, this intake of God's Word is pictured in a graphic way as the Lord commanded Ezekiel to eat a scroll (see also Ps. 19; Jer. 14; and Rev. 10). Getting into God's Word is like eating. In much of Europe, supper is a slow, wonderful affair that may last a couple of hours, designed to be lingered over and enjoyed. In America, we drive by the restaurant, grab the food through the window, and eat on the run. Something akin to that happens in Bible study. We're often in such a rush that we gulp down a quick passage, but we need time to chew, swallow, and digest it. If God is going to use us in His service, we must be serious partakers of His Word.

3. **God Sends Us on Our Way** (v. 3a). "And He said to me, 'Son of man, I am sending you. . . .'" In John 20:21, Jesus said, "As the Father has sent Me, I also send you." We say: But Lord, I have other plans! *You are sent.* Lord, I don't want to go there! *You're sent.* Lord, they might reject me. *Yes,* the Lord told Ezekiel, "I am sending you to a rebellious nation, and you shall say to them, 'Thus says the Lord God.' Whether they hear or whether they refuse—yet they will know a prophet has been among them" (see 2:3–5).

Conclusion: Jesus said, "As the Father has sent me, so send I you," and the question we must ask is, "Where is our cross? What does God want me to do?" We're knocked on our faces in worship—that's God's majesty. We're set

>>> sermon continued on following page

APPROPRIATE HYMNS AND SONGS

So Send I You, E. Margaret Clarkson/John W. Peterson; © 1954 Singspiration Music (Admin. by Brentwood-Benson Music Publishing, Inc.).

Go Forth for God, John Raphael Peacey/Erik Routley; © 1984 Hope Publishing Co.

I Want to Serve You, Duane Clark; © 1990 Clark Brothers Communications.

Lord Send Me, Don Moen; © 1991 Integrity's Hosanna! Music (Admin. by Integrity Music Group, Inc.).

We Will Serve the Lord, Doug Hanks; © 1991 Lambs in the Meadow Music (Admin. by Heaven and Earth Productions.).

on our feet to listen—that's God's message. We're sent on our way to evangelize—that's God's mission. When we get a glimpse of His majesty, devour His message, and respond to His mission, something happens to us. We become His tools on earth. And as for the world around us, whether they listen or whether they don't—yet will they know that there is a prophet among them.

FOR THE BULLETIN

❂ On October 26, 431, the Council of Ephesus drew to a close. This was the third General Church Council, summoned in the hope of settling the Nestorian controversy. ❂ October 26, 1466, marks the birth of Desiderius Erasmus in Rotterdam, Holland. After studying and teaching in the leading universities of Europe, he increasingly believed the church stood in need of reform. His Greek New Testament (1516) became one of the classics of Christian history and showed scholars (particularly a monk named Martin Luther) what the church should really be and teach. ❂ On October 26, 1529, Thomas More was named Lord Chancellor under King Henry VIII. More was a deeply religious man who opposed Protestants and refused to recognize King Henry as head of the Church of England. Henry imprisoned him in the Tower of London and later had him beheaded. ❂ October 26, 1751, marks the death of Puritan pastor, author, and hymnwriter Phillip Doddridge, a prolific writer whose best-known work was *The Rise and Progress of Religion in the Soul*. He died at age 58, at the height of his ministry, from tuberculosis. Among his hymns is "O Happy Day." ❂ October 26, 1813, is the birthday of Henry T. Smart, British organist who wrote the music for "Lead On, O King Eternal" and "Angels from the Realms of Glory." ❂ The International Red Cross was organized in Geneva on this day in 1863. ❂ Bible teacher R. A. Torrey died on October 26, 1928. ❂ Mother Teresa founded her first Mission of Charity in Calcutta, India, on this day in 1950.

STATS, STORIES AND MORE

Robert Grant became a member of Parliament, then a director of the East India Company. At age 50, he was named Governor of Bombay. He was a Christian, deeply devoted to missions, lending his support to missionaries in India. One day while studying Psalm 104, he compared the greatness of the King of kings with the comparatively pallid splendor he had so often witnessed of British royalty. Sir Robert Grant filled his heart with these verses, and from his pen came one of the most magnificent hymns in Christendom: "O worship the King, all glorious above, And gratefully sing His power and His love. . . ."

When missionary Francis Xavier entered Japan in the 16th century, he found people there who had already heard of Christ. They were descendants of Christians who long before had immigrated from China, Korea, and the Middle East. As Xavier preached, these people came back to the Lord, and a great Christian movement spread across Japan. Within a year, nearly 100,000 had experienced revival, and in time about three million Japanese came to Christ. It became known as the "Christian Century" in Japanese history. But then an evil dictator initiated a program of persecution which lasted 250 years and led many people to their deaths—estimates range from 100,000 to a million. It all began on February 5, 1597, in Nagasaki. Twenty-six individuals were led to a hill where 26 crosses had been crudely built. The oldest man was 64 years of age. The youngest was a 12-year-old named Ibaragi Kun. Shortly after they arrived, an official came and begged Ibaragi to recant his faith. The boy looked his persecutor in the eye and said, "Sir, it would be better if you yourself became a Christian and could go to heaven where I am going." Then he said five words that will live forever in Japanese church history. "Sir," he asked, "which is my cross?" The stunned official pointed to the smallest cross on the hill, and the boy ran and knelt in front of it. There on those crosses, he and the others died, launching one of the most terrible periods of persecution in the history of Christianity.

WORSHIP HELPS

Call to Worship:

Bless the LORD, O my soul! O LORD my God, You are very great: You are clothed with honor and majesty.... Bless the LORD.... Praise the LORD! (Ps. 104:1, 35).

Responsive Reading from Psalm 104:

Leader: O LORD my God, You are very great: You are clothed with honor and majesty, Who cover Yourself with light as with a garment, Who stretch out the heavens like a curtain.

Group: He lays the beams of His upper chambers in the waters, Who makes the clouds His chariot, Who walks on the wings of the wind, Who makes His angels spirits, His ministers a flame of fire.

Leader: You who laid the foundations of the earth, So that it should not be moved forever, You covered it with the deep as with a garment.

Group: He causes the grass to grow for the cattle, and vegetation for the service of man.

Leader: He appointed the moon for seasons; the sun knows its going down. You make darkness, and it is night, in which all the beasts of the forest creep about.

Group: O LORD, how manifold are Your works! In wisdom You have made them all. I will sing to the LORD as long as I live; I will sing praise to my God while I have my being.

Everyone: May my meditation be sweet to Him; I will be glad in the LORD.

Offertory Comments:

In his book, *Tortured for Christ,* Richard Wurmbrand wrote that he tithed even in his prison camp. "When we were given one slice of bread a week, we decided we would faithfully 'tithe' even that. Every tenth week we took the slice of bread and gave it to the weaker brethren as our 'tithe' to the Master."

Benediction:

May the glory of the LORD endure forever; May the LORD rejoice in His works (Ps. 104:31).

Additional Sermons and Lesson Ideas

Wise Workers
By Melvin Worthington

Date preached:

SCRIPTURE: 1 Timothy 4:1–16

INTRODUCTION: Those who would effectively serve the Lord need to heed the apostle Paul's admonitions to Timothy in 1 Timothy 4.

1. Discern the Times (vv. 1–5). Discernment is essential for Christians to be effective in their walk, witness, and work. They need to *read* the times, *redeem* the time, *rebuke* the times, and *rejoice* in the times.
2. Dedicated to the Task (vv. 6–11). Dedication to the task requires we *understand* the task, *undertake* the task, and be *unmoved* in carrying out the task.
3. Display the Traits (vv. 12–15). Displaying the traits involves our *walk,* our *work,* and our *wit.*
4. Develop Our Theology (vv. 1–16). The *source, soundness, stretching, scope,* and *structure* of one's theology are vital if he would be a wise workman.
5. Discipline of Thyself (v. 16). Paul admonishes Timothy to, "Take heed to yourself and to the doctrine. Continue in them: for in doing this you will save both yourself and those who hear you."

CONCLUSION: Take heed to yourself. Be wise. Be a worker approved of God.

How to Bless Your Children Real Good

Date preached:

SCRIPTURE: Proverbs 20:7

INTRODUCTION: This verse says that the children of righteous and blameless parents are blessed. The preceding verses (20:1–6) define what a righteous and blameless parent is.

1. One Who Avoids Alcohol (v. 1).
2. One Who Obeys the Law (v. 2). The righteous don't do things that bring down on them or their families the wrath of the "king"—the government.
3. One Who Doesn't Quarrel (v. 3).
4. One Who Is Hard-working (v. 4)—not lazy.
5. One Who Knows How to Draw Out the Thoughts of Others (v. 5).
6. One Who Gives Faithful Love (v. 6).

CONCLUSION: Blessed is the child with a parent like that!

Confidence in Sermon-building
An Interview with Dr. Timothy Warren
Professor of Pastoral Ministries,
Dallas Theological Seminary

You seem to have a very carefully thought-out definition for preaching.

I usually put "expository" at the beginning of it, so I would say that expository preaching is the communication of a biblical proposition discovered through a Spirit-directed, exegetical, theological interpretation of a text, and applied through the preacher by the Holy Spirit to a specific audience for the glory of God.

Some ministers are intimidated today because there are so many changes in the way preaching is done, with seeker-sensitive emphases, purpose-driven emphases, and an awareness of trying to reach a postmodern audience. What would you say to us pastors who feel an inadequacy about all this?

I would say, "Don't be intimidated by the people who want you to back off from a propositional statement of truth and from a clear application of that truth." Historically and biblically, the message has always been, "Thus saith the Lord," and if we really believe "Thus saith the Lord," then we have the right to speak propositionally. That is, we can say, "This is true. This is applicable in all times, in all cultures, to all people." And if it is true, then our job as preachers is to say, "And this is how it should show up in your life." Haggai didn't simply tell the people, "You need to get yourselves right with God." He said, "I want you to go up to the mountains and bring back wood for the temple, and I want you to build the house of the Lord." I can't think of any portion of Scripture that is not propositional, that does not have a worldview that can be stated in a single sentence, or that is not applicational. My opinion is that the people who are saying, "Back away from propositional preaching, back off from clear application," are people who, for whatever agenda, are telling us to do the opposite of what the Bible has done and the opposite of what we have historically done, in proclaiming the Christian message. Our message may be anti-culture, but that's not a new problem for preachers. That's the way it's always been.

Do people have an appetite for theology today?

D. A. Carson came to deliver some lectures at Dallas Seminary a few years ago and I asked him, "What do you think is the greatest need in preaching today?" He replied, "Biblical theology." I just about whooped, right there in our dignified faculty meeting! Absolutely, preaching has to be theological, whether it gets overtly expressed or whether it is expressed covertly in the development of the message.

You have expressed some concern over what you call a "reader's response" in Bible study and sermon preparation.

I don't think our major problem is denying truth. I don't think most of us would say, "You know, Paul was wrong here. We really need to correct his insight into this issue." Most of us make the error of looking at the text, responding to it from our perspective—from our culture, from our bias—and saying, "Okay, this is how it connects, this is how it relates to us today," and as Haddon Robinson has said, "rushing to relevance." Reader response hermeneutics is looking for something preachable and trying to make it quick and easy and relevant; and we're skipping steps when we do that. We skip exegesis. We skip theology when we do that. And it's so easy to do, because you look at the text and you say, "That's preachable. I know how I can make that connection." And even before we really understand the text, we find something to preach, and we rush off to that.

Let's say we have a minister who doesn't have much of a library, doesn't have training in Greek or Hebrew, but he's got a Bible and a legal pad. Briefly just give a summary of the steps he or she would take to go from that point to a sermon.

I would start out reading the whole book, reading the whole chapter, getting a good feel for the argument or development of the whole thing. This is one of the reasons why it's easier to preach through books than it is to preach topically or from the lectionary. Read through the book. I think that's the most important step, so that, having read through the whole book, you are not looking at your verse or your paragraph in isolation. You're seeing it in the whole flow. It's much more difficult to do a "reader response" interpretation when you get the whole big picture. The first step, probably the most crucial step, is to read the whole unit. Next, as you focus on your preaching text, I would take it sentence by sentence. If it's narrative, I'd try to identify how the plot develops. If it's an argument in an epistle, I would try to see how the argument itself

326 / NELSON'S ANNUAL PREACHER'S SOURCEBOOK

evolves. I'd go line by line, verse by verse, sentence by sentence. My goal is not to take my congregation through that, but for my own understanding. Once I lay out an outline for my passage, I try to summarize that in what's been called a "big idea statement" or, as I call it, an "exegetical proposition statement" that expresses inclusively and accurately the concept of that passage.

Next, I want to back off from the exegesis to a broader understanding of its theology and ask myself, "What are the theological issues that are at stake here?" If I'm doing a narrative passage like the story of David's adultery, I back far enough away to see that the theological purpose is something bigger and broader than simply "how to avoid adultery." I want to see what happens when God's leaders break covenant with Him, when they fall short of His standard for leadership. What effect does that have on the leader's life? On the spiritual community of God's people? So, after I've done exegesis, I move to thinking about the theological themes and motifs.

Finally, I want to ask, "What does this theological principle or proposition have to do with my audience?" What I end up preaching is not necessarily a through-the-text discourse as much as the theological proposition expressed in the text and applied to my audience, going back to the text only as much as I need in support of the principle that's relative today. Really, this involves those three moves, exegesis, theology, homiletics.

Would you just give two or three hints for preachers who would like to improve their delivery?

Probably the best thing they can do to improve their delivery is to get three or four people in the congregation—maybe an English teacher, maybe a drama or a speech teacher, but it could be anybody—who will give them feedback and critique, who will say, "This really worked, but that didn't work," and to accept their critique, to take it seriously. It doesn't have to be done every week, but maybe every month or so. Almost any layperson would be able to give you some very good insight into how to improve your delivery. The other thing would be to videotape and watch yourself. The worst thing in the world is to watch yourself preaching, but, if you can get beyond that to a helpful personal critique, it can be of great benefit. ✿

William Carey: The Power of Plodding

William Carey was a cobbler who lived, as one historian put it, "in a forgotten village in the dullest period of the dullest of all centuries." He was born in 1761 in Paulerspury, a rural village of eight hundred inhabitants north of London. His father was a poor weaver, working at a loom in his own cottage.

William was a sickly child, afflicted by numerous allergies and sensitive to the sun. He was also poorly educated. Entering adolescence, William frequently got into trouble, swearing, lying, and running with an undesirable group. At length, he was apprenticed to a shoemaker.

He found himself working alongside a senior apprentice named John Warr, a dedicated Christian who began faithfully witnessing to William, but the young man wanted nothing to do with religion.

Those were the days of the American Revolution, and King George III, hoping for divine assistance in his war efforts, proclaimed a day of national prayer for Sunday, February 10, 1779. Warr persuaded his young friend to join him for a church service.

The preacher spoke from Hebrews 13:13, urging his listeners to give their lives to Christ. The text spoke directly to William, 17, and from that day, the direction of his life changed. He was baptized and became a member of the local Baptist church. In time, he began to do some preaching and pastoral work in nearby Baptist churches.

In 1781, William married Dorothy (Dolly) Plackett, and within a year they bore a daughter, Ann. But fever swept through the Carey household. Their little girl died, and William nearly died also. He recovered at last, but the disease left him bald; for many years he wore a wig.

One day William acquired a book that had become a best-seller in England—Captain Cook's *Voyages*. Reading the accounts of the famous sailor's travels, William began thinking of overseas evangelism. On the wall of his cobbler's shop, he hung a homemade world map, jotting down facts and figures beside the countries.

During those days, most Protestants believed the Great Commission had been given only to the original apostles. Except for the Moravians, there was virtually no thought about missions in the church.

But William Carey began preaching about it. At meetings of Baptist ministers, he continually brought up the subject until they wearied of it. In one famous exchange, Dr. John C. Ryland, the man who had baptized him, said, "Young man, sit down! When God pleases to convert the heathen, he'll do it without consulting you or me."

Carey, deeply disturbed, authored a book justifying and explaining the imperative of Gospel evangelism. Published on May 12, 1792, it has become a classic in Christian history: *An Enquiry into the Obligations of Christians, to use means for the Conversion of the Heathens in which the Religious State of the Different Nations of the World, the Success of Former Undertakings, and the Practicability of Further Undertakings, are Considered.*

William was invited to preach to his fellow ministers on Wednesday, May 31, 1792, at the Baptist associational meeting in Nottingham. He spoke on the imperative of world evangelization from Isaiah 54:2–3, and it was in this sermon that he is quoted as having said: "Expect great things from God; Attempt great things for God."

The following morning there was a business meeting among the ministers, and William expected a resolution that would lead to establishing a missionary society. When no action was taken, William turned to fellow minister Andrew Fuller, gripping his arm, and asking "Is nothing again going to be done?"

Before the assembly dispersed at noon, it had been resolved on a proposition from Fuller "that a plan be prepared against the next Minister's Meeting at Kettering, for forming a Baptist Society for propagating the Gospel among the Heathens."

On Tuesday, October 2, 1792, fourteen men huddled in the back-parlor of widow Wallis' house in Kettering. Carey, now 31, reviewed the achievements of the Moravians and recounted the Bible's missionary mandate. By and by, a resolution was worded: "Humbly desirous of making an effort for the propagation of the Gospel amongst the Heathen, according to the recommendations of Carey's Enquiry, we unanimously resolve to act in Society together for this purpose; and as, in the divided state of Christendom, each denomination, by exerting itself separately, seems likeliest to accomplish the great end, we name this the Particular Baptist Society for the Propagation of the Gospel among the Heathen."

Andrew Fuller passed around his snuff box with its picture of Paul's conversion on the lid, taking up church history's first collection of pledges for organized, home-supported Protestant missions. And Carey immediately began planning to go to India.

That's when his problems really began.

But the end of the story is this: William Carey did go to India. He never took a furlough and never returned to England. He stayed for 41 years, dying there at age 73. When all was said and done, he had translated the complete Bible into six languages, and portions of the Bible into twenty-nine others. He had founded over one hundred rural schools for the people of India. He had founded Serampore College, which is still training ministers to this day.

He introduced the concept of a savings bank to the farmers of India. He published the first Indian newspaper. He wrote dictionaries and grammars in five different languages. He so influenced the nation of India that, largely through his efforts, the practice of *sati* (the burning of widows) was outlawed.

Most importantly, he launched the modern era of missions and laid the foundations for the modern science of missiology. One biographer, Mary Drewery, wrote: "The number of actual conversions attributed to him is pathetically small; the number indirectly attributable to him must be legion."

What was his secret? He once put it this way: "I can plod. I can persevere in any definite pursuit. To this I owe everything." ✿

Quotes for the Pastor's Wall

66 The preacher's first, and the most important task is to prepare himself, not his sermon. 99

—Martyn Lloyd-Jones

NOVEMBER 2, 2003

The Bad Girl Who Made Good

Date preached:

By Stuart Briscoe

Scripture: Joshua 2:1–21, especially verse 1b: So they . . . came to the house of a harlot named Rahab, and lodged there.

Introduction: In the conquest of Canaan, Joshua sent spies to determine the strength of Jericho. Arriving there, the men went to the house of the harlot Rahab, and she received them and made a remarkable confession of faith—that their God was the true God. She made it abundantly clear that she wanted to disassociate herself from her society and commit herself to the Lord. In the process, she became the means of helping the spies escape. They told her that if she would tie a scarlet cord through her window, she would be spared during the conquest. When we come to the New Testament, we find that Rahab is mentioned three times, which brings a new aspect to the whole story, letting us know that God does indeed work in unusual ways through unusual people to accomplish His eternal purposes. Rahab's transformation is one of the most remarkable in Scripture.

I. **The Factors that Contributed to Her Transformation.**
   A. **The Prudence of Joshua.** God had previously told Joshua, in effect, "You're going into battle and facing an appalling conflict, but you can be certain of one thing—you've already won!" Joshua said, "I am a man of God who believes the promises of God, but I'm also a general in the army, responsible for engaging in solid military practice." So he sent spies into Jericho to spy out the land. It's not a contradiction to believe the promises of God while, at the same time, going about in a practical way finding out how the promises of God are to be worked out. God accomplishes ends through means. Matthew Henry says that to ignore the means through which God works out His divine ends is not *trusting* God but *testing* God. If it hadn't been for the prudence of Joshua, the spies would never have met Rahab, there wouldn't have been a crimson cord in the window, and Rahab would not have been saved.

B. **The Providence of Jehovah.** The spies had all Jericho before them, yet God knew where there was a hungry heart. This is the overruling outworking of God's providence. He knows the *hungry heart*, and He is able to send a *suitable servant* to the hungry heart, and in the process, to accomplish *eternal ends*. You'll find many instances of this in Scripture. God says to you and me: "If you're in a situation of being a suitable servant, I am in the situation of working eternal ends in hungry hearts, and My eternal ends will be worked out through you."

2. **The Facts that Accentuated Her Transformation**
   A. **The Kind of Person She Was.** Rahab was a born liar. When soldiers come after the spies, she looked them straight in the eye and they believed her story. In so doing, she became a traitor who sold her city down the drain. She was a prostitute, a born liar, and a traitor.
   B. **The Kind of People She Belonged To.** She was a Canaanite, a people so rotten and mixed up that they were of no redeemable value.
   C. **The Kind of Profession She Followed.** She was a harlot, yet she became an ancestor of our Lord and a New Testament illustration of faith. These are the facts that accentuate her transformation. Maybe you feel your life is a mess. Perhaps you're a born liar. Perhaps you've got such inherent tendencies that you worry yourself sick. The Lord is looking for people just like you.

3. **The Fame that Followed Her Transformation.** Rahab is mentioned three times in the New Testament, as:

>>> sermon continued on following page

APPROPRIATE HYMNS AND SONGS

Hungry for You, Bonnie Low; © 1997 Parachute Music.

Lord Whose Love in Humble Service, Albert F. Bayly/Cyril V. Taylor; © 1942. Renewed 1970 Hope Publishing Company.

Make Me an Instrument, Larry Olson/Karol Baer; © 1989 Dakota Road Music.

The Solid Rock, Edward Mote/William B. Bradbury; Public Domain.

You Are So Faithful, Lenny LeBlanc/Greg Gulley; © 1989 Doulos Publishing (Admin. by Maranatha! Music.).

A. **An Illustration of Genuine Faith.** In Hebrews 11:31, she comes in the same breath as Joseph, Moses, Joshua, Abraham, and Samuel. Genuine faith is hearing the good news, recognizing it as truth, and responding to it.

B. **An Illustration of Gracious Forgiveness.** James 2:25 tells us that Rahab was justified, that God looked on her as if she had never sinned at all. God can cleanse us as pure as fresh-fallen snow.

C. **An Illustration of God's Faithfulness.** In Matthew 1:5, we find her in Jesus' genealogy. God knows how to get hold of broken, wasted, sinful lives and use them to work out His eternal ends.

Conclusion: I'm glad Rahab is in Scripture, for it reminds me that God finds and uses the most unusual people—like you, like me.

FOR THE BULLETIN

❂ On November 2, 1164, Archbishop Thomas Becket, 45, left England to begin a six-year, self-imposed exile in France, having been condemned by his erstwhile friend, King Henry II. ❂ While a student, John Calvin became leader of the Protestant (evangelical) group in Paris. When Nicholas Cop was elected president of Paris University, he asked Calvin to help him write his inaugural speech. The two men overstated the case, attacking Catholic doctrines in sharp tones, and a melee ensued. On November 2, 1533, Calvin escaped through a window by bedsheets and fled Paris disguised as a farmer. ❂ November 2, 1834, is the birthday of Harriett Eugenia Buell, author of the hymn, "I'm a Child of the King." ❂ Absalom Backus (A. B.) Earle, a New York preacher, struggled with periodic bouts of darkness and doubt, but by perseverance and prayer he began to experience victory. On November 2, 1862, he was in his room alone, pleading for the fullness of Christ's love, "when all at once a sweet, heavenly peace filled all the vacuum in my soul, leaving no longing, no unrest, no dissatisfied feeling in my bosom. . . . For the first time in my life, I had the rest which is more than peace." He went on to hold 39,330 services, travel 370,000 miles, lead 160,000 souls to Christ, and earn a total of $65,520 for his 64 years of ministry. ❂ In a letter dated November 2, 1917, British foreign secretary, A. J. Balfour, wrote: "HM government views with favor the establishment in Palestine of a national home for the Jewish people." This Balfour Declaration led to the establishing of Israel in 1948.

STATS, STORIES AND MORE

Philip Bray, executive director of Safehouse Outreach Ministries of Atlanta, understands the hard life. Despite growing up in a parsonage, he strayed from God. "I began drinking and drugging. Especially cocaine. I developed a $1,000-a-day habit, and I was in bad shape. I got involved with organized crime—the Dixie Mafia—to pay for my habit, and I was doing everything. I didn't just go from bad to worse, I went from worse to worst.

"One night I came home stoned after a party and turned on the television. There was my cousin, Billy Watson, on a religious program. I couldn't believe it. I idolized Billy. He owned nightclubs across the country and was involved in a lot of the bad things, but he had a lot of money and was successful, and I admired him because of that. Well, here he was on television, telling how Christ had changed his life. Every time I'd ever seen him, he'd been high or drunk, but here he was, sober, sharing his testimony. I decided he was scamming, just doing it for the money. Then I learned Billy would be speaking at my dad's church the following Sunday. I was furious, because I thought he was just trying to get money out of our people."

At his mom's pleading, Philip decided to attend and hear Billy's presentation. Philip was stoned when he took his seat on the back pew, and still angry. But that night Billy could hardly talk for crying. He kept saying, "I once was in bondage, but now I'm free. I tried getting off drugs and alcohol on my own, but I couldn't. Jesus is the only way to freedom."

On the back row, a sobered Philip listened intently. His anger melted away and the message took hold of his heart. "I took him up on it," said Philip. "That evening I gave my own heart to Jesus, and Jesus set me free."

—Adapted from *Lean on Me,* by *Kirk Franklin,* with *Robert J. Morgan*

WORSHIP HELPS

Call to Worship:

"Come now, and let us reason together," says the LORD. "Though your sins are like scarlet, they shall be as white as snow; though they are red like crimson, they shall be as wool" (Isa. 1:18).

Pastoral Prayer:

Dear Lord, we're so grateful to You this morning that we are alive, and we're thankful for all the things that have gone into our very existence. We're grateful that we're not only physically alive, but spiritually alert. We thank You that it is possible for a human being, part of the divine creation, to know the divine Creator. We thank You, dear Lord, that it is possible for an infinitesimal fragment of creation to know the One who is the beginning and genius behind it all. We thank You, Lord, that You have made it possible for us not only to know You in a shallow, superficial way, but for us to be constantly increasing in depth and experience of Yourself. That's why we gladly avail ourselves of any means to a deeper discovery of who You are, and what You can do, and what You want to do in and for and through our lives. That's why we're here this morning. We're thankful, dear Lord, that as we come together, we can have what the human heart needs, what the human mind craves—fellowship and friendship with You and with each other. Please bring glory to Yourself and blessing to each of us this morning, because we pray in Jesus' name. Amen.—*Stuart Briscoe*

Appropriate Scripture Readings:

- James 2:19–26
- Hebrews 11:30–40
- Matthew 1:1–6
- Isaiah 1:16–18
- Romans 3:21–26

Benediction:

We ask, dear Lord, as we leave this spot that our faith might be real, our love warm, our spirits refreshed, and our lives suitable by grace for the accomplishing of Your eternal ends this week. In Jesus' name. Amen.

Additional Sermons and Lesson Ideas

Beyond Today

Date preached:

SCRIPTURE: Revelation 19:1–21

INTRODUCTION: Discouraged by this week's headlines? Sometimes it helps to fast-forward to the end and remind ourselves of what is in store for us beyond today.

1. Joy (vv. 1–10). This is the chapter describing the return of Christ. In the first ten verses, heaven erupts in anticipation of His imminent appearance. Notice the fourfold "Hallelujah!"
2. Jesus (vv. 11–18). The returning Christ is pictured as a conquering hero descending on a white horse followed by the host of heaven. Notice His fourfold name: Faithful and True (v. 11), a Secret Name (v. 12), the Word of God (v. 13), and King of kings and Lord of lords (v. 16).
3. Judgment—Verses 19–21. His first coming was as a baby in the manger, but when it comes again it will be in battle dress to dispatch justice.

CONCLUSION: When the headlines seem most discouraging, lift up your heads! Your redemption draws near.

Overcoming Lust
By Peter Grainger

Date preached:

SCRIPTURE: 1 Corinthians 6:12–20

INTRODUCTION: Sex isn't evil—it was created by God for good—but it has never been so abused and misused. Our culture is engulfed with sinful, sensual, and sexual images, and we fight a constant inner battle to remain pure. God addresses this in this passage, stressing these things about our human bodies:

1. We Are Bought With a Price. See 1 Peter 1:18–19. When we come to Christ, we have a new Master and a new freedom. But we must ask ourselves this about our activities: Is it beneficial? Is it overpowering? The question isn't "Is it my right?" but, "Is it His Will?" (Hebrews 10:5–7; Matthew 26:39).
2. We Are Members of Christ. Our bodies are not made for sexual immorality, which is damaging both spiritually and physically, but for the Lord.
3. We Are Temples of the Holy Spirit. God's presence in the body gives us holiness (Ephesians 4:30), power (Romans 8:9–11), and redemption (Romans 8:22–24).

CONCLUSION: The challenge: To offer our bodies as living sacrifices (Romans 12:1–2).

NOVEMBER 9, 2003

A Cure for Nerves

Date preached:

Scripture: Psalm 23 (KJV)

Introduction: Preaching from the 23rd Psalm is one of my greatest joys because it is so beloved; but it's also one of my hardest jobs because it's so well-known. Verse one establishes the tone and theme: *The Lord is my Shepherd; I shall not want.* If the Lord is our shepherd, we have everything we need. If we are seeking His kingdom and righteousness, all will be added to us. As Psalm 23 unfolds, it answers the question: "We shall not lack what?" We shall not lack:

1. **His Peace in Life's Meadows—Verse 2.** The word *peace* occurs 429 times in the Bible. While it doesn't actually occur in Psalm 23, it is pictured in beautiful terms: *green pastures, still waters.* What four words in the Bible paint a lovelier picture of peace and tranquility? Whenever we hear them, we want to go to that place, to visit that meadow. That's the Bible's great cure for "nerves." (See Isaiah 26:3, John 14:27). The historian and writer, H. G. Wells, once said, "Here I am at sixty-five, still seeking for peace." If only he had known the Shepherd! But besides conveying an attitude of tranquility, do these figures of speech have deeper meaning? What do the pasture and the pond represent? The green pastures might exemplify the Word of God. There we find nourishment for our souls, the Bible being sweet pasturage. We feed and ruminate on the Word of God as sheep do on grass. We can furthermore say that the Holy Spirit is symbolized by the still waters. When a sheep has eaten her fill, she drinks water to aid the digestion and assimilation of that food through her system, just as the Spirit takes the Scripture on which we're meditating and applies it to our lives. The result is peace and strength. We are replenished. Our souls are restored.

2. **His Plan for Life's Pathways—Verse 3.** Our Shepherd also provides guidance, leading us in paths of righteousness, even in the smaller decisions of life (Proverbs 3:5–6). Here are six C's for finding God's will:

A. **Commit** your decision to the Lord in prayer.

B. Open the **covers** of the Bible and seek Scriptural direction.

C. Seek the **counsel** of those who know more about the matter than you do.

D. What are the **circumstances** indicating?

E. Is an inner **conviction** about this matter developing?

F. Finally, **contemplate** the issue. Think it through. God gave us a brain, and He expects us to use it to arrive at a wise and sanctified decision.

3. **His Presence in Life's Valleys—Verse 4.** Now we come to a subtle but important change of tone. Until now, God has been addressed in the third person; now the pronoun changes to the first person: *Thou art with me.* Corrie ten Boom used to say, "When Jesus takes your hand, He keeps you tight. When Jesus keeps you tight, He leads you through your whole life. When Jesus leads you through your life, He brings you safely home."

4. **His Provision on Life's Tableland—Verse 5.** In his book, *A Shepherd Looks at Psalm 23,* Phillip Keller suggests that at this point in Psalm 23, the shepherd has led the sheep from lower meadows where the grass is turning brown and the waters are drying up. Traversing the canyonous valley, they have ascended to the mountain plateaus or tablelands where the flock can graze through the summer as the shepherd keeps a close eye for predators. A table was prepared in the presence of enemies. God knows our needs, and when we put Him first He provides and protects. In the process, He tends to our hurts, anointing us with oil. He blesses us with abundance, making our cups overflow.

>>> *sermon continued on following page*

APPROPRIATE HYMNS AND SONGS

This Is the Day, Brian Howard; © 1978 Missions Hill Music.

Gentle Shepherd, William J. Gaither/Gloria Gaither; © 1974 William J. Gaither, Inc. (Admin. By Gaither Copyright Management.).

Guiding Light, Paul Baloche; © 1992 Integrity's Hosanna! Music (Admin. By Integrity Music, Inc.).

I Am a Sheep, Dennis Jernigan; © 1992 Shepherd's Heart Music, Inc. (Admin. By Word Music Group, Inc.).

5. **His Promises for Life's Journey—Verse 6.** If the Lord is our shepherd, we'll never lack for peaceful lives, righteous paths, divine protection, abundant provision, and, all along the way, His promises for life's journey—*Surely goodness and mercy shall follow me all the days of my life: and I will dwell in the house of the LORD forever.* Jesus must have been thinking of this when He said, "In my Father's house are many mansions. If it were not so, I would have told you."

Conclusion: One writer said Psalm 23 is so universal because it is so individual. We often ask, "Is the Lord your personal Savior?" Today the question is, "Is the Lord your personal Shepherd?"

FOR THE BULLETIN

✱ John Knox, leader of the Scottish Reformation, performed his last public act on Sunday, November 9, 1572. His health had failed, and his once trumpeting voice could barely be heard during his sermons. A successor had been chosen at his church, St. Gile's Cathedral in Edinburgh, and at his installation, Knox preached his last sermon, pointing out the mutual duties of a minister and a congregation. The following Tuesday, he was seized by a violent cough and declined rapidly. On Friday, November 14th, he rose from bed, thinking it was Sunday. He wanted to dress and go to church and preach. On Monday, November 24, he asked his wife to read from the passage "where I first cast my anchor"—John 17. About 11 o'clock that evening, he passed away. ✱ November 9, 1865, is the birthday of John "Praying" Hyde, missionary to India. ✱ Amy Carmichael arrived in India on this day in 1895, ill, but determined to serve Christ as a missionary of the Church of England Zenana Missionary Society. She remained in that land until her death in 1951, founding the Dohnavur Fellowship which ministered to abused children in India, and writing devotional classics. ✱ On November 9, 1938, Nazi thugs in Germany unleashed a campaign of terror against the Jews. As the police stood passively by, German mobs broke windows of houses and stores and brutalized Jews. There were 267 synagogues plundered, 7,500 shops wrecked, 91 Jews killed, and 20,000 arrested and sent to concentration camps. It was afterward known as "Kristallnacht" ("Crystal Night") because of the thousands of broken windows.

STATS, STORIES AND MORE

Psalm 23 occupies a curious place in the Book of Psalms, preceded by Psalm 22 and followed by Psalm 24. Psalm 22 is a vivid prophecy about the Crucifixion of Christ. Psalm 24 describes the Coming of our Lord in glory and power, presenting Him as a great King over the earth. Between the two is Psalm 23 with its green pastures and still waters. There's a famous little outline that says:

- Psalm 22 tells of the Savior's Cross.
- Psalm 23 tells of the Shepherd's Crook.
- Psalm 24 tells of the Sovereign's Crown.

Or we can think of it like this: Psalm 22 tells us of the sufferings on Mount Calvary. Psalm 24 tells us the glories of Mount Zion. Between the two we have a lovely valley with green grass, quiet waters, and grazing sheep—a pathway of righteousness leading from the cross to the crown under the escort of the Good Shepherd.

In his little book on the 23rd Psalm, published in 1899, the evangelist J. Wilber Chapman suggested we should learn to emphasize every word of this phrase. *The Lord*—literally, Jehovah—the Eternal, Self-Existent God, the King, Eternal, Immortal, Invisible. This Jehovah, this Lord *is*—present tense, right now, at this moment. The Lord is *my*—a personal pronoun; He is mine today and He is yours today. It doesn't say, "The Lord is a shepherd," or "the Lord is the shepherd," but "the Lord is *my* shepherd"—and what a difference that little pronoun makes. The Lord is my *shepherd*. Jesus called Himself the good shepherd, and Peter called Him the chief shepherd. All that an ancient, oriental shepherd was to his sheep, the Lord is, and more, to you and me.

Many people don't realize that sheep have terrible eyesight. Their eyes are dull and cloudy, and they can't see far down the path. They need a shepherd to guide them. Jesus said in John 10 that His sheep follow Him because they know His voice.

WORSHIP HELPS

This is the day the LORD has made; We will rejoice and be glad in it *(Ps. 118:24).*

Scripture Reading Medley:

The LORD is my shepherd; I shall not want. There is no want to those who fear Him. The young lions lack and suffer hunger; but those who seek the LORD shall not lack any good thing. They shall not be ashamed in the evil time, and in the days of famine they shall be satisfied. For the LORD God is a sun and shield; the LORD will give grace and glory; No good thing will He withhold from those who walk uprightly. Do not seek what you should eat nor what you should drink, nor have an anxious mind. For all these things the nations of the world seek after, and your Father knows that you need these things. But seek the kingdom of God, and all these things shall be added to you. [a] My God shall supply all your needs according to His riches in glory by Christ Jesus. *(Pss. 23:1; 34:9–10; 37:19; 84:11; Luke 12:29–31; Phil. 4:19)*

Benediction:

May God's goodness and mercy follow you every day and hour this week, and may we dwell in the house of the Lord forever. Amen.

Kids Talk

Tell the children that you're going to act out a verse in the Bible, and you'd like for them to guess what verse it is. Then lift a cup and saucer out of a small plastic tub and begin pouring water into it from a pitcher. When the cup is full, pause, look at the children, then keep pouring until the water flows over the cup and saucer and splashes into the tub. When they guess Psalm 23:5—*My cup runneth over*—tell them that that's the way God pours His blessings into our lives. He gives more to us than we can receive.

Additional Sermons and Lesson Ideas

It Was for My Benefit

Date preached:

By Ed Dobson

SCRIPTURE: Isaiah 38:9–20

INTRODUCTION: If you've ever faced illness, you'll identify with Hezekiah's song of praise in Isaiah 38, after God healed and extended his life. Verse 9 gives the setting, and Hezekiah sang:

1. Lord, I Really Don't Want to Die (vv. 10–12). Thank God for heaven, but we don't really want to die. At least, not yet!
2. Lord, I'm Weary With Struggling (vv. 13–14). He fell asleep, hoping to wake up finding his terrible illness had been a bad dream. Instead, the opposite happened. He didn't get better but worse.
3. Lord, What Can I Say? You Healed Me! (vv. 15–17). Between verse 14 and 15, the Lord healed him, and, though speechless, he still managed to give four benefits of illness: It teaches humility (v. 15); teaches dependence on God (v. 16); was for my benefit (v. 17, NIV); and taught me about the Lord (v. 17b).
4. Lord, Here's What I'm Going to Do (vv. 18–20). Hezekiah resolves to spend the rest of life praising God and speaking of His faithfulness.

CONCLUSION: Some of you are facing illness. Let's pray now for God to grant healing as He wills.

How to Keep Your Marriage from Going to the Dogs *Date preached:*

SCRIPTURE: Philippians 1–4 (Selected verses)

INTRODUCTION: The Philippian church, though strong, was having internal stresses— just like a lot of Christian marriages today. Paul's four chapters of advice to the church would serve us well as husbands and wives.

1. Philippians 1: Pray for the growth of your partner. Ever prayed for your mate as Paul did in Philippians 1:3–6?
2. Philippians 2: Let your first concern be the happiness and well-being of your mate. See especially verses 3 and 4.
3. Philippians 3: Beware of outside influences. Notice verse 3: Beware the dogs. We must guard against unhealthy relationships outside of marriage, platonic friendships, pornography, etc.
4. Philippians 4: Work hard to get along with each other. Like Euodia and Syntyche.

CONCLUSION: And greet one another with a holy kiss!

NOVEMBER 16, 2003

SUGGESTED SERMON

No Gains Without Pains

Date preached:

By Peter Grainger

Scripture: 2 Timothy 2:3–7, especially verse 3: You therefore must endure hardship as a good soldier of Jesus Christ.

Introduction: The his book, *Holiness,* Bishop J. C. Ryle wrote: "I will never shrink from declaring my belief that there are no spiritual gains without pains. I should as soon expect a farmer to prosper in business who contented himself with sowing his fields and never looking at them till harvest, as expect a believer to attain much holiness who was not diligent about his Bible-reading, his prayers and the use of his Sundays. Our God is a God who works by means." This principle not only applies to holiness, but to Christian service. Take Paul, for example. The secret of his success was "God's grace plus hard work" (1 Cor. 15:9–10). Here in 2 Timothy, his labor was shortly to be ended by an executioner's sword, so he was entrusting the Gospel work to his younger protégé, Timothy, telling him at the beginning of chapter 2 to entrust it to other faithful men who will pass it on to others as well. In the next verses Paul illustrated his point using three metaphors from the Roman Empire, each emphasizing a different aspect of the principle "no gains without pains."

1. **The Soldier, Characterized by Devotion (v. 4).** The Christian as a soldier is a familiar image in Paul's writings, not just because soldiers were a familiar sight in every town and outpost of the empire, but because Paul spent years in close proximity to them. He often described the Christian life as a warfare, but the emphasis here is more specific, on a devotion to duty that inevitably means hardship. The Greek word implies suffering. Sharing the gospel always draws opposition from its enemies, and some of Paul's trusted "soldiers" had recently deserted him in Asia (1:15). He reminded Timothy that suffering is the badge of authenticity for genuine disciples. We must be ready for action and prepared to fight and suffer. We can't afford to be entangled in civilian affairs. There has been much discussion as to what Paul meant here by *the affairs of this life,* but the key

lies in the word *entangles.* It is not just sin that entangles but other things which, while legitimate, may hamper our effectiveness for Christ. A test for any activity we're considering is: Will it hamper my Christian service? Paul added that motive for this suffering is our desire to please Christ, our commanding officer.

2. **The Athlete, Characterized by Discipline (v. 5).** Here is another of Paul's favorite metaphors. In this instance, he emphasized the need for single-mindedness and discipline. The literal translation says that the athlete does not qualify unless he competes lawfully. In the ancient world, this word described a professional athlete. In the Greek games, the athletes had to swear on oath that they had completed a full ten months of rigorous training before they were allowed to compete in the race. So the Christian is one who is disciplined in his or her personal life and walk with God. There is no short-cut to glory, only rigorous discipline. Yet how many of us think we can get by with a minimum of effort. For some, the Christian faith is little more than a Sunday hobby, despite what they profess with their lips. Becoming good disciples means dedicated discipline over as many years as God gives us. The only alternative is to drop out of the race and become a spectator or critic—and there are plenty of those around.

3. **The Farmer, Characterized by Diligence (v. 6).** In the first century (and in many places today), farming was all hard, back-breaking manual labor. The word *hardworking* implies toil that produces weariness or exhaustion. The farmer doesn't just drop seed into the ground then retire to the Bahamas for

>>> sermon continued on following page

APPROPRIATE HYMNS AND SONGS

Arise, My Soul, Arise, Charles Wesley/Lewis Edson; Public Domain.

Front Lines, Dave Billington; © 1992 Desert Springs Music.

I'm a Soldier, Geron Davis; © 1992 DavisSongs (Admin. By SpiritSound Music Group.)

Army of God, Kevin Prosch; © 1990 Mercy/Vineyard Publishing.

Onward, Christian Soldiers, Sabine Baring-Gould/Arthur Seymour Sullivan; © Public Domain.

a few months. He is out and about every day at all hours, tending, weeding, caring, cultivating the precious crop. There isn't much glamor in working in the pouring rain at the end of a long day. But it's absolutely necessarily if we're to reap a plentiful ingathering (Prov. 20:4 and 24:30–31), and it is worth it, for we will share in the ultimate harvest.

Conclusion: There are no gains without pains, but the gains more than compensate for the pains. In the final chapter of this letter Paul writes that he has fought the good fight—he has maintained devotion, discipline, and diligence—and is ready for the crown of righteousness which has been laid up for him. May that be our experience, too, whenever He comes or calls!

FOR THE BULLETIN

❋ Augustine, sixth century missionary to the British Isles, was ordained as the first Archbishop of Canterbury on November 16, 597. ❋ Saint Hugh of Lincoln was a noble bishop who, due to the death of his mother when he was eight, was raised in a convent. He later became abbot of an English monastery, and his reputation as a wise and holy man spread widely. In 1185, he was made Bishop of Lincoln. He denounced the mass persecution of Jews in England, and was fearless in making his case before both mobs and civil authorities. He died on this day in 1200 in London. ❋ Ever wonder why September (Sept = seven) is the ninth month, October (oct = eight) is the tenth month, etc.? On November 16, 1621, the Vatican adopted a new calendar which made January 1 the beginning of the calendar year, instead of March. ❋ November 16, 1662, is the birth of Samuel Wesley, Sr., father of John and Charles. ❋ On November 16, 1895, as Samuel Francis Smith, 88, hurried to catch a train to fulfill a preaching engagement, he collapsed and died. Years before, while translating a patriot German hymn, he had been inspired to write the words of the hymn: "My country, 'tis of Thee." ❋ On November 16, 1903, missionaries Wiley and Eunice Glass arrived in China. There was no one to meet them, and they didn't know the language.

STATS, STORIES AND MORE

Newsweek Magazine ran an article analysing why Tiger Woods is the world's greatest golfer, and why he dominates the course as he does. The magazine asked a dozen of world-class athletes—including Wayne Gretzky, Martina Navratilova, Joe Montana, and Michael Jordan (a close friend of Woods's—what it takes to be the best of the best. The answers were compiled into five rules:

1. Genius Is 99 Percent Perspiration. It all begins with good, old-fashioned hard work. There is no magic pill. "At this level, talent is a given. But Tiger works harder than anyone out there," says tennis great Martina Navratilova. The magazine said, "Tiger's habit of pounding golf ball after golf ball long into the twilight—often during tournament play—has already become part of his legend. During his so-called slump earlier last year (2001), Woods claimed he was simply working on shots he would need specifically for the Masters in April. People rolled their eyes, until he won the Masters. (Joe) Montana, like Woods, understands that such preparation pays off biggest in critical situations—moments when a bout of nerves could disrupt even the most basic play.

2. Let the Other Guy Get Nervous. Tiger Woods has an almost creepy ability to keep cool. He lets the other guy's butterflies become a weapon on his behalf.

3. Don't Just Dominate—Intimidate. It's no accident that Tiger often pulls out a blood-red sweater for his Sunday charges, just as it wasn't chance that Dale Earnhardt preferred dark sunglasses and drove a black and white stock car that looked like a 200 mph pirate ship.

4. Have a Sense of the Historic. Tiger doesn't just want moments of glory. He has an innate sense that he can't be a legend without them.

5. Never, Ever Be Satisfied. Most athletes work the hardest when they're trying to reach the top, but Tiger has seemed only more committed to improving his game since leaving the competition in the dust.

WORSHIP HELPS

Call to Worship:
Oh, Come, let us sing to the Lord. . . . Come, let us worship and bow down. . . . Come, let us rejoice in Him. . . . Let us come boldly before the throne of grace! *(Ps. 95:1, 6; 66:6 NIV; Heb. 4:16).*

Pastoral Prayer:
As we come into Your presence, Lord, we do so humbly, because when we have any conception of You at all, that's the only way we *can* come. You told us that if we will humble ourselves under Your mighty hand, you will exalt us in due time. But You've also warned us that if we insist in exalting ourselves, You Yourself will accept responsibility for humbling us. We'd rather humble ourselves than have You do it. We'd rather have You exalt us than trying to exalt ourselves. So we come humbly in repentance, confessing the things we have done that we never ought to have done. We confess there have been demands that You have presented to us that we have blatantly ignored. We thank You that Your patience is inexhaustible and that Your longsuffering is intended to lead us to repentance. May we never despise the riches of Your grace. We're thankful, Lord, for the gift of Your Word and its principles that outline for us how we are supposed to live on earth. We ask that You will say what needs to be said and do exactly what needs to be done in our hearts today, for our good and Your glory. In Jesus' name. Amen.
—*Stuart Briscoe*

Kids Talk

Talk to the children about their sports, and yours. You might have your running shoes, golf club, or ball glove. How many play soccer? Little League? It takes practice, doesn't it? It takes hard work discipline to be a good ball player. Tell them it takes discipline to be a good Christian, too—regular habits of Bible reading, prayer, and church involvement.

Additional Sermons and Lesson Ideas

Living with People
By Kevin Riggs

Date preached:

SCRIPTURE: 1 Peter 3:8–12

INTRODUCTION: Our relationship with Christ will enhance our relationship with others. In the extended passage, Peter has been dealing with various relationships. Now he gives six principles concerning living around others.

1. Strive for unity (v. 8)
2. Show compassion (v. 8)
3. Love as brothers and sisters (v. 8)
4. Practice humility (v. 8)
5. Be courteous (v. 8)
6. Work at being a blessing (v. 9)

CONCLUSION: Why should we live this way? First, it is the secret to a good life (vv. 10–11); and second, it is what the Lord expects of us (v. 12).

Gregarious Giving

Date preached:

SCRIPTURE: 2 Corinthians 8:13–9:5

INTRODUCTION: This passage falls into three sections, each one giving us a different guiding principle for the way the apostle Paul directed his own stewardship campaign

1. The Principle of Equity (vv. 13–15). Paul felt there was something wrong among his churches when some Christians were overly wealthy while others were starving. He believed those with greater resources had an obligation to help those suffering from want. In other words, God provides some people with more money that they might be of greater help. There should be equality of sacrifice.
2. The Principle of Honesty (vv. 16–24). Here Paul reassured the Corinthians about his handling of the monies raised. He wanted to avoid any criticism about the way the funds were handled.
3. The Principle of Charity (9:1–5). We're prone to ask ourselves, "How little can I get by with? What is the least amount I can reasonably promise to give?" But the Lord does not want gifts "grudgingly given."

CONCLUSION: God wants eager, enthusiastic, generous gifts—and givers.

NOVEMBER 23, 2003

Owl or Eagle?

Date preached:

Scripture: Psalm 103:1–5, especially verse 1–5: Bless the LORD, O my soul; and all that is within me, bless His holy name!

Introduction (vv. 1–2). Let's buck the trend. Instead of focusing on turkey and football, let's spend a few moments this Thanksgiving season giving thanks. Let's say: "Bless the Lord, O my soul, and all that is within me, bless His holy name!" Psalm 103 is a chapter in the Bible with no clouds, devoted exclusively to counting our blessings, to lauding our Lord and Savior; it's one prayer in the Bible with no dismal moods, no petitions, no problems—just praise. We haven't time to study the entire psalm, so let's look at the preamble—verses 1–5. It begins: "Praise the Lord." To whom is he speaking? To himself! King David is giving himself a pep-talk. When was the last time you talked to yourself like this, saying: "Self, you've been down in the dumps, fretting, faint-hearted. Shake it off. Cheer up! Count your blessings!"

1. **The Courtroom (v. 3a).** What blessings should we count? In these verses, the Lord takes us on a little tour, and the first stop is the courthouse to remind us we've been declared "Not guilty." God forgives all our sins. Later, in verses 11 and 12, the psalmist uses a graphic comparison, telling us God's forgiveness is as high as the heavens; that He removes our sins as far as east from west. His love and forgiveness is as infinite and inexhaustible as the universe.

2. **The Hospital (v. 3b).** Next we tour the hospital, for God heals our diseases. Psalm 103 is not asserting that it's *always* God's will to heal *all* our diseases *physically* in *this* life; that runs counter to the overall teachings of Scripture and to our actual experience. God *can* and often *does* give healing in answer to prayer; but even Paul wasn't healed of his thorn in the flesh. God said instead, "My grace is sufficient for you." But what of Paul now? If we had a telescope to look into heaven, we'd see him healthy, happy, and disease free. There's no cancer in heaven, no heart disease, no diabetes. God will heal us in this life or through the process of death, but in either case "by His stripes we are healed" (Isa. 53:5).

3. **The Slave Market (v. 4a).** Now to the slave market to remind us we've been purchased and set free—redeemed. In past days, cruel masters threw slaves into deep holes where they sunk in brackish mud. The holes were sealed shut, and the slave was left hungry, terrified in the darkness amid rats and rodents. That's a picture of the eternal condition Satan desires for us. But Christ saw us when we were enslaved to that cruel master and purchased us with His blood. We're redeemed from darkness and the pit.

4. **The Palace (v. 4b).** Where do we go next? From the pit to the palace, to the throne room. We are crowned with love and compassion. In the Tower of London are the British crown jewels. The Imperial State Crown, the one Queen Elizabeth wears for state functions, is covered with 3,733 jewels, including 2,000 diamonds, 200 pearls, 17 sapphires, 11 emeralds, and 5 rubies. It is perhaps the most precious collection of stones and jewels on earth. But when we come to Christ, He crowns us with something infinitely greater—His love and compassion. He wore a crown of thorns that we might wear a crown of glory.

5. **The Banquet Hall (v. 5).** Now we visit the Banquet Hall where God satisfies our mouth with good things. He meets our needs. What needs do you have? Financial? Physical? Emotional? Do you need peace and strength? When we seek first the kingdom of God, all these things are given us.

>>> *sermon continued on following page*

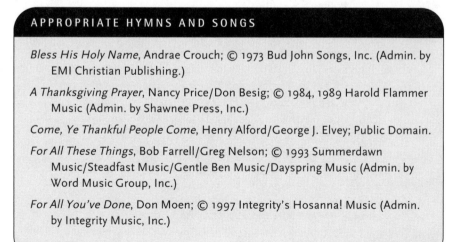

APPROPRIATE HYMNS AND SONGS

Bless His Holy Name, Andrae Crouch; © 1973 Bud John Songs, Inc. (Admin. by EMI Christian Publishing.)

A Thanksgiving Prayer, Nancy Price/Don Besig; © 1984, 1989 Harold Flammer Music (Admin. by Shawnee Press, Inc.)

Come, Ye Thankful People Come, Henry Alford/George J. Elvey; Public Domain.

For All These Things, Bob Farrell/Greg Nelson; © 1993 Summerdawn Music/Steadfast Music/Gentle Ben Music/Dayspring Music (Admin. by Word Music Group, Inc.)

For All You've Done, Don Moen; © 1997 Integrity's Hosanna! Music (Admin. by Integrity Music, Inc.)

When He is our shepherd, we shall not lack. When we delight ourselves in the Lord, He fulfills our desires.

Conclusion: In the previous psalm—Psalm 102—the psalmist was afflicted and troubled. In his pessimistic state, he sees himself as a brooding, lonely old owl—sad, silent, grim (Ps. 102:6). But one chapter later as he remembers to praise the Lord, how does he feel? Like an eagle—strong, majestic, soaring (Ps. 103:5). The next time you're needing a pep talk and there's no one around to give it to you—learn to strengthen yourself in the Lord. Tour God's blessings, and learn to say: Bless the Lord, O my soul, and all that is within me bless his holy name.

FOR THE BULLETIN

✿ November 23, 1596 marks the beginning of Japan's Kirishtan Holocaust when nearly 100,000 Japanese Christians were murdered (some estimates set the number at closer to a million). In A.D. 1549, when Francis Xavier, the Jesuit missionary, arrived in Japan, he met some people who had known of Christ from ancestral sources. Many of these responded with enthusiasm to become Christians, and within a year 10,000 people were following Christ. Eventually an estimated three million became part of the Kirishtan movement, and this time was dubbed "The Christian Century." But at the end of the sixteenth century, the government unleashed a persecution against the church which decimated organized Christianity. It began on November. 23, 1596, when 26 indigenous Japanese Christians were arrested in Kyoto. On the following February 5, they were crucified on a hill outside Nagasaki. The youngest was twelve years old. ✿ On November 23, 1654, the French mathematician, Blaise Pascal, committed his life to Christ while reading John 17. He jotted his impressions on a parchment: "From about half-past ten in the evening until about half-past twelve, FIRE! God of Abraham, God of Isaac, God of Jacob, not of the philosophers and scholars. Certitude. Feelings. Joy. Peace. This is eternal life, that they might know thee, the only true God, and the one whom Thou hast sent, Jesus Christ. Pascal sewed the paper inside his coat lining and often in moments of temptation slipped his hand over it to press its message into his heart. ✿ On November 23, 1873, D. L. Moody opened his evangelistic campaign in Edinburgh, Scotland. ✿ Hymnist and Baptist minister, Robert Lowry, died on November 23, 1899.

STATS, STORIES AND MORE

Campbell Morgan said that Psalm 103 was perhaps the most perfect psalm of pure praise to be found in the Bible; Charles Spurgeon said, "It is one of those all-comprehending Scriptures which is a Bible in itself, and it might alone almost suffice for the hymnbook of the church."

In 1 Samuel 23:16, David was in deep trouble. Several disasters had befallen him, and he was distraught. His friend Jonathan came and "strengthened his hand in the Lord." Later, in 1 Samuel 30, David again found himself in terrible distress. This time Jonathan was unable to come, and there was no one to encourage him. First Samuel 30:6 says, "David strengthened himself in the Lord." This is an important technique to learn. Sometimes there's no one around us to uplift us, and we must learn to encourage *ourselves* in the Lord. We must learn to give ourselves pep-talks, to talk ourselves out of depression and despair. That is what Psalm 103:1 teaches us.

"As the heavens are high above the earth, so great is His mercy" (Ps. 103:11). If, in the scale of things, earth were the size of a grape or marble, the sun would be the size of a beach ball 163 yards away. Jupiter would be about the size of a grapefruit, five blocks up the road. The nearest star would still be 24,000 miles away. If the earth were a grape, the Milky Way, reduced to proportionate size, would still be 55 billion miles wide. Who can imagine the size of the universe? Who can tell how high the heavens are above the earth? Who can measure the distance between east and west?

WORSHIP HELPS

Call to Worship:

Bless the LORD, you His angels, who excel in strength, who do His word . . . . Bless the LORD, all you His hosts, You ministers of His, who do His pleasure. Bless the LORD, all His works, in all places of His dominion. Bless the LORD, O my soul! (Ps. 103:20–22).

Pastoral Prayer:

We praise you, dear Father, for another day. We rejoice and are glad in it. We will rejoice and glad for the fellowship of God the Father, Son, and Holy Spirit. Our hearts, minds, and mouths are full of thanksgiving as we say, "Bless the Lord, O my soul, and all that is within me!" Now bless us, and make us a blessing. Bless each member of our families. Guard us and guide us in matters great and small, and use us to extend and strengthen the kingdom for Christ and His glory. We pray with thanksgiving in Jesus' name. Amen.

Reader's Theater (Can be used as a Scripture Reading Medley or Responsive Reading)

Reader 1: I will say to my soul, "Soul, you have many goods laid up for many years; take your ease; eat, drink, and be merry." But God said to him . . .

Reader 2: "Fool! This night your soul will be required of you; then whose will those things be which you have provided?"

Reader 3: So is he who lays up treasure for himself, and is not rich toward God.

Reader 1: Bless the LORD, O my soul; and all that is within me, bless His holy name!

Reader 2: Bless the LORD, O my soul, and forget not all His benefits:

Reader 1: O my soul, march on in strength!

All: Praise the LORD!

Reader 3: Praise the LORD, O my soul!

Reader 1: While I live I will praise the LORD; I will sing praises to my God while I have my being. The LORD shall reign forever—your God, O Zion, to all generations.

All: Praise the LORD!

(Luke 12:19–21; Ps. 103:1–2; Judg. 5:21; Ps. 146:1–2, 10)

Additional Sermons and Lesson Ideas

Looking Through Bars

Date preached:

SCRIPTURE: Selected Verses in Colossians

INTRODUCTION: Is it hard to be thankful in your circumstances just now? What if you were in prison? The book of Colossians, written by Paul in prison, has four chapters—and seven references to thanksgiving!

1. Be Thankful for Other Christians—Colossians 1:3. For those exhibiting faith and love in Christ
2. Be Thankful for Kingdom Citizenship—Colossians 1:12. We are qualified in Christ to share in the inheritance of the saints of the kingdom of light.
3. Be Overflowing with Thanksgiving—Colossians 2:7. This verse contains three analogies. We are plants (rooted), houses (established and built), and fountains (overflowing). An inner spring of thanksgiving should bubble up.
4. Be Thankful for the Peace of Being in the Body of Christ—Colossians 3:15.
5. Be Thankful in Song—Colossians 3:16. We're to sing with grace (gratitude, thanksgiving) in our hearts to the Lord
6. Be Thankful in Your Work for Christ—Colossians 3:17
7. Be Thankful in Prayer—Colossians 4:12

CONCLUSION: Two men looked through bars. One saw mud; the other saw stars. Even in prison, we can experience seven-fold thanksgiving!

Pray!

Date preached:

By Drew Wilkerson

SCRIPTURE: 1 John 5:14–15

INTRODUCTION: Abraham Lincoln wrote, "I have been driven many times to my knees by the overwhelming conviction that I had nowhere else to go. My wisdom, and all that about me, seemed insufficient for the day." Do you feel your prayers are connecting with God? If not, put John's counsel to work.

1. Be confident when you approach God (v. 14)
2. Ask anything you want of God (v. 14)
3. Seek to know if what you're asking for is the will of God (v. 14)
4. Believe that you are heard by God (v. 14)
5. Expect that your answer will come from God (v. 15)

CONCLUSION: Prayer is a relationship God wants to develop with His children. It needn't become stale or boring. All we need to do is be intentional and full of assurance. As much as we need to pray, God wants to answer our prayers.

A THANKSGIVING SERMON

Sweet Peas

Scripture: 2 Peter 1:2–4

Introduction: After evangelist D. L. Moody passed away in 1899, his great Northfield Bible Conference Center in Northfield, Massachusetts, came under the management of the popular Bible expositor, G. Campbell Morgan. In the middle of the busy 1904 Bible conference season, Howard Morgan, Campbell's three-year-old son, became desperately ill and wasn't expected to survive. As his family attended to him at his bedside, the multitudes attending the summer Bible conferences prayed earnestly for his recovery. One day Howard turned his face toward his mother and requested she sing a hymn for him, one he had often heard in some of the Bible conference sessions. "Sing to me about the sweet peas," he asked. She didn't understand which hymn he had in mind, but when she hesitated, he added, "You know, the sweet peas, gift of God's love." Then she understood he was referring to Peter Bilhorn's famous hymn, "Sweet *Peace*, the Gift of God's Love." Well, in counting our blessings, it seems that so many of them begin with the letter "P." God has given us a cornucopia of "Sweet P's," and I'd like to remind you of some of them today, so that we can thank God for the gifts of His love.

1. **His Pardon—Isaiah 55:7.** All of us have, to a lesser or greater extent, ruined our own lives. We all have areas of moral failure and sin. Not a person here has lived a life free from mistakes and regrets. But in a way we cannot fully comprehend, God through Jesus Christ became sin for us, bearing our guilt, that we might have a complete and irreversible pardon through the power of His shed blood (Isa. 1:18; 1 John 1:9).

2. **His Purpose—Isaiah 14:27.** Sometimes when we slow down enough to think, we become troubled, and we ask ourselves the great philosophic questions of life—Why am I here? What is the meaning of life? Does my life really have meaning and purpose? Millions of people spend their money on alcohol, drugs, and entertainment just to fill the void and emptiness of a purposeless life. But Isaiah 14:27 tells us that the Lord of

Hosts is a God of purpose, and Psalm 139:16 tells us that we fit into His purposes, that is, that He has a meaningful purpose for our lives.

3. **His Precepts—Isaiah 40:8.** Without the Word of God we would be sheep in a desert, without pasture. We would be hungry children without food. We would be pilgrims without a map. We would be questioners with no answers. Thank God for His infallible Word!

4. **His Providence—Isaiah 46:9–10.** God watches over this world, and He watches over His children, working all things together toward the fulfillment of His purposes and His will. To the child of God, there are no accidents. We travel an appointed way (Ps. 139:16).

5. **His Provision—Isaiah 33:16.** John and Sophia Ironside were ardent Christian workers, but when John died suddenly at age 27 of typhoid fever, Sophia was left with two small boys and no income. One of the boys, Harry Ironside (later the world-famous Bible teacher and the pastor of Moody Memorial Church), watched his mother closely. On one occasion, Sophia gathered her two sons to the table for breakfast, but their plates were empty, and there was only water to drink. "We will give thanks, boys," she said. Closing her eyes, she prayed a prayer she based on Isaiah 33:16, saying, "Father, Thou hast promised in Thy Word, 'Your bread shall be given you, and your water shall be sure.' We have the water, and we thank Thee for it. And now, we trust Thee for the bread, or for that which will take its place." Just as she finished praying, the doorbell rang, and the boys ran to the door to find a man there. "Mrs. Ironside," he said, "I feel very bad. We have been owing you for months for that dress you made for my wife. We've had no money to pay you. But just now we're harvesting our potatoes, and we wondered if you would take a bushel or two on account of the old bill." In a few minutes, the potatoes were sizzling in the frying pan, and the boys had answered prayer for breakfast. How wonderfully God has promised to meet all our needs (Ps. 23:1; Matt. 6:33; Phil. 4:19).

6. **His Presence—Isaiah 41:10.** This is one of the sweetest promises in the Bible. As it is put in the hymn "How Firm a Foundation": "Fear not, I am with thee / Oh, Be not dismayed / For I am thy God; I will still give thee aid. / I'll strengthen thee, help thee, and cause thee to stand / upheld by my gracious, omnipotent hand."

7. **His Peace—Isaiah 26:3–4.** The words here "perfect peace" are, literally from the Hebrew, "shalom, shalom." It indicates a deep kind of peace which Isaiah later describes as a river of peace (Isa. 48:18). As the afore-mentioned hymn writer, Peter Bilhorn, put it:

> *There comes to my heart one sweet strain,*
> *A glad and a joyous refrain,*
> *I sing it again and again,*
> *Sweet peace, the gift of God's love.*

Conclusion: What thankless people we would be to remain depressed and full of self-centered pity when we have all of God's sweet P's to enjoy. Thank You, Heavenly Father! Thank You, Holy Spirit! Thank You, God the Son! Thank You for Your pardon, Your purpose, Your precepts, Your providence, Your provisions, Your presence, and Your peace!

Quotes for the Pastor's Wall

❝ No, I do not become discouraged. You see, God has not called me to a ministry of success. He has called me to a ministry of mercy. **❞**

—Mother Teresa

Quotes for the Pastor's Wall

❝ In every pew there is a broken heart.

Speak often on suffering and you will never lack

for a congregation. **❞**

—Joseph Parker

NOVEMBER 30, 2003

Caleb, the Magnificent

Date preached:

By D. James Kennedy

Scripture: Joshua 14:6-15, especially verse 12: Now therefore, give me this mountain of which the LORD spoke in that day; for you heard in that day how the Anadem were there. . . . It may be that the LORD will be with me, and I shall be able to drive them out as the LORD said."

Introduction: Some characters in Scripture make only cameo appearances, yet they are well worth our scrutiny. One such is Caleb. Without doubt, the most outstanding quality in his life was his unswerving faith that made him an unshakable optimist in the midst of a pessimistic people.

Background/Narrative: The Israelites had escaped Egypt by God's out-stretched arm. He led them through the Red Sea and into the howling wilder-ness, to Mount Sinai where they remained about a year before marching toward Canaan. From Kadesh Barnea, Moses sent 12 men to spy out the land. They returned with conflicting reports. The majority said in effect: "Indeed, it is a great land flowing with milk and honey, BUT . . .," and they discussed the frightening presence of the Amalekites, the Jebusites, the Amorites. They were especially alarmed at the Anakim—giants in the land. Leaping to his feet, Caleb said, "Let us go up at once and take possession, for we are well able to overcome" (Num. 13:30). But the negative majority caused the people's hearts to melt, and they grumbled against Caleb, and Joshua. The people might have stoned them but for the intervention of the Lord, who sentenced the nation to years of wandering. Finally the new generation entered Canaan and waged war. When time was near for allocating the conquered land, Caleb approached Joshua and said, in effect: "Before this allotment begins, I have something to say. A promise was made. Though it may not be written in stone, it is engraved in my heart." He rehearsed the events of years earlier, and explained how God had made a promise to sustain him and bring him into the land his seed would inherit. Caleb intended to collect on that promise because he was a man of faith—a faith that made him an inveterate optimist. But did he want fertile plains and sloping hills? A lovely pasture? The choic-est spot in Israel? No. He said, "Give me this mountain (of Hebron)." What was in Hebron? The Anakim—the giants before whom most of the Israelites trembled. "Give me this mountain. . . the Anakim were there. . . . It may be that the LORD will be with me, and I shall be able to drive them out" (Josh. 14:12). And he did just that!

Application: The physical battles of the Old Testament are foreshadowings of our own spiritual battles. We're fighting the "Canaanites, the Amorites, and the Jebusites"—the unbelievers of this world. We aren't trying to put them to death, but to bring them to life. In the midst of them, we still encounter giants. We need people in the church today who aren't afraid of the "Anakim." Wouldn't it be wonderful if there were Christians with the faith to seek to win college professors, civic servants, and commercial leaders to Christ? Caleb had that kind of faith, and we can say three things about it:

1. **Caleb's faith was based on the promises of God.** Five times in today's passage, Caleb said, "The Lord said. . . The Lord said. . . The Lord said. . . ." Faith is the personal appropriation of the promises of God.

2. **Caleb's faith produced Godly living.** Five times we're told that he "wholly followed" the Lord (Num. 32:11, 12; Deut. 1:36; Josh. 14:9, 14).

3. **Caleb discovered through faith the secret of perpetual youth (Joshua 14:10, 11).** In the spiritual realm, through faith we find eternal life in Jesus Christ. But also, as we follow God and turn from the sins and vicious habits that debilitate life, we find we'll live to an older age much healthier.

>>> *sermon continued on following page*

APPROPRIATE HYMNS AND SONGS

Trust in the Lord, Gary Sandler; © 1992 Integrity's Hosanna! Music (Admin. by Integrity Music, Inc.)

Trust, Try and Prove Me, Lida Shivers Leech; © 1923. Renewed 1951 Broadman Press (Admin. by Genevox Music Group.)

Unto Thee, O Lord, Charles F. Monroe; © 1971, 1973 Maranatha! Music.

We Trust in the Name of the Lord Our God, Steven Curtis Chapman; © 1994 Sparrow Song/Peach Hill Songs (Admin. by EMI Christian Music Publishing.)

He Brought Me Out, Henry J. Zelley/Henry L. Gilmour; Public Domain.

The fervent faithful Christian, however old in years, dies young, even as Caleb did.

Conclusion: Have you appropriated that promise of eternal life as a free gift by the grace of God through faith in Christ? If not, please do! If you have, then I challenge you to join the army of the Calebs. Look the "Anakims" squarely in the eye and by the Spirit of God and by faith in our Lord, say, "We are well able to overcome them." Together as the army of Calebs, may we say, "Now, therefore, give me this mountain."

FOR THE BULLETIN

❀ On November 30, 30 BC, Cleopatra, queen of Egypt, committed suicide.
❀ On November 30, 722, Boniface was consecrated bishop. He was the English "Apostle to the Germans." ❀ On November 30, 1215, the Fourth Lateran Council convened for the final time. This was the council that first defined the term "Transubstantiation" with reference to the Lord's Supper.
❀ Following the death of Protestant King Edward VII, his half-sister, Mary Tudor, rose to the throne. On this day in 1554, she restored Roman Catholicism to England. Hundreds of Protestants perished, as chronicled in John Foxe's *Book of Martyrs.* ❀ John Bunyan was baptized on November 30, 1628. ❀ The hymn "Jesus Calls Us O'er The Tumult" is sung for the first time on this day in 1852. ❀ John Clough sailed from Boston as a rookie missionary to India on November 30, 1842. He and his wife were placed on a discouraging station called "Forlorn Hope," in the area of Telugu, but as John faithfully preached the Gospel, conversions multiplied. Fifteen months later two Indian preachers stood in a river and began baptizing the converts. When they grew weary, other preachers relieved them. By five o'clock 2,222 had been baptized, and the baptisms continued for two more days. ❀ James Gilmore, a lonely, single missionary in China, asked God to give him a wife, "and a good one, too." Seeing a picture of an attractive young lady back in England, he immediately wrote to her, proposing. Though Miss Emily Prankard had never heard of Gilmore, upon receiving his letter she felt a leading to accept. In time, she sailed for China, and on November 30, 1874, the two met for the first time. They were married and had a very successful lifetime of marriage and ministry together.

STATS, STORIES AND MORE

How tragic that many people reach 65, retire, and wonder if their usefulness is over. So many great things have been accomplished by those who are long past that age. The artist Titian (pronounced Tish-ian) painted one of his greatest paintings, "The Battle of Lepanto" at age 98. The Earl of Halsburg prepared a revised version of the totally of English common law, amounting to 20 volumes, when he was 90. Goethe finished *Faust* at age 82. Galileo made some of his greatest discoveries at age 73. Cato, the Roman, influenced the Roman Senate more after the age of 80 than in all the years before. J. Hudson Taylor, the great missionary to China, was opening new fields for the Gospel in China. George Mueller, of Bristol Orphanage fame, at age 90, expanded his orphanage. Polycarp, at age 86, refused to deny his Savior and went to the stake, saying, "Eighty and six years have I served Him and He has never failed me. Will I deny him now?" Dr. Jonathan Goforth, the great missionary to China, wrote to his children on his 75th birthday: "You must not wonder at me even at 75, eager to remain here in the high places of the Field, for the opportunities of service were never greater and the outlook for a great harvest never brighter than now."
—D. James Kennedy

There are three kinds of evangelism. The first is "downhill evangelism." We evangelize or cross spiritual swords with those who are inferior to us, physically, mentally, socially, economically, or in some other way. Second, there is evangelism on the plane when we deal with our peers. Not too many of us are willing to do this. But third, there is "uphill evangelism" in which we seek to win those who are superiors educationally, intellectually, physically, socially, politically. Where are those who are willing to cross swords with the professors in our colleges? Or the editors of our magazines? Or our Congressional leaders? Or our mayors and governors? Where are those willing to cross swords with the leaders of our corporations?
—D. James Kennedy

WORSHIP HELPS

Call to Worship:

Trust in (the Lord) at all times, you people; Pour out your heart before Him; God is a refuge for us *(Ps. 62:8).*

Scripture Reading Medley:

Where can wisdom be found? And where is the place of understanding? Man does not know its value. God understands its way, and He knows its place. . . . The LORD gives wisdom; from His mouth come knowledge and understanding; He stores up sound wisdom for the upright; He is a shield to those who walk uprightly. Who is wise? Let him understand these things. Who is prudent? Let him know them. For the ways of the LORD are right; The righteous walk in them. . . . Therefore whoever hears these sayings of Mine, and does them, I will liken him to a wise man. The wisdom that is from above is first pure, then peaceable, gentle, willing to yield, full of mercy and good fruits, without partiality and without hypocrisy. If any of you lacks wisdom, he should ask God, who gives generously to all without finding fault, and it will be given to him. . . . The Spirit of the LORD shall rest upon Him, the Spirit of wisdom and understanding, the Spirit of counsel and might, the Spirit of knowledge and of the fear of the LORD. *(Job 28:12–13; 28:23; Prov. 2:6–7; Hos. 14:9; Matt. 7:24; James 3:17; 1:5; Isa. 11:2)*

Closing Prayer:

O God, we know that the devil has no happy old men or old women, for, though sin has its pleasure for a season, for them the season is long past and there is nothing to look forward to but the fiery judgment of God Almighty and the wrath to come. Lord, help us to be men and women of faith; faith in the living, risen Christ who died for us. O god, by that faith make us men and women of courage. Lord make us Calebs for our day, for there are still giants to be slain. For Christ's sake. Amen.—*D. James Kennedy*

Additional Sermons and Lesson Ideas

The Lord Lives
By Peter Grainger

Date preached:

SCRIPTURE: 1 Kings 17:1–3

INTRODUCTION: These are very bleak days for our world, spiritually and morally, but God still works in dismal, sinful times. As Elisha declared, "The LORD God of Israel lives."

1. The Word of the Lord Declared. "Neither dew nor rain will fall." This was a word of confirmation (Deut. 11:13–17) and of challenge (James 1:17; Matt. 5:45; Jer. 14:22). It was also a declaration of war.
2. The Blessing of the Lord Withheld. God's judgment is seen, not just in what He sends, but in what He withdraws, in this case rain and common grace (Rom. 1:24–28; 2 Thess. 2:6). It was also a warning to individuals and to society.
3. The Prophet of God Concealed. Verses 2–3 are a fresh word for Elijah. He was hidden—and so was the Word of God (Amos 8:11–12).

CONCLUSION: In a bleak age, the Lord still lives, and it is vital for us to hear to and respond to His Word (Heb. 3:7–8).

Principles for Partners
By Melvin Worthington

Date preached:

SCRIPTURE: Genesis 2:18–25; Ephesians 5:22-33; Colossians 3:18–21

INTRODUCTION: The escalating number of divorces and maritial breakups threatens the good of the family and of society. Husbands and wives must:

1. Leave and Cleave. Both husband and wife must leave their parents and cleave to each other.
2. Love and Cherish. Husbands and wives should love and cherish each other as long as they both shall live.
3. Listen and Communicate. Many explosive situations would be avoided if husbands and wives listened and communicated with each other.
4. Lead and Compensate. Husbands and wives must understand their roles and make the necessary adjustments to fulfill that role.
5. Be Loyal and Considerate. Loyalty to one's spouse and consideration for each other pave the way for marital bliss.
6. Live and Contribute. Learning to live together in harmony and honesty requires practice, patience, and perception.

CONCLUSION: A renewed focus on biblical precepts and principles will provide a positive solution to the dilemma of the family in today's world.

DECEMBER 7, 2003

Loving God with Your Mind

Date preached:

By Michael Duduit

Scripture: Luke 2:17 with Matthew 22:35-37: But Mary kept all these things and pondered them in her heart.

Introduction: This is the season of jingling bells and jangled nerves. The rush and expense of the holidays often leave us with little time to do what Mary did—to ponder these things in our hearts. We become too preoccupied to think. But thinking is a very God-ordained activity. Jesus said we should love the Lord our God with all our . . . minds. So this morning, at the onset of this great season, let's get a grip on our perspectives by looking at the Lord's great commandment as recorded in Matthew 22:35–37. Elsewhere in Scripture Jesus quoted the "Shema" as it appears in Deuteronomy 6:5. But here He altered it slightly to say we should love God with our minds. Maybe the particular Pharisee to whom He was speaking was proud of his mental agility, and he needed to understand that his mind was meant for devotion to God. What, then, does it mean to love God with your mind? The word translated "mind" was a common Greek term, *dianoia*, conveying several ideas:

I. **Loving God with Your Mind Involves Your Intellect.** A common meaning of this word involves human thought or intellect. The ability to reason is a gift of God, and using that gift is an act of worship, as we see through Mary's example. If God deserves our best—our greatest love, our deepest commitment, our highest service—that is no less true of our minds. Sometimes we're tempted to produce less than the best our minds can deliver. For example, there's the young person in school who feels pressure not to be "the brain" in class. Some kids say it's not cool to be academic achievers. Then there are those who expect God to directly reveal everything, and they don't use their minds to adequately process His Word. Others fear intellectual pursuits because they're afraid they might learn something damaging to their faith. Real education, however, doesn't harm a person's faith because all truth is God's truth. What can damage young people are the secular, materialistic presuppositions of many university faculties. It's possible to use our minds to try to create thrones for ourselves, bowing before the altar of ego. That's why it's essential to let Scripture be our guide; The Bible is our judge, not the other way around. God calls us to use our intellect to His glory.

2. **Loving God with Your Mind Involves Your Attitudes.** Another common use of *dianoia* involved a "way of thought" or "disposition"—a person's attitudes and perspectives about life. Hugh Downs observed, "A happy person is not a person in a certain set of circumstances, but rather a person with a certain set of attitudes." Much of what we accomplish in life is determined by our attitudes. When we come to faith in Christ, we receive a new mind, new thoughts, new attitudes. In fact, the Greek word for repentance, *metanoia*, literally means "a change of mind." As Christians, we think differently about life and have a new attitude because Christ lives in us. Our attitudes are reflected in things we say and do. Can you imagine saying, "Sure he's flunking all his classes, but he has such a good attitude about school!" That makes as much sense as Linus telling Charlie Brown, "I love humanity. It's people I can't stand!" What is on the inside—the kind of person we truly are—will inevitably surface in our words and actions. Are you loving God with your attitudes? Do you have an attitude of loving concern toward others?

3. **Loving God with Your Mind Involves Your Will.** Several ancient writers used the word *dianoia* to describe the will. Loving God with your mind means placing your will under His control. It doesn't mean you won't

>>> sermon continued on following page

APPROPRIATE HYMNS AND SONGS

Come, Thou Long Expected Jesus, Charles Wesley/Rowland H. Prichard; Public Domain.

Joy to the World, Isaac Watts/George Fredrick Handel; Public Domain.

Lord, Come This Christmas, Andy Parks; © 1990 Mercy/Vineyard Publishing.

Comfort, Comfort Now My People, Johannes Olearius/Louis Bourgeois/ Catherine Winkworth; Public Domain.

Celebrate the Child, Michael Card; © 1989 Birdwing Music/Mole End Music (Admin. by EMI Christian Music Publishing.)

have to make any decisions; but it does mean you'll seek to make decisions that honor God. No decision has greater consequences than how we'll respond to Christ's call. Surrendering your life to His lordship means accepting His authority over your life. We accept His rule and agree to submit ourselves in obedience to His will.

Conclusion: In Matthew 27:22, Pilate asked, "What shall I do with Jesus who is called Christ?" That may be the most important question posed in the entire Bible, and it is a question which can only be answered with a decision. If you've never given your life to Christ, you can make that decision right now and propel your life forward in a new direction.

FOR THE BULLETIN

❋ The prophet Zechariah received a vision from God on this day in 518 B.C., as recorded in Zechariah 7:1. ❋ On December 7, 43 B.C., the Roman orator Marcus Tullius Cicero was executed. ❋ December 7, 374, St. Ambrose, 34, was ordained and consecrated as Bishop of Milan. He had never considered the ministry. As governor in Milan, he was seeking to guide the city toward a replacement for its deceased bishop. When the populace couldn't agree on a suitable candidate, a child's voice was heard, "Let Ambrose be bishop!" The crowd took up the cry, and Ambrose was drafted against his will. He gave himself to his task, however, with all his heart and became a powerful church leader, and was largely responsible for Augustine's conversion. ❋ The great Irish missionary hero, Columba, was born on December 7, 521. With 12 companions, he established himself on Iona, a bleak, foggy island just off the Scottish coast. He built a crude monastery that soon became a training center for missionaries, one of the most venerable and interesting spots in the history of Christian missions. From Iona, Columba made missionary forays into Scotland, converting large numbers. An entire tribe of pagans, the Picts, were won to the faith. ❋ December 7, 1807, marks the death of William Carey's deranged wife, Dorothy. ❋ On December 7, 1941, Japanese planes attacked the American naval forces at Pearl Harbor, Hawaii. Missionary activity around the world was disrupted, and missionaries in China were particularly endangered, especially the children at the MK boarding school in Chefoo.

STATS, STORIES AND MORE

The human brain weighs only three pounds, yet it is the most complex structure in the body. The brain encases more than 100 billion cells, and is capable of sending signals to thousands of other cells at speeds of more than 200 mph. Over its lifetime the brain will establish trillions of connections within the body. All that power—and we still manage to forget where we put our car keys! The human brain really is an incredible machine. It goes far beyond any man-made computers in terms of its complexity and capability. Your brain serves as the command and control center of your body, enabling your various organs to function while simultaneously helping you operate at an intellectual level, retaining facts, learning to reason, thinking. The mind is one of God's most incredible creations. That's why I've always been fascinated with this statement by Jesus, that we are to love God with all our minds.
—*Michael Duduit*

A wildlife organization offered a bounty of $5,000 for each wolf captured alive. Sam and Jed decided they'd start hunting for wolves, and they began spending their days scouring the forests and mountains. One night they were exhausted and fell asleep right in the woods dreaming of all the money they were going to make. Suddenly Sam awoke to see that they were surrounded by fifty hungry wolves. He jabbed his friend in the side and said, "Wake up, Jed. We're rich!" That was a positive attitude!—*Michael Duduit*

Someone Once Said:
- Every temptation comes to us via our thoughts.—*Erwin Lutzer*
- The mind of man is the battleground on which every moral and spiritual battle is fought.—*J. Oswald Sanders*
- Our defeat or victory begins with what we think, and if we guard our thoughts we shall not have much trouble anywhere else along the line.—*Vance Havner*
- Self-control is primarily mind-control.—*John Stott*
- Every kidnapping was once a thought. Every extramarital affair was first a fantasy.—*Leslie Flynn*

WORSHIP HELPS

Call to Worship:

Praise the LORD! I will praise the LORD with my whole heart, in the assembly of the upright and in the congregation (Ps. 111:1.)

Scripture Reading:

And now . . . what does the LORD your God require of you, but to fear the LORD your God, to walk in all His ways and to love Him, to serve the LORD your God with all your heart and with all your soul, and to keep the commandments of the LORD and His statutes . . . ? Indeed heaven and the highest heavens belong to the LORD your God, also the earth with all that is in it. . . . Be stiff-necked no longer. For the LORD your God is God of gods and Lord of lords, the great God, mighty and awesome, who shows no partiality nor takes a bribe. He administers justice for the fatherless and the widow, and loves the stranger, giving him food and clothing. Therefore love the stranger, for you were strangers in the land of Egypt. You shall fear the LORD your God; you shall serve Him, and to Him you shall hold fast, and take oaths in His name. He is your praise, and He is your God, who has done for you these great and awesome things which your eyes have seen (Deut. 10: 12–21).

A Word About the Offering:

We should remember today that all that is happening around us in this church—this building, these ministries, these missionaries— all this is the result of God's people worshiping Him through the giving of their tithes and offerings. We don't have secret sources of income. There are no great benefactors who pay for all this. It is just people like you and me, giving to the Lord from what He has given us, and He uses it to do all that we see happening around us in and through this church. Thank you for being a part of it!

Benediction:

O Lord our Lord, we worship You today, and we love You with all our heart, mind, soul, and strength. Bless us this week with deeper love and greater faith. In Jesus' name, Amen.

Additional Sermons and Lesson Ideas

The Three Gifts
Date preached:

Scripture: Matthew 2:9–12; Romans 5:1-5

Introduction: As we prepare for Christmas, we notice some gifts at the cradle of the Christ child. Three are for Him—gold, frankincense, and myrrh (Matt. 2:11). But on the other side of the cradle are three other gifts, His to us. There is an exchange of gifts on Christmas. He gives:

1. A Life that Is Forgiven (Rom. 5:1). We are justified by faith and have peace with God.
2. A Life that Is Forever (Rom. 5:2). We rejoice in hope of the glory of God. "Hope" here is a reference to the return of Christ and our life in glory with Him.
3. A Life that Is Fortified (Rom. 5:3–5). We persevere in tribulations, strengthened by His love which is shed abroad in our hearts by His Spirit.

Conclusion: Receive Christ's gifts. He came all the way from heaven to give them to you.

Jesus' Little Sermon on Prayer
Date preached:

Scripture: Luke 11:1–13

Introduction: The disciples had seen Jesus perform miracles and preach great sermons, but they didn't say, "Lord, teach us to preach, teach us to perform miracles." But observing Him in prayer, they asked, "Lord, teach us to pray." Jesus gave them:

1. A Pattern (vv. 1–4). "When you pray, say: 'Father, hallowed be your name, your kingdom come. Give us each day our daily bread. Forgive us our sins, for we also forgive those who sin against us. And lead us not into temptation.'" The "Lord's Prayer" of Matthew 6 tells us to include praise in our prayers, and to ask for things that will advance God's kingdom, meet our physical and spiritual needs, and protection from temptation and testing.
2. A Parable (vv. 5–9). We should pray with the importunity of a man knocking at midnight who will not be denied until his request is granted.
3. A Promise (vv. 10–13). "Everyone who keeps on asking, receives; and the one who keeps on seeking, finds; and to the one who keeps on knocking, the door will open" (Williams).

Conclusion: Don't stop praying about that need or burden. None of your prayers are lost or forgotten. Sometimes we must persevere in persistent, I-will-not-be-denied prayer. As Jesus said later, "We should always pray and not give up" (Luke 18:1).

DECEMBER 14, 2003

"I Have Come"

Date preached:

Scripture: John 6:38–40, especially verse 38: For I have come down from heaven, not to do My own will, but the will of Him who sent Me.

Introduction: Even as we're singing about "joy to the world" and "peace on earth," our world is filled with wars and rumors of wars. How we need to understand the great peace initiative of heaven! Some of the most helpful information about our Lord's mission comes from His "I have come" statements. That phrase, occurring 13 times in the Gospels, is significant because it presupposes Christ's preexistence. The Lord Jesus is distinct from everyone else, in that He possesses a double nature—both God and man. He has always existed and always will. He is eternal in the heavens, thus His coming to earth was pre-planned. He looked down on this planet, saw a need, and said, "I am going to be born to meet that need." Thus the importance of the "I have come" statements.

1. **He Came to Represent a Father** (John 5:43): "I have come in My Father's name." The ceiling of a cathedral in Europe was beautiful but so lofty it was difficult to study. The rector put a tilted mirror near the floor, allowing visitors to study the grandeur of the ceiling at their level. Christ is the image of the invisible God, at our level. (See Heb. 1:3; John 1:18; and Col. 1:15.)

2. **He Came to Kindle a Fire** (Luke 12:49): "I came to send fire on the earth." This passage (vv. 49–53) can be boiled down to three words: fire, baptism, and division. Christ came to kindle a fire, undergo a baptism, and create a division. The baptism was His baptism into suffering, His death on the Cross. The division is between those who would receive Him and those who don't. But what did He mean by bringing fire on the earth? In Luke 3:16, John the Baptist said the Messiah would set fire to earth and burn the chaff, fire being a biblical symbol for judgment. Christ came to deal with and destroy the force of evil in the world. In Luke 12, He was saying in effect: "I have come to deal with sin and judge evil. I'm going to kindle a fire and cleanse this world of evil. In the process I am going to be plunged into suffering, and the world will be divided over Me. Everyone must accept Me or reject Me."

3. **He Came to Preach a Message** (Mark 1:35): ". . .because for this purpose I have come." The content of that message is given in Mark 1:14—the good news! This is that wonderful old Greek word: *euaggelion*. The prefix *eu* means good; the stem word *angel* means message. This is one of the Bible's great words, yet it seems an understatement. If you were trapped in a collapsed cave, running out of air, shut in claustrophobic darkness, minutes from death, and you heard workmen breaking through the rubble to rescue you, would you call that "good news"? Here we are, separated from God by sin, trapped on a doomed planet, facing death and hell. And God Himself became a man, dying in our place, rising from the dead to give us life. Is that good news? Yes, but it's more than good news. We don't have a word to describe it. The angels put it: "Behold, I bring you good tidings of great joy which shall be to all people. For unto you is born this day in the city of David a Savior."

4. **He Came to Illumine a World** (John 12:46): "I have come as a light." The world is a drab, miserable place, filled with sin's darkness. But Jesus came, offering His indescribable gift. His presence dispels the gloom, lighting up our world and our lives.

5. **He Came to Enrich Us** (John 10:10): "I have come that they might have life . . . more abundantly." Two cities in New York drew water from nearby mountains. One depended on a lake that tended to dry up during droughts. The other got its supply from a lake in the Catskills that

>>> sermon continued on following page

APPROPRIATE HYMNS AND SONGS

O Come, O Come Emmanuel, John M. Neale/Henry S. Coffin/Thomas Helmore; Public Domain.

Thou Didst Leave Thy Throne, Emily E. S. Elliott/Timothy Richard Matthews; Public Domain.

Emmanuel, Bob McGee; © 1976 C.A. Music (Admin. by Music Services.).

And the Glory of the Lord, Larry Pugh/George Frederick Handel; © 1982. 1986 Lorenze Publishing Co.

Arise and Shine, David J. Pedde/Jon Lugo/Laurey Berteig; © 1995 Music Pendulum Publishing.

never went dry, fed by underground streams. They could never exhaust that lake. Many of us forget we have endless supplies of grace, joy, peace. We don't have to worry about our spiritual reserves, but we've got to tap into them by faith. If we're committed to Christ and walking in the Spirit, we have an ocean of God's blessing to draw from every day.

Conclusion: He came for you! He knew you before you were born, and He loves you. He came to give you good news, to light up your life, to give you abundant life. Let this Christmas be the one you really celebrate!

> O come to my heart, Lord Jesus,
> There is room in my heart for Thee.

FOR THE BULLETIN

❋ December 14, 872, marks the death of the Italian pope, Adrian II, the last married pope, who died at about age 80. ❋ On December 14, 1417, Sir John Oldcastle, one of John Wycliffe's strongest supporters and a Lollard leader, was captured, suspended over a slow fire by chains, and roasted to death for his faith in Christ. ❋ December 14, 1836, is the birthday of hymn writer Frances Ridley Havergal, born in the rectory at Astley, Worcestershire, England. Her father, Rev. William Havergal, was an Anglican clergyman who devoted himself to improving the church music in England, and who himself wrote over 100 hymns. Frances struggled throughout her twenties and thirties, pulled in one direction by the acclaim of great London crowds who loved her singing, and in another direction by the Holy Spirit. Then one day at age 36 she read a booklet entitled "All For Jesus," which stressed the importance of making Christ King of every corner and cubicle of one's life. Frances made a fresh, complete consecration to God. Today she is best known as the author of such hymns as "Like a River Glorious," "Take My Life and Let It Be," and "Another Year is Dawning." ❋ On December 14, 1853, through the efforts of zealous Wesleyians, the Illinois Institute opened its doors for the first time. Seven years later, amid financial struggles, the trustees requested help from the wealthier Congregationalists. Jonathan Blanchard, Presbyterian pastor and academic, was appointed president. He approached Warren Wheaton for a large donation of property and offered to name the school Wheaton College. "That will at least save your heirs the expense of a good monument," Blanchard said. Wheaton College has been training students ever since "For Christ and His Kingdom."

STATS, STORIES AND MORE

In a recent newsletter, missionary and college president George Murray of Columbia International University, Columbia, South Carolina, wrote of the many holiday seasons he had spent overseas. He and his wife were missionaries in southern Europe for thirteen years. Not long after their arrival in Italy as rookie missionaries, the holidays approached and they were faced with their first Christmas away from home and family. They experienced genuine homesickness. They longed for familiar sights and sounds and smells—like pumpkin pie and cranberries, which were unknown commodities in the Mediterranean basin where they now lived. They missed their family gatherings. They missed their childhood traditions. They badly wanted to go home for Christmas.

Then one day as George was meditating on the meaning of Christmas, it hit him: Christmas isn't about going home. It's all about leaving home. That's what Jesus did. He deliberately left the comfort and security of His heavenly home to come to this sin-filled world. He was obeying His heavenly Father. He was representing God to this world. He said, "I have come down from heaven, not to do My will, but the will of Him who sent Me. Behold, here I am. I have come to do Your will, O God."

WORSHIP HELPS

Call to Worship:

Do not be afraid, for behold, I bring you good tidings of great joy which will be to all people. For there is born to you this day in the city of David a Savior, who is Christ the Lord (Luke 2:10–11).

Scripture Reading / Hymn Story:

Psalm 98:4–9 says: Shout joyfully to the LORD, all the earth; break forth in song, rejoice, and sing praises. . . . Shout joyfully before the LORD, the King. Let the sea roar, and all its fullness, the world and those who dwell in it; let the rivers clap their hands; let the hills be joyful together before the LORD, for He is coming to judge the earth. With righteousness. . . .

Isaac Watts was an odd little 18th-century Christian known as the "Father of English Hymns." When as a teenager he grumbled about the music in his church, his father told him to write his own songs if he thought he could do better. So he did. His new-fangled hymns were met with resistance, but he pressed on. In 1712, some friends invited him to spend several weeks in their home, recovering from an illness. He stayed 36 years, during which he devoted himself to publishing a volume of hymns based on the biblical psalms. He studied each psalm, then prepared his poetic version in the light of the New Testament, thus giving David's psalms a decidedly Christian slant. As Watts studied Psalm 98, he thought of the Christmas story. Verse 4 seemed to beautifully describe the joy that engulfed the world on the night Christ was born. Verse 6 spoke of the Lord as a King. Verse 7 exhorted all nature to sing. Verses 8 and 9 spoke of His coming to rule the earth with truth and grace. Out of his enraptured meditation came Watts' version of Psalm 98, ringing with these words:

Joy to the world! The Lord is come;
Let earth receive her King;
Let every heart prepare him room,
And heaven and nature sing.

Additional Sermons and Lesson Ideas

Anticipation

Date preached:

SCRIPTURE: Luke 2:21–30

INTRODUCTION: Recall how eagerly you anticipated Christmas as a child? Simeon was like that, for it had been revealed to him he wouldn't die before seeing the Christ. Perhaps God gave us this story to teach us to eagerly anticipate His return.

1. We Should Study the Second Coming Passages. Be students of Matthew 24–25, 1 and 2 Thessalonians, and the Book of Revelation.
2. We Should Visualize His Return. When you see the sun rising in the east or setting in the west, picture the Lord's Coming in clouds of glory.
3. We Should Pray for His Return. The last prayer in the Bible is "Even so, come, Lord Jesus!"
4. We Should Work Until He Comes. When we stand around waiting for someone to arrive, time drags by. As we remain busy, they appear before we know it. Jesus told us to stay occupied until He returns (Luke 19:13).

CONCLUSION: As we celebrate Christmas this year, keep a Simeon-like lookout for His return. Even so, come, Lord Jesus!

Looking for Christmas

Date preached:

By Drew Wilkerson

SCRIPTURE: Matthew 2:1–12

INTRODUCTION: C. S. Lewis defined hope as "a continual looking forward to the eternal world." This describes the Magi. They were hoping to find the King of the Jews; they discovered Jesus, the Son of God. We must be willing to look for the Christ of Christmas with eyes wide. The Magi show us how.

1. We Must Look Willingly (vv. 1–2). The journey ahead is difficult, but the reward is unbelievable. To find Christmas we must willingly look with renewed hope.
2. We Must Search Carefully (vv. 3–8). Only by a careful search for the Christ will we find life's answers. This is what the Magi did.
3. We Must Hope Expectantly (vv. 9–11). Martyn Lloyd Jones wrote, "It is a fundamental principle in the life and walk of faith that we must always be prepared for the unexpected when we are dealing with God."
4. We Must Change Radically (v. 12). The Magi were warned in a dream not to return home by the same route. At the close of every Christmas season, this should be our same desire.

CONCLUSION: Look for Christ this season with a renewed adventure and make the discovery of a lifetime. Christmas is for every child of God who longs to get a glimpse of the baby and realize they have found the Savior of the world.

DECEMBER 21, 2003

Good News of Great Joy

Date preached:

By Peter Grainger

Scripture: Luke 2:8–20, especially verse 8: Now there were in the same country shepherds living out in the fields, keeping watch over their flock by night.

Introduction: I've often wondered what difference it might have made if Jesus had been born when Elizabeth II was Queen of England or George W. Bush was President of the United States, rather than when Caesar Augustus was Emperor in Rome. One thing is sure—it still would not have made headlines. News bulletins are for world events, and our Lord's birth was in obscurity. The first people to hear were shepherds. There were senators in Rome, princes in Jerusalem, and philosophers in Athens. But there were shepherds living out in the fields, and to them the wonderful news was given. It was indicative of how God works even today. Notice three features:

1. **An Unexpected Surprise** (v. 8). They were minding their own business, or rather, their own sheep—just another day in their lives, another night in their shepherding. Probably the most exciting thing that happened was a visit from a marauding wolf, which is why they kept watch. Suddenly an angel appeared, and a bright light, the glory of the Lord, filled the sky. The creation story in Genesis begins in a similar way, with God speaking in the darkness. Throughout history, God brings light into human darkness. The prophets looked forward to the day when the people walking in darkness would see a great light. But for these shepherds it was an unexpected surprise. God still breaks into human history in unexpected ways to bring light into our darkness. He comes to those not expecting or even seeking Him. He comes to those going about the ordinary business (and busyness) of living. Shepherds were not highly esteemed in those days. The very nature of their work precluded regular observance at temple and synagogue. Their honesty was not rated highly (they weren't allowed to stand as witnesses in court). God still surprises people like that today (1 Cor. 1:27–29). Some of you can look back to last Christmas and you are surprised to find yourselves here today. Who would have dreamt that God

would meet you and bring you into His family? Others here are perhaps still in the dark, going about your business with little thought of angels and glory and God. He longs to break into your life. This Christmas could be a great surprise for you as you understand for the first time what it all means.

2. **An Unusual Sign** (v. 12). Bethlehem may have been a "little town," but finding the right baby wasn't easy, so the shepherds were given an identifying sign—not just a baby wrapped in swaddling cloths, for most babies would be in that state. The identifying sign would be a baby lying in a manger. This baby was in an animal feeding-trough, His first bed. The New Testament word "sign" means not just an identifying mark, but something that has in itself significance. So what is the "significance" of the manger? It indicates the depths to which the Son was willing to stoop in love (2 Cor. 8:9). It marks the beginning of the life of one who was a man of sorrows and acquainted with grief. It marked the kind of lifestyle He would adopt in His earthly ministry (Luke 9:58). He was born a Savior in a manger, and He died a Savior on a cross. The manger also meant the shepherds could visit Him freely. Spurgeon says: "We might tremble to approach a throne, but we cannot fear to approach a manger."

3. **An Unbelievable Story** (vv. 17–18). These shepherds were the first Christian missionaries. They had seen the Christ, and they told everyone what had happened to them. The good news about Jesus is something to

>>> sermon continued on following page

APPROPRIATE HYMNS AND SONGS

O Little Town of Bethlehem, Phillips Brooks/Lewis H. Redner; Public Domain.

Unto Us, Larry Bryant/Lesa Bryant; © 1987 Stonebrook Music Company (Admin. by EMI Christian Music Publishing.).

Hark, the Herald Angels Sing, Charles Wesley/Felix Mendelssohn; Public Domain.

Love Came Down at Christmas, Christina G. Rossetti; Public Domain.

Like Christmas All Year Round, Dennis Jernigan; © 1992 Shepherd's Heart Music, Inc. (Admin. by Word Music Group, Inc.).

be shared, and the best people to share it are ordinary folk who have had a personal experience with Him. You may not know everything, but if God has unexpectedly broken into your life, you have something to share. We have some*one* to share—a baby in the manager, a man on the Cross, a returning King!

> *O holy child of Bethlehem, descend to us we pray;*
> *cast out our sin and enter in; be born in us today.*
> *We hear the Christmas angels the great glad tidings tell;*
> *O come to us, abide with us, our Lord Immanuel.*

FOR THE BULLETIN

❀ December 21 marks the traditional death of the apostle Thomas in India. He was reportedly killed "in the 30th year of the promulgation of the gospel," by Brahmins who were seeking to end his evangelistic activities. Learning he was in a cave, they went to the mountainside, saw him through the narrow opening, on his knees with his eyes closed, in a rapture so profound he appeared to be dead. They thrust a lance through the opening, wounding him mortally. ❀ Thomas Becket, Archbishop of Canterbury, was born on this day in 1118. ❀ Hernando Cortes and the conquistadors slaughtered and enslaved thousands of the Aztecs and Incas. On December 21, 1511, at the risk of his own life, Pastor Antonio des Montesinos stood before his church in Hispaniola and thundered against the conquistadors: "I have climbed to this pulpit to let you know of your sins, for I am the voice of Christ crying in the desert of this island, and you must not listen to me indifferently. You are in mortal sin; you not only are in it, but live in it and die in it because of the cruelty and tyranny you bring to bear on these innocent people." ❀ On December 21, 1620, the 103 Pilgrims aboard the Mayflower landed at Plymouth Rock. ❀ December 21, 1795, is the birthday of Robert Moffatt, Scottish pioneer missionary and Bible translator to South Africa. ❀ Pastor and hymnist, John Newton, died on December 21, 1807. One of his famous hymns had this stanza: "But to those who have confessèd, / Loved and served the Lord below, / He will say, 'Come near, ye blessèd, / See the kingdom I bestow.'"

STATS, STORIES AND MORE

"Would it have been fitting that the man who was to die naked on the cross should be robed in purple at His birth? Would it not have been inappropriate that the Redeemer who was to be buried in a borrowed tomb should be born anywhere but in the humblest shed, and housed anywhere but in the most ignoble manner? The manger and the cross standing at the two extremities of the Savior's life seem most fit and congruous the one to the other."
—*Charles H. Spurgeon*

A man, dying of an incurable disease, received an urgent telegram from a far off town. It was from a physician who wired, "Come at once. Cure discovered." The man scarcely took time to pack. He jumped in his wagon and traveled as hard as he could, finally reaching the town where the physician resided. But it was Christmas Eve, and he arrived just as the town's people had gathered in the square for the singing of carols and to await the arrival of Santa. He got stuck in the parade. People were clogging the streets, children were every-where, bands were playing, candy was flying through the air. As the man stopped to unwrap a piece, he watched the commotion. In the center of the square was the biggest tree he had ever seen, the brightest lights, the biggest gifts, the loveliest decorations, the fattest Santa. Fireworks were exploding, and the whole world seemed to be celebrating. He tarried and watched, and in the hurly-burly of that night the man became so caught up in the crowd that he was herded into the grand hotel for Christmas cheer before going to bed. That night, drained by the crowds and stricken by his illness, he perished in his sleep. He had been so caught up in the festivities that he had forgotten about the physician. He had been so involved in the celebration that He had forgot-ten the Savior.

Kids Talk

Have a rocking chair, if possible, on the stage and ask the children to gather around for the reading of the Christmas story. Tell them you're about to read them the most wonderful story of all, then read to them the traditional King James rendering of Luke 2:1–20. In the background you might want some soft Christmas music; and following the reading, have the children join you in a verse of "Away in the Manger."

WORSHIP HELPS

Call to Worship:
Oh, come, all ye faithful! Oh, come let us adore Him, Christ the Lord!

Pastoral Prayer:
Our Heavenly Father, if we could light a million candles today, it would not equal the warmth and light in our hearts as we recall the events of our Lord's birth in Bethlehem. We thank You for the Christ child, for the manger and swaddling clothes, for the angelic chorus, for the shepherd's wonder, for the star in the sky, for the wonder of that Babe. We thank You for our Lord's childhood in Nazareth, for His teaching in Galilee, and for His death at Calvary. We've been forever changed by His resurrection from the garden tomb, and we worship Him today, enthroned in the heavens. Lord, may we never lose the wonder. Now, be near us, Lord Jesus, we ask you to stay close by us forever, and love us, we pray. In Jesus' name, Amen.

Word of Welcome:
When Mary and Joseph visited Bethlehem, there were great crowds—and no room for them in the inn. Today there are great crowds at our church, but there is plenty of room for you. We want you to feel welcome and to know how happy we are that you've joined us for this "Birthday Celebration" for our Lord Jesus Christ. May God bless each of you.

Benediction:
May we, like the shepherds of old, publish abroad the wonderful news—Christ the Savior is born!

Additional Sermons and Lesson Ideas

The Christmas Spirit

Date preached:

SCRIPTURE: Luke 1:26–38

INTRODUCTION: Don't overlook the role of the Holy Spirit in the Christmas story. He was responsible for:

1. The Conception of Christ in the Virgin's Womb (v. 35).
2. The Perception of Christ in the Peoples' Eyes. The people on the scene only understood the significance of what was happening as the Holy Sprit explained and revealed it to them. (See Luke 2:25–32).
3. The Reception of Christ in the Sinners' Hearts. There were those ready to receive Christ. Zechariah's family, for example. Every member of this family was said to be filled with the Holy Spirit: Zechariah in Luke 1:67; Elizabeth in Luke 1:41; and John in Luke 1:15.

CONCLUSION: The same Holy Spirit is pleading with you. What better time to come to Christ?

How to Have a Christian Christmas

Date preached:

SCRIPTURE: Leviticus 23:22

INTRODUCTION: As we celebrate our Christmas holiday, it would be a good idea to look at Leviticus 23 and see how God designed the holidays (holy days) for His people Israel. What purpose does a day like this serve?

1. Worship (Lev. 23:1–2, 4, 27, 35–36, 41). These were feasts to the Lord, special days for extended worship and praise.
2. Rest (Lev. 23:7–8, 21, 25, 28, 30–31). These were days when normal work activities were suspended.
3. Teaching Children About God (Lev. 23:14, 21, 31, 42–44). It's easy to give our children the toys and trees of Christmas, without giving them the truth about Christmas. It's one thing to place them on Santa's lap, and another thing to place them at Jesus' feet.

CONCLUSION: This year, let's make Christmas a holy day, not just a holiday.

DECEMBER 28, 2003

SUGGESTED SERMON

The Dream of Beginning Again   *Date preached:*

By Michael Duduit

Scripture: Exodus 2:11–15, especially verse 15: Moses fled from the face of Pharaoh and dwelt in the land of Midian; and he sat down by a well.

Introduction: Have you written your New Year's Resolutions yet—those annual decisions to slim down, shape up, sort through, and generally get our lives back in order? There's something about starting a new year that drives us to make resolutions. We like the idea of leaving behind an old year, with its mistakes and frustrations, and beginning afresh.

Background: In today's passage, Moses needed a fresh start as he sat by that well in Midian. He'd been miraculously adopted into the family of Pharaoh, with access to the best schools in antiquity. He was prince of Egypt. Now at midlife, he found himself alienated by a well in Midian. Ever been by a well, wondering what went wrong?

1. **His Exile Was Caused by His Own Impetuous and Violent Reactions.** Sometimes we find ourselves by those wells because of things we've done. Maybe we intended the best, but a combination of our actions and other circumstances caused a disastrous outcome.

2. **His Exile Was Also Caused by Others.** Moses looked around to see that no one was watching before he killed the Egyptian, but the story got out. Who could have blabbed? The Hebrew worker he'd saved! The very person Moses risked himself to save had disclosed the incident. Sometimes those we're trying to help are too busy saving their own skin to worry about ours.

Moses took up residence in the desert, married, and become a shepherd. Forty years passed, and the story resumed to reveal some vital truths that can help us as we seek to begin again.

Scripture: Exodus 3:1–4, 10

1. **Moses' New Beginning Was Initiated by God's Call.** After four decades in the desert, Moses didn't go looking for God; God sought out Moses. The Lord isn't interested in our sitting by wells the rest of our life. Has tragedy disrupted your life? It's often after those events that God uses us most.

2. **Moses' New Beginning Was Made Possible Through His Own Response.** Everything that was about to happen was dependent on Moses' willingness to act on God's call. At first, he resisted. Notice his excuses:

    A. **I'm nobody (3:11).** Have you ever felt like saying, "I won't amount to anything"? The Lord replies: "It doesn't matter who you are; all that matters is who I am, and I'll be with you" (3:12).

    B. **I don't know enough (3:13).** "I don't even know Your name, God." God's response: "I'll tell you what you need to know" (3:14–15). In following Christ, we don't know everything that's coming; faith moves on the information already given, and trusts Him to provide the knowledge we need as we need it.

    C. **I'm not a good speaker (4:10).** "I'm not ready for a new beginning, God; it might require something I've never done before." God's response: "I'll help you speak, and I'll also give you a helper to speak for you" (4:14–15). God will provide whatever we need to carry out His call.

3. **Moses' New Beginning Faced Barriers.** God gives us fresh starts. There are barriers to overcome, but they can be overcome with God's help.

>>> *sermon continued on following page*

APPROPRIATE HYMNS AND SONGS

Love Divine, Charles Wesley/John Zundel; Public Domain.

Another Year Is Dawning, Frances R. Havergal/Samuel Wesley; Public Domain.

O the Deep, Deep Love of Jesus, Samuel Trevor Francis/Thomas J. Williams; Public Domain.

Let's Sing Unto the Lord, Carlos Rosas/Roberto Escamilla/Elise Eslinger/George Lockwood; © 1976, 1983, 1989 The United Methodist Publishing House.

Alpha and Omega, Robbie Trice; © 1984 Songs of Promise (Admin. by EMI Christian Music Publishing).

A. **Age can be overcome.** Think you're too old to change? Moses was 80 when he experienced the dream of beginning again.

B. **Uncertainty can be overcome.** All his excuses reflected uncertainty about the future. In the face of uncertainty, God assures us He'll not send us anywhere without going with us, nor call us to a challenge He doesn't equip us to meet.

4. **Moses' New Beginning Required Two Things.** There are two requirements if we're to truly begin again:

A. **Beginning again requires putting the past behind you.** Things that bound you in the past must be released to move forward into God's future. Have you experienced broken dreams, broken relationships, broken promises that left you by a well in Midian? Let go and move on.

B. **Beginning again requires beginning.** After all is said and done, you have to act. You have to keep on swinging.

Conclusion: Only you and God know the pain of your past. But He does know, and He'll help you to overcome any barrier that stands in the way of a new beginning. A new year is beginning, filled with amazing potential. Make it a new chapter in your life. Allow God to produce a new beginning through the power of His love and grace.

FOR THE BULLETIN

❋ On this day nearly a thousand years ago, December 28, 1065, Westminster Abbey opened and was dedicated in London, built by Edward the Confessor, the last of the old Anglo-Saxon kings, as a memorial to St. Peter. Unfortunately, Edward was unable to attend the dedication, being ill a few miles away. He died shortly afterward, and his remains are interred behind Westminster's High Altar. ❋ John Wycliffe, the "Morning Star of the Reformation," suffered a debilitating stroke while presiding over the Lord's Supper of Sunday, December 28, 1384. He was carried to his bed, where he passed away on December 31. Forty-one years later, still hated by his enemies, his bones were exhumed, burned, and thrown into the river.

❋ December 28, 1798, marks the birthday of Charles Hodge, one of America's greatest theologians, who studied the old and familiar Scriptures with fresh excitement. Three thousand pastors prepared for ministry in his theology classes at Princeton, and multitudes have benefited from his three-volume *Systematic Theology*. ❋ On December 28, 1993, South Africa's white parliament, sitting for the last time, buried apartheid, voting 237 to 45 to adopt an interim constitution leading to majority rule after the staging of the country's first all-race election.

STATS, STORIES AND MORE

Winston Churchill had nearly reached the height of political power in Britain early in his career; by the age of 33 he was a cabinet minister and one of the nation's most popular speakers. Yet a series of events and unpopular positions caused Churchill to lose his political standing and become a subject of ridicule and rejection. By the early 1930s, he had been excluded from the seats of power. Churchill's prophetic warnings about Adolf Hitler were ignored by an English public that preferred to hear comforting words of peace. When Britain was plunged into World War II, Churchill was already 65 years of age, eligible to retire on a government pension. Yet that is the moment when the nation turned to him, and Churchill became the prime minister who inspired the British people to remain firm during the darkest days of the war.
—*Michael Duduit*

Babe Ruth was an all-time home run champion, with 714 major league home runs. Did you know he was also the all-time strikeout champion? He struck out almost twice as often as he hit home runs. He knew that he had to risk striking out in order to hit those home runs. When asked for the secret of his success, he replied, "I just keep on swingin' at 'em!"

Kids Talk

Show the children a beautiful new 2004 calendar. Flip through the pages and show them that they are all blank. Tell the children, "Nothing has happened yet on these pages. We haven't lived these days yet. We haven't made any mistakes or committed any sins. All the pages are still blank, and we don't know what lies ahead. Let's lay this calendar before the Lord and pray right now, asking God to bless every day of this coming year."

WORSHIP HELPS

Call to Worship:
This day is a day of good news! This day is holy to the LORD your God! *(2 Kings 7:9; Neh. 8:9).*

Suggested Scripture Readings:
- Acts 7:30–34
- Hebrews 11:23–29
- 2 Corinthians 5:17

Hymn Story:
This is the last Sunday of the year, a wonderful time to think about the love of our Lord who always gives His benedictions to the year's end, and His blessings to the year about to begin. It was on this day, December 28, in 1925, that old Samuel Trevor Francis died at age 92. He was the author of the hymn, "O the Deep, Deep Love of Jesus." As a child, Francis took up poetry, and at age nine he joined the choir of his local church in the town of Cheshunt, England. But it was in London that he was converted as a teenager. He later wrote, "I was on my way home from work and had to cross Hungerford Bridge to the south of the Thames. During that winter's night of wind and rain and in the loneliness of that walk, I cried to God to have mercy on me. I stayed for a moment to look at the dark waters flowing under the bridge, and the temptation was whispered to me, 'Make an end of all this misery.' I drew back from the evil thought, and suddenly a message was borne into my very soul: 'You do believe on the Lord Jesus Christ?' I at once answered, 'I do believe,' and I put my whole trust in Him as my Savior." He spent the next 73 years telling the world about the "deep, deep love of Jesus."

Additional Sermons and Lesson Ideas

The Wonder of Christmas and New Year's Day
By Kevin Riggs

Date preached:

SCRIPTURE: Luke 2:52

INTRODUCTION: Luke 2 begins with the birth of Christ and ends by giving us a picture of His perfect humanity. We, too, should be developing in wisdom and stature, and in favor with God and man. As we prepare for a New Year, let this verse give you areas in which God wants you to grow:

1. Intellectually, in Wisdom. Many of us quit learning the moment we finish our formal education. But we should always be challenging ourselves, stretching our minds. (See Prov. 1:7; 18:15; 24:5; 28:2.)
2. Physically, in Stature. This involves taking care of our bodies—exercising, eating right, resting. God cares about this aspect of our lives. (See 1 Cor. 3:16–17; 6:19–20; 9:26–27.)
3. Spiritually, in Favor with God. This defines the core value system and spiritual life. (See 1 Tim. 4:8.)
4. Socially, in Favor with Man. This involves working on relationship skills, becoming friendlier, learning to understand before being understood, reconciling, and serving. (See Rom. 12:18.)

CONCLUSION: 2004—the year for Christlikeness!

Passing On the Timeless Message
By Peter Grainger

Date preached:

SCRIPTURE: 2 Timothy 2:1–2

INTRODUCTION: The Christmas shepherds were the first evangelists, taking the news of Christ's birth to all they met. But they weren't the last. The transmission that propels the gospel from one generation to another is explained in 2 Timothy 2:1–2.

1. From Jesus to Paul. The teachings of Jesus were entrusted to the apostles (Acts 2:42), including Paul (1 Cor. 15:1–11; Gal. 1:11–12).
2. From Paul to Timothy. The message Paul preached was heard and learned by Timothy in the presence of many others (1 Tim. 6:20; 2 Tim. 1:13–14).
3. From Timothy to Reliable Men. Men who were dependable (1 Cor. 4:1–2).
4. From Reliable Men to Others. Which includes, through the passing of time, you and me.

CONCLUSION: The gospel is not something we come to church to hear; it is something we go from church to tell!

WEDDING SERMON

A Traditional Wedding

Dearly beloved, we are gathered together here in the sight of God and in the face of this company, to join together _____ and _____ in holy matrimony, which is an honorable estate, instituted of God, signifying unto us the mystical union that is betwixt Christ and His church, which holy estate Christ adorned and beautified with His presence and first miracle that He wrought in Cana of Galilee, and is commended in the Holy Scriptures to be honorable among all men: and therefore is not by any to be entered into unadvisedly or lightly; but reverently, discreetly, advisedly, soberly, and in the fear of God. Into this holy estate these two persons present come now to be joined.

Of all the sacred earthly ties, it is marriage above all which must display and embody the words of St. Paul the Apostle, who said in the thirteenth chapter of First Corinthians:

> Though I speak with the tongues of men and of angels, but have not love, I have become sounding brass or a clanging cymbal. And though I have the gift of prophecy, and understand all mysteries and all knowledge, and though I have all faith, so that I could remove mountains, but have not love, I am nothing. And though I bestow all my goods to feed the poor, and though I give my body to be burned, but have not love, it profits me nothing.
>
> Love suffers long and is kind; love does not envy; love does not parade itself, is not puffed up; does not behave rudely, does not seek its own, is not provoked, thinks no evil; does not rejoice in iniquity, but rejoices in the truth; bears all things, believes all things, hopes all things, endures all things.
>
> Love never fails. But whether there are prophecies, they will fail; whether there are tongues, they will cease; whether there is knowledge, it will vanish away. For we know in part and we prophesy in part. But when that which is perfect has come, then that which is in part will be done away.
>
> When I was a child, I spoke as a child, I understood as a child, I thought as a child; but when I became a man, I put away

childish things. For now we see in a mirror, dimly, but then face
to face. Now I know in part, but then I shall know just as I also
am known.

And now abide faith, hope, love, these three; but the greatest
of these is love.

And now _____ and _____, if thus you love each other and are prepared to unite your lives in this manner, will you please join hands.

_____, do you take this woman as your wedded wife, to live together after God's ordinance in the holy estate of matrimony, to love her, comfort her, honor, and keep her in sickness and in health; and, forsaking all others, keep yourself only unto her, so long as you both shall live? (The man shall answer, "I do").

_____, do you take this man as your wedded husband, to live together after God's ordinance in the holy estate of matrimony, to love him, comfort him, honor, and keep him in sickness and in health; and, forsaking all others, keep yourself only unto him, so long as your both shall live? (The woman shall answer "I do").

Then you are each given to the other, to have and to hold from this day forward, for better for worse, for richer for poorer, in sickness and in health, to love and to cherish, till death shall you part, according to God's holy ordinance.

Those whom God has joined together let no man put asunder.

Shall we pray: O Eternal God, Creator and Preserver of all mankind, Giver of all spiritual grace, send Your blessing upon these Your servants, this man and this woman, whom we bless in Your Name; that they, living faithfully together, may surely perform and keep the vow and covenant betwixt them made, and may ever remain in perfect love and peace together. Look mercifully upon them, that their home may be a haven of blessing and of peace; through Jesus Christ our Lord. Amen.

Forasmuch as _____ and _____ have consented together in holy wedlock, and have witnessed the same before God and this company, and thereto have given and pledged their troth, each to the other, and have declared the same by giving and receiving a ring, and by joining hands; I pronounce that they are husband and wife.

WEDDING SERMON

A Scriptural Wedding

Dear family and dear friends, we are assembled here today to unite _____ and _____ in holy matrimony. They have requested your presence on this memorable occasion so that you can share with them the pledging of their everlasting love. For my part, the best advice I could give to them is the counsel that comes from God's Word.

The Bible alone is an infallible lamp for your steps and a light for your path. So I would like to limit my own remarks today to just three words: "In Your Marriage . . ." and to those three words I will attach a handful of passages from the Word of God, appropriate to this occasion.

So let me say: In your marriage, be like-minded, being one in spirit and purpose, doing nothing out of selfish ambition or vain conceit. But in humility consider the other better than yourself. Both of you should look not only to your own interests, but also the interests of the other. Let this mind be in you which also is in Christ Jesus.

In your marriage, may He who has begun a good work in you carry it on to completion until the day of Christ, for unless the Lord builds the house they labor in vain who build it. And may He strengthen you out of the riches of His glory with all power through His Spirit in your inner being, for His grace is sufficient for you.

I urge you then to live a life worthy of the calling you have received. Be completely humble and gentle; be patient, bearing with one another in love. Make every effort to keep the unity of the Spirit in the bond of peace.

And in your marriage, put off falsehood and speak truthfully to one another. In your anger, do not sin. Do not let the sun go down while you are still angry, and do not give the devil a foothold. Do not let any unwholesome talk come out of your mouths, but only what is helpful for building each other up according to your needs.

In your marriage, rid yourselves of all bitterness, rage and anger, brawling and slander, along with every form of malice. But be kind and compassionate to one another, forgiving each other, just as in Christ God forgave you.

In your marriage, search the Scriptures. Study to show yourselves approved unto God, rightly dividing the Word. Continue in the things you have learned, because you know those from whom who have learned them, and how from infancy you have known the Holy Scriptures which are able to make you wise for salvation through faith in Jesus Christ.

And in your marriage, when you pray, go into your room, close the door, and pray to your Father who is unseen. Then your Father, who sees what is done in secret, will reward you. Pray without ceasing, be joyful always, and give thanks in all circumstances, for this is the will of God in Christ Jesus concerning you.

Do not forsake the assembling of yourselves together in worship and in the church, as the manner of some is; but may your light so shine before men that they might see your good works and glorify your Father who is in heaven.

Be joyful in hope, patient in affliction, faithful in prayer. Share with God's people who are in need. Practice hospitality. Be careful to do what is right in the eyes of everybody. If it is possible, as far as it depends on you, live at peace with everyone. Let no debt remain outstanding except the continuing debt to love each other.

In your marriage, sanctify Christ Jesus as Lord, trusting Him with all your heart, leaning not on your own understanding. In all your ways acknowledge Him, and He will direct your paths.

And may He lead you in paths of righteousness for His name's sake. May goodness and mercy follow you all the days of your lives. May God pour out His Spirit on your offspring and His blessings on your descendants.

And so in your marriage, may the Lord bless you and keep you. The Lord make His face to shine upon you and be gracious to you. The Lord lift up His countenance upon you, and give you peace.

If you then, _____ and _____, have freely and deliberately chosen each other as partners in this holy estate and know of no just cause why you should not be so united, in token thereof, will you please join hands.

_____, do you take _____ to be your wedded wife? To love her, to honor her and cherish her in this relationship, and leaving all others, cleave only unto her, in all things a true and faithful husband. (The man shall reply: "I do.)"

_____, do you take _____ to be your wedded husband? To love him, to honor him and cherish him in this relationship, and leaving all others, cleave only unto him, in all things a true and faithful wife? (The woman shall reply, "I do").

Then you are each given to the other for richer or poorer, for better or worse, in sickness and in health, as long as you both shall live.

WEDDING SERMON

A Wedding for God's Servants

Dear friends, we have gathered here to celebrate the uniting of _____ and _____ in holy matrimony. All of us who know this couple love them, and we reckon it a great blessing to witness the exchanging of lifetime vows between these two who are devoted to Christ and His kingdom.

Today, _____ and _____, I would like to give you a passage of Scripture upon which to build your marriage and your ministry. In the Philippian letter, chapter 2, verses 14 and 15, we read these words: "Do all things without complaining and disputing, that you may become blameless and harmless, children of God without fault in the midst of a crooked and perverse generation, among whom you shine as lights in the world, holding fast the word of life, so that I may rejoice in the day of Christ that I have not run in vain or labored in vain."

Keep Your Poise

There are four truths here that can serve as four cornerstones for your home. The first phrase in this passage talks about your poise, your composure, your self-possession and self-control: "Do all things without complaining and disputing."

This doesn't mean that you cannot discuss differences or work through problems. But it does mean that you realize you can damage your marriage by harsh and angry words, a nagging spirit, an argumentative demeanor, and splinters of bitterness. When the Lord says here, "Do everything without complaining or arguing," He wants us to know that the word *everything* includes washing dishes and taking out trash and making beds and changing diapers and earning paychecks and entertaining guests and making choices. He is thinking about paying bills and avoiding debt and making sacrifices for each other. Do all things without rancor and abiding anger. Be poised and gentle and wise.

Guard Your Purity

The next phrase cuts even more deeply into our hearts, for it deals with purity. "Do all things without complaining and disputing, that you may become blameless and harmless, children of God without fault." The Bible teaches that the power of the Lord Jesus Christ through His indwelling Holy Spirit can give us consistent victory over known sin. We may not be perfect in this life, but we can remain pure and holy through His power that works so mightily within us. Always be vigilant and watchful for the moral traps of the devil. Instead, let the Word of Christ dwell in you richly through daily personal Bible study as you teach and encourage one another with all wisdom and as you sing psalms, hymns, and spiritual songs with gratitude in your hearts to God.

Find Your Place

The third cornerstone for your marriage is your place. Wherever the Lord takes you, you can be certain it will be in the middle of a crooked and depraved generation. "Do all things without complaining and disputing, that you may become blameless and harmless, children of God without fault in the midst of a crooked and perverse generation."

Fulfill Your Purpose

And why? That brings us to the fourth cornerstone of your home. His purpose for you: He is going to place you in the middle of a wicked generation so that there, amid the sin and shame of our age, you can shine like stars against a blackened universe, holding out the word of life to those appointed to receive it.

The text says: "Do all things without complaining and disputing, that you may become blameless and harmless, children of God without fault in the midst of a crooked and perverse generation, among whom you shine as lights in the world, holding fast the word of life."

How wonderful to have a marriage that displays the joy of Christ to those who see it. How wonderful to be partners together in the Lord's kingdom. As you dedicate your home to the Lord Jesus, He will use you in ways greater than you know. He will use you mightily, but the full results of your work for Him will be known and calculated only on the other side of the Jordan.

We know not what the encircling years will bring, nor how life and labor will unfold before you. But whatever the passing seasons hold, you must always remember to keep your poise, guard your purity, find your place, and fulfill your purpose as the Lord guides and guards you.

Now _____ and _____, as I lead you in exchanging your vows as husband and wife, will you please join your right hands.

_____ , will you repeat after me: *In taking this woman to be my wedded wife before God and these witnesses, I promise to love her, to honor her and cherish her in this relationship, and leaving all others, cleave only unto her, in all things a true and faithful husband, as long as we both shall live.*

_____ will you repeat after me: *In taking this man to be my wedded husband before God and these witnesses, I promise to love him, to honor him and cherish him in this relationship, and leaving all others, cleave only unto him, in all things a true and faithful wife, as long as we both shall live.*

Then you are each given to the other for richer or poorer, for better or worse, in sickness and in health, till death shall you part.

Quotes for the Pastor's Wall

" To love to preach is one thing, to love those to whom we preach is quite another. **"**

–Richard Cecil

FUNERAL MESSAGE

The Twinkling of an Eye

Today we have gathered in honor and memory of _____.

(Personal comments)

Introduction: Such a heartfelt occasion as this points us to the future, to the promises of God as revealed in Scripture, and to the coming day of resurrection victory. We're naturally focusing on the passing of our loved one, but God also wants us to focus on the coming of His beloved Son. There is a chapter in God's Word that is wholly given to the resurrection of Christians, and it is of great encouragement in times like this—1 Corinthians 15, the "Resurrection Chapter" of the Bible.

Scripture: 1 Corinthians 15:51–57

1. **We Have Been Caught (v. 56).** Paul uses a rather graphic and unpleasant metaphor. He says that we have been stung by the law, sin, and death. The law reveals God's character and His requirements for our lives. Sin occurs as we break those laws, and death is the result of sin, for it separates us from the God of life. This is the terrible, tangled web in which every human is caught, and this is the way every generation in history has ended. If we could shave off the first six feet of the soil of this planet we would find the bones and the dust of virtually every human being who has ever lived. Funerals and memorial services are occasions when we must all face the truth about living and dying.

2. **We've Been Bought (v. 57).** But never forget that verse 56 with all its morbidity is followed by verse 57 with all its victory. Thanks be to God through our Lord Jesus Christ who gives us the victory! Death is swallowed up in victory, for we've been bought with a price, we've been redeemed. In Christ Jesus, we've been saved. Now, if there is a victory, there must be an

enemy. Over what have we have gained victory in Christ Jesus? It is victory over death, as we see in the verses that immediately precede verses 56 and 57. In these verses, the Lord is teaching us about the coming resurrection.

3. **We've Been Taught (vv. 51–55).** These verses teach us what will happen when Christ returns. We are not all going to be asleep when He comes back. In other words, when the Lord Jesus comes to earth again, He will meet a generation of Christians who are still alive, waiting eagerly for Him. It might be this generation. It may be you and me. We shall not all "sleep," but some will be sleeping. Notice the word "sleep" which Paul uses as a synonym for death. It is the Greek word κοιμάω (*koi-ma'-o*), a very common word in the Bible for those who pass away in Jesus. The Bible is highly reluctant to use the word "dead" to describe those who pass away in Christ. Do you remember what Jesus said to the disciples about Lazarus? "He is sleeping, and I am going to awaken him out of his sleep." When Jesus died on the Cross, Matthew's Gospel tells us there was an earthquake, tombs opened, and the bodies of some of the saints who were sleeping awoke and arose and went into the city of Jerusalem. When Stephen was stoned to death in the Book of Acts, he fell on his knees, prayed for his attackers, then fell asleep. First Thessalonians 4 talks about those who are "asleep in Jesus." The early Christians took this word κοιμαρω and attached another word to it meaning *place—sleeping place*, and it has become our English word *cemetary.* Christians are never buried in a graveyard. They are placed in a sleeping room to await the day when the body will be roused from its slumber by the alarm clock of God's trumpet. When the trumpet sounds, whether we are alive or sleeping, we will be changed. Paul says three things about this change:
   A. Its suddenness—in a flash; in the twinkling of an eye.
   B. Its timing—when the trumpet sounds at the return of Christ.
   C. Its nature—our human bodies will be transformed. Instead of being corruptible, they will become imperishable. Instead of dying, they will become immortal.

Conclusion: Martin Luther once said, "Even in the best of health we should have death always before our eyes. We will not expect to remain on this earth forever, but will have one foot in the air, so to speak." This is a day of sadness, but while there are tears in our eyes, there is joy and hope in our hearts, for death has been swallowed up in victory.

FUNERAL MESSAGE

He Does All Things Well

Scripture: Mark 7:37: And they were astonished beyond measure, saying, "He has done all things well."

Today we have gathered in honor and memory of _____.

(Personal comments)

Introduction: An old hymn by Anna L. Waring comes to mind today:

> *In heavenly love abiding, no change my heart shall fear.*
> *And safe in such confiding, for nothing changes here.*
> *The storm may roar without me, my heart may low be laid,*
> *But God is round about me, and can I be dismayed?*
>
> *Wherever He may guide me, no want shall turn me back.*
> *My Shepherd is beside me, and nothing can I lack.*
> *His wisdom ever waking, His sight is never dim.*
> *He knows the way He's taking, and I will walk with Him.*

That phrase, "He knows the way He's taking," is the basis for my remarks today. God knows what He is doing. He doesn't make mistakes, especially of this magnitude. As the people of our Lord's day put it, "He does all things well."

We don't always understand His means or His methods. He has purposes to which we are not always privy, but we know He does all things well.

His ways are not our ways and His thoughts are not our thoughts, but He does all things well.

He allows winds to blow and storms to rage. Sorrows and tears befall us, and our ways may wend through darkness and difficulty. But as for God, His ways are perfect. He works all things together for good. The Bible says, "Our times are in His hands."

A. W. Tozer once wrote, "To the child of God, there is no such thing as an accident. He travels an appointed way. Accidents may indeed appear to befall him and misfortune stalk his way, but these evils will be so in appearance only and will seem evils only because we cannot read the secret script of God's hidden providence and so cannot discover the ends at which He aims. . . . The man of true faith may live in the absolute assurance that his steps are ordered by the Lord. For him, misfortune is outside the bounds of possibility. He cannot be torn from this earth one hour ahead of the time which God has appointed, and he cannot be detained on earth one moment after God is done with him here."

He does all things well, and He asks us to trust Him. We can trust Him through sunshine and shadows. When we cannot trace His hand, we can trust His heart.

It is normal, however, to occasionally ask "Why?" Though God may not always answer our "why" questions, He listens to them and responds in the wisest ways.

1. Moses asked: "Lord, why have you brought trouble to this people?"

2. Gideon asked: "Why then has all this happened to us?"

3. Naomi said: "I went out full, and the Lord has brought me home again empty. Why?"

4. Nehemiah asked: "Why is the house of God forsaken?"

5. Job said: "Why have you set me as your target?"

6. David said: "Lord, why do you cast off my soul? Why do You hide Your face from me?"

7. Jeremiah asked: "Why is my pain perpetual and my wound incurable?"

But the greatest "Why" in the Bible was uttered by the Lord Jesus Christ on the Cross when He said, "My God, My God, why have you forsaken me?" And there is something about that "Why" that swallows up all the others.

Because Jesus gave Himself on the Cross, we can trust Him to have answers to all our other "whys."

Vance Havner once said, "You need never ask 'Why?' because Calvary covers it all. When before the throne we stand in Him complete, all the riddles that puzzle us here will fall into place and we shall know in fulfillment what we now believe in faith—that all things work together for good in His eternal purpose. No longer will we cry 'My God, why?' Instead, 'alas' will become 'Alleluia,' all question marks will be straightened into exclamation points, sorrow will change to singing, and pain will be lost in praise."

One thing we do know: The death of a Christian doesn't seem as tragic to God as it does to us. To us it is separation and sorrow. To God it is:

1. A promotion.

2. A release from the burdens of earth.

3. Early furlough from the battle zone.

4. Relocation to a better climate.

5. Instant transport to the celestial city.

6. To depart and be with Christ, which is far better.

7. To be absent from the body but present with the Lord.

Our friend has beaten us to heaven and is more alive than ever, for God is not a God of the dead, but of the living. We don't understand all of God's purposes, but we know He does all things well, and we must just leave it there, in His love.

> *In heavenly love abiding, no change my heart shall fear.*
> *And safe in such confiding, for nothing changes here.*
> *The storm may roar without me, my heart may low be laid,*
> *But God is round about me, and can I be dismayed?*

FUNERAL MESSAGE

To Die Is Gain

Today we have gathered in honor and memory of _____.

(Personal comments)

Introduction: If we were able to write an epitaph for ourselves or for our departed loved one, we could do no better than to use the words found in Philippians 1:21: "For to me, to live is Christ, and to die is gain." The Bible's perspective about death and dying is different from our own, and nowhere is it stated better than in this passage:

Reading from Philippians 1:21–26: "For to me, to live is Christ, and to die is gain. But if I live on in the flesh, this will mean fruit from my labor; yet what I shall choose I cannot tell. For I am hard-pressed between the two, having a desire to depart and be with Christ, which is far better. Nevertheless to remain in the flesh is more needful for you. And being confident of this, I know that I shall remain and continue with you all for your progress and joy of faith, that your rejoicing for me may be more abundant in Jesus Christ by my coming to you again."

The Bible here speaks of death as:

1. **A Profitable Venture**—*To die is gain.* "Gain" was a financial word, used by the Greeks to indicate a windfall, a bonus, a welcome increase in value, net worth, or condition. We think of death in terms of loss, but the Bible pictures death in terms of gain. In Scotland, when the Presbyterian Covenanters were slain for their faith, they would often climb the scaffold shouting, "Goodbye world! Goodbye pain! Goodbye suffering! Goodbye sorrow! Goodbye heartache! Welcome life! Welcome joy! Welcome heaven! Welcome eternity! Welcome Jesus!"

2. **A Tempting Option.** When Paul said, "I am hard-pressed . . . ," he used a word that implied a sense of equal pressure being placed on both sides, as

though someone had a rope around one hand and someone else had a rope around the other, and he was being pulled in both directions. In other words, he felt pulled to remain in this life so that he could be of service to the church; but he felt equally pulled toward heaven. If you asked him, "Do you want to die right now? " Paul would have said, "I just don't know. I'm being pulled in two directions on that question."

3. **An Improved Location**—*I have a desire to depart and be with Christ.* The word "desire" is a strong word, indicating an intense longing. And the word "depart" was a metaphor drawn from the act of a ship setting sail. It was sometimes used by the Greeks for loosing the moorings in advance of sailing. On other occasions, this word was used to describe breaking up camp. I read that during World War II, when the Royal Air Force stood between England and destruction, and when the lives of its pilots were being sacrificially spent, they never spoke of a pilot as having been killed. They always spoke of him as having been "posted to another station." That's the idea here. Death is viewed as a profitable venture, a tempting option, an improved location, and . . .

4. **A Better World**—*Which is far better. . . .* If you could see our friend now, we'd know this was true. No pain. No tears. No lapses of mind or memory. Present with the Lord, reunited with those loved ones gone before, heirs of eternal life and heaven!

Conclusion: All of this was captured in a hymn written by a Swiss hymnist named Henri Abraham César Malan (1787–1864):

No, no, it is not dying
To go unto our God;
This gloomy earth forsaking,
Our journey homeward taking
Along the starry road.

No, no, it is not dying
Heaven's citizen to be;
A crown immortal wearing,
And rest unbroken sharing,
From care and conflict free.

No, no it is not dying
To hear this gracious word,
"Receive a Father's blessing,
Forevermore possessing
The favor of thy Lord."

No, no it is not dying
The Shepherd's voice to know:
His sheep He ever leadeth,
His peaceful flock He feedeth,
Where living pastures grow.

Special Services Registry

The forms on the following pages are designed to be duplicated and used repeatedly as neeeded. Most copy machines will allow you to enlarge them to fill a full page if desired. Since they also are included in the CD-ROM in the back of the book, you may use that digital file to customize the forms to fit your specific needs.

Sermons Preached

Date	Text	Title/Subject

Sermons Preached

Date	Text	Title/Subject

Marriages Log

Date	Bride	Groom

Funerals Log

Date	Name of Deceased	Scripture Used

Baptisms / Confirmations

Date   Name   Notes

Baby Dedication Registration

Infant's Name: _____

Significance of Given Names: _____

Date of Birth: _____

Parents' Names: _____

_____

Siblings: _____

_____

_____

_____

Maternal Grandparents: _____

Paternal Grandparents: _____

Life Verse: _____

Date of Dedication: _____

Wedding Registration

Date of Wedding: _____

Location of Wedding: _____

Bride: _____

Religious Affiliation: _____

Bride's Parents: _____

Groom: _____

     Religious Affiliation: _____

     Groom's Parents: _____

Ceremony to be Planned by Minister: _____ by Couple: _____

Other Minister(s) Assisting: _____

Maid/Matron of Honor: _____

Best Man: _____

Wedding Planner: _____

Date of Rehearsal: _____

Reception Open to All Wedding Guests: _____ By Invitation Only: _____

Location of Reception: _____

Wedding Photos to be Taken:_____ During Ceremony

               _____ After Ceremony

Other _____

Date of Counseling: _____

Date of Registration: _____

Funeral Registration

Name of Deceased: _____

Age: _____

Religious Affiliation: _____

Survivors:

Spouse: _____

Parents: _____

Children: _____

Siblings: _____

Grandchildren: _____

Date of Death: _____

Time and Place of Visitation: _____

Date of Funeral or Memorial Service: _____

Funeral Home Responsible: _____

Location of Funeral or Memorial Service: _____

Scripture Used: _____Hymns Used: _____

Eulogy by: _____

Other Minister(s) Assisting: _____

Pallbearers: _____

Date of Interment: _____Place of Interment: _____

Graveside Service?: _____Yes   No _____

Subject Index

Abiding in Christ, 61, 397

Aging, 361

Angels, 275

Anxiety, 95, 151, 165, 289, 336ff

Baptism, 278-79

Basil, 104-05

Bible study, 247

Brainard, David, 253

Bunyan, John, 236-37

Call to missions, 65, 84-85

Calvin, John, 158, 213

Carey, William, xviii, 327-29

Carmichael, Amy, 5, 52, 54, 113, 338

Cartwright, Peter, 59, 126-29

Change, 25ff

Christ-likeness, 82, 193, 227, 387

Christmas, 369, 370-73, 375, 379,
    381, 387

Church, 67

Commitment, 205, 287, 321, 373

Communion, 112-13

Conversion story, 117, 275, 333

Creation, 36ff, 39, 310ff, 367

Criswell, W.A., xv

Cross of Christ, 112-13, 126-29, 205,
    379

Dale, R. W., 148-50

Death, 119, 158, 159, 280ff, 395-401

Depression, 2ff, 30, 35, 207

Discouragement in ministry, 164

Doctrine, 208ff

Easter, 13, 114ff, 119, 220ff

Emptiness, 263

Encouragement, 214ff, 217, 219

Evangelism, 81, 160-62, 243, 272ff,
    285, 291, 361, 387

Exercise, 68-70

Faith, 8ff, 92ff, 106ff, 109, 124, 151,
    205, 238, 285, 287, 358-60

Fathers, 174ff, 179

Funerals, 395-401

Giving, 134, 212, 242, 300, 322, 347

God, care of, 165

God, holiness of, 65

God, presence of, 101

God, promises of, 247

God, provision of, 109, 355

Goforth, Jonathan, 65

Gospel, 91, 278-79

Grace, 77

Guidance, 103, 249, 336

Heaven, 7, 41, 61, 280ff, 335, 400-01

Hell, 97, 103, 280ff

Hilton, Conrad, xvi

Holiness, 65

Holy Spirit, 166-68, 215, 235, 381

Home and family, 136ff, 157, 172,
    173, 174ff, 179, 195, 250-52, 254ff,
    323, 341, 363

Illness, 42, 43, 341

Illustrations, use of, xvii-xviii

Influence, 160-62, 218

Insecurity, 135

Interpersonal relationships, 147, 157,
    195, 254ff, 347, 351

Jesus Christ, 72ff, 91, 119, 190ff,
    370-72, 386

Jones, E. Stanley, 151

Journaling, 51

Joy, 145, 202, 220ff, 223, 225, 376-78

Judgment, 103

Knox, John, 338

Kuhn, Isobel, 188-89

Lay ministry, 19, 307, 323, 342ff

Leadership, 190ff, 193, 208ff, 213,
    214ff, 358-60

Lord's Supper, see "Communion"

Love, 136ff, 139, 386

Luther, Martin, 59
Marriage, 157, 195, 243, 250-52, 254ff, 341, 363, 388-94
Martyrdom, 71, 321, 350, 378
Missions, 180-81, 196-200, 249, 327-29, 373
Missions, call to, 182ff, 327
Moody, Dwight L., 17
Mothers, 136ff
Mothers' Day, 136ff
New Year's Day/New Beginnings, 2ff, 277, 382ff, 387
Olford, Stephen, xiv
Palm Sunday, 106ff, 111
Parenting, 323
Parker, Joseph, xvi-xvii
Patience, 130-32, 152ff, 240
Patrick, 84-85
Peace, inner, 151, 336, 354-57
Perpetua, 71
Prayer, 41, 49, 52, 141, 171, 177, 207, 213, 238, 250-52, 253, 296ff, 353, 369
Preaching, expositional, xiii-xiv, 211, 228, 229, 292-94, 316-17, 324-26
Preaching, use of notes in, 148-50

Pride, 190ff, 193, 217, 259, 315
Problems, 269
Prodigals, 11, 98ff, 177, 308-09, 333
Profanity, 47
Repentance, 44ff, 100, 183
Revival, 265, 285, 299
Ridderhof, Joy, 241
Satan, 56, 230ff, 233
Scripture, power of, 5, 36ff, 120ff
Second Coming of Christ, 25, 147, 375
Sex, 335
Shyness, 213
Sin/temptation, 123, 219, 335, 367
Spiritual warfare, 56ff, 120ff, 230ff
Stress, 86ff, 133, 142ff, 145, 336ff
Sunday/Lord's Day, 171
Thanksgiving, 353, 354-56
Tongue, 77, 291
Tradition, 26ff
Trials and troubles, 7, 50ff, 120ff, 188, 189, 269, 302ff, 341, 398
Voice, care for, 68-70, 295
Weddings, 388-94
Working for Christ, see "Lay ministry"
Worship, 62ff, 105, 111, 202, 238, 301, 302ff, 348-50

Scripture Index

Genesis 1:1, 61, 310ff
Exodus 2:11-15, 382ff
Exodus 15:22-27, 112
Exodus 31:12, 13, 171
Leviticus 23:22, 381
Deuteronomy 10:12-13, 125
Joshua 1:1-2, 72ff
Joshua 2:1-21, 330ff
Joshua 3:5, 241
Joshua 6:1-27, 238ff
Joshua 14:6-15, 358ff
Judges 6:1_7:25, 30ff
Judges 16:1-21, 219
1 Samuel 1, 207
1 Samuel 3, 235
1 Samuel 3:1-10, 195
1 Samuel 17:38, 39, xv
1 Kings 17:1-3, 363
2 Kings 5:1-19, 225
Ezra 1:1, 187
Ezra 7, 187
Nehemiah 1:1-4, 266ff
Nehemiah 8:8, xiii
Nehemiah 8:10, 225
Job 1:1-12, 230ff
Psalm 2, 25
Psalm 3, 67
Psalm 16:5-11, 115
Psalm 19, 36ff
Psalm 23, 336ff, 339
Psalm 23:3, 103
Psalm 27, 135
Psalm 37:3, 109
Psalm 42-43, 2ff
Psalm 46, 86ff
Psalm 50:15, 309
Psalm 95:15, 125
Psalm 98:4-9, 374
Psalm 103:1-5, 348ff
Psalm 103:11, 351
Psalm 104, 321
Psalm 139:23, 24, 41

Proverbs 3:5, 7
Proverbs 3:15, 243
Proverbs 20:1-7, 323
Ecclesiastes 11:1-6, 271
Isaiah 6:1-8, 62
Isaiah 38:9-20, 341
Lamentations 3:1-26, 35
Ezekiel 1, 301
Ezekiel 1:28-2:3, 318ff
Ezekiel 22:1-31, 315
Daniel 5, 207
Hosea 3:1, 157
Hosea 14:1-9, 277
Jonah (whole book), 182ff
Jonah 2, 35
Matthew 2, 369
Matthew 2:1-12, 375
Matthew 6:19-24, 97
Matthew 7:13-14, 280ff
Matthew 7:28, 243
Matthew 7:28-29, 92ff
Matthew 9:9-13, 78ff
Matthew 9:35-38, 19, 249
Matthew 13:34, xvii-xviii
Matthew 22:35-37, 364ff
Mark 1:1-11, 166ff
Mark 1:2, 3, 44
Mark 5:21-43, 152ff
Mark 7:24-30, 8ff
Mark 7:37, 397-399
Mark 9:33-35, 271
Mark 10:35-45, 190ff
Mark 11:1-11, 111
Mark 11:20-26, 106ff
Luke 1:26-38, 381
Luke 2:8-20, 376ff
Luke 2:17, 364ff
Luke 2:21-30, 375
Luke 2:52, 387
Luke 11:1, 213
Luke 11:1-13, 369
Luke 15:11-32, 98ff

Luke 16:19-31, 97
Luke 18:1-8, 13, 296ff
Luke 19:13, 147
Luke 19:28-44, 111
Luke 24:13-35, 119
John 2:1-11, 260ff
John 4:43-54, 285
John 5:1-30, 301
John 6:1-68, 286ff
John 6:35-40, 14ff
John 6:38-40, 370ff
John 6:45, xiv
John 7:38, 253
John 10:4, 249
John 12:1-11, 259
John 14:15, 277
John 14:28-31, 202ff
John 15:1-11, 61
John 17, 338, 350
John 20:1-3, 13
John 20:1-10, 114ff
John 20:20, 223
Acts 1:3, 285
Acts 1:8, 180, 181
Acts 1:9-11, 25
Acts 2:25-32, 115
Acts 4:8-13, 278-79
Acts 4:36, 219
Acts 5:12ff, 265
Acts 5:17-33, 272
Acts 5:31, 309
Acts 11:24, 214ff
Acts 13:32-38, 115-16
Acts 20:28, 141
Acts 26:19-23, 307
Romans 1:1-7, 265
Romans 12:16-18, 254ff
1 Corinthians 3:1-4, 83
1 Corinthians 6:12-20, 335
1 Corinthians 9:24-27, 20ff
1 Corinthians 13, 136ff
1 Corinthians 15:51-57, 395-396
2 Corinthians 1:8-11, 302ff
2 Corinthians 1:10, 305
2 Corinthians 5:17-21, 291

2 Corinthians 8:13_9:5, 347
Galatians 1:3, 4, 165
Galatians 6:1-10, 315
Ephesians 1:1, 67
Ephesians 5:8, 160-62
Ephesians 5:18, 235
Ephesians 5:25, 195
Ephesians 6:4, 174ff
Ephesians 6:10-20, 56ff
Ephesians 6:18, 49
Philippians (whole book), 341
Philippians 1:18-30, 142ff
Philippians 1:21-26, 400-01
Philippians 2:5, 19
Philippians 4:10-20, 49
Colossians 3:22-25, 179
Colossians 4:12, 141
1 Timothy 4:1-16, 323
2 Timothy 1:5-7, 213
2 Timothy 2:1-2, 387
2 Timothy 2:3-7, 342ff
Titus 1:5-9, 208ff
Titus 2:11-15, 77
Hebrews 1, 91
Hebrews 2:14-31, 119
Hebrews 10:22, 128
Hebrews 12:23, 307
Hebrews 13:13, 327
James 1:1-27, 120ff
James 3:7-12, 291
James 4:7-10, 259
James 4:13-17, 135
James 5:7-11, 130ff
1 Peter 1:13, 83
1 Peter 3:8-12, 347
2 Peter (whole book), 247
2 Peter 1:2-4, 354ff
2 Peter 3:17-18, 244ff
1 John 2:20, xviii
1 John 5:14-15, 353
3 John, 147
Revelation 19:1-21, 335
Revelation 20:11-15, 103
Revelation 21, 22, 7

SOFTWARE LICENSE AGREEMENT

CAREFULLY READ THE FOLLOWING TERMS AND CONDITIONS BEFORE USING THIS SOFTWARE. USING THIS SOFTWARE INDICATES YOUR ACCEPTANCE OF THESE TERMS AND CONDITIONS. IF YOU ARE NOT IN AGREEMENT, PROMPTLY RETURN THE SOFTWARE PACKAGE UNUSED WITH YOUR RECEIPT AND YOUR MONEY WILL BE REFUNDED.

LICENSE

The SOFTWARE may be used on a single machine at a time. This is a copyrighted software program and may not be copied, duplicated, or distributed except for the purpose of backup by the licensed owner.

The SOFTWARE may be copied into any machine-readable or printed form for backup, modification, or normal usage in support of the SOFTWARE on the single machine.

You may transfer the SOFTWARE and license to another party if the other party agrees to accept the terms and conditions of this Agreement. If you transfer the SOFTWARE, you must either transfer all copies, whether in printed or machine-readable form, to the same party or destroy any copies not transferred; this includes all modifications and portions of the SOFTWARE contained or merged into other software and/or software programs.

YOU MAY NOT USE, COPY, ALTER, OR OTHERWISE MODIFY OR TRANSFER THE SOFTWARE OR DATABASE(S) OR ANY ADD-ON PRODUCT'S TEXT EXCEPT AS EXPRESSLY PROVIDED FOR IN THIS LICENSE.

IF YOU TRANSFER POSSESSION OF ANY COPY OR MODIFICATIONS OF THE SOFTWARE TO ANOTHER PARTY, EXCEPT AS EXPRESSLY PROVIDED FOR IN THIS LICENSE, YOUR LICENSE THEREUPON IS AUTOMATICALLY TERMINATED.

LIMITED SOFTWARE WARRANTY

LIMITED WARRANTY. *Nelson Electronic Publishing* warrants that, for ninety (90) days from the date of receipt, the computer programs contained in the SOFTWARE will perform substantially in accordance with the *User's Guide*. Any implied warranties on the SOFTWARE are limited to ninety (90) days. Some jurisdictions do not allow limitations on the duration of an implied warranty, so the above limitation may not apply to you.

CUSTOMER REMEDIES. *Nelson Electronic Publishing's* entire liability and your exclusive remedy shall be, at our option, either (a) return of the price paid or (b) repair or replacement of SOFTWARE that does not meet *Nelson Electronic Publishing's* Limited Warranty and that is returned to us with a copy of your receipt. This Limited Warranty is void if failure of the SOFTWARE has resulted from accident, abuse, or misapplication. Any replacement SOFTWARE will be warranted for the remainder of the original warranty period or thirty (30) days, whichever is longer. Outside the United States, neither these remedies nor any product support services are available without proof of purchase from an authorized non-U.S. source.

NO OTHER WARRANTIES. To the maximum extent permitted by applicable law, *Nelson Electronic Publishing* and its suppliers disclaim all other warranties, either expressed or implied, including, but not limited to, implied warranties of merchantability and fitness for a particular purpose, with regard to the SOFTWARE and the accompanying written materials. This Limited Warranty gives you specific legal rights. You may have others, which vary from state to state.

NO LIABILITY FOR CONSEQUENTIAL DAMAGES. TO THE MAXIMUM EXTENT PERMITTED BY APPLICABLE LAW, IN NO EVENT SHALL *NELSON ELECTRONIC PUBLISHING* OR ITS SUPPLIERS BY LIABLE FOR ANY DAMAGES WHATSOEVER (INCLUDING WITHOUT LIMITATIONS, DAMAGES FOR LOSS OF BUSINESS PROFITS, BUSINESS INTERRUPTION, LOSS OF BUSINESS INFORMATION, OR ANY OTHER PECUNIARY LOSS) ARISING OUT OF THE USE OF OR INABILITY TO USE THIS PRODUCT, EVEN IF *NELSON ELECTRONIC PUBLISHING* HAS BEEN ADVISED OF THE POSSIBILITY OF SUCH DAMAGES. BECAUSE SOME STATES DO NOT ALLOW THE EXCLUSION OF LIABILITY FOR CONSEQUENTIAL OR ACCIDENTAL DAMAGES, THE ABOVE LIMITATION MAY NOT APPLY TO YOU.

Should you have any questions concerning this Agreement, please contact:

Nelson Electronic Publishing
Thomas Nelson, Inc.
501 Nelson Place
Nashville, TN 37214-1000
615/889-9000